Meridians feminism, race, transnationalism

VOLUME 21 · NUMBER 1 · APRIL 2022

BLACK FEMINISMS IN THE CARIBBEAN AND THE UNITED STATES: REPRESENTATION, REBELLION, RADICALISM, AND RECKONING

Ginetta E. B. Candelario

Editor's Introduction

"we the scapegoat in a land built
from death. no longitude or latitude disproves
the truth of founding fathers' sacred oath:
we hold these truths like dark snuff in our jaw,
Black oppression's not happenstance; it's law."
—Ashley M. Jones, "All Y'all Really from Alabama"

"Black women have been writing, joking, and 'me too'ing themselves into
existence."
—Constance Bailey, "Signifying Sistas: Black Women's Humor and Intersectional Poetics"

As a scholar of Afro-Latinidades, it is a particular pleasure for me to offer
Meridians readers this issue devoted to "Black Feminisms in the Caribbean
and the United States: Representation, Rebellion, Radicalism, and Reckoning." This curated conversation about Black feminist liberation strategies, which vary and move across time and place, is aptly illustrated with
cover art by Haitian artist Mafalda Nicolas Mondestin, *Ann fè on ti pale* (*The
Meeting*). *Ann fè on ti pale* is a Haitian Kreyol expression that means "let's chat
about it" or "we should chat" (pers. comm., August 29, 2021), and, apropos
of that invitation, we open the conversation with "Vodou, the Arts, and
(Re)Presenting the Divine: A Conversation with Edwidge Danticat," an
especially timely and insightful interview that Kyrah Malika Daniels conducted in January 2020.[1] As our readers well know, a global COVID-19 pandemic emerged just after this interview took place and dramatically

MERIDIANS · feminism, race, transnationalism   21:1 April 2022
DOI: 10.1215/15366936-9554035 © 2022 Smith College

changed the course of all our lives, but it has been most unforgiving in much of the global South and its diaspora. Simply stated, the United States and Europe have the highest quality and most resourced health-care systems in the world, but there, as throughout society, institutional racism produces devastating and deadly outcomes for Black, Indigenous, People of Color (BIPOC) communities. After a brief period of seeming relief due to the development of several effective vaccines, a COVID-19 mutation into the "Delta variant" emerged in June of 2021, and in January 2022 the "Omicron" variant also emerged, testing the effectiveness of the vaccines and claiming new demographics as victims, including children who were previously largely untouched by the virus. As of this writing,[2] more than 80 million people have contracted COVID-19 and 977,000 people have died in the United States (Worldometer 2021), with BIPOC folks disproportionately represented in both counts.

To make matters worse, US mainstream media and Republican Party–elected officials such as Texas Lt. Governor Dan Patrick routinely blame BIPOC folks for COVID-19 surges due to their supposedly lower vaccination rates, despite recent polls indicating that BIPOC vaccination rates are higher than Whites, even with the greater structural barriers they face and despite their historically grounded, sociologically sound distrust of the health-care system (Starr 2021). Indeed, it is right-wing media that continues to promote anti-vaccination propaganda to its largely White audience, including bizarre claims that Ivermectin, a veterinary deworming treatment, is preferable to the now fully FDA approved vaccines as a preventative measure and/or treatment (USDA 2021). Similar ideologically driven patterns appear globally, in which right-wing and nationalist leaders and other elements across the world blame vulnerable populations for the virus's spread and promote dangerously ineffective alternative treatments.

In Haiti, if these universal pandemic-related challenges weren't difficult enough, the summer of 2021 also brought the assassination of President Jovenel Moïse on July 7, another devastating earthquake on August 14 that took two thousand lives, and the brutal tropical storm Grace on August 17. With this context in mind, Edwidge Danticat's reflections on the perennial assaults on sovereignty, peace, and well-being that Haiti and Haitians have suffered and overcome thanks to their spiritual traditions and practices are critical counters to persistent anti-Haitian attitudes and discourses in the media and public sphere. This engaging and focused Interview—conversation, really, as Daniels's insightful comments position her more as interlocutor than interviewer—offers a rich and revealing window into Danticat's thinking about and connection to Haitian spiritual traditions and practices and their relationship to the natural world; ruminations about various faiths' rituals of death, dying, and honoring ancestors; and poignant comments on her own experiences of losing and keeping a connection to loved ones through dreams and creative work. As Danticat succinctly puts it in closing the interview, "We're not just rectifying old narratives, we're writing our own narratives, fully within ourselves."

In her Essay "Beyond Tragedy: Black Girlhood in Marlon James's *Book of Night Women* and Evelyne Trouillot's *Rosalie l'infâme*," Annette Joseph-Gabriel exemplifies Danticat's perspective with her analysis of two novels about enslaved Black girls' coming of age in Jamaica and Saint Domingue. These "resistive tragedies," Joseph-Gabriel argues, narrate the chipping away at slave societies' social orders because, "even if they do not overcome the forces of slavery," the girls "exceed the limitations that slavery places on their bodies, their imaginations, and their futures." These novels also exemplify the "spiralism" characteristic of Haitian and other Caribbean narratives. Unlike linear (read Eurocentric/White) notions of time and tragedy, spiral theories of historical and social change hold that stasis, and progressive and regressive shifts, can—and often do—occur simultaneously, allowing for "a continuous, dynamic engagement between past and present."

Next, we turn our attention to the U.S. context of Black girlhood and survivance beginning with Nia McAllister's poem, "Consort of the Spirits, *after Ntozake Shange*." Although the term *survivance* emerges from Native American Indian studies in the United States rather than from Black studies, it effectively captures the affect and vision of this richly evocative poem. "Survivance is an active sense of presence, the continuance of native stories, not a mere reaction, or a survivable name. Native survivance stories are renunciations of dominance, tragedy, and victimry" (Vizenor 1999: vii). McAllister builds on Ntozake Shange's evocative assertion that "a woman with a moon falling from her mouth, roses between her legs and tiaras of Spanish moss, this woman is a consort of the spirits," to narrate survivance as more than mere survival, as her repeated refrain "They call this survival"—followed by refutations to that hegemonic framing—illustrates.

Similarly eschewing hegemonic conventions and notions of survival, Kenly Brown, Lashon Daley, and Derrika Hunt's collectively written, transdisciplinary, and multi-methodological Counterpoint essay, "Disruptive Ruptures: The Necessity of Black/Girlhood Imaginary," coins the term "'Black forward slash Girlhood' to signal both an abstract configuration and a lived embodied experience of Black girlness that is in dialogue with global imaginings." Through three different case studies, Brown, Daley, and Hunt center both fictional and real Black girls' narratives and understandings of their girlhood experiences. By documenting the fictional Judy Winslow's (and/or actress Jaimee Foxworth's) unacknowledged disappearance from *Family Matters*, valorizing the poetry of a demonized Black girl enrolled in a California continuation school who asserts "the only demon in me is this crooked society," and the testimony of a sixteen-year-old girl working in a Jamaican resort, this Black feminist collective text showcases "the kaleidoscopic mosaics of Black girls' knowings . . . across time, space, and geographic boundaries."

We follow this with an In the Archives feature that departs from our usual archival document and research note. "Carlota's Hum: An Archive Fiction" by interdisciplinary poet and scholar Alana Pérez is, as the author explains in her introduction, an attempt "to retell" the documented true story of Carlota lucumí of the Triunvirato sugar mill in the province of Matanzas, Cuba, who organized a "traveling rebellion that freed over three hundred enslaved people" in 1843. Pérez offers our readers a retelling of this story that centers the "queer relationship" between Carlota and Fermina, another enslaved woman with whom Carlota was evidently in love with, while also "referencing Yoruba and Cuban Santeria practices" from which they drew strength and support. The Cuban context of and contributions to transnational Black feminism is also taken up by Laura Lomas in her Essay "Afro-Latina Disidentification and Bridging: Lourdes Casal's Critical Race Theory." Lomas's title also references the recent targeting of critical race theory by right-wing ideologues in the United States who have launched a disinformation campaign to prevent the teaching about the long history and ongoing social fact of racist interpersonal and structural violence at home and abroad.

Lomas recounts Casal's personal and political biography, one in which Casal elaborated a "radicalized" Cuban (im)migrant commitment to global freedom struggles in the 1960s and 1970s. This commitment was rooted in her experiences as an Afro-Asian, tacitly lesbian, Hispanic-Black-identified feminist who moved across and through worlds and geographies recovering and recounting the central role of Blackness, anti-Blackness, and Blacks in Cuban history, society, culture, and politics. Moreover, through Casal's case, Lomas offers an important contribution to our understanding of how Black women from the "Hispanic" Caribbean played active roles in the development of transnational Black feminisms; pushed White feminist projects to address imperialism, capitalism, and racism; and held their own societies similarly accountable. This under-recognized story offers a useful contemporary reminder to be aware of the ideological framings embedded in recent U.S. media coverage of the unprecedented mid-July protests against food and medicine shortages that broke out in Havana.

While it appears that the "leaders of this new movement are 'a cross-section of Cuba and they are younger, darker, and female'" (Ellis 2021) and that the genesis and outcome of these dramatic public challenges to the Cuban revolutionary regime remain to be seen, what is already clear is that, as with Haiti, mainstream U.S. media readily replayed its old narratives about the island and unhesitatingly echoed the anti-revolutionary sentiments of Miami's conservative Cuban exiles. "Propelled by the '#SOSCuba' hashtag, the *New York Times* and other usual suspects rushed to report, aghast, on a Cuban security crackdown in response to the protests, characterised by the jailing of dissidents and alleged human rights violations," noted Belén Fernández (2021), *Jacobin Magazine* contributing editor. "While such critiques are not in and of themselves invalid, they would surely hold more moral traction were they not issued by the media mouthpieces of a country that has long operated an illegal prison-cum-torture centre on Cuban soil" (Fernández 2021). Tracing a similarly complex tangle of national history and family genealogies, Elizabeth Pérez's poem "Remittances" conveys the painful inability of those bound by blood ties—"relatives with whom they share intimate racialized and gendered histories"—to overcome the legacy and ongoing denial of Cuban anti-Blackness, and instead find themselves "debating the relevance of revenants" in post-Soviet revolutionary Cuba.

By contrast, in "La Reina de Fusión: Xiomara Fortuna Coming of Age in the Dominican Republic," Rachel Afi Quinn helpfully contextualizes Fortuna's *Testimonio* about the evolution of her leftist Black feminist race consciousness; her experiences of Blackness and anti-Blackness in the Dominican Republic and abroad; and how she made these manifest in her music and performance. Fortuna, who grew up in Monte Cristi, Dominican Republic, as the darkest child in a large light-skinned, middle-class family, had established herself early on as a "willful girl" insistent on getting the best education she could and on accessing every opportunity available to her—but these were circumscribed in a country that, despite being the "cradle of Blackness in the Americas" (Torres-Saillant 1999: 55), continues to promote negrophobic ideologies, policies, and practices (Candelario 2007, 2016). Nonetheless, "rather than a story of childhood trauma and marginalization because of her blackness," a trip to Jamaica and revolutionary Cuba fostered a clearly articulated antiracist feminist consciousness in Fortuna whose "clear-eyed take on what it has meant for her to navigate Dominican society as a rebellious Afro-Dominican woman of her generation" infuses her culture work.

This was most recently exemplified in Fortuna's decision to perform and receive the Medalla al Mérito en el Área de las Artes (Medal of Merit in the Arts) barefoot. This powerful symbolic gesture evokes not only another transnational Black queen of world music who signaled class-consciousness similarly—Cape Verde's "Barefoot Diva" and "Queen of Morna," Cesária Évora (August 27, 1941–December 17, 2011)—but also Fortuna's identity as a Black Dominican woman who rejects the racism, classism, sexism, and heteronormativity of Dominican power elites, even, perhaps especially, when receiving presidentially bestowed awards of national recognition. As one supportive commentator put it, "Es una mujer de la raza negra que se ha caracterizado por defender las causas sociales y tener siempre presentes sus antecedentes y el sufrimiento a que fueron sometidos los esclavos traídos de África" (Quiñones 2017).[3] Arguably, Fortuna's cheeky response to elite outrage—that she lacked the appropriate footwear for the event, a fact belied by her meticulously styled hair and attire—also exemplifies what Constance Bailey brings to our attention in "Signifying Sistas: Black Women's Humor and Intersectional Poetics."

In this Cultureworks essay, Bailey examines texts that range across time from the eighteenth century to the present, and across genres—from poetry to speeches, and novels to television comedy show—to argue that these exemplify "black comediennes' intersectional consciousness" and use of "wit to subtly differentiate their lived experiences from those of White women" and Black men. Whether signifying and satirizing White women's racism, or "symbolically castrating" Black male aggressors, Bailey argues that Black women's comedy moves beyond documenting their "specific bodily experiences of racism" to metabolizing them critically and defanging their perpetrators publicly, even if to an "audience [that is] often oblivious to the intensity of their critique." This oblique yet powerful signifying strategy is also evident in the visual poem by S. Erin Batiste,

"Longer, Love," which mocks (up) an advertisement for hair products featuring a light-skinned Black woman with smooth, wavy hair above whom the rhetorical question "do you want love" floats. The poet rejects the original advertisement's misogynoirist (Bailey 2013: 26) message that natural Black women's hair must be made to conform to White aesthetics by visibly erasing/whiting out text such that the anti-Black message is transformed to one affirming Black women's self-love, asserting, "You are . . . your mirror" so "reflect love." As I read them, together the title, visuals, and text of "Longer, Love" enact Black femme disidentification, affirming the universal human desire to be loved, while rejecting the racist-sexist basis on which Black women's lovableness is premised and creating something new for those who want it: "Mail coupon now."

Also concerned with the complex politics and poetics of Black femme self-love, Jennifer Williams's Media Matters essay, "Apologizing to Chavers: #Blackgirlmagic's Resilience Discourse and the Fear of Melancholy Black Femme Digital Subjectivity," delves into the contentious debate unleashed when Linda Chavers's 2016 article criticizing the #BlackGirlMagic hashtag was published in *Elle* magazine. Chavers (2016) argued that, rather than empowering Black girls and women, the hashtag not only reproduces the trope of Black women's superhuman strength and imperviousness to pain but also harms them by disavowing their flawed humanity, imperfect bodies, and abjection. Simply stated, Chavers argued that "#Blackgirlmagic does not change the regularity of Black death and destruction." This did not sit well with many Black women who took to social media to reject Chavers's argument and to attack Chavers herself, going even so far as to question her Black identity and her mental health. Williams explains that, although she too initially joined the chorus of "vitriolic" critics, she now stands with Chavers in noting that, while there is an understandable appeal to the hashtag's celebration of "the overcoming actions of" individuals, that celebration implicitly reinforces contemporary respectability ideologies and allows "the misdeeds of the state and society" to remain unexamined and naturalized. Thus, Williams concludes, "Black people must envision other techniques and tools" that "generate Black liberatory possibilities" by allowing Black women to "identify with the whole of their humanity and emotions—including the sacred, the profane, and the abject."

Along these lines of saying one thing and doing another, Malia Lee Womack's In the Trenches essay, "An Intersectional Approach to

Interrogating Rights: How the United States Does Not Comply with the Racial Equality Treaty," carefully narrates and analyzes the contradictory facts of the United States' participation in international movements to articulate and promote human rights policies, on the one hand, and its long history of violating its residents' human rights on the other. Specifically, Womack analyzes how United States' reservations, understandings, and declarations (RUDs) about the International Convention on the Elimination of All Forms of Racial Discrimination (ICERD) claim that "US policies and government institutions are fully consistent with" ICERD yet fail to acknowledge "that its institutions are systematically racist." Moreover, the United States routinely fails to ratify human rights conventions, exempts itself from norms and obligations that contravene its interests, and refuses to proactively pursue and/or promote its residents' economic, social, and cultural rights as required by ICERD. It does so because ICERD notions of rights contravene normative US ideologies of freedom and equal opportunity that frame outcomes as resulting from personal decision making by individuals and deny the role played by White supremacist, patriarchal, settler-colonial, and capitalist social structures and systems in producing those outcomes for individuals and communities alike. By contrast, Womack deploys intersectionality theory to narrate how the "profoundly racist/sexist design of US legal and policy frameworks . . . assure[s that] women who are Black experience profound oppression" in and through the health, education, and housing system in explicit and implicit violation of ICERD. Womack argues hopefully that "applying an intersectional analysis to ICERD holds the United States more accountable to the treaty, which can maximize its effects."

Taking a related but different tack on addressing the legacy and ongoing fact of intersectional violence experienced by "racially minoritized" people internally and relationally, "Sisterhood Birthed through Colonialism: Using Love Letters to Connect, Heal, and Transform" is a joint memoir by Jamaican Raquel Wright-Mair and Puerto Rican Milagros Castillo-Montoya that exemplifies the listen, affirm, respond, and affirming inquiry method for "reckoning with this being a part of our personal history, whether we like it or not." These US-based colleague-friends, who both identify as racialized minority women, took part in a Black heritage tour of the Netherlands presenting their research on global racial equity in education. The tour included a visit to the Museum Van Loon, which showcased "a powerful exhibit on Suriname" that elicited powerfully disturbing emotions in the authors even months after their encounter with it. In response, they decided to "unpack this experience with [one] another in the form of love letters" that movingly model "witnessing ourselves in each other."

Finally, apropos of this call to draw on the power of diasporic (self) love to foment decolonial politics and practices large and small, we close this issue with a poem by Teri Ellen Cross Davis, "Black Berries." Drawing on the Black anti-colorism adage "the blacker the berry, the sweeter the juice," this poem's narrator travels from the United States to Ireland and Kenya, "exploring the journey from wonderment to acceptance to love" of Black (er) and dark skin. As with "Longer, Love," this poem affirms that Black beauty must be appreciated on its own terms, and that sometimes means leaving the United States behind. Freed from the U.S. context, in Mombasa, Kenya, the narrator "chased [her] color, taunted it to come out and play," sharing her joy and wonder that "melanin [is] a blessing," a sweet experience indeed. And in keeping with that celebratory sentiment, *Meridians* is thrilled and heartened by the historic confirmation of Ketanji Brown Jackson to the Supreme Court of the United States on Thursday, April 8, 2022. That the moment came to pass despite the trenchantly misogynoirist efforts of the Republican senators and was presided over by another Black woman history maker, Vice President Kamala Harris, made the occasion even sweeter. Here's to Black feminisms across the Americas!

Notes

1   This is the third interview with Danticat that we publish in *Meridians*; the first one was in 2001 (Danticat 2001) and, as it happens, I conducted the second one for the journal following the October 2003 "Women of Hispaniola" round table organized by then-Editor Myriam Chancy in order to celebrate the 200th anniversary of Haitian Independence (Candelario 2004). That event, *Caribbean Women Writers, Voices from Hispaniola: Haiti and the Dominican Republic*, was held at Smith College and featured Chancy, Danticat, Nelly Rosario, and Loida Maritza Pérez.

2   March 2022.

3   Translation: "She is a Black woman who has been characterized by her defense of social causes and always being aware of her ancestors and the suffering of enslaved Africans brought to this place."

Works Cited

Bailey, Moya Zakia. 2013. "Race, Region, and Gender in Early Emory School of Medicine Yearbooks." PhD diss., Emory University.

Candelario, Ginetta E. B. 2004. "Voices from Hispaniola: A Meridians Roundtable with Edwidge Danticat, Loida Maritza Perez, Myriam J. A. Chancy, and Nelly Rosario." *Meridians* 5, no. 1: 68–91.

Candelario, Ginetta E. B. 2007. *Black behind the Ears: Dominican Racial Identity, from Museums to Beauty Shops*. Durham, NC: Duke University Press.

Candelario, Ginetta E. B. 2016. "La ciguapa y el ciguapeo: Dominican Myth, Metaphor, and Method." *Small Axe* 20, no. 3 (51): 100–102.

Chavers, Linda. 2016. "Here's My Problem with #BlackGirlMagic." *Elle*, January 13. www.elle.com/life-lofe/a33180/why-i-dont-love-Blackgirlmagic/.

Danticat, Edwidge. 2001. "Edwidge Danticat, an Intimate Reader: Interview with *Meridians* and Jessica Horn." Interview with Jessica Horn. *Meridians* 1, no. 2: 9–25.

Ellis, Amy. 2021. "Faculty Experts Examine Historic Cuba Protests and What May Come Next." *FIU News*, July 21. news.fiu.edu/2021/faculty-examine-historic-cuba-protests-and-what-may-come-next.

Fernández, Belén. 2021. "SOS: A Plea for Freedom from the Media Narrative on Cuba." *Al Jazeera*, July 29. www.aljazeera.com/opinions/2021/7/29/sos-a-plea-for-freedom-from-the-media-narrative-on-cuba.

Jones, Ashley M. 2020. "All Y'all Really From Alabama." https://poets.org/poem/all-yall-really-alabama.

Quiñones, Alfonso. 2017. "Xiomara descalza." *Diario libre*, March 10. www.diariolibre.com/revista/musica/xiomara-descalza-IY6526082.

Shange, Ntozake. 1996. *Sassafras, Cypress, and Indigo*. New York: Picador.

Starr, Terrell Jermaine. 2021. "Poll: Black Americans Are Getting Vaccinated at Higher Rates than Whites." *Root*, August 25. www.theroot.com/poll-black-americans-are-getting-vaccinated-at-higher-1847554349.

Torres-Saillant, Silvio. 1999. "Introduction to Dominican Blackness." Dominican Studies Working Paper Series 1. New York: City College of New York, CUNY Dominican Studies Institute.

USDA (United States Food and Drug Administration). 2021. "Why You Should Not Use Ivermectin to Treat or Prevent COVID-19." www.fda.gov/consumers/consumer-updates/why-you-should-not-use-ivermectin-treat-or-prevent-covid-19.

Vizenor, Gerald. 1999. *Manifest Manners: Narratives on Postindian Survivance*. Lincoln: University of Nebraska.

Worldometer. 2021. "United States Coronavirus Cases." www.worldometers.info/coronavirus/country/us/ (accessed September 10, 2021).

Kyrah Malika Daniels

Vodou, the Arts, and (Re)Presenting the Divine
A Conversation with Edwidge Danticat

Abstract: Few conversations with the renowned Haitian novelist Edwidge Danticat have delved into the subject of religion in Haiti and the representations of Vodou in her fiction and nonfiction writing. This interview with Danticat explores her religious upbringing, Vodou and interfaith dialogue, and representations of Haitian religion in the media and in the world. Other topics discussed include Haitian sacred space and the environment, Vodou as a matriarchal religion, and divine archetypes present in her body of writings. Drawing from an Africana religion framework, the questions posed here consider the religious import of Danticat's literary works as "sacred texts" of Haiti and the Haitian *dyaspora*.

On January 4, 2020, Kyrah Malika Daniels interviewed Edwidge Danticat at her home in southern Florida to explore the subjects of Vodou and interfaith dialogue, her religious upbringing, representations of Haitian religion in the media and in the world, sacred space and the environment, and divine archetypes present in her body of writings.

Kyrah Malika Daniels (KMD): Thank you so much for meeting with me today. Your writings have had a profound impact on me and so many others, and it's an honor to sit down with you and discuss the role of religion in your life and work.

MERIDIANS · feminism, race, transnationalism   21:1 April 2022
DOI: 10.1215/15366936-9554046 © 2022 Smith College

Edwidge Danticat (ED): Yes, of course. I'm looking forward to the conversation.

KMD: I'd like to begin by asking about how you were raised religiously, both in Haiti and later in the United States. I know that your beloved uncle and aunt raised you, and your uncle was a Baptist minister. How did this religious upbringing influence you?

ED: I was basically raised in church. My family is originally from a very small village in the mountains of Léogâne called Beauséjour (it literally means, nice stay). Their first migration was from that small rural village to the city of Port-au-Prince. And within the family, I'm sure there was Vodou, at least on my father's side. We have always heard mystical stories about my grandfather, who fought against the United States occupation of Haiti between 1915 and 1934. He was a Caco. In these stories, we were told that he knew all of the secrets of the night. I think there was a lot of mythology about men like my grandfather. It was understood that you had to have special gifts to be part of the Caco rebellion, because you were mostly rural people fighting a world power that was occupying your country. The story in the family was that this was not a battle you could fight alone. You needed your ancestors there with you. You had to call on the past. You had to call on the spirits of those who'd won our first battle for independence in 1804. You had to have not just physical gifts, but also spiritual ones. Those were the types of stories I grew up hearing about my grandfather and men like him. After my grandfather died, his children, my father included, moved to Port-au-Prince in the 1940s. They moved to a neighborhood called Bel-Air, and that's where they all joined the Protestant church. My uncle became a Baptist minister. I don't know what my family's official spiritual practice was before that. Aside from those stories, they never really talked much about their religious past. By the time I was born, my father was Baptist, Haitian Baptist. At least back then, Haitian Baptists were a very serene kind of Baptist, compared to say, African American Baptists, whose worship more resembled Haitian Pentecostalism, the fierier brand of Protestants.

The first church our family attended was L'Église Baptiste des Cités, which was run by Pastor Luc Néré. He was quite well-known in Haiti by the time I was born. When I got christened in his church as a baby, I was given a small Bible with my name written in it. My parents kept that Bible for me until I was an adult. Pastor Néré was attacked by Jean-Claude Duvalier's henchmen in the 1980s. In fact, Néré partially inspired the preacher who is arrested in my book, *The Dew Breaker* ([2004] 2007). My uncle was a deacon in his church, then eventually started his own church around the time that my father moved to the United States and left me in my uncle's care. At that time, my brother and I became part of the minister's family and had to attend every service, including weddings, baptisms, and funerals.

I remember some weekends we had Friday night Bible study, a Saturday morning funeral, a wedding on Saturday afternoon, and then Sunday services all day and into the evening. At some point, my uncle built a house behind the church in Bel Air, but before that, we lived some distance from the church. And right next to this first house was a *peristil* [Vodou temple]! Every once in a while, there were these programs on the radio where they would play Vodou music, and we couldn't listen to that. It's kind of like the stories that some African American performers share about being raised in the church and becoming secular singers, and not being allowed to listen to secular music at home as children! But whenever there were Vodou ceremonies at the *peristil* next door, my brother, cousins, and I would climb to the roof of our house—it was a flat roof and a kind of playground for us— and we would look down into the *lakou* [Vodou family compound] next door where the *peristil* was. That was really my initial exposure to Vodou, watching the ceremonies in the *peristil* next door. We couldn't see everything, but from that perspective you could see a lot of what was out in the open, the dances and some of the rituals. And I was as intrigued about the transformation of people in that religious context as I was with the church I grew up in. Because you could see people during the week who were selling water on the street, who were *machann* [market vendors]. But then in both spaces [the church and the *peristil*], they suddenly take on this kind of regal authority when they're serving the spirit in their different religious communities. So, for instance, my father, who was a cab driver in New York, was also deacon in a local church, and when he wore his white suit to serve communion on Sunday, he was very different than the person he was when he was driving other people around the city.

I remember watching the transformative power of these roles in these parallel contexts. The woman who's the *machann* was so powerful as a *manbo* [priestess] in the *peristil*, and the rest of the week she did herbal work and other similar things. She was suddenly like a queen in the ceremonial context! It was the same way with people in the Protestant church, becoming transformed. There was something about both religions that seemed to elevate the person in their individual context. As a child, I was very intrigued by that transformation.

And I also saw certain parallels with Pentecostals. I had an aunt who belonged to the Pentecostal Church. They sang. They danced. They often wore white. They caught the spirit, and fell into trance. They spoke in tongues. They fell on the ground and they made predictions about the future, as some voice other than their own was speaking *through* them. It seemed to me they were doing similar things. So that also made me think —*Wow! This parallel is very interesting.* At that time, though, there wasn't much tension between the two groups [Christians and Vodouizan], at least not in our neighborhood. There were always attempts to convert and preach to people who practiced Vodou, but it didn't seem that aggressive, at least to my young eyes. There was still a sense of you do your thing, I do my thing . . .

KMD: Do you feel there was a certain coexistence?

ED: Yes. People also knew each other intimately outside religious contexts. We were neighbors. We were friends, in some cases, family. It wasn't a war. If you were sick, you visited each other. If you knew someone was hungry and you had a little extra food, you still sent it their way. There wasn't fighting. And in my own mind, I couldn't help but linger on certain echoes.

KMD: That's a beautiful way to put it, that there were echoes. I'm fascinated by how people were still neighbors despite their religious differences. Perhaps there wasn't complete understanding between *Vodouizan* [Vodou devotees] and *Pwotestan* [Protestants] during this time, but people made a choice to look the other way, because even with somebody else's different religious orientation, *tout moun se moun* [everyone is human, everyone deserves respect].

ED: Yes! It seemed like, this is what *you* do, and this is what *we* do. Back then, my uncle had something called *kowòt*, a very early morning service, sometimes starting at four o'clock in the morning. I know that the neighborhood was cursing my uncle because he would be broadcasting these early morning services over a loudspeaker! But the Vodou ceremonies could also go late into the night for days at a time in a very densely populated neighborhood, so folks got equal air time, and both sides got their share of complaints [laughs].

KMD: So, would you say that your first memory or first experience with Vodou was looking from the roof of your home into the *lakou* next door?

ED: Absolutely. In fact, I can still see it in my mind to this day. I was intrigued by how it all worked, because when there weren't ceremonies, there were still people coming through [the *lakou*]. Some people would treat the space like a hospital; they came for help with physical ailments and sometimes received herbal baths. Some people came for mental or spiritual help. Often, they were people from the neighborhood, and sometimes they were people we had never seen before. So there was a continuous flow. The *manbo* was obviously an authority figure in the way that my uncle was for his flock, and people came to her for different services the way that they came to my uncle for prayer, advice, and even financial support. The best way to ignite a kid's imagination is by telling them not to be interested in something. So, I was up there with my brother and cousins, and we would be watching the *peristil* from the roof of my uncle's house. That was my first exposure, watching what was visible, what wasn't inside, watching parts of the ceremony and the daily comings and goings from the roof of my uncle's house.

KMD: That's so interesting: *watching what was visible.* Because there's this whole inside world that is happening behind closed doors in the *peristil* that's not visible.

ED: Yes, and I realized this early on, that there were layers to it. Recently, I was having a conversation with a friend, and she said, "Vodou is lost, everything is lost . . . " But reflecting on these memories growing up, I said to her, "There's so much that you don't *see!*" So I can't say if it's lost or not. Others who are practitioners or have more knowledge are in a better position to speak on these things, but even when I was a child, I always sensed that what we were seeing was the part that was meant to be seen. Even then I realized that there was this whole other layer behind closed doors, too.

KMD: Building upon this conversation, what was your first academic introduction to Vodou? For instance, Claudine Michel (2016) writes about her academic entrée into Haitian Studies and her study of Vodou specifically in her article "*Kalfou Danje*." Do you remember your first time reading about Vodou in a text, whatever genre that might have been?

ED: I think it was Maya Deren . . . no! No, first it was Katherine Dunham (1969). I had read a little bit of Zora Neale Hurston's *Tell My Horse* (1938), but I remember thinking, *Oh, she's being really critical* [laughs]. And later, I read Laënnec Hurbon's *Voodoo: Search for the Spirit* (1995), Leslie Desmangles's *The Faces of the Gods: Vodou and Roman Catholicism in Haiti* ([1992] 2000), and Colin [Joan] Dayan's *Haiti, History, and the Gods* (1996).

KMD: Yes, I actually prefer teaching Zora's writings about African American Hoodoo and Conjure rather than Vodou. I don't love the way that she writes about Haitian religion.

ED: Until I read *Nan Dòmi* [*An Initiate's Journey into Haitian Vodou*, Beaubrun 2013], and I read it very recently, I didn't realize how much we were missing an intimate and personal Haitian perspective. I think what Mimerose Beaubrun offers is the perspective of a Haitian woman—it might be different than other people's experiences, as it's a very singular journey the way that she explains it to us, as she is discovering all the layers herself—but, to my knowledge, we have not had this perspective in print before, the particular way she's written about her experience of initiation.

KMD: You're right. Until recently, maybe the past twenty to thirty years or so, there weren't a great deal of Vodou publications in the United States written by Haitians. And as for the Vodou texts published in Haiti, few of them have been translated into English, of course.

ED: We certainly have not had these intimate, first-person narratives from a Haitian perspective. And especially not from a translated text [Mimerose Beaubrun's book was first published in French in 2010]. I don't know of any except *Nan Dòmi*, but that could be my own limitation.

KMD: I have to admit I found certain principles that Beaubrun highlighted somewhat unfamiliar to me. I remember her specifically mentioning, "Vodou is ultimately about nothingness," which is what her teacher, Aunt Tansia, had shared with her. That sounded very much like Buddhism, and I wondered whether she had also practiced Buddhism at some point in her life. Someone also reminded me that her initiatory work was in her home-town of Ouanaminthe, which is not only a borderland with the Dominican Republic but is also in the north. Vodou is very different in the north versus the south. So much of the research, including my own, is conducted in Port-au-Prince and the south, and so certain regional differences do emerge.

ED: This is something that I also face in what I write. I think we have to allow for individual and regional differences in the Haitian stories we tell. I think what you are saying is extremely powerful here, and it's something that a lot of people might not be aware of. They might think of Vodou as being practiced the same way everywhere in Haiti, when actually, as with everything else, everyone's journey might differ based on the geographical region and area, or even the person initiating them.

KMD: How do you define your religious orientation today? Do you feel drawn to a particular tradition, or do you find yourself following a few spiritual paths?

ED: I am still Baptist, though a lot of people I know have said that I am a bad one. I was Unitarian for a while, and I still attend Sunday services when I can in a very small church in my neighborhood. I sometimes visit larger churches. I don't always agree with everything I hear. I know a lot of progressive Catholics who feel the same way, but still attend mass. I strug-gle with the contradictions for sure, with my own and that of others, but I'm glad that I had this upbringing where you knew there was a power greater than yourself, and I have been very comforted at many difficult moments in my life by prayer.

KMD: How did your husband grow up religiously speaking, and how has that influenced the girls' upbringing?

ED: My husband grew up Catholic, but he does not have a religious practice now. I bring my daughters to church with me. They are not being brought up as strictly religious as I was, but I want them to have a sense that they are not the center of the universe and that the world is bigger than them. I do think that any kind of gathering of like-minded spiritual people is commu-nity. Ultimately, I would like them to find their own spiritual "homes" when they are older.

KMD: I'm interested in pursuing a future project that traces a genealogy of matriarchs, trying to identify the last site where we can trace Vodou in our family tree. I know for my family it's been several generations of distance, but I also know that there are a few stories that seemed to have crept down the lineage. For instance, family lore says that my great-great-grandmother recounted an experience of being taken somewhere where a man dressed in all red danced while loud drums filled the air. To me, that suggests this could have been a *fèt* or *dans* [ceremony or ritual dance] for the *lwa* Ogou [the *lwa* of war, iron, diplomacy]. It could also be other things but . . .

ED: But there are very few dances where someone would have been wearing all red! [laughs] That's really interesting as a starting point. Did you ever press for more details?

KMD: I did, but unfortunately that's all we know of her direct experiences with Vodou. I'm hoping to uncover more about my family's relationship to the tradition in future interviews with our elders. This leads me to ask, are there any particular *lwa* or spirit energies whom you feel played an important role in your family's life? Any saints for instance who played a key role in the family lineage? More broadly, were there other people or even distant family members you knew who were involved in Vodou?

ED: In the Protestant church, an important part of the conversion stories of former Vodouizan is often a confession of the spirits they've left behind. Let me tell you, if you ever want to fill up a church or a service, you have someone who used to be a Vodouizan who has converted share their testimony! I saw newly converted people do this in my uncle's church all the time, but, as I mentioned before, in my family they never talked about their religious past. My mother's family was very Catholic initially, and then they became Jehovah's Witnesses. My mother's name was Rose, and I know she was named for Saint Rose de Lima, which was the patron saint of Léogâne. Her middle name was Souvenance.

KMD: Souvenance? Wow! Souvnans![1]

ED: Believe me, just like you, I tried to ask all types of questions! *How did you get that name?* And she would only say, St. *Rose de Lima*, which was the patron saint of Léogâne. She didn't want to broach the other part.

KMD: In your uncle's role as minister and pastor, I understand that he would often perform funeral services. How did this affect you as a young girl, and later as a maturing young woman?

ED: My uncle performed the funeral services of all his church members. I also had a cousin who was an undertaker, so I got to attend many funeral services. Later on, as an adult woman, I had the privilege of dressing the aunt who helped raise me for her funeral, and I considered this a great honor. The most striking thing for me, though, about this proximity to death, both very early and also later in my life, is that I learned early on that death is indeed a part of life, that there is a continuity to life into death. I'm not sure I knew how to express it, but I quickly caught on that no matter what your belief system, when you die you are not completely gone. I registered all of that very early. The body is no longer here, but there's a continuation of who you are in some other form. I think I was getting the message both ways, from two traditions. The transition is painful because you're no longer interacting with the body, but in some ways, the person is still with you. I had my minister uncle saying, *this is not the end—you are going to Heaven!* And then next door at the *lakou*, they were returning to Ginen.

KMD: In your book *Brother, I'm Dying*, you mention that the same day you learned that your father was diagnosed with pulmonary fibrosis, you also found out that you were pregnant with your first child, a daughter.

ED: That was Mira, in 2004. Yes, that happened on the same day.

KMD: In previous writings and interviews, you have identified yourself as having a close connection to the cemetery, and to those who have passed. How do you feel like these experiences—regularly attending funeral services and linking your father's diagnosis with your daughter's new arrival—was an affirmation of this close connection to the spiritual realm?

ED: Again, I think it goes back to when I was younger. All of these things kind of merged. The circle of life became very real and tangible to me in that moment with my daughter coming and my father being told he was dying. Both of my parents, in their own way, believed so strongly in the eternal life as described in the Bible. That helped them to die more peacefully. They were not afraid. They were actually more afraid of causing us pain by dying. They also saw new life as another kind of continuity and renewal, which is why my daughter is named Mira, after my father. I feel like he waited to meet her. He died a few days after he held her for the first time, and as he held her, he said something like, "At least when this Mira is gone, another one will be there to take his place." And so that sense of continuity I think for me will always be there with my parents. It lives on in my children.

KMD: In Haiti, even Protestants and Catholics occasionally seek out local healers when they become ill. What was your family's relationship to traditional healing?

ED: My parents were both very serious about herbalists, more so than their interest in medical doctors. I write about it in *Brother, I'm Dying* (2008a). My dad was going to an herbalist as well as a pulmonologist, as he was dying of pulmonary fibrosis. I went with him to a couple of herbalists. One was Haitian, one was Jamaican. The Haitian herbalist, he had an apartment on Newkirk Avenue in Brooklyn, actually two buildings down from the church my parents attended. And I remember going to see him with my father—it was a small apartment in public housing, first floor, no appointments. People just showed up. Some people had been diagnosed with terminal cancer, and they swore he'd healed them. They came from all over to see him, even as far as Montreal, Canada. He did consultations by touch, and then he gave you herbs. My father also went to Chinese herbalists for a serious case of psoriasis. And the last herbalist he went to see was a Jamaican woman who did hair analysis. I went to see her with my father and didn't realize I was pregnant. She told me immediately that I was with child. So, this idea of seeking natural healing, that was something that carried over in both my parents' lives, not just from Haiti, but from rural Haiti. I was always a little worried about their vulnerability to charlatans [laughs], but my parents were devoted to natural medicine and natural healers. A lot of people in their church were too.

KMD: One of the reasons I'm interested in healing in Vodou and other Africana traditions is because a lot of people describe their devotion to a certain tradition, but when someone falls ill or the stakes are high, people become very "flexible" religiously speaking. They'll do whatever it takes to ensure their restoration of health.

ED: Yes, definitely. Here in Miami, there are young Haitian or Cuban herbalists who also do acupuncture for example and who combine different types of healing traditions from all over the African *dyaspora* [diaspora] and the rest of the world.

KMD: Traditionally to be a *manbo* or an *houngan* [Vodou priestess or priest], you had to acquire a deep knowledge of plants, medicines, and herbs. Today in the urban space, some people still have this knowledge, but when you're removed from the forest, you have to work harder to become a skilled herbalist.

ED: It's a tricky space too. Like my parents, I've also sought out herbalists and naturopaths at the same time as traditional doctors. And the doctors can really scare you because they're worried about negative interactions between the drugs you're taking and the traditional herbs. So, someone with this knowledge of plants now has to know how to make it work with traditional medicines to ensure they don't get into trouble. I remember reading a book about Paul Farmer, *Mountains beyond Mountains* by Tracy Kidder ([2003] 2011). I appreciated when Farmer said that when they went to Cange [a town in Haiti's Central Plateau] to open their clinic, they had the most success when they weren't resisting the traditional healers and began to seek their cooperation. The doctors went to see the healers; they talked to them about the herbs they were using, etc. They weren't saying to people, *you have to stop going there.* So that collaboration with the traditional healers was really important, and very smart to do.

KMD: Absolutely. I've often felt humbled when I interview healers who say that certain illnesses should be solved in the Western hospitals, and other conditions they explain they can offer treatment with local remedies. Some people mistakenly believe that traditional healing means a total *rejection* of Western medicine, when in fact many people in other parts of the world already integrate both healing systems—Indigenous medicine and Western medicine.

ED: I agree. The natural medicine folks we go to here in Miami always say that there are some acute issues they won't be able to help with. I have always appreciated that.

KMD: I'd like to shift now to some questions about how Vodou is perceived outside of Haiti. What do you think of the representations of Vodou in the Western world, specifically within the media? Do you feel that you've seen progress in the way that Vodou is represented today, and what falsehoods do you think continue to persist?

ED: It's so strange to me how little has changed! [laughs] With all the information out there, with all the people you can talk to, all the folks that you can consult with, we still get the same tropes in different types of media. You still read articles with seemingly smart people who say things like, *I'm going to Haiti to look for a zombie!* I'm like, *oh you haven't read the twenty-five other articles of people who've already done that?* It's bizarre that with all the Haitian and Haitian American scholars, all the people whom you can reach out to, that some people are still reaching for the same old tropes. Honestly, I can't say I've seen too much improvement in the representations, because what was attracting people back in the day, from the 1900s onward was the sensationalism, and that still happens. I think people still like this idea of Haiti as a "land of mystery." Even when they're trying, they can't seem to escape the tropes. There might be some that I have missed, but generally I think there is a lot of reaching back to what was written or shown before about Haiti and repeating those same things over and over again. That's why it's so good that now we have more Haitian American scholars emerging, people like Gina Athena Ulysse, and Charlene Désir, and people like you, among others. People who are younger, who have new intimate perspectives, people who can speak with nuance and offer us, in Gina's words, new narratives for Haiti.

KMD: Several times in your writings, you mention parallels between Vodou and the traditions of ancient Egyptians and ancient Greeks, for instance in your mention of funerary masks and mausoleums [*Create Dangerously*, 2010, and *After the Dance*, (2002 [2014])]. How have you made these connections, and how did they become apparent to you? What connections do you see between Vodou and other African Diaspora traditions or other "world religions"?

ED: I guess because of my upbringing, I have been looking for parallels between religions my whole life. As for ancient Egypt, I'm fascinated with it. I feel like it's the most direct afterlife blueprint, more so than the Bible, because the Bible makes you a promise. But with ancient Egyptian mythology, you'll be asked certain questions, and if you answer properly, you *may* be admitted. I also see some powerful resonances in how Haitians and ancient Egyptians prepared themselves for the afterlife and cared for their dead. In addition to what you've already mentioned, I think Japanese Shinto and Haitian Vodou, for example, have many striking parallels, including polytheism and a full awareness of ancestors, prayers, and ritual offerings.

KMD: The political scientist and *houngan* Patrick Bellegarde-Smith (2005) says that Japanese Shinto is one of the Indigenous traditions most closely aligned with Vodou.

ED: It's true—that blew my mind! The fact that there are these connections with religions like these all over the world is very powerful in demystifying certain aspects of African-based religions, including Vodou.

KMD: I want to ask about the presence of Vodou in your own writings. Which of your texts do you feel feature Vodou, or include significant references to the tradition? Has there been a chronological development in your writing about Vodou? Or is it rather the *genre* of writing that lends itself to the inclusion of Vodou? For instance, I found subtler reference to Vodou in your first book, *Breath, Eyes, Memory* ([1994]), though in *Krik? Krak!* (1995), there are numerous overt representations of Vodou. Is this because *Krik? Krak!* Is a collection of short stories? Or is it something entirely different— perhaps Vodou's presence in your writing is most connected to the characters' voices?

ED: It's interesting because I remember I went to Haiti with *Breath, Eyes, Memory*. I was doing a gathering with students, and someone said, *There's no Vodou in this book!* And I had to respond, *Literally, the family lwa is Èzili in the book! They say it several times!* [laughs] So I feel in some ways that *Breath, Eyes, Memory* has the most reference to Vodou. You have a family where the grandmother became Protestant but the rest of the family was very syncretic. The grandmother had her Bible, but Èzili was their family lwa, and the women wanted to be powerful—they wanted to be like her. I'm always very cautious. My knowledge is book knowledge; it's not knowledge of practice, so I also want to be respectful. I don't want to fall into the same traps of media representations. You read a book or you see a movie about Haiti, and it's like the characters suddenly hear the drums in the distance and have to somehow find their way to the nightly Vodou ceremony. I didn't want to be that person! In *Breath, Eyes, Memory*, it's so much a part of their daily life; they're not talking about Vodou all the time, but it's in their worldview. It's part of how they see the world. They move through the world as if, *this is how we live, these are certain things we do.*

Krik? Krak! is probably more overt. You had women who practiced Vodou in *Krik? Krak!*, especially in "Nineteen Thirty-Seven." And in a lot of those stories, for instance in "A Wall of Fire Rising" and "Nineteen Thirty-Seven," I was exploring Vodou as a form of resistance. Many of the characters definitely feel that this is how they survived. But they also suffer from the stigma, like when the gardener in "Between the Pool and the Gardenias" thinks to himself about Marie the protagonist: *This woman is a murderer because she found this dead baby on the street, and it must be a human sacrifice.* So, there's a back-and-forth about Vodou in that story, a conversation, if you will, about how it is perceived, even among Haitians. The mother at the end in "Caroline's Wedding," she's very Catholic, but in that story, she has her Vodou rituals, and then there's the silence about it. And I think that silence exists in a lot of Haitian families, including *dyaspora* families. The dilemma of writing about Vodou in literature, like presenting it in art, is not sensationalizing it, exotifying it, or portraying it as something that people take as your condemnation. That's also what I wanted to show in *Breath, Eyes, Memory*: the multiplicity of beliefs that we have as Haitians. But always in the back of our minds is our ancestral line, our lineage. That was the whole structure of *Krik? Krak!*: you come from this powerful lineage.

KMD: I read *Krik? Krak!* a long time ago and wrote about it in graduate school. In preparation for our conversation, I returned to it. I forgot how all of the stories weave together, how the women's lineage is being woven throughout. This becomes even more clear towards the end. These stories are not just puzzle pieces, but are beautifully braided together.

ED: Thank you so much. That was certainly the intent. The idea was for those characters to realize at the end that all these women are carrying you. But let me think again about your question: is the representation of Vodou in my work chronological?

KMD: Yes, has there been a change in your style of writing when it comes to the portrayal of Vodou in your earlier work versus your more recent writing? How does it become clear to you that certain characters must have a relationship with Vodou? And is there any difference in the relationship that men and women have with Vodou?

ED: Maybe, I don't know if there's been a change. I feel like you're probably right, the most noticeable Vodou might have been was in *Krik? Krak!* It was like assembling a village. There was a family line. Talking to you, I'm realizing that I consider Vodou to be matriarchal. [laughs]

KMD: Very much so! I definitely agree that Vodou is matriarchal.

ED: And so maybe for me, if I veer away from the women, then I veer away from Vodou. It feels to me extremely matriarchal. Especially in *Breath Eyes, Memory*, where Èzili was almost a character in the text, because she was such a presence for these women.

KMD: In preparation for this next question, I want to return to something you mentioned earlier before our interview. Did you mention that when reading *Breath, Eyes, Memory*, your mother asked you, *how did you know about this?*

ED: Yes, when she read it, the first thing she said was, *oh my God, people are going to think you're not a good girl.* But that was the sex stuff! [laughs] And then she said, *how did you know?* And I responded: *know what?* At that point, I was just reading broadly about Vodou. I was reading Maya Deren's *Divine Horsemen* (1953). She captured a lot in her writing, and she left behind these extraordinary images in her videography. Some of the visual material she's left us with is so powerful, so respectful. I was also reading Zora Neale Hurston's texts. But when I look back at *Breath, Eyes, Memory*, I think to myself, how did I write this, how did I even know this stuff? I was eighteen years old! But it's almost as if that family was always real. And maybe they were the people next door in that *lakou* of my childhood. Perhaps they were always with me.

But then I got a little shy after writing *Breath, Eyes, Memory*. I think it was because I worried about getting things wrong. I think, too, a lot of us were traumatized by *The Serpent and the Rainbow* experience [the 1988 film]—we didn't want to recreate those representations! And I'm curious with the next generation coming, of Haitian American creators, I mean. Will there be even more hesitation about plowing in and depicting Vodou if there is no direct experience or firsthand knowledge? Maybe we're all afraid of falling into the same traps as the foreigners. Or maybe it's a lack of exposure.

KMD: A lack of exposure to Vodou, that's definitely what comes to my mind. Looking around at the Haitian *dyaspora* today, some of us feel very proud of our Haitian identity, and yet a good number of people from my generation have never been to Haiti.

ED: Yes, sadly a lot of them.

KMD: This could be because of the fear their parents have, especially if they left under the Duvalier regime or under Aristide. But I'm also amazed to see all of the different responses to Vodou in this generation. I feel like there are a lot of people between the ages of twenty and forty who realize they have so many questions about Vodou that no one they know is ready or willing to answer. And my generation as well as the generation just below me are the first ones to grow up with *grandparents* who converted to Protestantism rather than parents. And unless they grew up with a *lakou* next door like yourself, their experience of being Protestant rather than Catholic in the United States allows for less room for the merging and blending of Vodou and Catholic traditions.

ED: There are not many platforms for interfaith dialogue, both among younger and older people in our communities. Haitian people of different faiths speak *at* each other, but not very often *to* each other, without one trying to negate the other. These conversations are not being had often enough in terms of the coexistence of religions in Haiti and in the *dyaspora*. At least not that I know of. So, in addition to our own internal narratives, many of us have also been exposed to the stereotypical narratives about Vodou, including the popular American narratives about it. You also have the *dyaspora* young people who *do* come to Vodou and are very powerfully engaged in the ancestral tradition, like you are. And others for whom it's more focused in a performance-oriented experience.

KMD: Yes! It can be very performative. And there's nothing wrong with that, but that's not quite Haitian Vodou. And that's not even the Vodou of the next generation. That's an adaptation of Vodou, which is equally valuable, but is definitely a transformation of the tradition. I also agree that there's something interesting happening with this new generation. I've been speaking about this with Dr. Charlene Désir, who's based here in southern Florida as well. She said so many young Haitians have been reaching out to her recently, saying, *Listen, I don't want to be initiated, but I do have questions about Vodou, and no one in my family will talk to me.* This is what we were saying earlier. Charlene and I have both done some podcasts and workshops independently, and recently we've been talking about doing a teaching series together about Vodou from an academic platform as well as a personal standpoint.

ED: People need to be hearing from you two, among others, and what you have to say. It's definitely an important dialogue to be had, because other people are using these misinterpretations of Vodou to harm us. For example, my uncle, the Baptist minister who died in immigration custody in the United States at eighty-one years old, had some herbal medicine on him at the airport. That medicine had been helping him for years. It was taken away from him at the airport, and the immigration official who took his medicine called it "Voodoo medicine." That person was acting on stereotypes that might have led to my uncle's death by taking away his medicine. That's just one personal example, but it reveals how misinformation and stigma can have terrible ramifications. And we can't be contributing to that as well.

KMD: Yes, and people need to hear from different age groups. There are so many Haitians who have questions about Vodou, and I think that if they learned the truth about these African-derived traditions and their complexities, they might demonstrate more interest. The reality is that we are also losing some of our Haitians to other sister traditions because Haitian parents so often refuse to answer questions about Vodou.

ED: Absolutely, yes. And frankly, I don't know that a lot of us have as open a door for conversation with our children about certain topics. However, I do think young Haitians are claiming their identity in their own way, so it would be wonderful if they can learn from each other, even if they practice different religions, even if they disagree. It would be great to see the young people having a conversation with one another that the older people have not necessarily had.

KMD: Moving to specific representations in your work, certain tropes keep emerging. It seems that the lwa [the spirits] and the ancestors can be found in *the forest, the river, the sea, and the cemetery.* Many Haitians explain that these are all sites where the spirits manifest, where they present themselves to humans. Could you speak to how these sites emerge in your texts, their connection to the spirits and to Vodou more broadly?

ED: I think growing up in the way that I did—with both the church and the lakou on the other side—I have always been extraordinarily fascinated by rituals, especially rituals of life and death. And that also goes back to the ancient Egyptians, and the Greeks as you mentioned. We all have these very elaborate ways in which we explain to ourselves *how* we come into this world. And that's what stories are, right? This is the realm I'm in. It was always interesting to me how we access continuity to rituals. I also see a lot of parallels between rituals and literary devices, in the sense that you can't just send somebody off. Think about all that we do to accompany the dead, and all that we do to help them transition. And there were things that might be linked to Vodou traditionally, but no matter what faith you practice, you honor the dead, and if you don't, or can't, it's seen as some type of disruption in the natural order of things, both for you and for them. My mother always said, *Yes, feet first—the dead come out feet first! You come out head first hopefully in birth, and you leave feet first.* And all these things that were rituals . . . how did she know? How do we know certain things? Because they're passed on from the people who came before us, and if we pass them on, they'll live on after us.

So the more I learned about Vodou, about the connection to the water . . . they say that after about one year and one day following someone's death, there's a ritual involving water [*wete mò nan dlo*].[2] For me, these types of rituals were what I found really powerful. And the connection of the rituals to nature, to the earth, to the soil, to the water. There are many religions in which you have earth, fire, water, certain types of stones. In Christianity, you have the Resurrection of Lazarus and later Christ himself returning from the dead, which reminds us that our focus should not be on the physical form—rather we must recognize our human transitions "from dust to dust." Even with the family in *Breath, Eyes, Memory,* rituals are what carries them from generation to generation, what connects us to this physical space, though not all the rituals are healing to them. Certain rituals become very complicated, and sometimes muddled in migration, but what we do carry with us is memory. Just like after crossing over on the slave ships, "New World" Vodou ceremonies emerged. So, for me, all of these things are connected. Religious practices like Vodou, this connection to nature, and then, of course what comes in the afterlife. In some religions, what happens in the afterlife is a choice, in some places, it's just where you end up. The connection to these essential elements of nature are key for me when I write and when I am trying to describe someone's life and journey, or even when I am trying to imagine that for them. Because whatever faith we practice, we're always looking for physical manifestations of spirit where we are, and how these things can filter through via dreams and visions.

KMD: I want to ask you a few specific questions about representations of Vodou and divine archetypes, especially in *Krik? Krak!* (1995) and *After the Dance: A Walk through Carnival in Jacmel, Haiti* ([2002] 2014). In both *Krik? Krak!* and *The Art of Death: Writing the Final Story* (2017), you mention the power of butterflies to carry messages. I also want to ask about the importance of sacred trees such as *sabliye* and *mapou* as mentioned in *After the Dance*. How did you learn about the power of butterflies to carry messages? And what are the connections between spirits and trees?

ED: Well the thing is, my grandmother—my mother's mother—lived in Léogâne but *Lavil Léogâne*. Their side was the fancy side of my family; my grandmother had her parlor and everything. But every time she saw a butterfly land, she would say, *I wonder who's visiting?* And I still do that! Especially if . . . sometimes you'll have a relentless butterfly who just won't leave you! [laughs] So I always connected the presence of butterflies in my work to my grandmother's visitations. In C. S. Lewis' *A Grief Observed* (1961), which I read after my parents died, he says to his wife as she's dying of cancer something like: *Promise me that if there's any way you can signal to me where you are, you will.* And his wife replies, *I promise you, I'll pierce the veil of heaven to reach you.* Or something like that. I've always had this strong belief that this veil is not as thick as we think. That there is a kind of fluidity between life and death. And I feel like it manifests in ways like that, in fireflies, in butterflies, through marvelous and fragile creatures in nature. The ancestors and the dead speak to us. I strongly believe that.

So, for me, that comes from my grandmother. A butterfly was never an annoyance to her, you were *never* supposed to squash one for sure—that was a high crime! Even though she was Catholic, she was such a strong believer in nature, such a strong believer that nature could allow people who were on the other side to reach us. And butterflies were one such presence. It's such a perfect metaphor that I think it's almost a cliché. But when you look at such a beautiful creature—so fragile. And I do think that there's a way that we communicate amongst ourselves, between the living and the dead. I think from her I got the sense that the butterfly was one way of communicating. It's obvious to me that we're not alone here. I mean you don't just emerge and go away. There's some kind of lineage. How could somebody spend their whole life loving you, and then just disappear, bye! [laughter] There has to be a way that they can love you from wherever they are. I'm always looking for ways that this manifests itself in the real world. I think that's the challenge of every faith, any faith. Faith in nature, faith in the people we love. As if to say, *please give me a sign—spirit or being—that you have not forsaken me!*

KMD: That we're not alone. And what about trees? In "Children of the Sea" (*Krik? Krak!*), the protagonist sits under the banyan tree . . .

ED: Well the *banyan* tree is like a version of the *mapou* or silk cotton tree. Like the *mapou*, there are certain trees that are sacred for sure. I wrote a children's book called *The Last Mapou* ([2013] 2019) with Édouard Duval-Carrié—it was published in French, English, and Kreyòl. There was one story that I heard about the mapou, I don't remember the source, but I think it goes back to the Taínos and Arawaks [Indigenous people of Hispaniola]. Among their many creation myths, one explains that they were all in a cave, and an Arawak person went out one day and realized, *Oh there's a world here!* But another version explains that the Taíno all lived in this silk cotton tree [the *mapou*] and that one day they just emerged from this tree. Again, you see this connection to nature. Trees were the first temples of any kind. One of the great things about the *mapou*, and I outline it in the children's book, is how it self-generates. And there's *so few* of these trees left! They're just magnificent trees. In other tree lore, there's the forgetting tree (*sabliye*) that we are told enslaved people were made to walk under in order to forget their past on the African continent before they arrived in the so-called New World. One of the things that I've also been fascinated by, and have written a little bit about in *After the Dance*, is the misuse of Vodou in the political space. Like with François "Papa Doc" Duvalier taking on the outward personality of the spirit Bawon Samdi in order to scare the Haitian population (Smith 2012).[3] This was yet another negative revision of Vodou. It's the same thing with the *mapous* and the anti-superstition campaigns of the 1940s, how those trees were cut down, contributing further to the deforestation of Haiti. The symbolism that trees afforded for Haitians and Vodouizan couldn't be allowed to exist. I love how when someone who touched a lot of people dies, people say that a mapou has fallen. But in classic Haitian irony, there is also a proverb that says when the mapou falls, the goat eats the leaves, meaning we can all be humbled.

KMD: In *After the Dance*, you write about a woman who shares her knowledge of *flè kouwòn lavyèj* [Flowers of the Virgin's Crown], and she explains that these are the tears of the Virgin. How might these associations with the *lwa*, the spirits, affect our relationship to the natural environment around us? For instance, you quote the late Ati Max Beauvoir as having said that in Haiti there are lands we recognize as belonging to the first ancestors [*After the Dance*].

ED: Like the *boutilyes* (Danticat [2002] 2014: 107–8).[4] I mean this question is so important now, I find, because there's such an abuse of our environment. I recently wrote this essay called "Pristine Paradise" for a Caribbean issue of a journal called *A Stranger's Guide* (2019). I felt awkward about it, but I decided I just had to write about trash! Last summer, we were in Haiti, and there are places we've visited before, just beautiful rivers, that are now full of trash. I've always had this practice when I go into a river, you salute the river—but the river is full of trash now! And the wider ocean is full of trash. I feel like if we could adopt a spiritual approach to our environment, that would be wonderful. Because even cemeteries are full of trash! Really, I found that quite unsettling. On that same trip, we were coming from La Marine Ayisyènn, closer to the water side near Gressier (near Léogâne). The man who was driving with us was maybe sixty years old, and it was nighttime. We were looking out from the car and we saw this shimmering water in front of us, and we thought, *what is that?* It was *bottles* bobbing in the water. It looked like a silver river, but it had just rained, and it was all these empty plastic bottles were floating on a kind of river in the middle of the street. The man who drove with us said that he had never seen something like this despite having lived in Haiti his whole life. So goodness—it would be great if we started thinking of our entire land as sacred again, as the Taíno and Arawak did, as something not to be defiled. But can we even do that in this globalized age? The plastic stuff is literally dumped there, all the bottles, all the non-biodegradable trash from elsewhere. We did not create all this trash, and the pollution of the land is not entirely our fault, but it is a kind of desecration. It feels like this is one of so many ways Haitian life is abused and attacked by outsiders, who just dump their trash in the country, make us buy all this stuff with all the packaging, and lead us to imitate their Western approach to consumption and waste.

KMD: Definitely, like the introduction of all these plastics, which we didn't used to have.

ED: Yes, and now styrofoam!

KMD: We used to have krich (clay vessels) which we would drink water out of, which can be repaired when they break, and can keep water cool when buried under the earth. And now instead, we have all these foreign and local sache dlo [plastic bags of water].

ED: Yes, I can't help but think of that as a kind of desacralization of our space . . . even sacred spaces have trash. So, for me, that's the next frontier. I see the sea as a space of memory for us. We don't have landfills, so they are [the river and the sea] completely desacralized, completely disrespected. I mean it's really not the fault of Haitians. It used to be that the local trash, people would pile it in their yards and the pigs would eat it. But then foreigners killed the pigs (Farmer 1995)![5] And their foreign pigs or hybrid pigs don't eat peels! The environmental degradation is killing everything that's under our feet. The trash is another layer of tragedy. But if we think of it in a religious context and a healing context, these destructive acts that affect the environment are not just killing us, they're moving us farther away from nature, from what we should consider sacred.

KMD: That's a powerful way to think about it: environmentalism is the next frontier.

ED: Yes, it's kind of obsessed me, because I think about the Arawaks and the Taínos, for example. We're a long way from them, and bless their spirits, but the land they left us, the land that was taken from them, then reclaimed by us, this land—in addition to all the past foreign invasions—the physical land keeps getting attacked in different ways, and there are so many types of environmental abuse. All this dumping of plastics and other outside trash on our land can't help but remind you of how much we have lost.

KMD: Thinking about the ocean as sacred, what inspired you in "Children of the Sea" (*Krik? Krak!*) to write about the heaven of Agwe's underwater palace? And what does Afrik-Ginen, the mythic realm beneath the sea, represent for Haitians?

ED: I always thought at the time that I was writing that story . . . I kept thinking of the Middle Passage. At that time, there were a lot of Haitians arriving in the United States by boat. It was the early 1990s, after the first coup against Aristide. People were just dying, like in "Children of the Sea" and in "Caroline's Wedding," the first and the last story respectively in *Krik? Krak!* Every day, there was a boat that didn't make it. And I kept thinking about the Middle Passage. Again, it's this yearning to imagine an afterlife. There were so many of our ancestors who perished at sea, in that *first* journey. So it was comforting to me to imagine those people embracing these new people who were trying to make this very dangerous journey from Haiti to Miami. It's so far back now, I think that for a lot of people the boat crisis seems distant. But at that time in the 1990s, every week there was a boat. And we learned there were all these people who had left Haiti, but never arrived. The Coast Guard was intercepting just a small percentage of them. I was a student at Brown University at that time, and there were some folks who made it and were relocated to Providence by Catholic Services. I remember spending time with some of them, in their homes, in the church I went to on Sundays. It was kind of like the intensity of the European migration now. Some of the harrowing details they described in their journeys made it into "Children of the Sea." As for the idea of a possible afterlife in an underwater place, I kept thinking of the sea as a reunion with our ancestors from the Middle Passage who jumped off those ships in defiance, in order to swim back to Ginen. And Ginen could be under the water, it could be this other home [Guinea] back in Africa. This makes the idea of dying at sea slightly more bearable, because it meant that you had not lost your path, and that you were not alone, that there are others there to receive you, to embrace you *anba dlo*, under the waters, beneath the sea.

It's like if you died in a fire, your spirit could rise from the flames in some other form, like Boukman was said to have risen. That kind of hope was important for me to allow my characters to have.

KMD: You mention rising in flames . . . I want to ask about the accusations of women with sacred powers. In "Nineteen Thirty-Seven" (*Krik? Krak!*), Josephine's mother Défilé is accused of being a *lougawou*,[6] and she is imprisoned in Port-au-Prince. She tells her daughter the story of her escape during the 1937 massacre at the Dominican border and recounts how she and other women flew with wings of fire across Rivyè Masak, the Massacre River. Where did the inspiration for this story come from? And what are the consequences of our women being accused of witchcraft for their mystic powers?

ED: There were a couple of cases that I knew of when I was growing up of women being accused of being *lougawou*, as Marie-José N'Zengou-Tayo explains (2000).[7] And when I started studying feminist theory, we were introduced to the archetype of the crone, who is in many cases a woman who is "unaccounted for" in the community. And I thought, *that's what the lougawou was! She was a kind of stigmatized crone.* The person accused of being a lougawou is usually an old lady who lives alone. In other African traditions, it would be the woman outside the village who didn't have family. It felt as though it was also punishment for a person being dis-attached, or rather unattached from society. So that came from the accusation stories that I had heard. I have to confess that the first time I heard of a *lougawou*—a woman who can fly with wings of fire—it seemed *so cool*. I thought, *let me be one!* [hearty laughter] Everyone said I was out of mind! But I thought, that sounds like the coolest thing! You get to leave this body and fly in the night sky, and then you come back to your body, unless some vicious person pours pepper on the skin. It really sounded like a kind of superhero to me.

[Reflective now] But those accusations are nevertheless real and dangerous. And as I said, it made complete sense when I started studying feminist theory—I thought, this is a way of punishing women for not having traditional types of attachments. Most people who are accused of witchcraft fall into that category and are being stigmatized or persecuted for not being married and not having children. Ironically, people see it as a way of protecting children. So this story ["Nineteen Thirty-Seven"] is the *extreme*—what could have possibly happened in that situation. The whispers, the name calling, the people who say everybody knew that so-and-so was a *lou-gawou*. I was always sure that these women were misunderstood. That there must be something powerful about them that everybody's afraid of. And that's also what I wanted that story to convey: that there was something very powerful about this Défilé—like her original namesake—be it her trauma or something else, but also the way that she triumphed over her trauma, which had not defeated her but had given her special gifts. And because people didn't understand or because they couldn't control her and her gifts, they decided to punish her instead.

KMD: You also delve into the negative connotations of Vodou, especially among Haitians. In "Children of the Sea," the young girl wants to send *wanga* to exact revenge on the Tonton Macoutes who have attacked the Radio Six. In "Between the Pool and the Gardenias" (*Krik? Krak!*), Marie is attracted to the abandoned baby Rose, but she's worried that there may be women who have put this baby in her path as *wanga* sent to capture her. And Marie's employers think she may be a *manbo*, which "holds the country back," while the gardener accuses her of killing a child and calls the gendarmes on her. What calls you to write about *wanga* and these negative representations of Vodou?

ED: I was trying to reflect a kind of attitude that really exists and is actually quite common. If I were writing it now, some of the anti-Vodou Haitian characters in the stories might be saying the types of things we heard Pat Robertson and others say after the January 10th earthquake, that we as Haitians are "cursed" because we made a pact with the Devil for our independence. Some of the characters in "Between the Pool and the Gardenias" see Vodou as a class thing; it's something that "those people" practice, which they actually say explicitly in the story. I remember why I wrote "Between the Pool and the Gardenias." I actually saw a dead baby on the street in Port-au-Prince, and the thing that I was most fixated on, besides the massive tragedy of it, was that she had pieces of white thread in her tiny pierced earlobes. Someone had pierced her ears, though there wasn't an earring. That's how it was when I was young; my mother did the same thing. When I was younger, when you pierced a small child's ear in Haiti, you'd put a thread to hold the place, if you didn't have earrings to put in the hole. So this little girl, this dead baby, had two threads in her ears. And I remember thinking, *oh my God, someone loved her enough to pierce her ears, but* *she died and they couldn't bury her.* So that's what this character, Marie, saw and thought to herself, *oh this baby, I want a baby, and here's this baby, I can at least love this baby . . . until it's buried.* And because she practices Vodou, this act of kindness is distorted and misinterpreted as *wanga,* or some act of human sacrifice.

KMD: Relatedly, how have you learned about *travay mistik* [ritual work]? Characters like Caroline and Gracina's father in "Caroline's Wedding" stuffed snakes into bottles, while their mother made a charm to make the father remain in love with her. The characters ask, "What kinds of charms will you give your daughters to ward off evil?" ([1995] 2015: 183) What is the role of *travay mistik* in Vodou? Are there similarities in other traditions as well, or is this something unique to Vodou?

ED: You tell me . . .

KMD: I think all religions have some version of *travay mistik*! When people feel spiritually vulnerable, we pray to our god(s), our spirits, and our ances-tors to offer us guidance, provide strength, remove obstacles, grant us blessings. So prayer is one form of ritual work. And many devotees feel their prayers are more likely to be answered if they also take matters into their own hands. So we enact different rituals to attract love, to ensure success in work, to protect ourselves from enemies, to heal our loved ones. Do you feel this is something your characters embody in their own *travay mistik*?

ED: I definitely see the link between vulnerability and the reach for rituals in *travay mistik.* Some of my characters operate from that position. Since we can't always see, hear, and touch the forces, including God, we seek relief, answers, blessings, guidance, and strength through rituals. Church services and ceremonies help us to connect [with these forces] because they offer us a bridge. And these rituals represent visual or aural manifesta-tions of our desire to connect with the invisible world. You learn early on in Sunday school for example—at least I did—that what is seen is temporary, but what is unseen is eternal (2 Corinthians 4:18). So you're supposed to focus your energy on the things that are unseen, rather than the things that are seen. We often inherit traditional rituals and practices that are part of this quest, in whatever way we interpret it, perhaps through family lore, like the women in *Breath, Eyes, Memory*. Also, living here in Miami, you hear radio advertisements for people who advertise their services, their *travay mistik*, as *manbo* and *houngan* for people to go see before their court dates or immigration appointments. There is an open commercialization of Vodou and *travay mistik* as a commercial or practical service, which I guess was always true. Even some Protestant ministers—I've seen a few white ones on TV do this—will offer blessed bottles of water, for example, to bring in money or cures as a commercial *travay mistik* service.

KMD: Some of your characters, mothers especially, create ritual baths for their daughters ("Caroline's Wedding"). What is the role of ritual baths in Haitian culture?

ED: Oh, sacred! We should probably differentiate further, even more than the "religion versus worldview." For me again, it goes back to the rituals. I don't know that every mother whom I write about knows why she does it. It's as if, my mother tells me to do something and I'm like, *okay I'm sitting on this bucket full of leaves because you told me to!* [hearty laughter] *And the water is really hot!* And then sometimes there are words that are said over you, but you don't know what they are.

Again, with the rituals, there's some beautiful mixtures—no matter what religion the person is practicing now, there are some threads that they accept. This is part of our daily lives because these are things that were passed on; we don't know even how far back they go. I really enjoy writing that element into my stories. Obviously, the mother was operating on so many levels there but never bothered to explain! It's kind of like the younger people who are saying, *I have so many questions.* I think in many ways the parents plant the questions. Because you're expected to respect or to honor certain practices without explanation. And some people will go to books and look them up and understand. Or some people will have friends from the Haitian tradition or other traditions, and they'll see echoes in them. But a lot of younger Haitian people are just operating in a void.

KMD: I'm thinking about the importance of dreams in Vodou and the rituals associated with dream interpretation. Many of your characters experience mystic dreams and receive visitations from ancestors and loved ones ("Caroline's Wedding" and "Between the Pool and the Gardenias"). What is the importance of dreams in Vodou?

ED: In many different belief systems, I see dreams as an ancestral conversation. I always have. . . . When my mom passed away, a friend called me and
asked, *Have you dreamed about her or is she still traveling?* And I said, *You know, I
haven't dreamed about her yet.* And then a couple of nights later, I had this
dream of my mom in this beautiful pink coat—she had a pink coat when
she was young—I had a pink coat somewhat like it, but not the same. I saw
her in her pink coat, just looking young and beautiful. And I remember
thinking in the dream, *So you've arrived!* And she nodded. And I thought,
Yeah, that was a communication, we were talking, as much as we're allowed. And
later, I realized that, okay so the rules of this are that we're not going to have
long chats [laughs], but you'll check in every now and then, right? So yes, I
see dreams as something *ancestral.* I also think dreams are one of the many
ways that the veil between this world and the next is pierced. And there are
manifestations in nature, beautiful creatures, like butterflies and fireflies.
But I think dreams are probably the most direct for sure. I know people who
have said, *You know, I know I need to be initiated, because I've had a series of dreams.*
And that's how that message is communicated to them. But again, rituals
can connect worlds and also manifest as literary devices. They offer a wealth
of possibilities. And when you're talking about art and sacred healing, these
things are connected. Art as ritual can lead to a kind of healing, certainly
psychological healing. I've had moments where I feel something after I wake
up from a dream and I realize my health has been helped through dreams
that I've had. You know you wake up differently. So yes, I think the dream-
scape is where we're most open and where that veil between life and death,
as others have written, is most easily pierced.

KMD: Returning to "Nineteen Thirty-Seven," a weeping Madonna appears
in the story. She's probably the icon that stayed with me most throughout
the entire collection. Where did the inspiration for this weeping Madonna
come from? Specifically, would you align her with either the Mater Dolorosa
(Èzili Freda) or the Black Madonna of Częstochowa (Èzili Dantò)? I have
some ideas about her, but of course would like to hear your own thoughts.

ED: Well I had just come out of *Breath, Eyes, Memory* with that family. The
mother in "Nineteen Thirty-Seven" for me is definitely a Freda, like the
Mater Dolorosa, the suffering Mary, the weeping Madonna figure with the
tears. I had just come from the tragic ending of *Breath, Eyes, Memory* and
maybe was grieving that family. When I wrote the story "Nineteen Thirty-

Seven," I was still carrying that grief with me, literally the way that the women were carrying a physical figurine of the Madonna. And I feel that all my female characters carry this presence: that's their *lwa*, Èzili Freda. I had just read about people who were faking weeping Madonnas—they had the formula! So what you do, you make sure she has a little crease under the eye and you put the oil inside the wax, and when the wax melts, the Madonna will cry. I thought, *Oh this is really fascinating.* And I started with that opening line, *My Madonna cried.*

KMD: Yes, that unforgettable opening line.

ED: But it's also about having a physical heirloom which you pass on through generations. To me, that was a very precious thing for that family, which they didn't otherwise have. And that's why they fought so hard to keep the Madonna, as a physical manifestation of their lineage. Just like some people have a saint in their house, but theirs is this crying statue. The mom, Défilé, inheriting the statue is momentous because that's what she has to pass on to her daughter Josephine. So tell me what your theory was . . .

KMD: Mater Dolorosa [Our Lady of Sorrow] is definitely the saint who came to mind, who is associated with Èzili Freda. Because I think Èzili Dantò has a distinct pain that she carries, it manifests very differently. Dantò's pain manifests more as anger.

ED: Right, anger.

KMD: . . . which is why Dantò comes to ceremony *epi l ap rele amway* [she hollers]! I think part of it is her pain, her battle wounds, her being ostracized, her emotional labor for her sister. And then here you have Mater Dolorosa, Èzili Freda, this weeping Virgin Mary, who weeps for *so many* reasons. Who weeps because the world is not perfect, because her devotees don't always remember to do the things that she wants them to do, who weeps because there is endless suffering in the world.

ED: Yes, and the people carrying her are literally carrying the suffering in this case. Also, you know in my day [laughs], there was much more written about "syncretism" than there is now. What some people were practicing in public versus what was actually happening in their inside world, there could be a significant difference. In this family too, you could see how that statue has meant so many different things at so many different times to them. That to me was also very important to show. And what will the statue, the Madonna, mean to the next generation?

KMD: In "Nineteen Thirty-Seven," the Massacre River dividing Haiti and the Dominican Republic serves as both a site of mystic healing as well as a mausoleum for the dead. This same theme emerges in *After the Dance*, when you mention your poet friend Rodney Saint-Eloi, who dips his hands in rivers to connect to the dead. In this way, do rivers operate similarly to the sea as a resting place for the dead?

ED: I see the sea as an international site of memory we share with other African Diaspora people. And that's definitely why I try to make that connection with "Children of the Sea." I think there's a woman who's written a novel about it, what happens when all our different people who were either dumped into the sea or were pushed from those ships during the slave trade, what happens when they create a nation under the sea. This idea that at least there'll be ancestors waiting to receive those who were making the journey [from Haiti to Miami or Africa to the Americas] when they disappeared into the sea was somehow reassuring.

As for rivers, I wrote an essay (2008b) about going to the Rivyè Masak [Massacre River] when I was writing *The Farming of Bones* (1998). When I visited the border, I kept looking for a plaque of some sort. But I got there and I saw people washing clothes, donkeys drinking. . . . And you have to realize, this is also a kind of memory, but for the living. The fact is that this river is still here, and that its being put to use is in itself a kind of living memorial. During my visit, the bridge over the river was maybe the height of a two-story ceiling. And when I spoke to the older people who had lived nearby, they would say, *Mezanmi, jou masak la, rivyè a te rive men wotè! Li te touche pon an!* [My friends! In the days of the massacre, the river was this high! It reached the bridge!]. I mean, if it were true, the town would have been underwater. And in fact, this bridge of the 1990s wasn't even there at that time [in 1937]. But as they were talking, these elders were in their seventies, some of them in their eighties; I realized that their memory was *magnified* to match the catastrophic event.

I remember thinking and writing, *Water has no memory*. Then I remembered Toni Morrison [(1988) 1998] saying that water is always trying to get back where it was. She was talking about how the Mississippi River was straightened out in some places to make room for houses and how the river would occasionally "flood" these places, and she mused, "'Floods' is the word they use, but in fact it is not flooding; it is remembering. Remembering where it used to be. All water has a perfect memory and is forever trying to get back to where it was" (199). Writers are like that, she said. We are always remembering where we've been and the "route back to our original place." She said it was emotional memory, "what the nerves and the skin remember as well as how it appeared. And a rush of imagination is our 'flooding'" (199). I suppose survivors are like that too, and for these survivors of the massacre this was both their remembering and their flooding. So, for me, part of the power of that river was that, like those survivors, it was still there. And it was still being used. There wasn't a gate there, so I stood and gazed at the river. People were still bathing in it. And maybe because there weren't these other formal structures of memorials or plaques or statues, I felt like the fact that the river was still full of life was what it was *meant* to do. And water is precious! Not just this veil between the earth and under there. We don't have that much potable water. And there it was.

KMD: Your work leads me to think about these rivers as a site of renewal and healing but also a site where the dead traverse. Mirrors excite me because they're so connected to water. I'm fascinated by mirrors, and interestingly, the idea that a mirror breaks and brings seven years of bad luck comes from the European understanding that the mirror was a portrait and a reflection of your soul. And so, if you broke the mirror, you broke your soul. African Americans in the United States who encountered this lore came up with remedies to rid themselves of these curses (Daniels 2017). One ritual included burying the pieces of the mirror under the earth, which is compelling to think about in terms of growth and renewal. Another solution involved throwing the pieces of broken glass into the river. So one reflective surface begets another. It's very much in tune with how people of African descent seem to understand that, no matter what misfortune befalls you in life, it can be remedied or at least addressed.

ED: That's powerful. I remember reading *Dust Tracks on a Road* ([1942] 2006), Zora Neale Hurston's autobiography. In Zora's household, before the dead took their last breaths, clocks and mirrors were to be covered to allow time to stand still and to stop departing spirits from seeing their reflections and staying put among the living. Before she died, Zora's mother told her not to let the clocks and mirrors be covered, because her mother had not yet made peace with dying.

KMD: When you're newly initiated in Yorùbá traditions—specifically in Cuban Lukumí—you cover the mirrors in your home because spirit contact could be too easy, you could be too vulnerable to spirit visits at first.

ED: Oh wow. In my new book, *Everything Inside* (2019), there's a story ["In the Old Days"] where the father dies and the family covers all the mirrors. I was always intrigued by the notion that spirit can escape through the mirror. Or could be distracted by it.

KMD: Earlier you mentioned an interest in secret societies. What inspired the women's mystic banter and coded language from the Massacre River in "Nineteen Thirty-Seven"?

ED: Oh, the secret codes? I was reading about *Bizango*. I can't remember the source now, but I remember that to get through certain spaces, in Bizango society, they have to test you with language to make sure you're one of them. I said to myself that the women in the story in my story should also have certain codes so they can recognize each other, even in the dark. That's where that comes from.

KMD: This code resonates powerfully with Haitian initiation rites. In the final stage of initiation, *pran ason*, initiates are tested on their knowledge of the *ason* [ritual rattle]. While the details cannot be revealed to outsiders, the language of rattles is effectively a series of proverbs and riddles. Each motion of the rattle has a gesture and accompanying proverb, which requires the appropriate rattle answer. In essence, it's a language of mirrors. So when I read this passage, I was mesmerized. This idea of testing someone not simply to gauge their connection to community, but also their dedication to spirit, was very familiar.

ED: Oh wow. I don't know if this comes from the practices of all secret societies, but there's also this protective element. Especially in the context of "Nineteen Thirty-Seven," there's this way in which the characters feel, *We have to protect ourselves against people who might want to hurt us, or people who* might want to infiltrate our community. The code is also a way for them to identify the faces of people whom they don't know, but who might belong to their group, people who might have inherited the honor without having had a chance to meet every member of the society! What appealed to me most was how much the codes broadened the society. Like if she met one of these women in Brooklyn and she knew the answers to the code, she would be accepted as part of that sisterhood. I think that was also the mother's gift to the daughter: expanding for her the notion of what a sisterhood is and can be. And what do we pass on? We pass on language. We pass on rituals. We pass on stories, and certainly, the healing practices. We pass on remedies. That's what makes for a society like theirs. From modern African American Greek letter societies to all types of societies, these codes reveal a sense of, *this is how you enter*, and there are things you have to learn before we allow you to enter.

KMD: In *After the Dance*, you write a chapter beautifully and hauntingly titled "Carnival of the Dead." Here, you refer to cemeteries as a "post-life *lakou*" and a "kinship of the dead." What do you mean by these terms? You also mention that you have always loved cemeteries, that you find them to be "altars and entryways for the dead." Can you say more about this?

ED: Well there's something I've always found so powerful in cemeteries as a kind of permanent home. In *One Hundred Years of Solitude* (1967), Gabriel García Márquez wrote that you don't really belong to a place unless you have someone under the ground. I guess I have always subscribed to that. There's this sense that people are there in the cemeteries and at the same time they are not. I was just in New York over the holidays, and we went to the cemetery on my mother's birthday. And there was this duality: I know the body is there, and this macabre realization, *I don't know what state the body is in now*. But I also know that she's *not* there. In Jacmel, what was amazing to me about that cemetery is that you could tell the history of the town through that cemetery. And the place is small enough, you can even tell the class dynamics. Based on the size of the tombstones, where they were located, you can see the financial status of the families. Cemeteries are great introductions to the town.

KMD: Haitian *Kanaval* features many masks, which, as you point out, are featured in several of your writings, especially *After the Dance*. I've taught

After the Dance in my carnival class and the students love it. The class focuses on connections between West African masquerade, Caribbean carnival, New Orleans Mardi Gras, and other Black Atlantic festivals. I think your book is a wonderful way for students to engage with Haiti as it brings Jacmel *Kanaval* to life. Of course, masks are connected to European carnival as well as African masquerade and festival traditions. How do masks play an important role in both Haiti's secular and sacred life?

ED: The only place I've really seen masks active and lively is in the Jacmel *Kanaval* (carnival), which I love. I have seen both physical and psychological mask shedding there, in terms of how people behave! It used to be said that carnival was one of the few times people could freely mix class-wise, though now it's become a little more stratified with the fancy stands and special access floats versus the people walking on the ground. Jacmel is small enough, it's easy to be in close proximity with one another. Jacmel showed me that if we had the means, we'd do even more with carnival in Haiti than we do now. We might be on the scale of Trinidad or Brazil if the means were there.

KMD: I think there's so much that we can learn from Vodou and other earth-based traditions about medicinal plants and indigenous science, broader definitions of gender and sexual identity, and the value of sacred dance, storytelling, and embodied knowledge. I hope that in the future, Vodou remains as dynamic and open to change as it always has been, while still holding strong to *rasin nou*, our roots. We can continue to honor our traditions of Vodou songs, dances, visual arts, healing rituals, and also enter a new era. It would be so powerful for Haitians in the next generation to take ownership of our legacy and portray Vodou as it really is—in literature, on the stage, in visual arts, on podcasts, and in films to share with the world what the *real* face of Vodou looks like. That way, we could underscore the truth of Haitian religion: that Vodou is ultimately about healing and balance. So, as we conclude, what do you think Vodou can teach us— what can it offer the world? And what do you hope for Vodou and Haitian religion(s) in the twenty-first century?

ED: I think we can definitely learn a great deal from looking at how deeply Vodou is woven into our stories of resistance. We should definitely stop the blame and the persecutions, as they can result in real harm as we saw with how many Vodouizan were murdered after the 2010 earthquake and in other historical moments. We also need to have a *real* interfaith conversation between people of different religions in Haiti and in the *dyaspora*. Our national motto is *L'union fait la force* [unity creates strength]—we should be able to coexist, and to respect the faith that each of us practices. I don't know that I can or should ask things of Vodou, however, I would like to ask something of those who depict it, in the arts for instance. We're often on the defensive and are trying to prove ourselves either through Vodou or counter to it. I'm yearning to see more written about Vodou that does not have what Toni Morrison called the "White gaze." In our case I guess it would be the "outsider gaze." Where it doesn't just feel like we're writing about Vodou to rectify what has been said by others in the past, but where we're writing about it more organically. Like you and other Haitians and Haitian Americans have done, for example. I would love to see more of that. It's the same thing of [marginalized people] not writing to prove we're human. And I think with Vodou, like you said we're always on the defense, like, *No we do not pin dolls to kill people!* And it's hard, because people are still writing about these stereotypical tropes. I feel like we need to shake those shackles off, to say, *We're not just rectifying old narratives, we're writing our own narratives, fully within ourselves!*

We have spoken of Vodou's sister religions . . . I've been to Bahia, Brazil, and when I was there, people were celebrating February 2nd, the day of ceremony for the *orixá Iemanjá* [Candomblé spirit of motherhood and the ocean]. So many people in the city were dressed in white, with thousands and thousands of people walking to the water to launch these boats filled with flowers. It was such a beautiful procession. And I thought, *Oh my goodness, could that even happen in Port-au-Prince?* Maybe it has and I'm not aware of it, but I wonder, would people be able to do that so freely in Haiti? And whether you're participating or not, you'd be able to partake in the beauty of it, just as you might be watching a church revival. Watching that happen so peacefully in Bahia reminded me of that balance I remember from my childhood, what I first saw in the *lakou* from the roof of my uncle's house when I was a girl. A kind of peaceful coexistence and respect between religions that made a most incredible impression on the little girl I was then, that contributed significantly to my own evolving spiritual education, and that formed the woman I have become today.

KMD: What a beautiful place to end. Thank you so much for your generosity.

....

Dr. Kyrah Malika Daniels is assistant professor of art history, Africana Studies, and theology at Boston College. Her first book (*Art of the Healing Gods*, forthcoming) examines sacred art objects used in Haitian and Congolese healing ceremonies. Daniels currently serves as vice president for KOSANBA, the Scholarly Association for the Study of Haitian Vodou.

Notes

1 Souvenance (French) or Souvnans (Kreyòl) is a temple and pilgrimage site near Gonaïves in northern Haiti. Souvenance is the center of the Dahomean lineage in Vodou. Along with the temples of Soukri (Kongo lineage) and Badjo (Nago/Yorùbá lineage), also in Gonaïves, Souvenance is one of Haiti's most visited pilgrimage sites.

2 *Wete* [retire] *mò nan dlo*, literally, means to call the dead from the water. This ritual occurs one year and one day after an ancestor's death, or several years after the death of many ancestors, and the ceremony can be elaborate and expensive. The soul is "caught" in a clay vessel known as a *govi*. In the *govi*, the ancestral spirit regains the ability to speak for herself once again, and thereafter serves as counsel and guide for her living family.

3 Before his presidency "for life" between 1957 and 1971, Dr. François "Papa Doc" Duvalier was a medical doctor and conducted ethnography about Vodou during his studies at the Faculté d'Ethnologie in Port-au-Prince. He became notorious for manipulating the tradition and making people fearful of Vodou. He modeled his attire after the lwa *Bawon Samdi* (a key *Gede* spirit of life, death, and sexuality), wearing somber black-and-white garments, with a black hat and dark sunglasses. Duvalier sinisterly declared that, like *Bawon Samdi*, he too had control over the life and death (and sexuality) of all Haitian people. See Katherine Smith's (2012) "Genealogies of Gede."

4 Danticat (2002: 107–8) explains that the late Vodou Ati (national religious leader) Max Beauvoir recalled that the forest of mountains in Seguin, Haiti, were referred to as *boutilye*, meaning "land of the first ancestors."

5 For more on the devastating Haitian pig slaughter of the 1980s, see Paul Farmer's (1995) *Uses of Haiti*.

6 In Haiti, *lougawou* are defined as mystic women who fly at night with wings of flames and attack children. (The French term *lougarou*, werewolf, is a false cognate and does not render the same meaning.) Socially vulnerable citizens, such as elder women and unmarried women, are most likely to be accused of being a *lougawou*.

7 Haitian literary scholar Marie-José N'Zengou-Tayo (2000: 128) recounts: "In July 1987, an angry mob stoned an old woman to death along the Pétionville-

Port-au-Prince road: she had been discovered stark-naked in the early morning by passers by and accused of being a 'lougarou.'"

Works Cited

Beaubrun, Mimerose. 2013. *Nan Domi: An Initiate's Journey into Haitian Vodou.* San Francisco, CA: City Lights.

Bellegarde-Smith, Patrick, ed. 2005. *Fragments of Bone: Neo-African Religions in a New World.* Champaign: University of Illinois Press.

Daniels, Kyrah Malika. 2017. "Mirror Mausoleums, Mortuary Arts, and Haitian Religious Unexceptionalism." *Journal of the American Academy of Religion* 85, no. 4: 957–84.

Danticat, Edwidge. (1994) 1998. *Breath, Eyes, Memory.* New York: Vintage Books.

Danticat, Edwidge. (1995) 2015. *Krik? Krak!* New York: Soho.

Danticat, Edwidge. 1998. *The Farming of Bones.* New York: Soho.

Danticat, Edwidge. (2002) 2014. *After the Dance: A Walk through Carnival in Jacmel, Haiti.* London: Random House Group.

Danticat, Edwidge. (2004) 2007. *The Dew Breaker.* New York: Vintage Books.

Danticat, Edwidge. 2008a. *Brother, I'm Dying.* New York: Vintage Books.

Danticat, Edwidge. 2008b. Preface to *Massacre River,* by René Philoctète. Cambridge, MA: New Directions.

Danticat, Edwidge. 2010. *Create Dangerously: The Immigrant Artist at Work.* Princeton, NJ: Princeton University Press.

Danticat, Edwidge. (2013) 2019 [2013 English edition, *The Last Mapou*]. *Dènye pye Mapou A,* illustrated by Édouard Duval-Carrié. Brooklyn, NY: One Moore Book.

Danticat, Edwidge. 2017. *The Art of Death: Writing the Final Story.* Minneapolis, MN: Graywolf.

Danticat, Edwidge. 2019. "Pristine Paradise." *Stranger's Guide: The Caribbean,* no. 3.

Danticat, Edwidge. 2019. *Everything Inside: Stories.* New York: Vintage Books.

Dayan, Joan [Colin]. 1996. *Haiti, History, and the Gods.* Berkeley: University of California Press.

Deren, Maya. 1953. *Divine Horsemen: The Living Gods of Haiti.* New York: McPherson.

Desmangles, Leslie G. (1992) 2000. *The Faces of the Gods: Vodou and Roman Catholicism in Haiti.* Chapel Hill: University of North Carolina Press.

Dunham, Katherine. (1969) 1994. *Island Possessed.* Chicago: University of Chicago Press.

Farmer, Paul. 2005. *The Uses of Haiti.* Monroe, ME: Common Courage.

García Márquez, Gabriel. (1967) 2006. *One Hundred Years of Solitude,* translated by Gregory Rabassa. New York: Harper Perennial.

Hurbon, Laënnec. 1995. *Voodoo: Search for the Spirit.* New York: Harry N. Abrams.

Hurston, Zora Neale. (1938) 2008. *Tell My Horse: Voodoo and Life in Haiti and Jamaica.* New York: Amistad.

Hurston, Zora Neale. (1942) 2006. *Dust Tracks on a Road.* New York: Amistad.

Kidder, Tracy. (2003) 2011. *Mountains beyond Mountains: One Doctor's Quest to Heal the World.* London: Profile Books.

Lewis, C. S. (1961) 1996. *A Grief Observed*. New York: HarperCollins Publishers.

Michel, Claudine. 2016. "Epilogue: *Kalfou Danje*: Situating Haitian Studies and My Own Journey Within It." In *The Haiti Exception: Anthropology and the Predicaments of Narrative*, 193–208. Liverpool, UK: Liverpool University Press.

Morrison, Toni. (1988) 1998. "The Site of Memory." In *Inventing the Truth: The Art and Craft of Memoir*, edited by William Zinsser, 183–200. Boston: Mariner Books.

N'Zengou-Tayo, Marie-José. 2000. "Rewriting Folklore: Traditional Beliefs and Popular Culture in Edwidge Danticat's *Breath, Eyes, Memory* and *Krik? Krak!*" *MaComère: Journal of the Association of Caribbean Women Writers and Scholars* 3: 123–40.

Smith, Katherine. 2012. "Genealogies of Gede." In *Extremis: Death and Life in Twenty-First-Century Haitian Art*, edited by Donald Cosentino, 84–99. Los Angeles: Fowler Museum of UCLA.

Annette K. Joseph-Gabriel

. . . .

Beyond Tragedy

Black Girlhood in Marlon James's *The Book of Night Women*
and Evelyne Trouillot's *Rosalie l'infâme*

Abstract: This study explores the relationship between past and future in neo-slave narratives that feature Black girl protagonists. Marlon James's *The Book of Night Women* tells the story of six enslaved women and their youngest recruit Lilith, as they organize a slave revolt in Jamaica at the end of the eighteenth century. In *Rosalie l'infâme*, Evelyne Trouillot traces the legacy of women's resistance in Saint Domingue through the eyes of her young protagonist Lisette in this same period. James and Trouillot examine Black girls' coming of age through collective intergenerational acts of resistance that reappear throughout their texts as a cyclical and irreversible momentum toward freedom. This narrative framing challenges retrospective readings of slave revolts as always doomed to failure and encourages readers to reflect on the possibilities that each of these moments held, to create new futures by destabilizing the foundational laws of slave societies.

. . . .

Resistive (adj.): Capable of or characterized by resistance; having a
tendency or disposition to resist something or someone.
—*Oxford English Dictionary*

. . . .

Neo-slave narratives invite critical reflection on time. Slavery in the Atlantic world is the temporal location from which these texts examine various scenes of horror, trauma, and resistance. They also engage productively and provocatively with a range of other genres as they narrate and account for the past. The slave narrative is by turns a predecessor to be emulated

MERIDIANS · feminism, race, transnationalism   21:1 April 2022
DOI: 10.1215/15366936-9554057 © 2022 Smith College

and a constraining force whose limits are to be examined and disrupted. Likewise, the Gothic offers tropes that, when replicated and reimagined, allow for an examination of violence, force, coercion, and the instability of supposedly immutable social roles (Harrison 2018). Tragedy in turn serves as both a literary genre and a mode of narrative emplotment by which we are to read "the slave past [as] provid[ing] a ready prism for apprehending the black political present" (Best 2012: 453).[1] Neo-slave narratives are therefore haunted texts that grapple with the unfinished business of the past, not only in their content but also through their form (Gordon 2011).

Examining the tropes of tragedy in neo-slave narratives proves particularly fruitful for thinking through the question of Black agency in entangled pasts and presents. In *Metahistory*, Hayden White (1973) argues that the tragic mode of emplotting history often concludes with "the resignations of men to the conditions under which they must labor in the world. These conditions, in turn, are asserted to be inalterable and eternal, and the implication is that man cannot change them but must work within them. They set the limits on what may be aspired to and what may be legitimately aimed at in the quest for security and sanity in the world" (9). Tragedy, as White defines it, is the protagonist's ultimate reconciliation with his powerlessness, his inability to alter his place within the laws that govern human existence. Thus tragedy as mode of emplotment allows for an examination of the limits of human action. As David Scott (2014: 33) so cogently argues in *Omens of Adversity*, "it is not the suffering or misery or even death as such that summons the tragic effect (Aristotle's moral emotions, fear and pity) but, rather, the characteristic structure of *action* in human conduct that propels the hero with irreversible momentum toward it" (emphasis in original).

The power of tragedy for the author of the neo-slave narrative lies precisely in this ability to explore the nature of agency in a social, political, and economic system that was premised on absolute agency for some and no agency for others. That the condition of slavery appeared "inalterable and eternal" then—and perhaps even now—is an idea that animates many contemporary renderings of the slave past. Stephen Best (2012: 454) traces the intellectual genealogy of the "neoslavery" critical turn and summarizes its core contention as follows: "the present that most African Americans experience was forged at some historical nexus when slavery and race conjoined, and in the coupling of European colonial slavery and racial blackness a history both *inevitable and determined* proved the result" (emphasis mine). The tragic mode of accounting for a past that is "inevitable and determined" allows authors of neo-slave narratives to examine the nature of resistance by focusing on the struggle waged by actors who are themselves shaped and constituted by the very system they seek to overthrow. It also already dooms resistance to failure, holding up the tenacious afterlives of slavery as evidence that "transformative projects issue almost invariably in disaster" (Forter 2019: 100).

In emphasizing these two elements, that is, the generic mode of tragedy and its preoccupations with time, my primary concern here is with the temporality of the possibilities of human action. If scholarship on temporality in neo-slave narratives has focused almost exclusively on the relationship between past and present and on the neo-slave narrative as an act of memory, it is perhaps because the tragic mode precludes all possibility of a future beyond present horror (Beaulieu 1999; Rushdy 1999).[2] What futures are possible, imminent, foreclosed, and still unimaginable in fictional accounts about slavery?

To examine Black agency past, present, and future, I turn to two Caribbean neo-slave narratives whose emphasis on Black girl protagonists coming of age in slavery allows us to interrogate what lies beyond both the narrative's present and our own. In Marlon James's (2010) *The Book of Night Women* and Evelyne Trouillot's (2013) *Rosalie l'infâme*, Black girls bear the brunt of slavery's violence. They also spearhead some of the most consequential attacks against the institution. In both novels, time recurs as a powerful rhetorical tool for highlighting Black girls' resistance to both their present conditions of slavery and slavery's denial of their futures. Through the experiences of their young protagonists and narrators, both novels disrupt the generic conventions of classical tragedy that undergird so many neo-slave narratives, producing a hybrid form that both engages with tragedy and moves beyond it to imagine futures after slavery.

This attempt to reach beyond tragedy is at the heart of *The Book of Night Women*'s story of six enslaved women who orchestrate a slave revolt in Jamaica and their reluctant young recruit, an enslaved girl named Lilith. It is also central to *Rosalie l'infâme*'s recounting of the legacy of women's resistance in Saint Domingue through the young protagonist Lisette's marronage. Both texts use tragedy to narrate the history of resistance in the Caribbean, notably as they emphasize their protagonists' struggle for freedom within and against the severe limitations placed on their agency as enslaved girls. They also reimagine the "narrative shape" (Forter 2019;

Scott 2004) of tragedy by presenting Black girl protagonists who, even if they do not overcome the forces of slavery, exceed the limitations that slavery places on their bodies, their imaginations, and their futures.

This reshaping of notions of tragedy in both writers' works results in what I am calling resistive tragedy in order to emphasize its departure from and rewriting of the laws of classical tragedy. In resistive tragedy there is no ultimate moment of reconciliation with one's place in a greater, inalterable system as White asserts. There is instead a continuous cycle of resistance that chips away at the organization of power in slave societies. Resistive tragedy engages with the tragic form, draws on it to elaborate the limitations placed on human action in slavery, and therefore "refuses the narrative contours, the naïve, almost teleological optimism about rebellious overthrow" that characterizes revolutionary romance (Forter 2019: 102). This is crucial to recognize, lest we romanticize the catastrophic slave revolt that comes to pass in *The Book of Night Women* and the imminent revolution that hovers on the horizon of *Rosalie l'infâme*. At the same time, resistive tragedy also makes room for imagined futures that are not simply—or not solely—more of the same.

Resistive tragedy therefore refuses the eternal pessimism of classical tragedy, the hopelessness that the seeming intractability of slavery and its enduring legacy would impose on the emplotment of the history of revolution and resistance in the Caribbean. The narrative framing of resistive tragedy challenges retrospective readings of slave revolts as always doomed to failure and encourages readers to reflect on the possibilities that each of these moments held, to create new futures by destabilizing the foundational laws of slave societies. To limit our understanding of neo-slave narratives to a relationship between past and present is to ignore the authors' use of the past, in their presents, to imagine futures that might have been or might yet be.

The Book of Night Women and *Rosalie l'infâme* also depart from classical tragedy's focus on the singular male hero struggling against his immutable destiny. As ambivalent as Lilith is about her enlistment in the enslaved women's planned revolt, her story, as told by Lovey, is ultimately intertwined with theirs. Likewise, Lisette's narrative is bound up in the stories about her mother, Ayouba; her great-aunt, Brigitte; her godmother, Augustine; and her grandmother, Charlotte, as they return repeatedly to their collective origin story of capture, the Middle Passage aboard *La Rosalie* and their lives and deaths on the plantation. The protagonist in each story is not a lone individual struggling against divine (in)justice but, rather, a Black girl coming of age in a community of women who refuse the resignation and acceptance of slavery as the overarching power structure that governs their lives and relationships to one another. As Renée Larrier (2009: 142) shows, these narrators "counter Edouard Glissant's observation that slavery was a struggle without witness" by telling their stories in the present.

If I have emphasized narrative shape, form, and contours, it is because in resistive tragedy, the teleology of romance as linear movement toward triumph over adversity and the cyclical nature of tragedy's ever futile struggle against power come together productively in the form of the spiral. Struggles for freedom in James's and Trouillot's novels are characterized by both cyclical and forward movement, motion that shows both the limits of and possibilities for resistance in slave societies. At the end of both texts, freedom is deferred but remains a possibility, awaiting what James's narrator, perhaps channeling James Baldwin, calls "the fire next time" (James 2010: 259).

Examining the spiral as a rhetorical device in Caribbean literature necessitates an acknowledgment of Spiralism as a literary movement (Glover 2011). The three pioneers of Spiralism, Frankétienne, Jean-Claude Fignolé, and René Philoctète, conceived of the spiral as a rhetorical, formal, philosophical, and aesthetic tool for literary and cultural production in Haiti from the mid-1960s. The spiral became for them a way to engage with temporality, language, and creation. Given the particularity of this movement, located within the specific space of Haiti during the Duvalier years, neither James nor Trouillot would claim to be spiralists, and my goal here is not to claim them as such. Rather I aim to examine their specific uses of a spiral narrative structure in their novels to conceptualize time on the slave plantation.

In *Closer to Freedom*, Stephanie Camp (2004) urges us not to abandon resistance as an interpretive lens but, rather, to complicate it. In naming James's and Trouillot's tragedies as resistive, I want to suggest that the resistance to slavery's crushing power occurs both in the actions of their Black girl protagonists and in the form of the narratives they craft to account for those actions. By reaching beyond tragedy to offer glimpses of a future—even when the Black girl characters and narrators are ambivalent about these futures—both novels shift our attention away from triumph and failure and instead toward possibility as the means to apprehend the value and power of resistance.

It is perhaps not a coincidence that my reading of resistive tragedy emerges from two novels that feature Black girl protagonists. Childhood studies scholars have long persuasively argued that all disciplines benefit from paying critical attention to constructions of childhood and to children as thinkers and historical actors. As Corrine Field (2017: 272) writes, "Adult concerns about childhood are often broader meditations on the workings of power and dependency that implicate people of all ages" (see also Field et al. 2016). Black girls are central to thinking through the resistive possibilities of narrative time because of their unique positions in these texts as daughters who become mothers.[3] In both novels, filiation and motherhood on the slave plantation are at once tender and transgressive, comforting and violent, life giving and death dealing. Mothers and daughters commit unspeakable crimes, sometimes to each other (Sol 2008; Vásquez 2012). They facilitate rape (Circe), commit infanticide (Brigitte), burn an entire family including children (Lilith), and strangle would-be betrayers (Lisette). Simultaneously victims and perpetrators, Lilith and Lisette are both haunted by the smell of burning flesh that follows them long after the smoke has cleared. We would imagine that these blood-soaked tales would foreclose all possibility of a future beyond the immediate horror of slavery's violence, that the endings of both novels would indeed "offer no vision of what a future beyond the horror would/could look like, beyond the puzzling parting visions of the abject figures of widow and slave woman" (Harrison 2018: 2).[4]

Yet against insurmountable odds, Lilith and Lisette come of age, or more precisely, "come of (r)age," to borrow Lashon Daley's (2021: 1036) formulation of Black girls' navigation of historical and contemporary violence "in pursuit of survival, subjectivity, agency, and autonomy." Lilith and Lisette both become mothers, and the novels close with a one-sided conversation between mother and daughter as Lilith's daughter, Lovey, reveals herself to be the narrator of her mother's story, and Lisette promises her unborn daughter that she will be born free.[5] There is a future to be glimpsed here, as I show in my subsequent reading of temporality in both novels. Futurity via reproduction is certainly not uncritically celebrated in these novels, given the brutality of enslavers' co-optation of childbearing for their own nefarious ends. As Cecily Jones (2006: 19) reminds us, "Enslaved children were vital components of the reproduction of the institution of slavery." These closing scenes, centered as they are on the Black girl-turned-woman-turned-mother, are nevertheless productive, "not because they offer a lazy, symbolic representation of futurity, which reproduces a nationalist project of mothering driven by respectability, but because their narratives are capable of challenging such discourses while helping us to recognize the limits of such challenges" (Shoemaker 2018: 31).

My goal in this reading of resistive tragedy is not to substitute the Black girl for the lone white male heroic protagonist of classical tragedy but, rather, to read Black girls in relation. This essay focuses therefore on Black girls coming of (r)age in intergenerational communities of women, and on the forms of kinship that Black girls pursued, desired, and disavowed.[6] Sometimes Black girls submitted to the ministrations of older enslaved women's storytelling and healing rituals. At other times those practices had deadly consequences. As Lilith and Lisette each navigate their place as girls becoming women in the brutal world of the slave plantation, they find that supposedly linear transition from childhood to adulthood to be marked by repeated cycles of brutality. Their acts of resistance in turn offer imaginative possibilities for life beyond the recurring violence of slavery.

Imagining Futures Gone and Pasts to Come

In describing the temporality of their neo-slave narratives, both James and Trouillot refuse the label of historical fiction. They are particularly adamant about the restrictions of accuracy and veracity that the label of historical fiction imposes. They emphasize the creative process and the ability to imagine beyond the parameters of what retrospective analyses would deem to have been possible or not in the eighteenth century. Both writers also express the intertwining of pasts, presents, and futures in their work. James (2015) emphasizes this temporality when he says that his rewriting of women as the leaders of a slave revolt was inspired by the question "what if this happened?"[7] Here James imagines what could have been, the possibility of a different past, informed by the silences he encounters in his present.

For James (2015), as for many Caribbean writers, history has a central presence in his work: "Once I open my eyes all I see is stuff behind me." He argues also that "anybody from the diaspora who is writing any form of fiction who thinks he or she is not driven by history is kidding himself." His use of *driven* is significant because it points to that inevitable forward momentum that is also at work when one looks to the past and sees "the stuff behind." He emphasizes this inevitability elsewhere when he notes, "Somebody is telling this story, writing this story, somebody like me, is fated to be witness" (James 2009). To be fated to bear witness is to accept at most partial control over the task of serving as witness to the past. This idea of fate is central in his crafting of *The Book of Night Women* as resistive trag-edy. His narrator, Lovey Quinn, too will find herself fated to bear witness to the freedom struggles of her mother and the six enslaved women, passing their stories down in writing and through song.

For Trouillot, invoking the past in order to ask questions of the present is also about actively building a better future or what she describes as "a little more happiness down the road" (Danticat and Trouillot 2005). In an interview with Edwidge Danticat, Trouillot reflects on her poetry in the wake of deadly floods in Gonaïves in 2004. She articulates a relationship between past, present, and future similar to James's understanding of temporality in his work: "The Gonaïves tragedy can be considered a defin-ing event of our time. It's not just about mourning our dead, which we continue to do, but moving forward from the present, working to prevent similar catastrophes from happening in the future" (Danticat and Trouillot 2005). Trouillot situates her commemoration of the victims of the Gonaïves flood in the present and argues that creating a better future—not in the linear terms suggested by progress narratives but rather through a contin-uous, dynamic engagement between past and present—is central to that memory work. Mourning, for Trouillot, is not limited to the past haunting the present. It is a creative act that seeks to call into being a future that resists repeating the trauma of the past.

In their conversation, both Danticat and Trouillot draw on tragedy to explore the temporality of action and resistance in Haitian history and through literary production. Danticat asks, "Is there room to look at these sad and tragic moments the country has faced this year as cyclical, or sim-ply coincidental? Do we owe some psychic debt for which we are paying? Does the world owe us one?" (Danticat and Trouillot 2005). Danticat's questions here recall the rhetoric put forward by conservative evangelical preachers in the United States, that Haiti's political and economic diffi-culties are the result of some "original sin" committed during the Haitian Revolution (Danticat and Trouillot 2005). By asking if it is the world that owes a debt to Haiti, Danticat shifts that original sin from the Haitian Revolution to its aftermath. The seemingly cyclical nature of Haiti's politi-cal and economic problems comes not from mysterious spiritual forces but instead from the realities of imperial domination, including France's siphoning of Saint Domingue's natural resources, international isolation of the new republic, and the United States' undermining of Haiti's sover-eignty during its invasion of the country.

In their reflections on the way time unfolds in their novels, both James and Trouillot engage with the recurring legacies of slavery's violence in the Caribbean and in the process offer glimpses of the future—however bleak or hopeful—as possibility. Be it "bearing witness" as an act of preservation or working toward "a little more happiness down the road" as a creative act, both authors highlight the interplay of repetition and change in Caribbean history.

Black Girls' Freedom Dreams

The Book of Night Women draws from tragedy in its treatment of time. For the six women, time as spiral manifests itself in the cyclical nature of violence on the plantation. The narrator articulates this dual motion in her recurring assertion of walking in a circle:

> Every negro walk in a circle. Take that and make of it what you will. A road set before every negro, from he slip through the slave ship or him mother pussy, that be just as dark. Black and long and wide like a thousand year. And when a negro walk, light get take away from him so he never know when he hit a curve or a bend. Worse, he never see that he walking round and round and always come back to where he leave first. That be why the negro not free. He can't walk like freeman and no matter where he walk, the road take he right back to the chain, the branding iron, the cat-o-nine or the noose that be the blessing that no nigger-woman can curse. (James 2010: 118)

James's narrator expresses temporality through movement and yet rejects ideas of progress or stagnation as frameworks for understanding time on the plantation. She chooses instead to emphasize the spatial dimensions of temporality. Consequently, she equates the Middle Passage with a rebirthing of the African in the New World. She expresses the loss of agency that accompanies this movement because the enslaved person walking in a circle finds that it is the road that dictates the destination. The condition of unfreedom is manifested in the idea that it is time, that irreversible momentum along the road, that drives him, rather than his own intentionality. For the narrator, the end of this movement is always violent. In her evocative list of instruments of torture, we see the circular shape of each link in the chain, the hot, rounded tip of the branding iron, the O shape of the noose and the cat-o-nine as it curls through the air. Slavery is an unending cycle of violence. As the claim that "every negro walk in a circle" echoes across several of the novel's chapters, it both takes on a repetitive cyclical quality and moves the narrative forward.

Resistance too is inscribed within this spiral structure of time in a slave society. For example, as punishment for Lilith's spilling hot soup on a guest during the Montpellier New Year's Eve ball, the slaveholder Humphrey orders the overseer, Robert Quinn, to have her whipped at a scheduled time every day for about three weeks. In response to this repeated punishment, the six women undertake a collective act of intergenerational resistance through a nighttime healing ritual after each of Lilith's whippings. This ritual is worth quoting in its entirety here for its visual and aural representation of a woman-centered cycle of resistance to gendered forms of violence such as rape in the context of slavery:

> Two nights a week, six black womens go to Homer room and mix brine, comfrey and sinkle-bible to rub into Lilith back. Even Callisto. Homer and Pallas sing a song in a tongue that be known only to them. Then they sing like negro.
>
> Fi we love have lion heart
> Fi we love have lion heart
> Fi we love have lion heart
> Only fi you
>
> And the other womens come in on the back of the song.
>
> Fi we love will never die
> Fi we love will never die
> Fi we love will never die
> Only fi you
>
> Lilith will hear the song and feel the drum click on they tongue and heal her back. The womens light a secret fire and spirits dance on the wall. Olokun, owner of the seas and god of water healing, and even Anansi, the spider god and trickster. The womens call on Oya, the river goddess of the Niger and wife of Shango. They call on the river mama to plead to the god of thunder and lightning to cast a thunder-stone from the sky to the field and give them powers. The womens go to the river where Oshún be waiting. . . . The womens down by the river with Homer, ... Then later than that, Homer read to the womens and teach the womens how to read. (165–66)

The six women root their healing practice in a discourse of love that is as tenacious as the violence it seeks to counter. This tenacity is emphasized in the cyclical song structure. Their ritual of intergenerational healing is an act of spiritual flight. Through song and memory, they leave the here and now of the plantation and draw strength from an alternate myth of creation and power beyond the reaches of slavery's violence. However, this flight is not simply an escape fantasy. If, as Sheri-Marie Harrison (2018: 5) asserts, "the repetition of 'every negro walk in a circle' throughout *The Book of Night Women*, [is an] example of temporal collapse that wield[s] elements from the past to say something about the present," the six women's repetitive healing ritual collapses time in order to go beyond pasts and present to imagine liberatory futures. Thus Homer's strategic act of teaching the women to read is an example of forward momentum in the temporal spiral toward freedom. Amidst the recurring violence of whipping in the present, and the repeated returns to the past through song and myth, Homer leads the women in preparing for the revolution to come by teaching them to read. In describing Lilith's response to this ritual, the narrator's jarring use of the future tense "Lilith will hear the song" rather than the present tense "Lilith hear the song" again allows the future to slip into this ritual of calling on a mythical past as a source of strength to face a traumatic present.

Ultimately, James illustrates the spiral-like nature of resistive tragedy by situating the women's revolt within a larger history of continued resistance in the Caribbean. Their revolt is inspired by the Haitian Revolution and the wave of uprisings sweeping the Caribbean at the end of the eighteenth century. The narrator chronicles the cycle of revolts in Jamaica between 1702 and 1782—a total of sixteen—and shows that revolution takes on a cyclical quality similar to the repeated violence to which it responds. Likewise, the "six-tell-six" women spread the news of the island-wide uprising by instructing each woman on each plantation to tell six other women. As six tell six tell six, they set into motion an inevitable spiraling toward freedom.

These examples illustrate two central elements of resistive tragedy in *The Book of Night Women*: the emphasis on a collective protagonist, and the continuous nature of resistance in response to the constant cycle of slavery's violence. These core characteristics of resistive tragedy allow for a reworking of traditional notions of tragedy in ways that refuse resignation and silencing. According to White (1973: 9), "The fall of the protagonist and the shaking of the world he inhabits which occurs at the end of the

Tragic play are not regarded as totally threatening to those who survive the agonic test. There has been a gain in consciousness for the spectators of the contest." Within White's framework, the value of tragedy lies in spectators' ultimate awareness of the limits of human agency in resisting a greater power. Yet James shows that each revolt in the Caribbean, even when deemed unsuccessful, plays an important role in reshaping the nature of power in slave societies. That the result of slave rebellions in *The Book of Night Women* is that "white man sleep with one eye open, waiting for the fire next time" suggests that even those who hold power are redefined by the contest between master and slave (James 2010: 259). The contest conditions the very possibility of being for enslavers in the colonies.

Further, it is James's shift from a lone hero to a collective protagonist made up of a community of women that makes this challenge to White's framework possible. As the six women in Homer's room administer a healing salve to Lilith's back to counter the multiple violations of her body, their close physical proximity shows that in a slave society there can be no spectators. There is no chorus observing and narrating events at a safe distance or from a space external to the main action. In a slave society in which slavery is the raison d'être, as Michel-Rolph Trouillot (2015) argues, all are participants.

In *Rosalie l'infâme*, time as spiral is inexorable movement toward freedom through marronage. Lisette's coming of (r)age is shaped by a cycle of storytelling, a continuous engagement with the past in the present in order to prepare her for future flight from the plantation as an ultimate act of resistance. Three stories hold particular significance for Lisette, and she asks to hear them repeatedly: the story of the barracoons, the crossing aboard *La Rosalie*, and the story of her great-aunt Brigitte's resistance and death. Each one has a different significance for storyteller and listener. Lisette's grandmother Charlotte readily recounts the Middle Passage, beginning with the same formula each time and then pausing at the end of her introduction so that Lisette might choose the particular story she wanted to hear. Grann Charlotte's introduction to these stories maneuvers between the different spaces of trauma and healing that characterize the temporality of her capture and resistance:

> Toutes ses paroles commençaient de la même façon. "Ayouba, ta mère, n'avait pas encore compris le sens de sa destiné quand commença l'horreur. Nous étions au moins une vingtaine, des hommes jeunes, beaux et

forts, des femmes couleur de vie, la poitrine haute et belle, les rires aux yeux et les mains pleines. Libres. Brigitte aurait pu te dire comment nous avons été capturés, comment nous avons résisté; moi je veux seulement essayer de me rappeler la joie toute simple qui existait avant cette odeur de vagues, de vent et de sables vivants sous les pieds. Je ne veux penser qu'à ces images de dunes et d'épaules nues. Avant la capture et Rosalie l'Infâme. Parce qu'après je n'aurai rien de chaud à mettre dans ma mémoire, sauf le poids de ta main contre ma joue le jour de ta naissance." (Trouillot 2003: 32)

All her remarks began the same way: "Ayouba, your mother, had not yet understood the meaning of her destiny when the horror began. We were about twenty people, young men, beautiful and strong, young women, full of life, with high and beautiful chests, laughing eyes, and promising hands. Free. Brigitte could have told you how we were captured, how we resisted. Me, I only want to remember the simple joy that existed before, before the smell of those waves, those winds, and the sand moving beneath our feet. I don't just want to remember sand dunes and the bare shoulders of slaves. I want to think about the time before the kidnapping, before The Infamous Rosalie. Because afterward I'll have nothing warm to hold in my memory, except the weight of your hand against my cheek the day of your birth." (Trouillot 2013: 24)

Two elements of temporality are particularly striking in this narrative. First, Charlotte begins with the period of their capture: "when the horror began," a time in the past. Like the six-tell-six women's healing ritual, her return to the past through repeated storytelling is ultimately her attempt to create a future beyond the reach of trauma. This act of creation emerges in her shift from the simple past and past conditional tenses in her account to the future tense in her final sentence. For Charlotte, the desire to stock up positive memories for the future motivates the memory work of storytelling, even if for now her ability to speak that future only through negation ("je n'aurai rien") holds it in abeyance. For Lisette, going beyond her present moment of the trauma of her captivity to access a more uplifting origin narrative provides her with the framework she needs to conceptualize freedom and eventually undertake her marronage to a space in the future that exists beyond the plantation. The second striking element of temporality in Charlotte's narrative is the fact that Trouillot's narrator, like James's, emphasizes the spatial dimensions of the passage of time. The past is an imagined space located at once in the barracoons, aboard the slave ship, but also in "the sand moving beneath our feet," in those living spaces that exist beyond slavery as death.

However, if Charlotte is willing to rewrite their collective origin narrative and to locate it in a time before the Middle Passage, she refuses to oblige Lisette's requests for the story of Brigitte's resistance and death, and the story of the barracoons. Lisette notes, "Grand-mère se prêtait à ma requête, sauf lorsque je lui réclamais l'histoire de Brigitte et celle des barracons qu'elle gardait pour un jour spécial, à venir" (Trouillot 2003: 33; Grandmother would agree to my request, except when I demanded she tell Brigitte's story or the one about the barracoons that she was keeping for a special day, a day still to come [Trouillot 2013: 25]). Charlotte's response to Lisette is often "Un jour, je te le promets, je te parlerai de ces barracons, un jour où tu auras besoin d'ailes pour te porter au-delà du moment présent. Un jour, où ton besoin sera plus fort que ma peur de retourner là-bas, dans ma mémoire. Pas aujourd'hui" (Trouillot 2003: 33; One day, I promise you, I'll tell you about the barracoons; one day, when you'll need wings to carry yourself beyond the present moment. One day, when your need will be greater than my fear of going back there in my memory. But not today [Trouillot 2013: 25]). Brigitte's act of resistance—which we later find out is her killing of seventy babies born into her care as a midwife—is contained within the multiple ellipses of this exchange, suspended in the realm of the unspeakable. Her story for Lisette is a past that is yet to come, yet to be spoken into being. However, the promise of "un jour à venir" (Trouillot 2003: 33) bears a close resemblance to the noun l'avenir (the future). Thus, when Lisette finally learns the story of Brigitte, it provides the impetus she needs to undertake her marronage. Women's collective resistance, including infanticide and storytelling, functions as that invisible force that sends Lisette spiraling toward freedom. Revisiting spaces of trauma is an active engagement with the past in order to go "beyond the present moment."

Yet even as Trouillot seemingly gives her characters free rein to go beyond the hopelessness of their present conditions through their resistive imaginations, she also refuses to create the illusion of absolute agency in navigating the pasts, presents, and futures that shape her protagonist. Like James's negro walking in a circle, the women who arrive in Saint Domingue aboard the slave ship La Rosalie seem fated to keep returning to the site of their capture and uprooting from Africa. One striking example of this cyclical, involuntary return is the dream that Marie-Pierre relates to Lisette.

Lisette describes Marie-Pierre as an African-born woman who "semble faire partie de la terre tant elle est petite et tant sa peau a pris le craquelé rougeâtre des mornes. Elle sent le sucre de canne car elle passe sa vie à pousser les cannes entre les tambours à broyer" (Trouillot 2003: 95; seems an extension of the earth itself, with her small body, and her skin, a cracked reddish mountain hue. She smells of sugarcane since she spends her whole life pushing cane stalks through the rollers [Trouillot 2013: 86]). Marie-Pierre's proximity to the earth and the fact that she takes on the qualities of the plantation's landscape and architecture through her skin color and smell would suggest some form of reconciliation with her place and root-edness in her new space. Yet despite the seemingly harmonious continuity between Marie-Pierre, the physical terrain of Saint Domingue, and the brutal space of the sugarcane mill, the enslaved woman habitually leaves the plantation and returns to *La Rosalie* in her dreams.

Marie-Pierre's narrative, in addition to reinforcing the nuanced temporality of resistive tragedy, also engages with the (im)possibility of enslaved women's action and resistance:

Tu diras pour moi à Augustine que la nuit dernière je suis retournée sur *Rosalie l'Infâme*. Je ne voulais pas y aller, l'entrepont était couvert de gens luttant contre une terrible tempête. J'aurais voulu me sauver, j'ai essayé de me jeter à l'eau pour échapper aux bras qui m'agrippaient de partout. Mais tu sais comment les rêves peuvent parfois être de mauvaise foi et vous trimbaler de catastrophe en catastrophe. Soudain je me suis retrouvée à terre, dans l'obscurité des barracons, enchaînée à des chiens qui mettaient bas. Des bébés tout noirs et brillant sans arrêt leur sortaient du ventre. Je peux te l'avouer, Lisette, j'étais terrifiée. Puis j'ai vu Brigitte dans mon rêve, toujours aussi magnifique, toujours grande et belle, mais les larmes aux yeux. Je n'ai jamais vu pleurer ta grand-tante, même quand sur le bateau l'un des Blancs l'a frappée en pleine poitrine, même quand on l'a isolée et enfermée dans un réduit où elle devait rester courbée en deux et pouvait à peine bouger. Mais je l'ai vue pleurer dans mon rêve. Ses larmes tombaient comme des torrents drus et violents. Plusieurs nègres passaient dans les flots en hurlant, et je suppliais Brigitte d'arrêter ses larmes parce qu'on allait tous se noyer si elle continuait ainsi. Puis nous somme retournées sur l'entrepont, les eaux nous tombaient dessus et couvraient le bateau. C'était comme si on allait tous périr. C'est toujours la mauvaise foi des cauchemars ; ils s'amusent à vous tourner la cervelle.

Alors, j'ai hurlé moi aussi et je me suis réveillée en sueur. J'ai l'impression que je suis sortie trop tôt du rêve. Comme si j'avais manqué la fin! (Trouillot 2003: 96–97)

You'll tell Augustine for me that last night I returned to The Infamous Rosalie. I didn't want to go; the steerage was filled with people battling a terrible storm. I wanted to save myself, so I tried to throw myself into the waters to escape the arms that were clutching me from all directions. But you know how dreams can be dishonest and can put you through hell and high water. Suddenly I found myself lying on the floor, in the darkness of the barracoons, chained to dogs that were giving birth. Totally black, brawling pups were coming out of their wombs. Lisette, I admit I was terrified. Then I saw Brigitte in my dream, as magnificent as always, still tall and beautiful, but with tears in her eyes. I never saw your great-aunt cry, even when one of the whites punched her directly in the chest, even when they locked her up alone in a little cubbyhole, where she had to stay bent in half, barely able to move. But in my dream I saw her cry. Her tears fell in thick, violent torrents. Several slaves were screaming as they passed through the waters, and I begged Brigitte to stop her tears because we were all going to drown if she kept on crying. Then we turned around in the steerage; the waters were falling on us, dousing the ship. It looked like we were all going to perish. That is the bad faith of nightmares: they enjoy playing tricks on our minds. Then I screamed too and woke up drenched in sweat. I feel like I left the dream too soon and missed the end of it! (Trouillot 2013: 88)

This passage is but one example of Trouillot's use of rich imagery to evoke moments of stillness and quiet resistance amidst the turbulence, horror, and screams on the slave ship. Certainly, there is much to analyze here, including the terrible tempest that prefigures the violence into which the African captives would be delivered in the New World, a violent baptism that echoes Lovey Quinn's equation of the slave ship with the mother's pussy. Within this plethora of highly evocative imagery, I want to focus on the two women at the center of the dream, Marie-Pierre as narrator and Brigitte.

For Marie-Pierre, this dream is very much a tragedy. It is not the horror and death in and of themselves that create the tragic effect. Rather it is Marie-Pierre's helplessness and inability to effectively resist the forces that pull her to this tragic end. She cannot resist the unseen force, symbolized by myriad disembodied hands, that confines her to the ship. Nor can she control her physical location in the space and time of the dream. The dream, like James's road as time personified, takes on anthropomorphic qualities and propels Marie-Pierre from one catastrophe to the next. The verb that Marie-Pierre employs to characterize this motion, *trimbaler*, has strong connotations of movement that is met with resistance. It evokes the image of dragging someone from place to place against their will. This idea of will is significant for our understanding of the loss of agency that Marie-Pierre faces aboard the slave ship. Notably, her lack of control over her movements in the dream means that she is unable to free herself from the ship by jumping overboard to her death as she wishes to do. She has no agency over that most fundamental decision to live or to die.

Marie Pierre's powerlessness in turn throws into relief the resistive nature of Brigitte's killing of the babies that will be born into her care as a midwife once she arrives in Saint Domingue. The testimony of the Arada midwife, the historical figure on whom Trouillot bases her fictional character Brigitte, illustrates the challenge that this gendered form of resistance poses to notions of classical tragedy. According to the French physician and historian Michel Descourtilz (1809: 119–20), as the midwife approached the stake at which she was to be burnt as punishment for her crimes, she initially appeared repentant and then became defiant:

> [Elle] marchoit lentement, la tête baissée, lorsque tout à coup, par un excès de rage et de désespoir, arrachant une ceinture qui retenoit sa chemise: "Voyez, dit-elle, si j'ai bien mérité mon sort . . . . Ma qualité de sage-femme me donnant les occasions de tenir en mes mains les nouveaux nés . . . je plongeois à l'instant une épingle dans son cerveau . . . de là, le mal de mâchoire si meurtrier en cette colonie, et dont la cause vous est maintenant connue. Je meurs contente à présent que je n'ai plus rien à confesser, et vais rejoindre dans mon pays, tout ce que j'y ai quitté." A ces mots, elle s'élance avec intrépidité vers le brasier dévorant.

> She walked slowly with her head bowed, when suddenly, in a burst of rage and despair, ripping the belt that held her shirt: "See, she said, if I have deserved this fate. . . . My role as a midwife gave me opportunities to hold newborns in my arms . . . I plunged a pin in his brain . . . causing the lockjaw that is so murderous in this colony and whose cause you know now. I am dying happy now that I have nothing more to confess and I will be reunited in my country with all those I left behind." With these words, she threw herself toward the devouring flames. (translation mine)

The Arada midwife's initial slow, remorseful march to her punishment is that moment of reconciliation and resignation that characterizes White's definition of the narrative arc of tragedy. Yet the Arada woman, like Brigitte, engages in resistive tragedy by refusing this end to her story. The plethora of active verbs such as *arracher* (to rip), *plonger* (to plunge), and *s'élancer* (to hurl oneself) cast her as a central actor in this historical contest between enslavers and enslaved woman over the lives of seventy of Saint Domingue's children. The result of this contest, contrary to White's theory, is indeed threatening to the very order of the slave society. In revealing herself to be the cause of infant deaths by lockjaw, the midwife situates herself also as the arbiter of the newborns' fate. In challenging the idea of a just and deserved fate ("mon sort") meted out by the colonial judicial system, the Arada woman emphasizes the gendered nature of her resistance, asserting that it is precisely her capacity as a midwife that allows her to undertake these repeated acts of resistance. That she throws herself into the fire and moves voluntarily toward her death in a way that the fictional Marie-Pierre remains powerless to do reminds us that the story of the Arada woman is not romance but tragedy. She cannot triumphantly escape the punishment of the courts. However, she emphasizes the resistive nature of this tragedy by placing herself beyond the reaches of the slave society (*dans mon pays* [in my country]) after her death.

In *Rosalie l'infâme*, Brigitte's apparition in Marie-Pierre's dream symbolizes that same refusal of resignation that characterizes the Arada woman's story as resistive tragedy. Her violent torrential tears inundate the other captives as in a flood. This flooding may very well symbolize the moment of baptism that accompanies their birthing through the Middle Passage. It also approximates the ocean waves that Marie-Pierre hopes will sweep her away from the terror that awaits her. Thus Brigitte's tears evoke life in an atmosphere of death. This understanding of life through death informs her acts of infanticide.[8] In that still, quiet moment when she slips a pin into the baby's head to induce lockjaw and death, Brigitte, like Marie-Pierre, imagines death as deliverance from slavery, perhaps even as life beyond the reaches of slavery. To regain control over life and death is to attempt to restore the agency that slavery takes away. It is to imagine death as marronage.

Marie-Pierre's dream functions as a space of transformation and resistance because it is where Brigitte cries for the first time. The dream becomes a space that is constituted by slavery yet also exists beyond its reach. The sacred dream space of another enslaved woman becomes the only site at which Brigitte can finally weep for her sons, killed while trying to protect their mother from capture, and for the babies she kills in Saint Domingue. Marie-Pierre's involuntary return to the past creates a space to mourn the foreclosure of motherhood and the truncated futures of murdered children. If Brigitte's refusal to cry before her captors in her lifetime symbolizes her refusal to accept their total power and control over her, her ability to mourn in death signals yet another refusal, this time of the normalization of violence and death on which slavery is premised. In death, Brigitte reclaims that humanity that allows her to grieve for the murdered children, for futures that will never be.

Ultimately, in Marie-Pierre's and Brigitte's intertwined narratives, the end is always deferred. There is no neat conclusion, no clear moment of ultimate triumph over slavery and racialized domination. This deferred end also characterizes the plot of *Rosalie l'infâme*. The story ends with a pregnant Lisette's departure from the plantation to begin her journey west as a maroon, a journey enabled by her newly acquired knowledge of Brigitte's story. She flees with Brigitte's chord—its seventy knots representing each of the killed babies—resting against her stomach. She promises her unborn child, "enfant créole qui vis encore en moi, tu naîtras libre et rebelle, ou tu ne naîtras pas" (Trouillot 2003: 137; Creole child who still lives in me, you will be born free and rebellious, or you will not be born at all). Scholars have largely read these closing words with optimism, interpreting them as Lisette's choice of life over death (Jean-Charles 2016, 2018; Sol 2008). My reading of the ambiguity of the novel's conclusion aligns with Larrier's (2009: 143) assertion that "Lisette's closing words leave open the possibility that she may change her mind and assume the once-unspoken part of Brigitte's legacy." Resistive tragedy's intertwining of agency and lack thereof supports this more cautious reading. Brigitte's chord resting on Lisette's unborn child leaves open the possibility that, should freedom not be possible, the child will not be born. Lisette's road, like that evoked by Lovey Quinn, may very well bring her back to her great-aunt and to the terrible choice of infanticide as resistance. By closing the narrative on this note of life and death, ending and beginning, *Rosalie l'infâme* locates Lisette's and her daughter's freedom in that space where past, present, and future meet.

The Book of Night Women locates freedom in this same space. The novel ends with a sentence also found on its first page: "You can call her what they call her. I goin' call her Lilith" (James 2010: 417). Time as spiral has moved

Jamaica in circles and forward to a new moment that is neither the beginning nor end of slavery. In the four hundred odd pages contained between those two utterances of Lilith's name, the island has been rocked by an uprising, which does not overthrow the system of slavery but brings both slave owners and the enslaved to a new moment of reckoning with the levels of violence and brutality needed to quell resistance and maintain the status quo. These deferred endings convey the longevity of slavery and its legacies of imperialism and economic inequality that still haunt the Caribbean today. Yet resistive tragedy would have us read in these deferred endings, too, the multiple and continued possibilities for resistance, that ongoing spiraling toward freedom in which enslaved girls in the eighteenth century found a new place, a new way of being both within and beyond the reaches of slavery. The irreversible momentum of resistive tragedy continues to propel the Caribbean toward futures imagined and hoped for.

What does this future look like? James and Trouillot imagine it as an embodied future, present in the new generation of Black girls—Lovey and Lisette's unborn daughter—who will also locate themselves in the spiral toward freedom. I use the term *generation* here deliberately, to signal not just the passage of time but also the generative potential of alternate historical accounts to imagine new life even amidst death. For Lisette, the relationship between life and death, creation and destruction, is at the center of this freedom to come. As she recalls her rape by her enslaver's son, Raoul, a violent sexual encounter that marks a rite of passage for an enslaved girl in the brutal setting of the plantation, she notes: "Je sens la rage et la haine envahir mon chagrin et m'habiter de juste colère. Pour l'instant, une colère d'eau tranquille, petit vent léger sans parapluie. Mais avons-nous d'autres choix que les averses et les pluies torrentielles, les tremblements de terre où tout change de place et de saison?" (Trouillot 2003: 40–41; I feel the rage and hatred take over my sadness and settle into righteous anger. At the moment my anger is like calm water, a light breeze with no protection. But do we have any other choice than to accept the showers and the torrential rains, the earthquakes, when everything changes place and season? [Trouillot 2013: 33]). In Lisette's words we see motion once again. The initial inertia and immobility that characterize her rage gradually evolve into a powerful movement—symbolized by torrential rains and earthquakes—that is at once a destructive and creative force, shaking the very foundations of systems of oppression and inequality (*tout change de place* [everything changes place]). As Charlotte tells Lisette,

"Ton histoire doit veillier sous ta peau, à la pointe de tes cheveux. Chaque morceau que tu y ajoutes fait pousser des racines et des étoiles à tes rêves" (Trouillot 2003: 28; Your story must dwell, vigilant, under your skin, at the tips of your hair. Each piece that you add to it grows roots and stars for your dreams [Trouillot 2013: 20]).

History, seemingly dormant beneath the skin, has the power to bring forth new creations for Lisette, in much the same way as James's and Trouillot's engagement with history brings forth new futures, new possibilities for refusing the eternal pessimism about the potential for eradicating slavery's legacy of continued inequality in the Caribbean. Production and creation within moments of destruction recur in Caribbean historical fiction. If James and Trouillot reproduce elements of tragedy in both the content and form of their novels, their texts also offer us new ways to think about agency through their innovations on and departures from the genre of tragedy. They signal not only the past haunting the present but also the very possibility of being in the future.

· ·

Annette K. Joseph-Gabriel is an associate professor of Romance Studies at Duke University. She is the author of *Reimgaining Liberation: How Black Women Transformed Citizenship in the French Empire* (2020).

Notes

I am immensely grateful to the *Meridians* editorial team and to the anonymous reviewers for their labor under the difficult conditions of a pandemic. Their feedback and expertise remain invaluable for my ongoing thinking about time.

1   See, for example C. L. R. James's ([1963] 1989) reading of twentieth century African and Caribbean anticolonial thought through the prism of the Haitian Revolution. In more contemporary scholarship, Stephen Best (2012: 454) productively disrupts modes of reading that "predicate having an ethical relation to the past on an assumed continuity between that past and our present."

2   Beaulieu (1999: 156) closes her analysis of Black women's representations of life under and resistance to slavery by briefly gesturing to the possibility of seeing the future in the past. A notable exception is Margo Natalie Crawford's (2016: 79) evocation of the "post-neo-slave narrative" as a genre that thinks temporality otherwise by disrupting the conventions of the neo-slave narrative and examining, among other things, "the trauma of reproductive futurity."

3   The lives and experiences of Black girls have gone largely (although not entirely) unaccounted for in histories of the slave trade and slavery. Randy M. Browne and John Wood Sweet (2016: 213) note that between 1776 and 1808 "captives from the Bight of Biafra had about a 40% chance of being taken to Jamaica . . . [and] were more likely to be female—and particularly girls."

4   For a rich and generative reading of horror in *The Book of Night Women*, see also Forbes 2017.

5   Both James and Trouillot leave ambiguous the genders of their protagonists' children. Scholars largely read Lovey Quinn as Lilith's daughter, likely because she bears the name that her father, Robert Quinn, called Lilith. In the closing pages of *Rosalie l'infâme*, Man Augustine tells Lisette "Ce sera une fille" (It will be a daughter), and Lisette calls her "ma fille qui naîtra" (my daughter who will be born) (Trouillot 2003: 136–37).

6   On Black girls and varied forms of kinship see Field and Simmons 2019 and Owens 2019. Owens's analysis of Black girls' disappeared correspondence as "fugitive letters" offers a particularly productive avenue for reading some of the silences and obfuscation of the archive and for seeing the disruptive possibilities of Lovey's and Lisette's storytelling practices. On Black women's disavowal or refusal of kinship, see Glover 2021.

7   For a historical account of enslaved women's roles in revolution in the Caribbean, see Bush 2008.

8   For a discussion of enslaved women's midwifery practices, infanticide, and the misdiagnosis of tetanus as the leading cause of infant mortality in the colonies, see Barbara Bush's chapter "Slave Motherhood: Childbirth and Infant Death in a Cross-Cultural Perspective," in Bush 2008 (120–50).

Works Cited

Beaulieu, Elizabeth A. 1999. *Black Women Writers and the American Neo-slave Narrative: Femininity Unfettered*. Westport, CT: Greenwood.

Best, Stephen. 2012. "On Failing to Make the Past Present." *Modern Language Quarterly* 73, no. 3: 453–74.

Browne, Randy M., and John Wood Sweet. 2016. "Florence Hall's 'Memoirs': Finding African Women in the Transatlantic Slave Trade." *Slavery & Abolition* 37, no. 1: 206–21.

Bush, Barbara. 2008. *Slave Women in Caribbean Society, 1650–1838*. New York: ACLS History E-Book Project.

Camp, Stephanie. 2004. *Closer to Freedom: Enslaved Women and Everyday Resistance in the Plantation South*. Chapel Hill: University of North Carolina Press.

Crawford, Margo Natalie. 2016. "The Inside-Turned-Out Architecture of the Post-neo-slave Narrative." In *The Psychic Hold of Slavery: Legacies in American Expressive Culture*, edited by Soyica Diggs Colbert, Aida Levy-Hussen, and Robert J. Patterson, 69–85. New Brunswick, NJ: Rutgers University Press.

Daley, Lashon. 2021. "Coming of (R) Age: A New Genre for Contemporary Narratives about Black Girlhood." *Signs: Journal of Women in Culture and Society* 46, no. 4: 1035–56.

Danticat, Edwidge, and Evelyne Trouillot. 2005. "Evelyne Trouillot by Edwidge Danticat." *Bomb Magazine*, no. 90 (Winter). bombmagazine.org/article/2708/evelyne -trouillot.

Descourtilz, Michel E. 1809. *Voyages d'un naturaliste, et ses observations faites sur les trois regnes de la nature, dans plusieurs ports de Mer Français: En Espagne, au continent de l'Amerique septentrionale, à Saint-Yago de Cuba, etc.* Paris.

Field, Corrine T. 2017. "Why Little Thinkers Are a Big Deal: The Relevance of Childhood Studies to Intellectual History." *Modern Intellectual History* 14, no. 1: 269–80.

Field, Corinne T., Tammy-Charelle Owens, Marcia Chatelain, Lakisha Simmons, Abosede George, and Rhian Keyse. 2016. "The History of Black Girlhood: Recent Innovations and Future Directions." *Journal of the History of Childhood and Youth* 9, no. 3: 383–401.

Field, Corinne T., and Lakisha Michelle Simmons. 2019. "Introduction to Special Issue: Black Girlhood and Kinship." *Women, Gender, and Families of Color* 7, no. 1: 1–11.

Forbes, Curdella. 2017. "Bodies of Horror in Marlon James's *The Book of Night Women* and Clovis Brown's Cartoons." *Small Axe: A Caribbean Journal of Criticism*, no. 54: 1–16.

Forter, Greg. 2019. *Critique and Utopia in Postcolonial Historical Fiction: Atlantic and Other Worlds.* New York: Oxford University Press.

Glover, Kaiama L. 2011. *Haiti Unbound: A Spiralist Challenge to the Postcolonial Canon.* Liverpool, UK: Liverpool University Press.

Glover, Kaiama L. 2021. *A Regarded Self: Caribbean Womanhood and the Ethics of Disorderly Being.* Durham, NC: Duke University Press.

Gordon, Avery. 2011. *Ghostly Matters: Haunting and the Sociological Imagination.* Minneapolis: University of Minnesota Press.

Harrison, Sheri-Marie. 2018. "Marlon James and the Metafiction of the New Black Gothic." *Journal of West Indian Literature* 26, no. 2: 1–17.

James, C. L. R. (1963) 1989. "Appendix: From Toussaint L'Oeverture to Fidel Castro." In *The Black Jacobins: Toussaint L'Oeverture and the San Domingo Revolution,* rev. 2nd ed., 391–418. New York: Vintage Books.

James, Marlon. 2009. "Interview with Marlon James." Interview by Maud Newton. Maud Newton, April 17. maudnewton.com/blog/marlon-james-on-bossy-female-characters-and-more/.

James, Marlon. 2010. *The Book of Night Women.* New York: Riverhead Books.

James, Marlon. 2015. "Interview with Jamaican Novelist, Marlon James." Interview by Vladimir Lucien. The Spaces between Words: Conversations with Writers. http://www.spaceswords.com (accessed April 12, 2015).

Jean-Charles, Régine M. 2016. "Memwa se paswa: Sifting the Slave Past in Haiti." In *The Psychic Hold of Slavery: Legacies in American Expressive Culture,* edited by Soyica Diggs Colbert, Aida Levy-Hussen, and R. J. Patterson, 86–106. New Brunswick, NJ: Rutgers University Press.

Jean-Charles, Régine M. 2018. "Occupying the Center: Haitian Girlhood and Wake Work." *Small Axe: A Caribbean Journal of Criticism*, no. 57: 140–50.

Jones, Cecily. 2006. "'Suffer the Little Children': Setting a Research Agenda for the Study of Enslaved Children in the Caribbean Colonial World." *Wadabagei* 9, no. 3: 7–26.

Larrier, Renée. 2009. "In[her]itance: Legacies and Lifelines in Evelyne Trouillot's *Rosalie L'Infâme.*" *Dalhousie French Studies* 88 (Fall): 135–45.

Owens, Tammy C. 2019. "Fugitive Literati: Black Girls' Writing as a Tool of Kinship and Power at the Howard School." *Women, Gender, and Families of Color* 7, no. 1: 56–79.

Rushdy, Ashraf H. A. 1999. *Neo-slave Narratives: Studies in the Social Logic of a Literary Form.* New York: Oxford University Press.

Scott, David. 2004. *Conscripts of Modernity: The Tragedy of Colonial Enlightenment.* Durham, NC: Duke University Press.

Scott, David. 2014. *Omens of Adversity: Tragedy, Time, Memory, Justice.* Durham, NC: Duke University Press Books.

Shoemaker, Lauren. 2018. "Femme Finale: Gender, Violence, and Nation in Marlon James' Novels." *Journal of West Indian Literature* 26, no. 2: 18–33.

Sol, Antoinette Marie. 2008. "Histoire(s) et traumatisme(s): L'infanticide dans le roman féminin antillais." *French Review* 81, no. 5: 967–84.

Trouillot Evelyne. 2003. *Rosalie l'infame.* Paris: Olfert Dapper Stichting.

Trouillot, Evelyne. 2013. *The Infamous Rosalie,* translated by Marjolie Salvodon. Lincoln: University of Nebraska Press.

Trouillot, Michel-Rolph. 2015. *Silencing the Past: Power and the Production of History.* Boston: Beacon.

Vásquez, Sam. 2012. "Violent Liaisons: Historical Crossings and the Negotiation of Sex, Sexuality, and Race in *The Book of Night Women* and *The True History of Paradise.*" *Small Axe: A Journal of Criticism,* no. 38: 43–59.

White, Hayden V. 1973. *Metahistory: The Historical Imagination in Nineteenth-Century Europe.* Baltimore, MD: Johns Hopkins University Press.

Nia McAllister

Consort of the Spirits
after Ntozake Shange

Abstract: Drawing inspiration from the 1982 novel, *Sassafrass, Cypress & Indigo* by Ntozake Shange, the poem "Consort of the Spirits" celebrates the legacy of Black womanhood, ancestry, and resilience. The opening lines of Shange's novel read: "Where there is a woman there is magic." This phrase serves as the entry point for framing womanhood, specifically Black womanhood, as something extraordinary. In tribute, "Consort of the Spirits" guides readers on a journey through time and memory, depicting the tangible yet magical ways in which lineages of Black women have carried tools for their survival, protected their shared histories, and guided their descendants on a path toward a more liberated future.

There are roadmaps in my great-great-grandmother's braids.
She keeps seeds in there too
      because where we are going, home must come with us.

Tell me how your mother hides spices in the hem of her skirt,
tucks hymns behind her ears
      and calls it packing for tomorrow.

Do the women in your family hide rosewater in their saliva,
sage in between their thighs?
      Because how dare we sleep on strange land
      without blessing?

MERIDIANS · feminism, race, transnationalism   21:1 April 2022
DOI: 10.1215/15366936-9554068 © 2022 Smith College

There are black eyed peas in my auntie's coin purse.
She keeps moonlight in there too.
>   Because luck is far more precious than loose change.

Tell me how your sister folds indigo leaves between her toes,
smuggles cotton flowers under her arms,
>   and promises that where we are going there will be color.

Do the women in your family wrap beeswax around their
ring fingers,
>   tuck matchsticks in their collarbones,
>   and vow that we will never know darkness?

I carry a cowrie shell in the crook of my arm.
It sings when my twins are near.
>   I wear sea glass upon my ears because where we are going
>   there will be music.

They call this survival,
>   but we know better.
>   Where there is a woman there is magic.

They call this survival,
>   but we pack what we must
>   because what we return to may no longer be ours.

They call this survival,
>   but this ritual of making to leave
>   before knowing where we're headed is how
>   we birth futures.

They call this survival,
>   but the body is a compass
>   and we *are* each other's destination.

. . . .

Living at the intersection of Blackness, womanhood, art, and activism, **Nia McAllister** is a Bay Area–born poet, avid reader, and environmental justice advocate. Nia's writing has been featured in *Radicle* magazine, *Poets of Color* podcast, San Francisco Public Library's Poem of the Day, and *Painting the Streets: Oakland Uprising in the Time of Rebellion* (2022).

Kenly Brown, Lashon Daley, and Derrika Hunt

Disruptive Ruptures
The Necessity of Black/Girlhood Imaginary

Abstract: This article examines Black/Girlhood Imaginary, a transdisciplinary methodology that merges performance studies, Black studies, and education to research and theorize the capacious archives of Black girlhood. What the authors term *Black/Girlhood Imaginary* is a multivalent prism that aids in the recovery of the losses, the undermining, the layered violence, the joys, and the embodied experiences of Black girls. As a methodology, Black/Girlhood Imaginary weaves both the fullness and fissures of Black girlhoods, opening up the space for Black girls to recover their own images. The authors use the methodologies of Black/Girlhood Imaginary to analyze three case studies beginning with Judy Winslow's unexplained disappearance from the popular 1990s sitcom *Family Matters*. The authors then move into a literary analysis of a poem written by Paradise, a student, who theorizes state-sanctioned violence in her community. The authors end with a poem about Daniele, an employee embedded between diasporic economies. These case studies illustrate representations, perspectives, and experiences of Black girls in the kaleidoscope of the Black/Girlhood Imaginary.

Black/. We strategically write "Black forward slash Girlhood" to signal both an abstract configuration and a lived embodied experience of Black girlness that is in dialogue with global imaginings. The oblique line—the American English slash—symbolizes the space, the gap, the expectations, the interruption, the omission, the expansion, the theoretical downward slope, the jubilant upward reach, the implicit fall forward, and explicit push back created within and between culture's reconnaissance of Blackness and girlness. Used grammatically to mark both inclusivity and

MERIDIANS · feminism, race, transnationalism   21:1 April 2022
DOI: 10.1215/15366936-9554079 © 2022 Smith College

exclusivity, the slash between *Black* and *Girlhood* denotes the broad stroke with which we include varying notions of Blackness—notions that do not hinge on an essentialist notion of Blackness but, rather, a broader stroke, an expansion of the boundaries of Blackness deepened by the breadth and depth of Black girlhood that reaches beyond the flesh, nation-states, and political borders.

Girlhood. Let us pause here to give space to the volume of this word.

Girlhood is a layered mosaic, compounded by girls' experiences within social systems. In writing about girlhood, we are not implying heteronormative notions of girlness or girlhood; we are rather signaling to anyone who experiences life as a girl in mind, body, and spirit. The slash extends, or rather, leans toward girlhood, applying pressure to the word *Girl* with a capital G.

Imaginary. Stemmed from the word *image*, and rooted in the Latin term *imago*—a copy, likeness, equivalent, "im" to imitate. We see Black/Girlhood Imaginary as Jean Baudrillard's (1994) simulacra, a copy without an original. Mediated and circulated, this copy sometimes becomes blurred and fractured, separated into unidentifiable parts, and then mediated and recirculated again. In other instances, it is sanitized and enlarged, plastered on socially constructed billboards to be glimpsed from one's periphery.

Black/Girlhood Imaginary acknowledges the systemic fractures that produce and condition Black girlhood. Accordingly, Black girls strategize to subvert the sanitized image of society's failures mapped on to them to focus on the pixelated interstices where they live, theorize, and survive. Black/Girlhood Imaginary is the copy without an original—reconstructing sources of rupture into repair for the Black girl whose image then becomes her own.

Where We Enter

> To understand the complexity of black girlhood we need more work that documents that reality in all its variations and diversity. . . . It's vital then that we hear about our diverse experience. There is no one story of black girlhood.
> —bell hooks, *Bone Black*

We are a collective of Black women at top research institutions mapping the coordinates of our own spatial and material realities. From this position, we take up this work. As a collective, we honor the genealogy of other collectives like the Combahee River Collective (2014) and Corrine T. Field and colleagues (2016), whose theories, texts, and intellectual labor have inspired our work. Similarly, our politic is situated in both our Black womanhoods and girlhoods and is informed by how we see, document, theorize, remember, and name Black girlhood.[1] We acknowledge there is a range of complex factors, including body size/shape, skin color, sexuality, hair texture, ability, religion, class, beauty standards, age, and a host of other social structures that shape the way Black girls move through their social worlds. We enter this realm of imaginative study because there is an urgency and value in documenting Black girls.[2] We also understand that Black girlhood is too ephemeral, too capacious, too worthy to fit into the bounds of a theoretical project. As such, we are devoted to a praxis that centers Black girlhood as a nexus of lived and mediated forms of performance. When we sat down to reflect on Black girlhood, we were flooded with emotions, particularly grief. In a way, we felt like we were writing a eulogy. Why? Because writing about Black girlhood felt congruent with writing about death and its many wakes (Sharpe 2016). We acknowledge that our sentiments ranged from that of grief to celebration—and the gradient spaces in between, which both haunted and uplifted our work.

We have developed a transdisciplinary approach by merging performance studies, Black studies, and education to research and theorize the effervescent archives of Black girlhood. To discern the nuances of Blackness and girlness, we started from our own sensibilities as Black girls, which is to gather and talk. We met for several years laughing, discussing, and arguing about our embodied knowledges as Black girls and how to define our often-undefinable experiences. We also ate together, sharing meals while digesting and processing our memories. We celebrated together—birthdays, academic accomplishments, and life milestones. We traveled together, sometimes simply to a local workout class, other times halfway across the world. These intentional acts of love and care helped us cultivate our own Black feminist praxis through which we devised Black/Girlhood Imaginary.

We construct and excavate an imaginative space of Black girlhood that is simultaneously hypervisible and invisible, translucent and opaque. This spectrum of legibility is where we continue to labor. Through our ongoing conversations and research, we succumb to the ephemerality of Black/Girlhood Imaginary.

Critical Musings of Black Girlhood

The field of Black girlhood studies encompasses scholars from many academic disciplines.[3] Accordingly, we acknowledge that there is an array of texts that have been influential to the field. In this section, we examine three monographs that informed Black/Girlhood Imaginary's conceptual framework and methodological interests. Our list consists of *South Side Girls: Growing Up in the Great Migration* (2015) by Marcia Chatelain, *Between Good and Ghetto: African American Girls and Inner-City Violence* (2009) by Nikki Jones, and *Shapeshifters: Black Girls and the Choreography of Citizenship* (2015) by Aimee Meredith Cox. We immersed ourselves in these works while exploring how each author used Black feminist methodologies to highlight how Black girls advanced, subverted, and altered the economies, social structures, and educational systems within the inner city. Each text critically examines specific institutional and interpersonal spaces to interrogate how Black girls are positioned and position themselves.

In *South Side Girls: Growing Up in the Great Migration*, Chatelain (2015) explains how the construction of Black girlhood shifted in early twentieth-century Chicago in response to the city's economic, political, and social changes. Black girls and young women who had left the Jim Crow South migrated for higher wages and more educational opportunities, and to escape sexual violence in the workplace. However, when they arrived, educational, religious, and community-based reforms sought to rehabilitate and/or co-opt their femininity to advance the race. Black girlhood became integral to the success and progress of the Black community, where protection and well-being were tied to service. Otherwise, girls who were considered wayward[4] were marginalized objects of rehabilitation. The work of Chatelain is an important frame within Black/Girlhood Imaginary to capture how the voices of Black girls are used to elucidate the conditions surrounding their participation in daily life. From this work, we see how the same historical vulnerabilities affecting Black girls in Chicago of the early 1900s still affect the lives of Black girls in Philadelphia a century later.

Nikki Jones's (2009: 19) ethnography, *Between Good and Ghetto: African American Girls and Inner-City Violence* captures the ways Black girls and young women in Philadelphia strategize ways to stay safe that contrast with "traditional White, middle-class conceptions of femininity, and the gendered expectations embedded in Black respectability." Jones's commitment to building strong relationships with participants allowed her to explore "situated survival strategies"[5] (2009: 53): situational avoidance (e.g., avoiding certain areas at certain times) and relational isolation (e.g., loyalty to friends and willingness to fight on behalf of the friendship). Her analytical framing provides Black/Girlhood Imaginary with a detailed method to process how vulnerability and violence converge to shape Black girlhood. While Jones is interested in the ways Black girls and young women navigate violence, Cox (2015) examines how Black girls theorize and choreograph their bodies to shift from being understood as a statistic to being seen as human.

Through creative nonfiction, storytelling, and performance, *Shapeshifters: Black Girls and the Choreography of Citizenship* (Cox 2015) weaves the narratives of life-and-death situations experienced by dozens of young women who moved in and out of the Fresh Start Homeless Shelter between 2000 and 2008 in Detroit.[6] Cox conceptualizes the movement of Black girls as shapeshifting to convey "how young Black women living in the United States engage with, confront, challenge, invert, unsettle, and expose the material impact of systemic oppression. Shapeshifting is an act, a theory, and in this sense, a form of praxis that . . . reveals our collective vulnerabilities" (7). Cox intentionally grounds her analysis in theories and knowledge developed by the residents at the shelter. Janice Brown[7] shares her theory of *"missing the middle,"* which is "not just surviving like getting a job and getting a degree, but surviving by holding onto our truth. The truth you don't see on TV or in the papers like you should" (10, emphasis in original). Janice's perspective on where Black girls and women are situated in society is an important discovery in Cox's work. This discovery is also a key intersection for Black/Girlhood Imaginary that informs our methodological inquiries on Black girls' perspectives when they are perceived as social problems. Ultimately, Chatelain, Jones, and Cox demonstrate how Black girls survive, subvert, and shapeshift within, through, and beyond the matrices of violence.

Black/Girlhood Imaginary Methodology

What is required to imagine a free state or to tell an impossible story?
—Saidiya Hartman, "Venus in Two Acts"

In *Black Feminist Thought: Knowledge, Consciousness, and the Politics of Empowerment* (2002), Patricia Hill Collins characterizes a Black feminist epistemology as 1) lived experience as criterion of meaning, 2) dialogue, 3) ethics of care, and 4) ethics of personal accountability. Subsequently, researchers can incorporate knowledge created and used by Black women as an analytical proposition. Accordingly, we apply the methodology of Black Feminist epistemology—a mosaic, a fusion of creativity—informed by field and archival research, cultural meanings, embodied knowledge, and lived experiences of Black girls. Our methodology is intentional as we move beyond hierarchical rankings of knowledge production. We honor the knowings of Black girls and Black women beyond the realms of constructed sociopolitical and historical measures that fail to account for the epistemologies of marginalized people. Our method is one of making, memory, doing, and simultaneously of unmaking, rememory (Morrison 1987), undoing. For us, this work has more disruptive ruptures than closures.

When writing and engaging the lives of Black girls in various settings, conversations, and performances, their behaviors and theorizations shape our definition of Black/Girlhood Imaginary. In conjunction with our Black feminist episteme, we use writing as a praxis of survival and resistance in honor of our theoretical foremother Barbara Christian (1987: 61) who declared, "I can only speak for myself. But what I write and how I write is done in order to save my own life." Black/Girlhood Imaginary hinges on the axes of the personal, political, and the performative. It is steeped in the makings of possibility. We write with those of us at the shoreline because this work is critical, urgent, and necessary (Lorde [1978] 2007).

Our methodology is a type of recovery. The emergence of Black girlhood studies excavates, ruptures, and mends disjointed and dismembered histories and experiences of Black girls. Understanding how Black girls are often barred from girlhood, we imagine a space of ethnographies, discourse analysis, theories of movement, and imagery to rectify this rupture. Not meant as an exhaustive description and exploration of Black girlhood, our methodology reconciles the chasm within girlhood and brings to the forefront Black girlhood. We offer an imaginary space to consider several ways (by no means conclusive) to acknowledge, complicate, and engage how Black girls move, resist, and understand what girlhood means to them.

In the following pages, each of us draw from our research using the methodologies of Black/Girlhood Imaginary. These case studies illustrate representations, perspectives, and experiences of Black girls within each of our interdisciplinary traditions. Lashon Daley begins by analyzing Judy Winslow's unexplained disappearance from the popular 1990s sitcom, *Family Matters.* Kenly Brown offers a literary analysis of a poem written by Paradise,[8] a high school student, who theorizes state-sanctioned violence and resistance. Derrika Hunt concludes with a poetic meditation on the situated knowledges of Black girls by examining her encounters with Daniele,[9] a Black girl whose knowings emerge as a meaningful rupture. In the case studies, we deploy the imaginary at the interstices of Black performativity, state-sanctioned violence, and diasporic geographies.

A Disruptive Rupture within the Home:
The "Disappearance" of Judy Winslow
from *Family Matters*
Lashon Daley

As a Black performance and new media studies scholar who uses ethnography and object analysis as my primary methods, I reached back into my own Black girlhood to ground my disciplinary contribution to Black/Girlhood Imaginary. Because Black/Girlhood Imaginary privileges the narratives of Black girls, I chose a time during which these narratives were made more visible on the small screen. My experiences as a Black girl and as the youngest sister in a home that felt too full brought my cognizance back to 1989—to the release of the television show *Family Matters*.

I was six years old when *Family Matters* made its debut on September 22, 1989 during the American Broadcasting Company programming block known as TGIF. *Family Matters* featured the Winslows, a middle-class African American family in Chicago, Illinois. The family consisted of Harriette; her husband Carl, a police officer; their three children, Eddy, Laura, and Judy; Harriett's sister, Rachel Baines-Crawford and Rachel's son, Richie; and Carl's mother, Estelle "Mother" Winslow.

Through the lens of Black/Girlhood Imaginary, I record and theorize Judy's representation of Black girlhood, partly because of the popularity of the show, but also because, without this record, Judy's portrayal will continue to be read superficially, not only by fans but also by those who undervalue her representation. Her character embodies what Black girls experience when they are pushed out of their homes, often erased from their family's lineage, leaving an apparition in the familial spaces they once inhabited.

Judy's childhood encompassed a lot of time inside her family home, especially with her older sister Laura, to whom she often played sidekick. When she was not at Laura's side, she could be found with Eddie or somewhere in the home doing what the youngest siblings do best: quietly waiting their turn. For thirteen years, Judy waited patiently for her turn to engage with her family's dynamics. During that time, she made herself known through one-liners and quips, followed by running upstairs to her bedroom, where she would often remain until it was time for her next line or until she followed someone else downstairs.

I understood Judy's predicament. As the youngest of five siblings—three brothers and a sister—my status in my household was contingent on the hierarchical status of my older siblings, leaving me feeling like a supporting character.

In season 1 of *Family Matters*, Judy is cast as a precocious nine-year-old with an unwavering love for her family. Her quick wit and vibrant personality made her a steady sidekick to Laura's domestic adventures. Judy's storyline fluctuated between trusted sidekick and annoying little sister. Her jabs, comebacks, and side-eyes were peppered throughout the first four seasons. Then, nineteen episodes into season 4, thirteen-year-old Judy inexplicably vanishes from the Winslow household. Their family life continues as if she had never existed. Judy's disappearance was the first of its kind for a Black girl lead character on a family sitcom.

Season 4, episode 18, titled "Higher Anxiety" (Correll 1993), is Judy's second to last episode. Not having appeared throughout most of the episode, Judy finally makes her entrance from the kitchen at stage left during the final credits as she, her mother, father, and cousin Richie take their seats on the couch to watch TV. Although she is the first to leave the kitchen, she is the last to speak.

Judy waits to take her seat until Richie has taken his. Her mother is the last to sit down. Judy perches on the edge of the couch to create more room for her father. Rather than trying to accommodate his daughter, Carl takes up more than his share of space on the couch. Entering unannounced from stage right, Steve, their neighbor, and the main antagonist, walks into the frame and plops in the center of the group. Played by Jaleel White, Steve Urkel was originally slated to have a single appearance. However, he proved extremely popular with viewers and transformed what was supposed to be a one-off appearance into a star turn. In this scene, his endearing clumsiness gets Judy pushed off the couch, and then her father shoves her to the floor. Like Steve, Carl barely takes any notice. Carl glances at his daughter and then turns his attention to Steve. Judy is the only one who is peeved, yet she remains silent. Steve then begins to talk about the show he wants to watch. Disinterested, Carl, Harriet, and Richie peel themselves off the couch, Judy picks herself up off the floor, and they all exit stage right, leaving Steve to watch TV by himself. The episode ends with another quip from Steve as the audience laughs.

In episode 19, "Mama's Wedding" (Menteer 1993), Judy's final lackluster one-line question in the first minute of the episode is all that the viewer sees of her until she reappears in the last segment. Here, she is again upstaged by Steve as she prepares to walk down the aisle as the flower girl. After the wedding, Judy walks in procession with her family and is not seen again. For the last five episodes of season 4, Judy is absent. Her quick-witted comments, her need for recognition and validation, and her storylines fade into Black/Girlhood Imaginary, where she is recovered as a simulacra—a representation of Black girls whose narrative is centered on their disappearance and not how they were actually pushed out.

Judy unwittingly becomes a mediated avatar for Black girls who become translucent in their homes. She is seen, but only slightly. Her proxied body is a virtual stand-in for the phenomenon that Cox describes in *Shapeshifters: Black Girls and the Choreography of Citizenship* (2015). Cox writes, "As crowded or uncomfortable as a house could get with adults and their children, it always seemed to be the teenage young women who were displaced. Another body moved in, and the first one pushed out and made to figure things out in another place was one of the girls" (45–46). Judy's smiling face lingers in the opening credits until season 5 when Judy becomes a mere trace in her family home. She has no more desires, wants, or needs. She does not get dressed in the morning, does not rush out the door to catch the school bus, or appear for dinner. She does not mature into a young woman. She is not a being who longs to be seen or heard. Rather, she becomes ageless, a fluid body that allows family life to move unhindered through and around her. She does not take up space. Instead, there is more space for others to move about, to talk, and to engage.

Judy's performance in "Higher Anxiety" is the culmination of her reduction from an opaque body as a lead character to a translucent organism who can be pushed off a couch. Her translucency gave the producers a reason to remove her from the show—her value was not visible either to her sitcom family or to the audience. They saw no need to write Judy out of the storyline because it was easier to pretend that she had never existed. And because Steve proved to be so valuable to the show, he soon took over Judy's role. In other words, he became the intensified version of Judy. His ability to out-sidekick, out-sassify, and out-clumsify Judy literally pushed her character, and actress Jaimee Foxworth, out of the show. As a result, by season 5, Carl and Harriet were the parents of two children, in addition to Steve who had, by the end of season 1, begun inhabiting their home as if it were his own.

In the decades following her disappearance, Judy's face began to reappear in the most peculiar of places: milk cartons, T-shirts, and "missing" posters. As a result of syndication, fans like me, who were now older, were able to question Judy's sudden disappearance during their nostalgic trips down television memory lane. What we had not noticed before about her disappearance now caused us to question the show's choice and express concern. Why had we not noticed that a main character from our favorite television show had suddenly disappeared? Why did she disappear? Why was she not formally written out of the show? Who played Judy Winslow, and where is she now?

In 2021, twenty-three years after *Family Matters* ended and twenty-eight years after Judy was pushed out, fans continue to bombard the internet with theories, criticisms, and questions about her disappearance, and also about Foxworth. Almost every internet search reveals that Foxworth dabbled in the porn industry and became a heavy marijuana user in the years after *Family Matters*. She appeared on *The Oprah Winfrey Show, Celebrity Rehab with Dr. Drew, The Tyra Banks Show,* and *20/20* to tell her side of the story and her struggles after leaving the sitcom. At the beginning of 2020, Foxworth (now forty years old) did a tell-all interview with the YouTuber Armon Wiggins, describing her rise and fall as Judy Winslow. She detailed her audition, her stage fright and anxiety, her marijuana addiction, her move into the porn industry, and her present life and career. It is her most comprehensive interview to date and was long awaited, especially since fans have been piecing together their own versions of her story for years. In addition, she responds to not being invited to the 2017 *Family Matters* cast reunion photo shoot produced by *Entertainment Weekly*. In her interview with Wiggins (2020), Foxworth voiced her frustration:

> Certain people are going to have to speak up on my behalf because I've been speaking for so long. The one that plays Waldo [Shawn Harrison], when they did the whole thing [the *Family Matters* reunion], he actually called me. He was like *Do you know what we did?* I was like *Absolutely not.* He was like *Yeah, I was going to definitely call you and let you know that this happened because I didn't want this to be something that you looked at and it took you by surprise. I wanted you to know that we did this.* He told me the backstory of what happened and what people said while they were there and who stood up for me and all of that stuff. So when I did the interview [with *The Root*], it wasn't from a place of anger. It was a place of like *I have not talked about*

this. I get why they feel like they need to do this but enough! You get what I'm say-ing? Enough is enough. I was a whole daughter on the show.

For nearly an hour and forty minutes, Foxworth revealed important details about her time as a child star, and by doing so, she reclaimed Judy's story too. To reclaim her story and her image, Foxworth sells Judy memorabilia to nostalgic fans. She has a T-shirt for sale with an image of her as Judy on the front labeled "Missing," "Judy Winslow." The back reads "Found Her!," along with an image of herself as an adult.

Although Judy's narrative within the fandom has centered on her dis-appearance, Black/Girlhood Imaginary exemplifies how important it is to refract that narrative to find what was once lost and to recover what was once abandoned. Judy being pushed out rather than simply disappearing, puts her representation in conversation with intersectional frameworks like those of Cox and Monique Morris. Through Black/Girlhood Imagi-nary's refraction, Judy's translucency in the Winslow household is slowly moving back to opacity. As Foxworth and fans of the show continue to question Judy's being pushed out, and bring visibility to it, Judy is not only being given a future, but gaps of her narrative are finally being filled in. Even sites like Fanfiction.net and forums like Reddit.com continue to add to Judy's growing opacity because of fans writing fictional storylines for her. By beginning to recover Judy's subjecthood through Black/Girlhood Imaginary, this theoretical framework provides an opportunity to open conversations on how to begin the recovery process for Black girls like Judy, whose bodies remain apparitions within their family homes.

A Disruptive Rupture within Society: Paradise's Social Critique of State-Sanctioned Violence

Kenly Brown

As someone who practices humanist social science and centers Black feminist theories and Black girlhood studies, I examine the ways people make mean-ing with one another in their social worlds. I use ethnographic methods of participant-observation, direct observation, semistructured interviews, and informal conversations to capture the relationship between people and the communities and institutions they live in, work at, learn at, and move through (Emerson, Fretz, and Shaw 2011). Over the course of years of ethnographic fieldwork, I engaged, witnessed, and learned from Black girls enrolled in a California continuation school, H.B. Stowe Academy.[10] Continuation schools are an opportunity for students to recover academic credits to stay on track to graduate while learning in a smaller educational setting. While these schools are presented as an opportunity for students, continuation schools have been used as a "dumping ground" for Black, Native, Latinx, and other nonwhite youth from working-class neighborhoods (Nygreen 2013). Similarly, educators, students, and parents colloquially refer to H.B. Stowe Academy as the school where "the bad kids go" (Naledi, interview, February 7, 2017).

I cultivated a Black feminist love politic to witness and embrace mutual vulnerability with each Black girl to craft an expansive exploration of Black girlhood (Brown 2021; Nash 2018). Over time, I built rapport with a few of the girls to the point where they began to refer to me as a mentor rather than a researcher or ethnographer. The etymology of *mentor* is from the noun *mentos*, meaning "intent, purpose, spirit, or passion" (Snowber 2005: 345). It is with this intention and spirit that I began to learn how Black girls theorized and lived through the ruptures they disrupted.

I met Paradise at H.B. Stowe Academy in Dr. Jackson's Spanish class. At the time, she was a seventeen-year-old Black girl passionate about poetry and urban fiction. Sharing similar experiences with girls and young women centered in the works of Cox, Nikki Jones, Saidiya Hartman, and Toni Morrison, Paradise endured physical and sexual violence, was bullied in school, and experienced the heartache of losing loved ones too soon. She wrote prose to soothe her pain and to imagine what felt like an impossible future.

In one of her classes, Paradise pulled me aside to share a poem titled "My Society." She had written this poem soon after learning about the murder of Michael Brown at the hands of police officer Darren Wilson in Ferguson, Missouri. Paradise documents the ways in which Black youth are demonized by society and terrorized by law enforcement. She submitted her poem to a writing competition for students in her school district. Dr. Jackson proudly displayed her poem at the entrance of the classroom. Poetry is an analytic that can tend to the gaps and silences social science research grasps to uncover but cannot fully articulate (Dill, Rivera, and Sutton 2018). Eve L. Ewing (2018: 199) describes this distinction between social science and poetry: "As the social scientist asks *what is*, the poet asks *what may be*; as the social scientist tells what people *do*, the poet tells what people *are*" (emphasis in original). Paradise's poem illuminates what it is like to survive in a world that seeks your demise but also brings to life what it is like to live. Using literary analysis, I understand Black/Girlhood Imaginary's methodology of recovery through the art, moves, and calibrations Paradise expresses in "My Society."

My Society

Looking in my eyes
my society thinks they see the demon in me
A mother falls to the ground screaming
"I thought I was alive until they took the one thing that was
breathing in me"
american flag tears falls to her ears as she watches blue bullets
seeping in me
lying cold on the ground
a blank soul that took my last feeling from me
hiding behind their vest
afraid of my success
if it wasn't death
i would be trying to cop a plea
So many of my brothers shouting out let me free
We share different pigments but they're all attached to me
So if you weren't just looking in my eyes
you would see i'm a Masterpiece
influencing my youth teaching them peace like that's the key
Instead of watching violence destroy our city like a catastrophe
So as you look in my eyes it's a bright future you see the only
demon in me is this crooked society

Paradise captures the affective and material experiences of Black girls in the slash of Black/Girlhood Imaginary to signify the break between Blackness and girlness. Paradise illustrates this break in the first line to elucidate the friction between the state and herself: "Looking in my eyes / my society thinks they see the demon in me." At the genesis of the United States, slavery situated Black girls and women outside girlhood and womanhood using a "system of gendered and racialized economic exploitation and social control" (Haley 2016: 4). After the abolishment of slavery, legal statutes and social ideologies continued to frame and stigmatize Black girls as social failures. Hartman (2018: 470) unsettles perceived social failures ascribed onto Black girls in her conceptualization of their lives as wayward—"the wild thoughts, reckless dreams, interminable protests, spontaneous strikes, nonparticipation, willfulness, and bold-faced refusal [to redistribute] the balance of need and want and sought a line of escape from debt and duty in the attempt to create a path elsewhere." The wayward is the pressure applied to girl Black/Girlhood Imaginary to shatter the sanitized image the state deploys to exclude them from their girlness and constrain their Blackness. Paradise crafts a path elsewhere in "My Society" in her analysis of suffering and resistance from the vantage point of her community and family.

Paradise theorizes the suffering of people in her community at the hands of institutional failures, as opposed to the social failure of the individual: "A mother falls to the ground screaming / I thought I was alive until they took the one thing that was breathing in me' / american flag tears falls to her ears as she watches blue bullets seeping in me." The death of a child at the hands of the state, and Paradise's metaphorical death from the blue bullets, exemplify a linked fate between death and incarceration. I interpret the blue bullets as representative of the thirteen stars on the American flag that pierce her body—thirteen stars that signify thirteen colonies that foreclosed opportunity and liberty for those enslaved. Paradise illustrates the stakes in Black/Girlhood Imaginary to challenge the exclusionary, discriminatory, and violent practices embedded in a social order that thrives on the oppression of Black people. Her imagery of a bereaved mother falling to the ground is informed by her own loss of two brothers to the carceral state. Their incarceration left her mother grief-stricken because she could not protect them.

In elementary school, Paradise was inspired to write poetry when she heard Billie Holiday's "Strange Fruit" and learned about the civils rights movement. She was moved by the vulnerability and honesty of Holiday's protest lyrics and protesters in the civil rights movement to stand up against state violence. In "My Society," Paradise honestly and vulnerably captures the meaning of death and fighting for one's life in her contemporary moment in the following lines: "hiding behind their vest / afraid of my success / if it wasn't death / i would be trying to cop a plea." While the I in Black/Girlhood Imaginary is capitalized, the i in Paradise's poem embodies the truncation of self and tension between precarious freedom and survival for Black children and young people. While the i is lower case in Paradise's poem, the power of *eyes* holds the imaginary, in which the pixelated images of her girlhood come into view to unsettle society's image of Black girls as inferior.

The state weaponized this image to absolve itself of accountability to protect and serve them and their communities. Returning to Paradise's first line, "Looking in my eyes / my society thinks they see the demon in me," I understand *eyes* as initially mirroring back to society what it thinks it sees in Paradise—a demonic girl. She subverts this societal perception of her into a refractive image in the last line of her poem, "So as you look in my eyes it's a bright future you see the only demon in me is this crooked society." Thus the image refracted back to society from her eyes is in fact her light and their brokenness, corruptness, and demons.

Using poetry, Paradise refracts the violent conditioning of a social world that attempts to undermine her humanity by externalizing her own understanding of who she is and her community. Her poetic devices uncover social atrocities and iniquities to waywardly recover her perspective and love for herself and community within the slash, the chasm, the imaginary. In the following lines of her poem, "So if you weren't just looking in my eyes / you would see i'm a Masterpiece / influencing my youth teaching them peace like that's the key," is where the bend of the reflection refracts to create possibility. It is in the bend and the rupture where Paradise and I continue to cultivate and imagine a world through the prism of possibilities. She is now a mother to a beautiful Black son whom I met the day he was born. I saw her eyes reflect awe, caution, and resolve to raise and educate her Black son in a violent world. Paradise continues to write and theorize about a world that will not protect her or her son, and she persists to write a bright future for them in honor of their lives.

A Disruptive Rupture within Diasporic Dreams:
Daniele and the Politics of Knowing
Derrika Hunt

As a Black feminist scholar who qualitatively studies the plural relationships between schooling, education, and knowledge production, I disrupt the commonsense that schooling is the most legitimate entry to knowing. I illuminate how schooling has come to signify a set of dominant cultural meanings that valorize it as the most viable pathway toward knowing, while simultaneously erasing the historical and political implications of colonialism, imperialism, and capitalism embedded within the institution of schooling (Bowles and Gintis 2011). I attend to these nuances by situating the knowledges of Black girls as legitimate and valuable entry points to knowledge production. As such, I employ the Black/Girlhood Imaginary framework to accentuate how the kaleidoscopic mosaics of Black girls' knowings move across time, space, and geographic boundaries to offer valuable knowledge. To do this I reflect on a particularly moving experience that has shaped and informed my formal ethnographic work.

When I met Daniele, a sixteen-year-old girl working at a hotel resort in Jamaica, I observed how Black girls like her navigate interlocking systems of oppression and, specifically, how they know beyond schooling. While Daniele was only sixteen, she worked full-time at a hotel resort because she could not afford to attend school—the costs were too high materially and personally. It is in tracing the poetics of Daniele's particular experiences and axes of identity that I came to know the multitude of Black girlhoods beyond a U.S.-centric framework. Daniele's subversion of systems of oppression is an important reminder that the multiplicity of Black girlhoods warrants study and careful attention to get to the heart of Black/Girlhood Imaginary—a kaleidoscope through which we have the opportunity to zoom in to get a close look; the opportunity to zoom out to see from different angles; and finally, the opportunity to notice the dazzling patchwork of shapes, colors, and patterns collaging into what we deem Black girlhood.

Conventional theoretical works might position Daniele as an uneducated worker, but through the prism of Black/Girlhood Imaginary, I zoom in on the minutiae of pixelation to animate a new way of sensing Daniele—as a producer of significant knowledge and as a teacher (Alexander and Mohanty 2010). Positioning Daniele as a teacher disrupts the hegemony of a teacher requiring formal education to offer valuable contributions to theory and knowledge production. Daniele's life experiences and her keen sense of her own positions within the global world are valuable entry points to theory. Black/Girlhood Imaginary allows me to recuperate these misunderstood knowings and to reimagine them as important ruptures through which to imagine knowledge production (Valenzuela 1999).

Black/Girlhood Imaginary makes space to recuperate Black girls' ways of knowing as crucial spaces of education and knowledge production. Therefore, in my work, the distinction between schooling and education situates my own political commitments of working toward praxes of education that center multiple ways of knowing (Collins 2002).

Thus, I bring together poetry and personal experience to get a glimpse into the interiority of Black girlhood by way of Daniele's epistemology. I intentionally move beyond a U.S.-centric paradigm to investigate the plurality of Black girlhood imaginary beyond geographic and political borders. That is not to say that Daniele's story is representative of all Black girlhood, but it is to suggest that her story is an entry, a rupture, and a place of possibility where we can meditate on a mere fragment of Black girlhood.

This necessary meditation echoes Collins's suggestion that investigating subjugated knowledges is a critical intervention to disrupt conventional paradigms of knowledge production. Thus, we take seriously the task of centering Black girls like Daniele, because we believe that in doing so we are privy to insights that might otherwise be missed. All in all, investigating the plurality of Blackness and girlness ruptures static notions and makes space for us to see, feel, think, and imagine gradations of Black girlhood within and beyond.

I highlight the ways Black girls know, and I then situate these ways of knowing as sophisticated educational spaces that offer insight into another depth of knowing. The depths of knowing I am referring to are revealed when Daniele takes me to school—not to a building, but to the imaginary where she and I engage in deep study during our encounter (Harney and Moten 2013). Examining Daniele's racialized, geopolitical, and classed experiences offers a meaningful way to understand how Black girls' knowing disrupts the hegemony of knowledge production and serves as a prism through which to envision new possibilities for situating education, schooling and knowing. Daniele defies my own commonsensical notions of Black girlhood as she shares her own formulations about Blackness and girlness with me. Daniele necessarily disrupts static ideologies of Black girlhood, and it is by studying Daniele's disruptive rupture that I build a bridge toward recovery. This bridge is a site of possibility, a site of futurity, and a site to reimagine how the Black/Girlhood Imaginary offers Black girls space to learn each other, to see each other, and to ultimately recognize each other. I imagine that during our encounters Daniele and I began to recognize each other and witness firsthand the vastness of Black girlhood. The methodology of Black/Girlhood Imaginary equipped me with the tools to recover Daniele's knowing through a diasporic, spatial, and geographic lens. In this effort, I thread together a poetic musing of what I learned during my conversations with Daniele.

A Poem for Daniele

This is for Daniele.
and "*likkle Caribbean*"[11] girls everywhere
I can still hear Daniele's sharp laugh as
she looks at me and says,
"*Your American tongue, don't say words right.*"

We both giggled.

But deep down I felt uneasy.

"Say likkle again. And this time take out the "t" sound.

This is how we say it."

I practice saying "likkle," betraying the vernacular rules

that have been beaten into me throughout my life.

"And say my name like this, Dan-yell," she emphasizes.

I repeat after her, trying to teach my tongue to unlearn

the English imperialism ingrained in me.

Still looking through me, she smiles, and we both stare out at the

ocean as the waves come and go.

This poem is for Daniele and likkle Caribbean girls.

Daniele has the most beautiful brown eyes I've ever seen,

eyes that seem to be longing for something more.

She has a smile that lights up the dimmest room.

I met her when she greeted me as I walked into the lobby of the

hotel I was staying at.

"Hello ma'am" she says

with a sweet smile spreading across her face

being called "ma'am" feels strange

but how could I resist such a sweet invitation.

I walk over to the desk where she is sitting.

She invites me to sit,

as she gestures toward

the seat across from her.

I sit

and we talk for what felt like hours

with the Caribbean Sea roaring behind us.

Daniele—

the girl with the most beautiful brown eyes I've ever seen

Daniele—

the girl

with arms reaching for lands, they may never touch.

She tells me of her dreams to travel the world

with a heart that yearns for places it may never see.

She tells me that dreams like that don't come true

for girls like her,

girls born into poverty

Daniele—
Her dreams are still lingering in my heart.
Every time I walk to the lobby
I hold my breath and scan the space looking for her
and there she is each time.
Today she is sitting on the veranda of the hotel
watching the cruise ships as they come and go
*"Whenever I can get a break, I love to sit out here in the breeze
and dream."*
Day after day,
month after month,
year after year,
she watches,
she dreams.
Dreaming of one day coming and going like those ships,
dreaming of one day pushing through the waves
and overcoming the tides.
Daniele is a dreamer.
Today she tells me about her mother.
She laughs as she recounts her mother bickering about her being in
la la land.
Daniele is sitting, perched on the edge of the veranda
hoping, but deep down somehow knowing
in a way that only Black girls can know
that she may never be lucky enough to touch gold.
She peels away her dreams
the way she peels the flesh of a ripe mango
with her teeth
like swords
cutting through raw flesh
pushing her tongue through the ripeness.
"Oh, don't be silly," she says
"I'll be lucky if I even get to see the inside rooms of this resort."
She takes the mango seed and tosses it in a small wooden trash can
the same way she scatters her dreams overboard.
Looking at the ground, she fingers the creases in her blue uniform
skirt.
I wonder what she is thinking.

She's got sky-wide dreams
that only her heart can hold.
She casts them into the Caribbean Sea
leaving them to drop away
like her—
our ancestors did.
I wonder if those dreams will float back to Daniele
I want to tell her that she can be anything in this world,
but I'm still trying to work out exactly what that means.
in that moment I realized that while we are both Black girls
our lives, our realities are worlds apart.
I touch her hand,
offering my touch as a communion
and as I write this poem in her honor
I hope that by writing these words
I make a bridge toward Daniele.
This poem is but a small offering,
an ethereal request
for miracles to tide
in the Caribbean Sea for likkle girls like Daniele
because they are waiting at the shores of possibility.
As this poem breaks, so will Daniele and I.

Daniele, a soft-spoken worker with deep-brown eyes, who has a fragile relationship with economy that taught me something theory could not. She has learned how to maneuver the tangled webs of capitalism and imperialism. In her lived experiences she forges a critique of these systems while simultaneously navigating them. In the geography of her experiences, she intimately, painstakingly knows that capitalism, imperialism, and geopolitics are the very things that have constructed her as a worker while barring her from the paradise of her own home. Black/Girlhood Imaginary insists that girls like Daniele have much to teach about the precariousness and poetics of Black girlhood.

Daniele signaled our vastly different realities when she told me solemnly, "You will go, and I will continue working here." While sitting with Daniele's declaration of my own privilege to "go" while she did not have access to the same opportunities, I came to see the slash, the chasm, the fissures in Black/Girlhood Imaginary. Daniele knows that, while we may both be Black girls, our realities are an ocean apart. Daniele's declaration speaks to Black/Girlhood Imaginary's insistence that Black girlhood is too capacious to be confined to singular storylines, and it illuminates the complex ways Black girls navigate the conditions of their lives. Our lives detour at the site of economy and geopolitical location: Daniele being born in Jamaica, and I being born in the United States; Daniele's labor is demanded in a tourist economy that crafts Jamaica's beaches as vacation havens for the privileged, while ignoring the inaccessibility and exploitation it demands from girls like Daniele—the same inaccessibility and exploitation that allowed me to meet Daniele (Mignolo 2011). In our last encounter, Daniele and I discussed our experiences. "Just don't forget me," she said softly, half-smiling. I can still see her. *Daniele, I did not forget. Thank you for challenging me and compelling me to imagine the layers and complexities which I have now collaged into the Black/Girlhood Imaginary*—an imaginary that holds space for the poetics of Blackness and girlness, both lived and mediated within and through invisibilized systems of power.

Conclusion

In this article, we explored three case studies of Black girlhoods: the subjecthood of Judy Winslow and the lived experiences of Foxworth, an analysis of Paradise's poem on her vulnerabilities to state-sanctioned violence, and the poetics of Daniele's experiences and knowings. Black/Girlhood Imaginary works toward recovering and reconciling the narratives and experiences of Black girls. Through ethnography, discourse analysis, and theories of embodiment, we stand alongside—and sometimes in opposition to—various constructs and confines of Black girlhood. We readily imagine the (im)possibilities of Black girls' lives within the dialectics of young Black life. As a prism that refracts and reflects, Black/Girlhood Imaginary pursues the restoration of the simulacra—the copy without an original.

We refuse to see the lives of Black girls simply as abstract analyses. Instead, we see Black girls along the spectrums of hypervisibility and invisibility, opacity and translucency. Analytically, each of our interpretations and understandings of Black girlhood speaks to a co-current illustration of loss and dream making that is negotiated within the Black/Girlhood Imaginary. When Judy disappears from the Winslow household, it creates an opportunity to ruminate on why television writers and producers need to be held accountable for their narrative choices. Yet through

Black/Girlhood Imaginary, Judy becomes centered, and her narrative is understood not just as a disappearance but also as a Black girl who was pushed out of her home and, subsequently, a Black actress who was pushed out of Hollywood. Informed by the methodological intervention of Black/Girlhood Imaginary, Paradise's poem is taken up as a theoretical analytic. Her work explores how law enforcement conditions the life chances of Black youth, while illustrating how Black girls voice their position and resistance. Black/Girlhood Imaginary acts as a telescope through which to explore the constellations of Daniele's life, mapping how geopolitical, imperial, and capitalist desires shape her. Daniele intuitively resists. Daniele—your story reaches beyond the borders that seemingly divide us. Paradise—your prose shows us how Black girls can make meaningful words out of painful experiences. Judy—your lingering presence haunts the show that tried to erase you. We write this text with their collective knowledge as our guide. Thank you for helping us forge a methodology out of chaos.

Our transdisciplinary engagement with the work comes from a place of conviction that Black girlhood, in all its manifestations and complexities, deserves and requires our attention, support, and care. We recognize it is a challenge to untangle the totality of what could or should be covered within Black/Girlhood Imaginary. Nonetheless, we invite opportunities for further reflection, conversation, and analysis. As we conclude, we ask: What does the future hold for Black/Girlhood Imaginary as praxis and analytic? How should we continue to theoretically engage these deliberations as individuals and collectives? What tensions remain for us to tease out and puzzles for us to ponder as we move forward? What interventions are still required? What is at stake if we do nothing?

Kenly Brown is a postdoctoral fellow at Washington University in St. Louis in the Department of African and African American Studies. She earned her PhD in African diaspora and African American studies at the University of California, Berkeley. Kenly employs creative ethnography to capture the affective lives of Black girls.

Lashon Daley is an assistant professor of English and comparative literature at San Diego State University. She earned her PhD in performance studies from the University of California, Berkeley. As a scholar, dancer, storyteller, and choreographer, Lashon thrives on bridging communities together through movement and storytelling.

Derrika Hunt, the daughter of Sylvia Renée, is a University of California Dissertation Writing Fellow. She is completing her PhD in education at the University of California, Berkeley. As a visionary curator across multiple domains, Derrika aims to keep imagination and dreaming at the heart of her work.

Notes

We would like to thank Nikki Jones and LeConté J. Dill for their mentorship as well as for reading earlier drafts of our manuscript. We are appreciative of our peers in the "Researching Race, Gender, and Justice" course where Black/Girlhood Imaginary came into fruition. We are especially thankful to Kyneshawau Hurd, Ina Kelleher, Frances Gregory-Roberts, Elizabeth Löwe Hunter, Rashad Timmons, Caleb Dawson, reelaviolette botts-ward, and Ra/Malika Imhotep. In addition, we would like to thank the Center for Race & Gender (CRG) at the University of California, Berkeley, for the generous funding of our research, which allowed us to have generative conversations, host weekly meetings, and purchase necessary materials. We are grateful to Aimee Meredith Cox and Savannah Shange, whom we engaged with during our conversation series supported by the CRG. Thank you to the editors and reviewers for their in-depth feedback that helped strengthen our manuscript. We are also grateful to the National Women's Studies Association for choosing us to present our work. Thank you to the Ford Foundation and American Education Research Association for supporting this research.

This work would not be possible without the Black girls and women who shared their lives in generous ways: to Paradise and every Black girl I met at H. B. Stowe Academy, this work is made possible through your courage and imagination. To Jaimee, thank you for your courage to speak out about your experience in the entertainment industry. To Daniele, thank you. You are so much more than a lesson, and you deserve so much more than what I can offer on the page. Thank you for teaching me how to dream and imagine in limitless ways.

1　Ruth Nicole Brown (2013: 9) informs our articulation of Black girlhood in *Hear Our Truths: The Creative Potential of Black Girlhood* where she "deploy[s] Black girlhood as a political articulation that intentionally points to Black girls, even as I mean for Black girlhood to direct our attention beyond those who identify and are identified as Black girls."

2　"To be without documentation is too unsustaining, too spontaneously ahistorical, too dangerously malleable in the hands of those who would rewrite not merely the past but my future as well. So I have been picking through the ruins for my roots" (Williams 2013: 22).

3　Scholars are Ruth Nicole Brown (2013), Tamara T. Butler (2018), Marcia Chatelain (2015), Venus E. Evans-Winters (2014), Corinne T. Field, Tammy Charelle-Owens, Marcia Chatelain, LaKisha Michelle Simmons, Abosede George, Rhian Keyse in Field et al. (2016), Dominique C. Hill (2019), Monique W. Morris (2016), Savannah Shange (2019), and LaKisha Michelle Simmons (2015).

4   Here we use Saidiya Hartman's (2018: 475) conceptualization of *wayward* as "riotous, queer, disposed to extravagance and wanton living. This promiscuous sociality fueled a moral panic identified and mobilized by the city's ruling elite to justify the extravagant use of police power."

5   Jones (2009: 53) defines *survival strategies* as "patterned forms of interpersonal interaction, and routine activities oriented around a concern for securing their personal well-being."

6   Pseudonym.

7   Pseudonym.

8   Pseudonym.

9   Pseudonym.

10   Pseudonym.

11   All quotations are taken from my conversations with Daniele.

Works Cited

Alexander, M. Jacqui, and Chandra Talpade Mohanty. 2010. "Cartographies of Knowledge and Power." In *Critical Transnational Feminist Praxis*, edited by Amanda Lock Swarr and Richa Nagar, 23–45. New York: State University of New York Press.

Baudrillard, Jean. 1994. *Simulacra and Simulation*. Ann Arbor: University of Michigan Press.

Bowles, Samuel, and Herbert Gintis. 2011. *Schooling in Capitalist America: Educational Reform and the Contradictions of Economic Life*. Chicago, IL: Haymarket Books.

Brown, Kenly. 2021. "Love, Loss, and Loyalty: A Black Feminist Reading of Black Girlhood." In *Black Feminist Sociology: Perspectives and Praxis*, edited by Zakiya Luna and Whitney N. Laster Pirtle, 197–206. New York: Routledge.

Brown, Ruth Nicole. 2013. *Hear Our Truths: The Creative Potential of Black Girlhood*. Chicago, IL: University of Illinois Press.

Butler, Tamara T. 2018. "Black Girl Cartography: Black Girlhood and Place-Making in Education Research." *Review of Research in Education* 42, no. 1: 28–45.

Chatelain, Marcia. 2015. *South Side Girls: Growing Up in the Great Migration*. Durham, NC: Duke University Press.

Christian, Barbara. 1987. "The Race for Theory." *Cultural Critique* 6 (Spring): 51–63.

Collins, Patricia Hill. 2002. *Black Feminist Thought: Knowledge, Consciousness, and the Politics of Empowerment*. New York: Routledge.

The Combahee River Collective. 2014. "A Black Feminist Statement." *Women's Studies Quarterly* 42, nos. 3–4: 271–80. www.jstor.org/stable/24365010.

Correll, Richard, dir. 1993. *Family Matters*. Season 4, episode 18, "Higher Anxiety." Aired February 26, on ABC.

Cox, Aimee Meredith. 2015. *Shapeshifters: Black Girls and the Choreography of Citizenship*. Durham, NC: Duke University Press.

Dill, LeConté J., Bianca Rivera, and Shavaun Sutton. 2018. "Don't Let Nobody Bring You Down." *Ethnographic Edge* 2, no. 1: 57–65.

Emerson, Robert M., Rachel I. Fretz, and Linda L. Shaw. 2011. *Writing Ethnographic Fieldnotes*. Chicago, IL: University of Chicago Press.

Evans-Winters, Venus E. 2014. "Are Black Girls Not Gifted? Race, Gender, and Resilience." *Interdisciplinary Journal of Teaching and Learning* 4, no. 1: 22–30.

Ewing, Eve L. 2018. "The Quality of the Light: Evidence, Truths, and the Odd Practice of the Poet-Sociologist." In *Black Women's Liberatory Pedagogies: Resistance, Transformation, and Healing within and beyond the Academy*, edited by Olivia N. Perlow, Durene I. Wheeler, Sharon L. Bethea, and BarBara M. Scott, 195–209. Cham, Switzerland: Palgrave Macmillan.

Field, Corinne T., Tammy-Charelle Owens, Marcia Chatelain, Lakisha Simmons, Abosede George, and Rhian Keyse. 2016. "The History of Black Girlhood: Recent Innovations and Future Directions." *Journal of the History of Childhood and Youth* 9, no. 3: 383–401.

Haley, Sarah. 2016. *No Mercy Here: Gender, Punishment, and the Making of Jim Crow Modernity*. Chapel Hill: University of North Carolina Press Books.

Harney, Stefano, and Fred Moten. 2013. *The Undercommons: Fugitive Planning and Black Study*. New York: Autonomedia.

Hartman, Saidiya. 2018. "The Anarchy of Colored Girls Assembled in a Riotous Manner." *South Atlantic Quarterly* 117, no. 3: 465–90.

Hill, Dominique C. 2019. "Blackgirl, One Word: Necessary Transgressions in the Name of Imagining Black Girlhood." *Cultural Studies ↔ Critical Methodologies* 19, no. 4: 275–83.

Jones, Nikki. 2009. *Between Good and Ghetto: African American Girls and Inner-City Violence*. New Brunswick, NJ: Rutgers University Press.

Kincaid, Jamaica. 1991. "Girl." *San Francisco Examiner*, January 1.

Lorde, Audre. (1978) 2007. "Uses of the Erotic: Erotic as Power." In *Sister Outsider: Essays and Speeches*, edited by Nancy K. Bereano, 53–60. Berkeley, CA: Crossing Press.

Menteer, Gary, dir. 1993. *Family Matters*. Season 4, episode 19, "Mama's Wedding." Aired March 5, on ABC.

Mignolo, Walter D. 2011. *The Darker Side of Western Modernity: Global Futures, Decolonial Options*. Durham, NC: Duke University Press.

Morris, Monique W. 2016. *Pushout: The Criminalization of Black Girls in Schools*. New York: New Press.

Morrison, Toni. 1987. *Beloved*. New York: Random House.

Nash, Jennifer C. 2018. *Black Feminism Reimagined: After Intersectionality*. Durham, NC: Duke University Press.

Nygreen, Kysa. 2013. *These Kids: Identity, Agency, and Social Justice at a Last Chance High School*. Chicago: University of Chicago Press.

Shange, Savannah. 2019. *Progressive Dystopia: Abolition, Antiblackness, and Schooling in San Francisco*. Durham, NC: Duke University Press.

Sharpe, Christina. 2016. *In the Wake: On Blackness and Being*. Durham, NC: Duke University Press.

Simmons, LaKisha Michelle. 2015. *Crescent City Girls: The Lives of Young Black Women in Segregated New Orleans*. Chapel Hill: University of North Carolina Press Books.

Snowber, Celeste. 2005. "The Mentor as Artist: A Poetic Exploration of Listening, Creating, and Mentoring." *Mentoring & Tutoring: Partnership in Learning* 13, no. 3: 345–53.

Valenzuela, Angela. 1999. *Subtractive Schooling: U.S.-Mexican Youth and the Politics of Caring*. New York: State University of New York Press.

Wiggins, Armon. 2020. "Exclusive: Family Matters Star Jaimee Foxworth (Judy Winslow) Opens Up about Career as Child Star." The Armon Wiggins Show, YouTube video, 1:39:32, uploaded January 12. www.youtube.com/watch?v=jIPrepj3r1U.

Williams, Patricia. 2013. "On Being the Object of Property." In *At the Boundaries of Law: Feminism and Legal Theory*, edited by Martha Albertson Fineman and Nancy Sweet Thomadsen, 22–40. London: Routledge.

Alana Perez

Illustrations by Pamela Fernandez

· ·

Carlota's Hum
An Archive Fiction

Abstract: This archive fiction recounts an insurrection led by Carlota in Cuba. Lázaro E. Cosme's *Voces Negras: Desde la plantación* holds a chapter detailing the legend of Carlota of the Triunvirato sugar mill in the province of Matanzas, Cuba. The author uses these short four pages to guide her fictional retelling of this historical moment. Other scenes illuminate the ways Black women of the nineteenth century were deeply connected to the nature surrounding them, emphasizing the unique relationship Black and Brown women have had with the land through natural healing scenes and also referencing nature-based Yoruba and Cuban Santería practices. Additionally, other records of this legend explain that Carlota only had eyes for another enslaved woman, Fermina. Therefore, the author attempts to push queer imaginations of the two women, beyond the Atlantic and onto Caribbean land.

Introduction

Carlota and Fermina, las *rebeldes* of the province of Matanzas, Cuba. This is a real story about two women who led a traveling rebellion that freed over three hundred enslaved people of Matanzas. A rebellion borne out of Carlota's prayers and dreams before it ever touched land or spread across neighboring plantations like a storm. This is a story, fabulated, of how the enslaved easily communicated with gods and goddesses. This story pays homage to Black women's incessant will to fight against chattel slavery in Cuba.

MERIDIANS · feminism, race, transnationalism   21:1 April 2022
DOI: 10.1215/15366936-9554090 © 2022 Smith College

I wanted to encounter the archive and excavate a deeper, more intimate history. In the process, I had to figure and reconfigure time lines, maps, and characters and find new methods that would allow me to find something anew in the archive, while also writing against the lapses and silences. This archive fiction is in part a translation of Carlota's story often told or written in Spanish (Cosme 2016); it is a passing down of legend; it's another iteration of an oral tradition that attributes the love of two women during a historical uprising (*Tremenda nota* 2019); it's a resurrection of Black femme voices from the overwhelming silences of the archive. So, try to listen, as Carlota "[listens] for that song that is our song, that song that actually travels across diaspora, that song that might engender a new form of radical black politics" (Hartman 2008: 15). Like Carlota, I had to listen for the song that started in Carlota's homeland, brewed in her lungs. The song that carried her to Fermina made me understand their own radical movement, their own radical ways of loving, and how the two women came to repossess their own breath and access their own freedom.

"Carlota's Hum"

The revolution started on her tongue. Carlota lucumí, meaning of Yoruba origin, was the master of disguise. While she worked on the sugar plantation of Triunvirato, the air and the sugar stuck to her as she whispered plans to herself, as if reciting a prayer, and in a language that her overseeing masters had no way of picking up. She licked the sweat off her upper lip as it dripped down. The way she pursed her lips while she quietly plotted. The slaveholders of Triunvirato have kept Carlota since she was only a young girl; they didn't worry about her, she just talked to herself a lot. She was a good slave who did her work.

The revolution grew out of her palms and feet. On these plantations, the enslaved worked from the early morning to late night. At night, Carlota walked off from her post. Invisible. She knew her friends would have her back while she went off. When Carlota returned to her secluded section in the woods, she would dance when no one but the gods and goddesses were watching. Nights of the full moon were rare to sneak out on, but they were her favorite, and that's when she could see with the most clarity. She drew blueprints of the land she was forced to learn, and that she tentatively came to love. With her right pointer finger she drew the paths that would need to be taken for this planned escape. She marked all the spots where white guards, masters, and families might be on that day. These

Figure 1.

were her intentions for the full moon every time. The dirt riddled with her imaginations of anarchy, noise. After looking at the plan under the moonlight, sometimes she would laugh with excitement, other times she would cry from fear and disbelief that this is how hard she would have to fight. That she would have to make others bleed. But every time, after inscribing her fight in the warm earth's cool soil, she would walk some feet away from it, enough so she could not see it anymore and lay her body down, perhaps to meditate, manifest, or just to close her eyes and be able to call it rest.

On this particular night, she laid on the ground, closed her eyes, and hummed a song. Although she could not wait to bring *el temor* to Triunvirato, she could not wait to be somewhere far, somewhere quieter, somewhere with more space so she could let her voice carry. No more of that timid humming; no more muffling the spirit. She thought of that life for a moment much too short for her liking. Eventually, she walked back to her blueprint, stomped it out so no one would see it the next morning, and walked back to her quarters. The next day she would find a moment to share her imaginations of trouble that she and her companions would wreak on the plantation. She knew she could not do it alone; in fact, she did not want to do it alone.

Realizar, to carry out, to make real.

It took months for Carlota and her crew of fighters to make their dreams of freedom and, more importantly, their rebellion real, to make the blueprints rise off the dirt and watch it happen before their eyes. It took time.

For months they could communicate with each other only through the sound of their *tambores*. The coded percussion was the first way they made the blueprint-soil rumble. The messages in the rhythm made it all the way to neighboring plantations and sugar mills. It all sounded like aimless beating to the Spanish guards and masters.

Carlota, *la compositora*. She was known for being musically gifted, and surely, she composed some of the rhythm-messages that would pulse beyond Matanzas, Cuba.

No fue tarea de un día . . . It took time for the beat of the *atabal* to flow through other warm bodies; the drumbeat revving up hearts without ever having to utter a single word. It took time for Carlota's partner in crime, Eduardo of fula origin, to interpret the voice of the *atabal*, to make sure everyone understood what needed to be done.

"A message came in today through the drums," whispered Eduardo. "Something has gone terribly wrong in Alancía."

"What happened?" asked Carlota with her back arched toward the sun, ripping the weeds from the earth, trying to be inconspicuous.

"The Spanish caught slaves during a revolt . . . they got Fermina."

Just the sound of her name stopped Carlota from whatever she was doing. She rose slowly from her bend and walked calmly through the field. She let the sweat on her body settle for a moment before she let herself speak too soon, then asked, "Did they kill her?"

"No, but they have locked her up. The drums carried her screams. She is not safe, Carlota."

"Well, alright. We must move a day sooner than we anticipated. Gather folks around the *atabal* tonight."

"Sí, Carlota."

She reached for Eduardo's hand, "And remember fula, do not let the Spaniards have a hint of a clue." He kissed her hand gently, understanding that this news was not easy for her to hear and left to spread the word. Carlota stood alone in the same spot Eduardo found her, dizzied by the heat and the news, but she stood incredibly still.

During a visit to Alancía, a neighboring plantation to Triunvirato, Carlota met Fermina.

Carlota was a beautiful woman, a full woman who carried her chest high regardless of who she was around. She knew that many men had their eyes on her, and she didn't mind it, so long as they didn't touch her. For example, Eduardo was always captured by Carlota without her ever having to lay a finger on him. Perhaps it was the control in her tone, or the vibrato in her laughter. But when Carlota looked back at Eduardo, she saw nothing but a friend. And she knew very well that he was in love with her. But so what? It was like this with most men and women that became enamored with Carlota's magnetic draw. She was always too focused on her plans in the dirt and the visions in her eyes.

But on this visit, she met a woman named Fermina.

Carlota was accompanying her master's oldest son. He had forced himself on her the night before and today brought her by his side to go visit their neighbors because Carlota was the prettiest and healthiest slave they had to show off. When they arrived at the Alancía manor, Fermina was moving quietly through the home, speaking only when spoken to.

"Fermina, get over here," her master snapped in Spanish. "Take this negrita with you out back to help finish putting out the wet clothes. Us men have some business to discuss."

"Sí, señor." As she turned around, he slapped her ass and let out a throaty cackle. Carlota kept her eyes fixated on him for a quick second, thinking how she could have slapped him across the face, that gross crooked-toothed man. She made sure she was not staring long. She didn't want any problems today.

The two women walked to the backyard of the home together silently, promptly doing what they were told. Fermina was on one side of the clothesline and Carlota on the other. Carlota was humming a tune under her breath, as usual, trying to keep herself calm. Her stomach felt strange . . . she had not felt this naive feeling since she was a young girl in her homeland. Sometimes the feeling would tickle her when her mother used to braid her hair in a cool shade outside their small but cozy abode; the

Figure 2.

way her mother's fingers parted her hair into sections was always a moment of meditation for Carlota. Or like when a young boy had noticed her for the first time and handed her a fruit and said something stupid but simple like, "It's sweet. Just like you." It was this same feeling that was arising now in her belly; she was unsure of how to subside it, so she hummed.

Fermina was staring at her as her hands thoughtlessly flipped and flopped the wet clothes over the line. Of course Carlota could feel her eyes on her, and there was that feeling, tickling her again, that wouldn't go away.

Eventually, Carlota looked back at Fermina and nonchalantly said, "Yes?"

Fermina did not respond, but she smirked a little bit and looked away, continuing her chore. They continued about their business for a few minutes, and Carlota carried her traditional tune all the while. Then unexpectedly, a harmony was layered onto Carlota's melody. It was quiet and raspy. Carlota looked again to Fermina who was not looking back at Carlota. They harmonized for one entire round of the song, so quietly so that the men in the house would not notice or hear. No one would ever know or hear this moment but the two of them. But the air was so clear this day that even their whispered melodic moans vibrated through the trees, the leaves.

"How do you know this song?" Carlota asked in Spanish.

"I am lucumí too," Fermina responded in lucumí dialect. "My big sister used to sing it to me. My ear will never forget it." Carlota was so pleased and warmed by this response she could not help but smile. Her back was facing the house windows, so she knew no one could see. The two finished hanging all the clothes, but neither of their masters had come back out yet.

Carlota enjoyed the slight breeze coming in and watched how it caressed the clothes of a dirty man then said, "What do you think they are talking about in there? Did you overhear anything before we arrived?"

"They are probably telling their best sex stories or whose broomstick is bigger." Carlota was shocked by Fermina's mouth. Only a moment ago, she was quiet and keeping her head down. Her big childlike watery eyes did not match the fire and snap on that tongue. They stared at each other for a short moment before finally letting out a trifling giggle. Then she said, "Wait here a moment," and entered back into the kitchen. Carlota watched through the window as Fermina politely interrupted the men, asking them a question she could not make out from where she was standing. Nevertheless, she stared at Fermina. She was a pretty thing, earthly all on her own, but the olive dress she wore brought it out even more.

Fermina walked back out. Her skin was dark but just light enough to notice fresh bruises on her forearms and a nasty scar on her right hand. She said plainly, "Let's go," and led them out the backyard and around to the front of the house.

Carlota followed without question, although she was usually the woman giving orders. "And where are we going?"

"El Señorrr," Fermina said with tease in her tone, mimicking the Spanish accent "said I can take you with me. The men will be talking for another few minutes. Maybe even an hour. They poured some alcohol, so they said you can help me tend to the garden in the meantime."

"Well alright," Carlota responded.

And so they walked about half a mile to the garden. It was beautiful and quite abundant. Fermina was the only one who tended to it. The master's wife would often host small events and get-togethers there, and as Fermina would walk around delighting the Spaniard folks, she listened to the wife take credit for growing everything in the garden. One can imagine all the slandering things Fermina would riddle in her head as she kept a docile smile all the while. No one could ever see the flames simmering in her heart, and certainly not all the words she choked down without even the semblance of a gulp.

There was really nothing to tend to in the garden today, but it was the one spot she knew no one would bother them, especially today when the men seemed to be in a decent mood and too preoccupied with talking "business." Fermina was the only of the enslaved ever allowed in the garden too, so it was rarely heavily guarded. One day a field slave was caught trying to steal a piece of fruit from the garden, and the wife ordered the guards to cut both her hands off for everyone to see. Fermina snuck a few berries in her breasts the next morning and fed them to her when no one was looking.

"Come, sit here," Fermina said, patting a spot under a mango tree.

"Don't we have to do something?" asked Carlota.

Fermina pulled the ripest mango from the tree, "Yes, we will eat this mango," then she sunk her teeth in without a care and let the juice fall all the way down her neck and to her collarbone. She liked the natural scent it left on her. "Did you know the skin of a mango helps you to breathe better?"

"Yes, I did know," Carlota chuckled, "Give me that." She took her bite, and they continued this way passing the mango back and forth, as if they'd had this tradition for years.

"So you are from Triunvirato . . . but who *are* you? We received and heard messages through the *atabal* from Triunvirato."

"I am Carlota. I been organizing for those messages to be spread across all of Matanzas."

"Carlota . . . " Fermina paused, "Ah. Carlota. I have heard stories about you."

Carlota did not respond to this, but she hoped the rumors that had made their way to Fermina before she did were at least flattering. After a short silence, she asked Fermina, "So, you are willing to fight?" Their chewing filled the short silence that followed the question.

"To fight? I am ready to kill," Fermina looked at Carlota in her eyes when she said this. Carlota knew this wasn't a lie or an exaggeration. She took the mango out of Fermina's hand and bit it, her teeth grazing the mango pit. Fermina took the seed and buried it into the soil a few yards away from where they sat.

"You think you're ready to kill, eh?" Carlota stood up.

"It's not a matter of readiness," Fermina said. "It's simply what will be necessary."

They roamed around the garden, making small jokes while admiring all the colors Fermina had been able to cultivate in the garden, such a small space. Before leaving the garden to return to the manor, Fermina grabbed some heliconia flowers and placed them behind Carlota's left ear, then her right, then she did the same for herself. The bright red plant accented their facial features. "See, now we look like real warriors," she said.

Fermina took hers off before walking back to avoid any trouble with the white men. Carlota said she wanted to keep them on for some of the walk because she liked how it made her feel. Halfway there, she took them off and slid the flowers under her underwear over her right hip.

They entered through the backyard and could see through the kitchen window that the men's glasses were empty and they were laughing loudly, constantly trying to be louder than the other. Carlota and Fermina simply looked at each other, not knowing but also knowing what their nights might be like later. Carlota reached for Fermina's hand, squeezed it tight and whispered, "I will see you soon, and we will fight."

Fermina's eyes lit up and she smiled.

It had been six months since that first encounter between Carlota and Fermina in Alancía, and four days since Eduardo had relayed the news about Fermina. Carlota's spirit was rattled, and she wondered how long Fermina had actually been locked up. There was no more time to waste; today was the day. As always, Carlota took tally of all the celestial bodies that would be aiding them. She prayed to each, one by one.

It was November 3 of 1843, and Orisha Oya, storm goddess, sat atop the sun, unphased by the burn. A dark dominant streak of energy was coursing through bodies. Meaning, she was *the only force within nature that has the ability to change the face of the earth from her destructive winds.* Carlota knew this. Carlota and her army would not go quietly today, or unseen.

They would be mean today. With Ogun, warrior god, pounding against the moon's curves, making iron and moon dust fall from cosmic heavens upon the earth's soil, upon Carlota's army, smudging them like something blessed. There was no time to wait anymore. The message was clear. Their fists and feet were ready to move at their own pace, and quickly.

For Carlota, these transits brought about an intensity in her gut. It was the Orishas. The sun. The moon. It was Fermina. She thought about her every day. She heard her sweet voice, often cut through with a slight rasp: *To fight? I am ready to kill.* Carlota was too.

The drums, along with Eduardo's translation, informed those of Triunvirato the evening before to be ready and in position as early as Orisha Oya rose with the sun. Carlota, however, was in her position while the moon was still peeking through the clouds, making sure everything was in place. She looked up at the moon often, thanking Ogun and also Orisha Yemoja, mother of the moon. She gulped down tears several times, as if swallowing her own moons down to her stomach, but never for a second did she doubt what needed to happen today.

The plan this time was not only to burn the fields. They had to use all the elements, orchestrate a hurricane. Something so godly and horrible to put an end to the brutal treatment they have endured for far too long. Yes, they would burn, but also wash out the white, blow away the ashes, lift the earth. The plan was to be carried out, made real, exactly how Carlota had envisioned it. Carlota was at the front of the crowd, not afraid to be seen. She had the bright red heliconia flowers on either side of her ears. They were slightly dried out at this point, but nevertheless she kept them since the day Fermina had given them to her.

As Ogun kept pounding, pounding, pounding, on the moon through the still-dark morning and Oya followed in tandem, carrying the sun up, the white "masters" of Triunvirato were going to be the first to feel Carlota's hurricane army. The sharp waves that they did not see coming. Their silence was their best technique.

They set fire to the big white house first, and they lit the entire sky before the sun could. The lighting of the house initiated the ceremony. They screamed, hollered, hooted, laughed, cried, shooting prayers in their mother tongues to the sky. As white bodies came flailing out of the house and other parts of the manor, the rebels' machetes made wind. White blood shed like rainfall from the clouds, as if it were the moon forcefully moving blood around as if they were bodies of water.

Not one warrior from Carlota's army died on this first fight; they were protected. So they moved onward. The opening ceremony was complete.

"¡To Alancía!" Carlota screamed.

"¡Alancía!"

The army quieted down on their way there. Many took turns riding on the horses they stole, while the others walked. By the time they reached Alancía, Ogun's moon-beat was less present and Oya's sunlight burned the skies. The heat was beating on their backs and forcing their eyebrows to furrow.

They began to enter the Alancía mill from different sides, their bodies maneuvering and spreading through the land like a river. The enslaved of Alancía were expecting them, anxiously awaiting their arrival all morning and all day. News of the insurrection at Triunvirato had not made it to the Spaniards yet, so their defensive guards were down.

Carlota was the only one from Triunvirato who knew how to enter the backyard of the manor. While everyone else assumed their positions like silent clouds in the sky, she made her way to the heart of Alancía, the home. Her bare feet barely came off the grass. It was as if she were floating across, silently lurking through the backyard, eyes locked on the kitchen window where she once stared into and at Fermina, and then being reminded that Fermina had the soul power to pull Carlota from her center, causing her to even stare for that long. Even now, she thought she had seen Fermina's figure through the glass. But there was no one there in the kitchen. Carlota advanced a little toward the back door. Then suddenly she heard movement, so she stopped for a moment and gripped the handle of her machete tighter. It was hot against her bare chest.

She closed her eyes and kept gripping until she finally released and let out her breath and with it rang the song she always hummed. But this time, with words in lucumí. If the song brought her Fermina before, she prayed it would again. She sang loudly, so loud and so far that her breath was trembling the leaves and branches of the trees. And she lured the master from his home. He came out confused and aroused, absolutely entranced by the body dissenting before him. Her hands drew invisible lines in the air. Carlota kept singing her song as he stood there stupefied at the sight of her, and she smirked, she smiled. It was hard for him to react quickly as he marveled at the bright yellow dress that hung just beneath her breasts and the glimmers caught in the sunlight from her shining silver jewelry and her big swinging machete. As her voice echoed farther and rang louder, the other rebels hollered in response across Alancía. The air rang with echoes of love and abolition.

Just when the master was about to bark a threat at Carlota, she twirled in one breath, hooked her arm around his neck, pressed the front of her body firmly against his back, and licked his neck with her warm machete. Carlota could have laughed at the way he shook; *always giving deadly commands but can't take them,* she thought. All he could do was pant. If he made any hasty movement his head would go dangling. They stood there in an intimate silence.

Finally, Carlota whispered in his ear, "Adonde estas Fermina?"

"Sh-she is locked up in the basement."

"Take me to her, now!" Carlota's voice was as sharp as the machete edge holding this white man in place. They clumsily danced through the kitchen, past his stupid wife and damned kids, frozen like statues, and finally all the way down the dark basement. There was a candle hanging at the bottom of the staircase.

"Grab that." Carlota ordered him. If it were not for this small source of light, this dungeon would be utter darkness. She couldn't believe he would let Fermina sit in all that nothingness. She already knew what it felt like to be treated like nothing, but to be forced to sit in it too . . .

The light lit a short path through the basement. It revealed drops of blood that led to someone that looked like Fermina, curled up in a fetal position, naked on the cold ground. Her back, arms, and legs were all gruesomely carved into by the doing of a whip. Her feet were tied up with iron chains. The smell was foul. Carlota could not stand the sight. She tried to hold back her tears, but she could not swallow them all; it felt like trying to push rocks down her throat.

"Let her go!" she shrieked. Carlota released him from her hold but kept the sharp point of the machete touching his back, and he hurried to let Fermina out of her chains; his hands quivered as he fumbled for the keys. As soon as he unchained Fermina, he stepped away with tears in his eyes and let out a pathetic moan about to plead with Carlota. Before he could get the words out, Carlota unearthed a roar and slashed him across his stomach, bringing him to his knees and finished him with a blow to the skull and a final roar.

Finally, Carlota went and examined Fermina. Fermina's skin was horribly scarred, but her eyes were intact, and thank the gods and goddesses for that. Fermina stared at her once-master's limp and leaking body before her, then looked up at Carlota to find her staring right back at her. Carlota took one of the heliconia flowers from behind her ear and placed it behind

Fermina's. She reached for her hand and said, "Come on, warrior. Get up. It is time to fight now."

Fermina was utterly confused coming out of her deep rest. First she looked out the window and noticed how bright the night sky was. What we would call a night sky was still bright to her after being subjected to that moonless basement for nearly a month. As she adjusted herself in the strange bed, she could not help but freeze up for a moment as she realized she was laying in the guest bedroom of the master's home. How had she gotten here? She had cleaned it so many times, but sleep in it? Never. Who had laid her down? She attempted to get out of the bed, but her body let out a million screeches and moans that only she could hear. It hurt her body, her ears, and everything climaxed to her head, a pounding she could not move through. She got back in the bed defeated by her own body. She tried to wait for the pain to quiet down, until it was just her, the silence and her body that did not know how to lay in this bed, not comfortably at least. She stared at the ceiling and wanted to scream at its blankness, because it too could not explain to her why she deserved all the atrocities that led up to this moment. So she cried. She made terrible faces that revealed pain before this pain. She screamed at all the nothingness consuming her. She screamed at the silence, the ceiling, the pain she could not touch. She screamed at herself for surviving; she hated strength if this is what it looked like.

Downstairs, Carlota was preparing treatments that would instantly heal Fermina's tenderized body. During the time Fermina was asleep, Carlota's army had wiped out all of the white from Alancía. Somewhere in the mill, there were men and young boys digging into the earth to let those white bodies fall and rot.

After Carlota killed Fermina's captor and while the rest of the enslaved of Triunvirato handled the rest of the family and Spanish guards, she ran a bath mixed with a potion she was able to concoct with plants from the garden and the kitchen. With the right dosage, this blend sent Fermina into a deep restful sleep. Carlota knew Fermina had lost even that privilege locked down there, naked and in the cold. Carlota needed her asleep so that she could clean her wounds thoroughly without Fermina writhing the entire time.

Carlota and Eduardo carried her from the basement and up to the bathroom, but she was hallucinating and could not always clearly see what or who was in front of her. They gently let her body sink into the herb-filled tub and supported her head. Carlota and Eduardo watched as the water turned an iron red-brown and waited for the sleeping potion to take over her body, and for Fermina's eyes to close.

To wash her wounds she had used *jobo* fruit, *ponasí* plant, powder from the *curujey* plant and most importantly infusions from the ceiba tree. The sacred tree of the Yorubas. There was not a ceiba tree planted at Alancía, but Carlota had made sure to come prepared with her own infusions from Triunvirato. She had stood at the foot of the tree and asked for it to help her bring wellness to her beloved Fermina. This, Carlota hoped, would speed up the healing, so they could go on and fight together the next day. Carlota had also collected horsetail herb and seed shell from the bija tree in the garden; this would act as the antiseptic. From the house, she took garlic and onions; these would act as antibiotics for the wounds.

It had been about six or seven hours that Fermina was asleep. Her slow moans of agony and sobs carried their way downstairs, letting Carlota know she was awake and very much in pain again. So she went upstairs carrying her ingredients to heal Fermina physically and spiritually. Upstairs, Fermina was still paralyzed in the bed, staring up at the ceiling that was trapping her, wailing at it.

"Relax now, Fermina," Carlota eased her. "I am going to make you better." Then, she began to do her magic, the magic of her ancestors. She had finely grounded the horsetail herb and added very hot water until it became a paste. Similarly, she pounded the bark of the bija seed shell into a thicker paste for the fresher and redder flesh still seething on the backs of Fermina's thighs and her sacrum. "Lay on your stomach, Fermina," Carlota directed her gently.

First, Carlota rubbed the horsetail on the backs of her arms and upper back. She made sure to spread it evenly and slowly, paying close attention to how her fingers pressed into Fermina's flesh and the noises that she would make into the pillow. On this part of her body, Fermina let out relieving sighs; the cooling of the herb-paste on her upper body dragged some of the dark concentration of pain out of her. Carlota then placed pieces of cotton cloth to cover the paste over her skin.

"That feels nice," Fermina groaned.

"Don't speak so soon," Carlota chuckled. Then she proceeded to lift up the dressing in order to get to the worst of her wounds. She took a scoop full of the bija paste and rubbed it on the badly scarred bottom half of her body. For this part, Fermina had to bite into the pillow. Although it pained

Carlota to do this, she rubbed steadily until her entire body was covered in the medicine. Before she wrapped her bottom half with cloth, she took the ceiba tree infusion and sprinkled it on top, lightly whispering a prayer, and then proceeded to wrap Fermina's body tightly so the medicine would take. Once this was done, Carlota got in the bed next to Fermina and rubbed her gently over the cloth, while humming the tune that they sang together. Like that first day, Fermina stared at Carlota singing.

"Sing with me," Carlota said, looking back at her, "Don't be shy now." Their faces were the closest they had ever been. Carlota rubbed Fermina's cheek and picked the tune back up, "Come on, sing." Fermina closed her eyes and sang the harmony. As she closed her eyes, still all she could see was Carlota's face underneath the mango tree, how beautifully the sun was catching her that day. Fermina was smiling through her daydream and did not notice that Carlota had stopped singing because she was parting her lips so that they would meet Fermina's unscathed forehead. This was their first kiss. Fermina opened her eyes and quieted her harmony. Carlota kissed her right cheek, then her left and Fermina watched her every move, with those eyes that Carlota loved having on her so much. They allowed their lips to meet once and cradled each other for the rest of the night, while Fermina's body cooled and healed. They both slept quietly, knowing that in the morning it would be time to move again.

At sunrise, the roosters woke the two women. Fermina let out a stretch, bringing her arms over her head; it sent a rejuvenating feeling down her spine all the way down to her toes. She giggled deliriously at the feeling, amazed by how much better her body felt already, although it physically still looked torn and scathed. Her laughter was really what started Carlota's day, waking her from one of the most restful nights she'd had in years.

"And how are you feeling?" Carlota asked, rolling over to caress the woman she loved so easily.

Fermina sighed and replied, "I cannot wait to run today. Just run." So she got up with all of this restored energy, and bent her legs every which way. Enjoyed the glory of the cerulean blue skirt she put on, swirling beneath her, looking like the stretched sky. Carlota had brought it for her from Triunvirato. She was like new. Better still, she was like herself again. She could not help the widening grin across her face, neither could Carlota. The healing was so miraculous it was silly; they couldn't help but laugh as Fermina contorted her body all kinds of ways. "Oh, thank you Carlota, ife mi, thank you, thank you, *thank* you, my love. Your magic worked!"

Excited and energized, Fermina threw herself at Carlota on the bed, kissing her impatiently all over her face. They laughed and wrestled this way until everything in their bodies slowed down some, and their tongues and hands explored parts of each other that they hadn't before. They tousled, and they kissed, fucked all over that cursed room, making sure it was known that they had come, that they were there. Together, they woke up every part of their bodies, enjoying every twitch, moan, breath, gasp, tear, climax, and return.

Carlota saw this still as part of Fermina's healing. "Return, Fermina. Come."

The revolution was sparked between their bodies that morning.

Once they came to, they got dressed again and decorated each other in their battle gear. Carlota in yellow, Fermina in blue. They ran through the house like some excited little girls about to go start trouble with the young boys back home that they would childishly tease. They tried to revel in their giddiness before the realities of war set back in.

Later, Carlota had gathered everyone in front of the manor. Her and Fermina divided the growing group of rebels into smaller units that would have different chores before leaving for their next destination. One group would help Fermina collect and gather food from the garden and farmland. "Don't pluck the fruits so aggressively," she would repeat to the children and to the men too impatient to pick the fruit gently. Another group led by Eduardo was in charge of finding and collecting all the firearms on the plantation. Carlota led a group in Yoruba spirituals to ensure their protection in this next fight.

The next stop was the Ácana plantation, another mill that Triunvirato had communicated with through the *atabal* for some time, despite the two-and-a-half-kilometer distance. They were expecting the freed slaves' arrival. Once they arrived, they met up with the enslaved revolt leader of Ácana, Cristóbal lucumí. He rang the bell of the mill, which notified the rest of the Ácana rebels to congregate and begin their fight. The ring of the bell vibrated deeply through all their bodies from the start of their fight to the end. Of the two revolts Carlota had already led, this one was the one that made her realize that history was being made.

As Carlota fought on the field, she watched women with babies strapped on their backs swing their machetes so precisely; there was practice and pain in their blows.

A young boy ran deep through the woods, cradling his baby sibling. He didn't look back for a second, only forward, letting the tree leaves and branches slap his face, hoping to erase the sight of his father's murder. He didn't know where he was running to; he just needed to hide.

A group of friends hid in a distant barn where they often gossiped, told stories, or shared secret remedies. Today, they were quiet. Only their sniffles and murmured prayers filled the space.

A mother who lost her children long before this fight stared at all that came undone before her. All she could do was stand still and stare, trying to find the right words or emotions that could evoke so much disaster, so much beauty. But all she did was stare at it all. Suddenly, one of the younger rebels snatched her by the arm, leading her to a safer spot.

A Spaniard had managed to shoot and kill a couple of the rebels, which stirred the army even more. The Spaniard continued to shoot at them, but kept missing. He was out of bullets now.

"You are nothing without your bullets!" yelled one rebel.

"Nothing!" they all yelled and ran toward him until they caught him and forced him to the ground.

The main rebel who led the chase straddled him and put a dagger to his throat. "You'll look me in my eyes when I kill you."

Others laid around the dead rebels, any short moment they could, praying to Orisha Oya, praying for the rebels' safe rising and arrival to the afterlife.

Farther out from the battleground, two lovers embraced, thankful to hug and kiss even if only one more time.

Fermina was inside the house hurriedly stuffing her pouch with any useful ingredients or herbs for future medicines or spiritual offerings until she was suddenly pushed from behind. A woman's voice cursed in Spanish, "Get your dirty hands off of what's mine before I cut them off!" She looked disheveled, as she did not know how else to fight Fermina off. Fermina laughed and pulled the woman by her hand, laid it out on the countertop, pulled out her machete and chopped off her right hand like a piece of meat.

"Get *your* dirty hands off of me, before I cut them both off."

Scenes such as these repeated in variation all afternoon; the fight did not stop until every Spaniard was dead.

After this battle, they moved on to the *ingenio*, or the sugar mill, Concepción. Word of their traveling rebel army was slowly spreading, and so the master of the plantation locked away all of the enslaved. He had also ordered twelve of his best men to travel to the border of the property on horses to act as some sort of barricade. However, as the twelve men stood there with their firearms, they felt the horses becoming jittery and anxious. They could feel the trembling of the earth under their hooves. Over the horizon they began to see over one hundred escaped slaves.

"Do we shoot?" one Spaniard asked.

Across the way, one of the rebels let out a shot from a gun they took from their previous location.

"They have guns! Retreat! Retreat!" And with that the twelve men went fleeing back to the mainland. *Los sublevados* chased the men, knowing they would lead them to *ingenio* Concepción. Once they arrived, they wasted no time in attacking all the men and forcing them to inform them of where the enslaved were being hidden, killed them once they had the information they needed, and confiscated their firearms. They were able to free the trapped enslaved and added to their group of *sublevados*. They continued on this way all through three other *ingenios*: San Miguel, San Lorenzo, and San Rafael.

Their freedom hurricane washed and pummeled through the *ingenios* of Matanzas all the way into the new year, 1844, unrelenting. Led by Carlota, often with Fermina by her side, the army had accumulated over three hundred rebels, but certainly with some losses along the way.

After their combat in San Rafael, they camped out there for the night before moving onward. Many, including Carlota and Fermina, had not slept for days upon days. So many were hungry and tired. While most of them had gathered around a warm fire and sang along to the beat of los *tambores*, Carlota and Fermina laid nearby staring up at the moon and the stars; this is how they recharged.

"What's on your mind, Mina?"

There was silence for a moment. "I wish that we find a boat soon at one of these damned *ingenios*."

Carlota laughed.

"I'm serious, Lo! I'm tired of doing these white souls favors and giving them the easy way out. I want us to find a boat and some remote piece of land. It doesn't even have to be back home. You and I can start somewhere, like new."

"We are somewhere, right now," Carlota raised her arms above her head and took in a deep breath and on the exhale let out a loud hoot. "You hear that? I haven't heard my voice echo into the night like that in a very long time. Believe me, *ife*, we are much closer to 'somewhere' than we were before."

Fermina smirked, amused by Carlota's ability to always say the right thing. Then she shouted into the sky to hear her echo as well. They held hands, feeling how grateful the other was in that moment. To be able to lay by their beloved, decipher the constellations before them, howling vowels at the moon.

As sunset approached in San Rafael, the sky was still dark enough to blanket the dreams and insomniac thoughts of the rebels. Although they saw a plethora of visions, they did not see or anticipate what was coming toward them. They could never have imagined that their instinctual need and craving for freedom would bring about the terror that would reach them shortly.

The Spanish government had finally gotten the details of the uprisings that these free slaves had waged for months and were able to locate their most recent destination. On this January morning, the colonial system and order were afoot. The Spaniards came in hordes of their own, ready to remind the rebels of the discipline they needed.

Carlota and Fermina were still lying on the warm ground they had fallen asleep on, bodies tightly bound together by a thin blanket. The sound of horse hooves slapping and rapping against the cool of the earth echoed miles ahead, which only meant that white men ready to kill sat upon those horses. Carlota woke up first because she was not as heavy a sleeper as Fermina. The rumbling earth woke her in a fright; she immediately knew what was going on. "Mina," Carlota shook her lover, "Fermina! Wake up, *ife*, wake up!" Fermina finally did and felt the shaking of the ground. They both sprang up and ran toward the drums, picked them up, and banged and banged and hollered until people began to wake up and move.

But it was just too late and unexpected. There were so many of them scattered throughout the property; some slept through the signal entirely. By the time the Spanish troops arrived, the battle was already guaranteed to be an unfair fight. While the rebels had fought so hard to be free, the Spaniards came back even harder to ensure they would never dream so big again. The battle lasted a little over two hours. The Spaniards managed to kill fifty-four and imprisoned another seventy-seven rebels. Many other rebels managed to run and run and run. Unfortunately for Carlota and Fermina, they were captured and identified as the main leaders of these uprisings. It was worse that they were women, and even worse still that they were in love. That such revolution could be borne out of the love of two *negras*. So their punishment reflected the Spaniards' insidious displeasure for the whole thing.

The following morning, once some of the chaos had subsided, the Spaniards decided to put on a show. The governor of Matanzas even traveled to see. Carlota was tied by her feet and hands to horses, which when commanded, would run in opposite directions. Before this command was given, the Spanish commander made sure to round up all the remaining slaves around the display, explaining to them what happens when you try to break the law and order of things in Matanzas.

Two guards held Fermina closest to the display. She did not listen to a word of what the guard was saying. She was only tuned into the notes tripping out of Carlota's croaking breaths. Carlota was beaten so badly prior to this moment that all that came out of her was a hoarse hum. She sang the same spiritual that carried her to Fermina and through all these months of sweet rebellion, big and small.

Fermina heard her, began to sob and scream, but she could not escape the tight hold of the two guards. Carlota continued to sing over Fermina's guttural cries. The dissonance was palpable; the captives also knew this discordant song; they'd heard it before.

The command was given. Carlota kept humming, Fermina screamed. She hummed. She screamed.

Her body stretched and she kept singing until her body was not hers anymore. Her tune ripped apart. Cut short. Fermina could not even scream anymore at the brutal sight. All she could do was drop to her knees. Stare.

Only a piercing silence carried for the rest of Fermina's day. A silence that cut through the mundane clanging of the Spaniards' gear, or of the metallic chains reattached to her wrists and ankles. Fermina heard nothing but the emptiness banging in her chest.

Fermina had to wait a little over three months to see Carlota again. When Fermina's soul departed from earth, all she remembered was moving through a bright light that turned into opaque whiteness. So she roamed through it aimlessly. Her body was not her body, but more so a silhouette, and she took pleasure in how much lighter everything felt.

She was not sure where to go; there was no one there to guide her. As she kept floating around, she began to hear a distant voice. It was Carlota's; she was sure of it. Her spirit trembled, thumped as if she still had a heart that could beat. She began to move quicker through the blank space. As she neared the voice, her surroundings began to change as well. Eventually, she found herself on an island, like Cuba but quieter, fewer bodies, no big scary house. Just trees, water, sunlight, and small pockets of shade. Here, her

Figure 3.

body had returned to its full and more solid shape. Her feet could feel the warmth of the sand, her hands could touch the smoothness of her cheek. By the shore, she saw a boat. There was the tune again; she was getting closer. She walked slowly toward it until she encountered a peculiarly placed mango tree. It didn't make sense for one to be planted in the middle of sand, but apparently it made sense here.

Underneath it sat Carlota, singing their song, continuing the tune that was ripped from her when she was killed. Fermina approached the shade and calmly sat by her.

"Mina," Carlota smiled with closed lips while she purred her song and chewed on ripe mango. "I guess we made it to that somewhere," she passed the mango to Fermina, "I was saving the next bite for you."

They laughed and ate together peacefully under the mango tree.

Alana Perez holds a dual BA in creative writing and Africana studies from Rhode Island College. Currently, she is pursuing her MFA in poetry at the University of South Carolina. She's bridged her scholarly and creative interests through fellowships like the Schomburg-Mellon Humanities Institute and DreamYard Rad(ical) Poetry Consortium.

Laura Lomas

. . . .

Afro-Latina Disidentification and Bridging
Lourdes Casal's Critical Race Theory

Abstract: The exiled Cuban poet, editor, and feminist Lourdes Casal breaks with social scientific convention and identifies in the first person with "Hispanic Blackness," feminism, and Cuba in her essays about race and revolution. Her bridging of identity categories informs Casal's self-definition as a "radicalized" social scientist who sheds light on academic feminism's blindspots and who applauds the revolutionary recognition of Cuban culture as "Latin-African." Casal forges decolonial tools for dismantling the master's house by adapting feminist rhetorical strategies of self-inscription that make palpable the entrenched effects of anti-Black violence. Casal's scholarship practices what queer Cuban philosopher José Muñoz calls "disidentification." Against a tradition that dismisses women as monsters, she reformats Cuban and Black thought by assuming the role of Shakespeare and Fernández Retamar's Caliban. This essay invites the reader to remember Casal's 1970s essays as foundationally intersectional, decolonial, antiracist, and feminist.

The exiled Cuban social scientist, writer, and feminist activist Lourdes Casal breaks with social scientific convention and identifies in the first person with Blackness in her essays about race and revolution in Cuba. To forge tools for dismantling the master's house, she engages with Black and Cuban radical traditions through disidentification—or a reformatting of theories she found useful yet at the same time exclusionary or dismissive (Lorde 1984; Muñoz 1999: 9). Identifying as "Hispanic Black" in Black and Latin Americanist academic circles, as a third-world feminist who brought to light

MERIDIANS · feminism, race, transnationalism   21:1 April 2022
DOI: 10.1215/15366936-9554101 © 2022 Smith College

academic feminism's blindspots, and as a New York-Cuban who became a supporter and scholar of the Cuban revolution, Casal (1978: 62) unsettled the dominant logics of the places she made home. Her writings on race relations make the traumatizing effects of these logics undeniable as she diverged from common assertions that revolutionary Cuba was post-race.

For example, Casal gives the lie to the triumphant revolutionary claim in 1978 that racism belonged only to the pre-revolutionary past. Black revolutionary Blas Roca declared in the Cuban newspaper *Hoy* in July 1962: "Today there exist none of those manifestations of persecution, official or public contempt, segregation and discrimination that before was the rule of our country" (Blas Roca, qtd. in Cannon and Cole 1978: 15). In contrast to the enthusiasm of Terry Cannon and Johnetta Cole, Casal's scholarship models a way to address what Christina Sharpe (2016) has called the psychic "afterlives" of slavery that persist in projects Casal supported (such as the Cuban revolution or academic feminism). Concurring with Fidel Castro's iconoclastic televised statement that racism remains "a deep wound at the core" of Cuban and all societies defined by centuries of colonization, empire and enslavement, she expands on this view through disidentification and bridging (Castro, qtd. in Casal 1979c: 19). Antonio López (2012: 14, 151–52) generatively excavates what he calls an Afro-Cuban-American archive to show how diaspora often provided a necessary space for the cultivation of race consciousness, and Casal is fundamental to this archive.[1] This essay reveals Casal's (1979d) disidentification with thinkers and policies that perpetuated race-based exclusions, including her critique of the Cuban state's failure to implement affirmative action for Afro-Cubans.

Elaborating upon research by William Luis (1997, 2018); Antonio López (2012), Yolanda Martínez San Miguel (2015, 2017), Yolanda Martínez San Miguel and Frances Negrón Muntaner (2007) and Iraida López (2018) that recognizes Casal's significance, I illuminate Casal's indefatigable bridging of political divides, examine Casal's shifting self-definitions, and weigh them against contemporaries' and collaborators' interpretations. Finally, I argue that her theorizing of race relations in Cuba is informed by and contributes to then-emergent woman-of-color feminist scholarship and to twenty-first century critical race theory. The texts I draw upon here have circulated only to a limited extent in Anglophone U.S. scholarly discussions, as many of these writings remain untranslated, or in manuscript or periodical archives.[2] The transgressive insight of Casal's late writings persists in her awareness that race and other identity categories can become a trap or a distraction if not studied in relation to other categories such as class, gender, sexuality, language and geopolitical location, among other shifting, historically determined structures of power.

Bridging Political Divides

A charismatic and fearless activist in starkly divided Cuban exile circles in New York and New Jersey in the 1970s, Casal advocated dialogue and critically engaged interlocutors of all stripes and positions, whether right-wing exile or hard-line Castro supporter, liberal capitalist or socialist revolutionary, straight or queer, out or closeted, white or Black (or Asian), social scientist or poet, male or female, in Spanish or English, feminist or machista, island-based or in the diaspora (Martínez San Miguel and Negron Muntaner 2007; Luis 1997, 2018; A. López 2012; I. H. López 2018; Lomas 2018). A courageous critic, Casal ([1971] 1982) engaged opposing camps and created space for critical reflection, a strategy that was a hallmark of her feminism (DeCosta-Willis 1993). Her role as a feminist bridge—a term I take from Gloria Anzaldúa and Cherríe Moraga ([1981] 1983)—remains indispensable for us in the twenty-first century, particularly when political polarization, censorship, pinkwashing, toxic masculinity, and relentless imperialism continue to undermine only recently reestablished relations between the U.S. and Cuba.

Working at the intersections of Cuban, Black, and women's studies during the years when students of color and feminists were breaking down the doors and changing the composition of university faculty, admissions, and curricula in the 1970s, Casal practiced what we might now think of as Afro-Latinx or "Blacktino" criticism, even though the twentieth- and twenty-first-century field-defining anthologies in these areas have often neglected to mention her (Anzaldúa and Moraga [1981] 1983; Bell-Scott, Smith, and Hull 1982; Ramos 1987; Jimenez Román and Flores 2010; Johnson and Rivera-Servera 2016). Parallel to radical Black and Chicana lesbian and "third world" feminists such as Audre Lorde, Cherríe Moraga, Gloria Anzaldúa, and in networks with Cuban and Puerto Rican and queer artists and writers such as Dolores Prida, Víctor Fragoso, Mirtha Quintanales, and Anna Veltfort, Casal brought into being a progressive Cuban diaspora group characterized by dynamic women leaders, most of whom she personally recruited (Quintanales 1987: 181; Lorde 1984; Prida 1991; Anzaldúa and Moraga 1981; Martínez San Miguel and Negrón Muntaner 2007). As an academic, an editor of the magazine *Areíto*, and manager of INTAR, Max Ferrá's Latinx theater, she became the heart and soul of a progressive

Cuban diaspora in New York (De la Campa 2006: 138). On one hand, Casal (1973; Domínguez [1977] 1981) articulated literary personas with a lesbian or queer subjectivity in Spanish (Martínez San Miguel 2015, 2017). On the other, she wrote about race, revolution, and women's development for English-speaking academic audiences (Casal 1977, 1979c, 1979d, 1980b). Although not a subject of her scholarly essays, Casal's queer and Asian-diasporic perspectives surely also illuminated her self-definition, silences, disidentification, and bridging, but proper treatment of these topics exceeds the scope of this essay.[3]

Although Casal (1971a) mentions the UMAPS (Unidades Militares de Ayuda a la Producción), or camps in which artists, hippies, or LGBTQ people were forced to work and faced extreme violence between 1965 and 1968 in Cuba, she demurs on first-person accounts of sexism and homophobia in English, which might lead us to erroneously conclude she did not live by feminist and queer commitments. Afro–Puerto Rican lesbian and Black feminist scholars such as Juanita Ramos (aka Juanita Diaz-Cotto) and Elizabeth Higgenbotham have criticized white-dominant feminist assumptions of the primary salience of "a conflict between male and female values, etc., while racial ethnic communities are first of all in conflict with dominant culture people and their institutions" (Higgenbotham 1982; Ramos 1987).[4] Kelly Coogan-Gehr's (2011: 90) archeology of race politics and American exceptionalism in U.S. feminist scholarship observes that the white-dominant editorial strategy at Signs under Barbara Gelpi initiated a period of intellectual "disappearance" or ghettoization of U.S. Black feminist theory from Signs and the field, while problematically "blam[ing] Black scholars for their own marginalization." Ramos similarly argues that when feminists demand all-women groups, she says, "but what about racism," and asks white, first-world feminists to see that "third world women" could not avoid working with mixed-gender groups that focused on race, rather than sex and gender (Ramos, qtd. in Henry 1981: 3).

While Higgenbotham emphasized the marginalization of women of color in Signs, Casal's intervention at the legendary international women and development conference at Wellesley College in 1976, which placed Signs on the radar of international feminism, revealed the conference organizers' unacknowledged alignment of "development" with first-world capitalism. The organizers' frameworks reflected de facto first-world assumptions. Casal (1977: 318) articulated this critique through a series of rhetorical questions in a plenary session:

Can conferences on "development" properly be convened in "developed" countries? What is the proper input which participants from the less developed countries should have in decision making at the level of program planning, format selection, representation at the panel convener, panelist and discussant levels, etc.? . . . The absence of scholars from the socialist world underlined the need to analyze the conception of development which seemed to prevail at the conference, and, indeed, in the whole field of U.S. development studies.

Casal's comment on the absence of socialist and "developing" country perspectives echoes Higgenbotham's critique of a feminist intellectual project in which women of color did not have a role in defining the agenda. Beyond registering Casal's intellectual aplomb as a rising Black star with third-world, leftist commitments, Casal's inclusion in *Signs'* report on the Wellesley conference may reflect how her apparently external "third world" perspective proved more palatable for inclusion than a similar critique from women of color inside the United States, who criticized the effects of capitalist development upon Black women. After Casal began to question the suppression of race consciousness in Cuba and began to claim her Blackness and socialism as a Cuban-American, she lost favor within some circles. Her radicalization and race consciousness help us put into context the misogynistic and racialized caricatures of her that have appeared after her death, addressed below.

Just as Casal rarely speaks in the first person about her sexuality, she never openly assumes the identity of "revolutionary" in her academic writing. That she became a target of anti-Castro exile groups, a far-right branch of which operated near where she worked at Rutgers University in Newark, New Jersey, did not preclude her maintaining a dialogue with them.[5] As the first exiled Cuban authorized to return to the island in 1973, who wrote favorably about the revolution's advances on her return, Casal became something of a "*tabú*" among exiles, as she notes in an interview at the Library of Congress (Casal 1974, 1975; Dorn 1980). She disrupted the notion of Cuban exiles as a politically, culturally homogenous "model" minority (faithful to a white-dominant, sometimes white supremacist, patriarchal, and solidly conservative Republican politics). Instead, she constructed a space for a progressive or "professed socialist" exile minority (Bustamante 2015: 126). In the thick of the Cold War when the U.S. government surveillance and infiltration program known as COINTELPRO (Counter

Intelligence Program) was in full swing, Cuban right-wing groups (some actively engaged in violence) frequently responded to any deviations from the pro-embargo position with death threats, bombs, and political assassinations (Quiroga 2014: 824; Latner 2017).[6]

Although some of Casal's admirers and detractors characterize her as a "political proselytizer," or as part of a group of "insignificant pro-Castro acolytes," we should look beyond these reductive labels (Behar 2018: 6; Bustamante 2015: 90).[7] Like the fellow *dialoguero* Carlos Muñiz Varela, Casal deserves a "passport to history" (Casal 1981b: 110).[8] In the spirit of Casal's *areíto* for Muñiz Varela, this essay affirms her continuing relevance for feminist and critical race theory in the United States.[9]

How do disidentification and bridging inform Casal's theoretical contributions? Casal's late essays disidentify with Black and Caribbean intellectuals in order to foreground Black women's perspectives (Bryce-LaPorte 1981). She pushes Cuban leaders and friends back home to acknowledge and transform their bias against a working-class, Spanglish-speaking, queer, or hybrid diaspora (Casal 1980a). In the U.S academy she laughs in the face of those who would dismiss or disdain her because of her politics, body, race, or sex.

Casal's Self-Definition as a "Radicalized" Cuban Migrant

> Para mí el título de "revolucionario" es uno de lo más altos que existe y creo que su adjudicación depende de un juicio histórico acerca de la acción política que uno desarrolla y que no puede basarse en auto-ascripción, o "regalo" de amigos o enemigos.

> For me the title of 'revolutionary' is one of the most elevated that exists and I believe judgment belongs to history, based on political actions developed over time. It may not be based on either self-ascription or a "gift" from either friends or enemies.
> —Lourdes Casal, "Los revolucionarios 'ausentistas'"

> I carry this marginality, immune to all returns,
> too *habanera* to be *newyorkina*
> too *newyorkina* to be
> —even to become again—
>
> anything else.
> —Lourdes Casal, "For Anna Veltfort"

Casal humbly defines herself as "radicalized," as opposed to "revolution-ary" during the effervescence of late 1960s and 1970s New York City, where the formerly middle-class private school student from Los Sitios in 1950s Havana had become a Bronx social worker, a graduate student at the New School for Social Research, a Black social scientist, and activist (Herrera 2005; Domínguez 1995). Casal uses the term *radicalizado* (radicalized) in the unpublished speech from which I quote above, delivered at Columbia Uni-versity in June 1976, to redefine *revolucionaria* (revolutionary) away from Cold War binaries. This label refers not only to a Cuban national politics but also to radical social changes underway in U.S. cities and globally. The group of Cubans she calls radicalized—as an alternative to the worn-out label *progresistas* (progressives)—sought to embrace a worldly perspective "on the form of solutions to the crisis of advanced and dependent capital-isms" (Casal 1976a), without losing the distance necessary for critical study of the Cuban government. Casal's critical race theory engages not only with the 1959 revolution but also with a global decolonial process, as a supple-ment to ethnic studies and women's movements that, as Chandan Reddy (2011: 26–28) notes, began as radical Third World student strikes and resulted in embattled U.S.-focused interdisciplinary centers, programs, and units in U.S. universities.

Responding to charges that members of progressive Cuban groups were undercover lobbyists for the Cuban government, Casal (1976a) defines an independent position for herself as critic: "Yo no me considero 'revolucio-naria'" (I do not consider myself a "revolutionary"). This move places a critical distance between her position and that of the Cuban government. To colleagues and critics within the Instituto de Estudios Cubanos, Casal's (1976a) first impulse was to send [her accusers] "sencilla y castizamente al carajo" (simply and chastely to hell). But in a bid to maintain an open dia-logue among various Cuban exile political positions, which was a key premise adopted by the IEC's founders, she elaborates a definition of the "radicalized" Cuban migrant politics that informs the award-winning *tes-timonio* she helped produce as part of a collective along with other Cuban exiles such as Román de la Campa (Grupo Areíto 1978). In Mirtha Quinta-nales's interpretation of interviews with radicalized Cuban youth who formed part of the circles in which Casal traveled, she concludes that the migratory experience and the racializing treatment (and sometimes abuse of) Cuban exile youth contributed to their radicalization. Neither Quinta-nales nor Grupo Areíto discussed racial differences among the Peter Pan youth, who were, as part of the first wave of refugees, predominantly white or white-passing. Casal's groundbreaking research on the Cuban-American diaspora, however, centers the category of race.

Casal's thinking on race in Cuba drew on her experiences in Africa and the United States. Casal's travels to Africa in 1962 transformed her sense of herself as part of a heterogeneous African diaspora and honed an acute sense of her Cuban-ness as a form of Blackness (Casal 1962; López 2018; Lomas 2020). Casal's (1978) autobiographical essay, "Memories of a Black Cuban Childhood," published in the glossy *Nuestro: The Magazine for Latinos*, emphasizes how that journey to her "origin" jolted her into a more complex self-definition developed in her childhood, so much so that at the end of her life, she recommenced her affiliations with Santería, into which she'd been initiated as a child.[10] Casal's diaspora experiences reveal her affinities with other feminists of color in her orbit in this period, many of whom also had Afro-Caribbean roots. As Toni Cade (who later took the name Bambara) noted in 1970, the United States was "a country that has more respect for the value of property than the quality of life, a country that has never valued Black life as dear, a country that regards its women as monsters" (10). The Black liberation and transnational feminist movements of this period insisted that any revolution would have to address the systemic racism and economic disadvantages Black women still faced, one hundred years after Emancipation (7).[11] Given that both Casal and Cade worked at Rutgers, lived in New York, and traveled to Cuba in the 1970s, I imagine Casal in conversation with Cade, a colleague who might have prodded Casal to reengage with "her" revolution. Cade aptly describes microaggressions that also affected Casal.

Pro-revolution and pro-exile Cuban positions both prized wholeness and unity over an acknowledgment of race, gender, and sexual difference. Sectors of the exile community commonly reproduced an unacknowledged yet nonetheless pervasive anti-Blackness that characterized the neoliberal republic and the period after 1959.[12] The refusal to acknowledge race among exiles reflects what Casal and Rafael J. Prohías (1980: 101) describe as "certain normative forces within the Cuban refugee community tending to deny the existence of racial problems in prerevolutionary Cuba and among exiles." Casal's (1979b: 116) research exposes how the myth of a "golden" exile subtly reinforces tendencies that isolate Cuban Americans from coalition with other Latinx migrant and racialized communities (Portes 1969; Capó Crucet 2015).[13] Focusing on Miami and New Jersey, a section of Casal and Prohías's (1980: 98) "preliminary report" on the Cuban minority defines the "invisible Cubans" as "a highly at-risk group, potentially a victim of double or triple discrimination (in the case of poor black Cubans)" (Prieto 2018). Casal's research shows how Afro-Cuban women had the highest level of integration into the labor force of all other Cuban exile sectors (white male, Black male, white female), second only to U.S. African American women, with the distinction that Afro-Cuban women had less access to welfare and child care. Inserting the Black woman as subject of Cuban migration history and policy discussions imagines a way out of U.S. and Cuban exoticizing stereotypes that dehumanized Black women or denied the categories of Blackness or race altogether.

Despite nationalist and even occasional anti-imperialist rhetoric and greater heterogeneity than left-wing generalizations often admit, the anti-Castro Cuban exiles had few words of reproach for anti-Black discrimination, nor did they acknowledge white privilege. According to Bustamante's (2015: 73) research on an exile organization active in New York and New Jersey, Abdala, anti-Castro nationalist groups did not engage in "minority" ethnic politics. But the exiled Cuban writer Gustavo Pérez Firmat proudly mentions displaying the Confederate flag on his desk in North Carolina, even as he alludes to Casal's rhetorical structures from her most famous poem, "Para Ana Veltfort," in the next line of his memoir. Pérez Firmat (1995: 209) echoes and inverts Casal's oft-cited closing stanza (a translation of which is cited in my epigraph to this section): "Too *cubano* to ever become American, but too American to ever become anything else." This allusion to Casal's bridging of her Havana origins and her New York City residence defaces Casal's legacy by associating her oft-cited poem with Pérez-Firmat's version of the United States and a neocolonial Cuba, a version that saluted the pro-slavery Confederacy in the U.S. South (and thus, we surmise, would not oppose white supremacist institutions). Unlike Pérez-Firmat, who ends up writing in English and staying in the United States, Casal makes her way to Havana and never stops writing poetry in Spanish; this thwarts the dominant narrative logic of Cuban-American and Latinx migration, much as her affirmation of her Blackness challenges post-racial narratives of Cuba and Latin American *mestizaje* to which we shall return at the end of the essay.

Weighing Casal's Significance: Lightweight Acolyte or Enduring Intellectual?

If Casal defined herself as radicalized, well-placed peers, colleagues, and interlocutors have unsurprisingly divergent views of her enduring intellectual significance in Cuban and diaspora letters. Jorge I. Domínguez ([1977]

1981: 18), Harvard-based professor of government, describes Casal in no uncertain terms as a "marxist," unlike himself; yet he nevertheless found it a pleasure to struggle intellectually with her. The island-based Cuban historian and former diplomat Jesús Arboleya Cervera (2013: 42) similarly recalls Casal as "la más dotada de los intelectuales de su generación" (the most gifted of the intellectuals of her generation). The posthumous comment by the Afro-Panamanian, Smithsonian-based sociologist Roy Simón Bryce-Laporte (1981) underscores Casal's "spirit of daring and determination." She assisted him in conceptualizing a volume of essays on Black Caribbean migrant women and helped set the research agenda at the Smithsonian ethnic and migration studies institute that published some of her work on race and revolution. In an unconventional "obituary" appended at the end of Bryce-Laporte's (1981) volume where Casal's essay on Black Cuban women in the United States appeared, her editor and friend celebrates her decision about where to die.

Unlike leading Caribbeanists and Latin Americanists, including José Arrom, Carmelo Mesa-Lago, and Jean Franco, who helped create an award in Casal's honor at the Latin American Studies Association, another eminent Latin Americanist and a former contributor to *Areíto*, the Yale literary critic Roberto González Echevarría ascribes an amateur, sophomoric mediocrity to Casal. Through recourse to a dehumanizing anecdote that he describes as his "fondest memory" of Casal, González Echevarría (2010: 115) depicts Casal as a "self-deprecating" "dark mulatta" and a "black monster." González Echevarría portrays Casal and others involved with *Areíto* as dimwitted and underprepared: "No one in the group's leadership had a strong political, philosophical, or ideological education," and "the magazine's intellectual quality was not high" (114). The passage further discredits Casal by mentioning a "seesaw personal and political life," marked by an initial "fervent" anti-communism and by having worked for the Central Intelligence Agency, and "confusion" thereafter, which he judged as evidence of her lack of leadership and intellectual qualifications.

Although González Echevarría appears to single out Casal for praise in the midst of his invective against the Grupo Areíto as a whole, he ultimately targets her with hackneyed stereotypes that white culture has often assigned to Black women:

> Lourdes had a magnificent, self-deprecating sense of humor. She told me that one night, at my home, she had gone to the bathroom and not locked

the door, it being so late. While sitting on the toilet—she told me later with tears of laughter running down her face—my son Carlos, about three years old at the time, burst in, holding his penis in hand, ready to pee, "but when he saw that black monster sitting there, he turned and ran for his life." She had arrived after the children had gone to bed, so Carlos did not expect her to be there at all. Her guffaws would make her shake all over. This is my fondest memory of Lourdes. (115)

This remarkable scene evokes masculinity and whiteness under threat, with details about the professor's three-year-old son displaying his penis and then fleeing for his life. Leading into this intimate memory, González Echevarría remembers Casal as a formerly beautiful, spurned admirer of a straight male love interest (an echo of treatments of Gabriela Mistral as pining for an unrequited love [Fiol-Matta 2002: xvii]). The young son's awkward brush with Casal's body becomes linked in this anecdote to the boy's subsequent tragic death at the age of forty-four due to cancer. Emphasizing Casal's threatening "monstrous" body, the text renders her aggressive and vulnerable, with compromised boundaries, shaking all over, with abject tears streaming down her face. Ostensibly repeating his now dead son's verbatim report, the essay reduces Casal in her own words to a "black monster." This move displaces responsibility for the conjoining of these two terms to his innocent and pitiful son and to Casal herself. More than a confession or acknowledgment of sympathy, Casal's "howl-ing" laughter and black humor more likely signify here "the unfiltered venting of cultural and political anger" (Haggins 2007: 4). Casal may be reacting to an absurd Cuban tradition that blames Black women's *brujería* for endangering white children (Helg 1995: 112–13). The scene reveals Casal perceiving that she figures as, and could be remembered to posterity in terms of, these very stereotypes, to which she responds with uncontrolla-ble laughter.

Casal's skilled organization of a movement in favor of dialogue and re-established relations between Cuba and the United States demonstrated Casal's ability to call into question the U.S. policies of embargo and block-ade. Her intellectual and organizational work posed a threat to the project that many anti-Castro exiles, including González Echevarría, supported unconditionally later in his life. Imagined from Casal's viewpoint, the passage evokes an experience of psychic annihilation similar to Frantz Fanon's ([1952] 2008) description of the effect of a French child's racist outburst on the Martinican psychiatrist's persona. Like Fanon, Casal appears in this anecdote to be left "spread-eagled, disjointed, redone" (93). González Echevarría's text asserts the senior scholar's as the last word on Casal, which it should not be.

As noted above, the Latinx and Cuban diaspora queer theorist José Esteban Muñoz (1999: 9) defines *disidentification* as a strategic engagement with theoretical positions even when aspects of the theorist's ideas include patriarchal, sexist, racist views that annihilate or silence. As a "reformatting of the powerful theorist for her own project, one that might be as queer and feminist as it is anticolonial," disidentification "offers a Fanon, for that queer and lesbian reader [whose] homophobia and misogyny would be interrogated while his anticolonial discourse was engaged as a still valuable yet mediated identification" (9). Disidentification permits us to see Casal as part of an anticolonial theoretical project that recognizes and critically reformats Fanon from an Afro-Latina lesbian feminist angle, while drawing on Fanon's critique of racialized psychic trauma (Zimra 1984: 60; Tinsley 2010). Casal eloquently extends González Echevarría's Latin Americanist contributions while denouncing the suppression of race consciousness—as I discuss below. She defends militant decolonization and Black consciousness in terms that resonate with Fanon's. Casal, a queer Black feminist, works on and against these influential ideologies through a "dissing" that becomes part of her intellectual legacy.

Unspeakable Things Unspoken: Casal's Race Consciousness

> I caused a problem because it was impossible to understand how a radical black woman was also a Cuban exile.
> —Lourdes Casal, interviewed by Margaret Randall in *Breaking the Silences*

Although Casal (1976c, 1980b, 1987) researches women and gender relations in Cuban novels and in the policies of the Cuban revolution, "race" is the key critical lens for Casal's (1978, 1979c,1979d, 1980a) most daring and engaging essays. Building on her early journalism about the Black struggle for civil rights in the United States (Casal 1957a, b) and her critique of the Black Panther Eldridge Cleaver's column on the Cuban government in *Time* (Casal and Pérez-Stable 1976), Casal's (1978, 1979c, 1979d) writings on race relations document progress for Black Cubans while examining the effects of centuries of racism in Cuba, well after the celebrated official "end" of such discrimination. Parallel to her dauntless critique of academic feminism, Casal's accounts of inhabiting a racialized gender most evocatively probe the deep wounds at the core of Cuban society. On the verge of her repatriation, Casal (1979c: 20; 1979d: 5) breaks a still oppressive "conspiracy of silence" about race in Cuba and in the Cuban diaspora by publishing her essays on race in journals in London and the United States. Riffing on a long-standing tradition of Afro-Cuban organizing to recognize Black Cubans' foundational contributions, Casal (1979c: 24) defines Cuban culture as "undoubtedly Afro-Hispanic" (Carbonell 1961; Mirabal 2017).

Casal's critique of the transgenerational effects of racial terror in Cuba (and specifically of the after-shocks of Cuba's so-called Race War of 1912) permits her to grapple, too, with "contemporary" racism (circa 1979). It brings into focus the domestic scenes in which Black women survivors engage in the radical work of cultivating a strategic race consciousness and a critical race theory. Like the legal theory (Crenshaw et al. 1995; Delgado 1995) that began in the 1970s and exposed racist bias and practices in ostensibly color-blind institutions, laws, and policies, Casal in 1979 began to articulate an intersectional critique of persistent racism baked into Cuban culture and institutions, even when they claimed to be antiracist. Rather than reading Casal as "cashing in" when the Cuban government wanted to present itself as a safe haven for threatened Black radicals, I read Casal's theorizing of race relations as her swan song and a gift to the Cuban revolution and to the transdisciplinary fields to which she contributed.

As the only Black female professor of social psychology in her Department at Rutgers University–Newark in the 1970s; and as the only woman and only person of color in her engineering department when she started at the most prestigious private university in Havana, Santo Tomás de Villanueva; and as one of the few Afro-Cubans among the founders of the Instituto de Estudios Cubanos, Casal often played the role of the token Black woman in academic institutions from which Blacks as a rule had been excluded for centuries.[14] With this in mind, it behooves us to attend to how Casal investigates and explicates the costs of race consciousness and of its suppression. She makes visible Black Cuban women's critical perspectives—her own, her ancestors, and those of other women-of-color interpreters of the Cuban revolution, such as Elizabeth ("Betita" Martínez) Sutherland (1969)—so that her English-speaking academic readers, liberal advocates of "minority rights," her colleagues in Cuban studies across the political divides, and ultimately the Cuban government could neither sidestep nor minimize the ongoing effects of anti-Black racism.

Casal's interpretive essays on race bring into focus subtle forms of racism, the unverbalized performative gestures, such as pointing to or touching the forearm instead of referring to Blackness or white violence out loud. She denounces the sedimented anti-Blackness that made it nearly impossible to acknowledge or address racial discrimination, which, as Casal (1979c: 12) notes, "can be embedded in the institutionalized practices of a society on a level different than the legal." Casal authorizes her argument about the need for critical examination of racist behaviors by connecting the largely forgotten struggles of the Partido Independiente de Color (PIC) to the 1959 revolution's most urgent and difficult task: to address and redress anti-Black discrimination.

Casal's explicit adoption of "race" and "Blackness" as categories of research also performs a transgressive critique of the Cuban government's misguided position that racism ended in 1961, two years after Fidel Castro's televised speeches. This naive conclusion draws on José Martí's flatfooted claim that racial equality would arise spontaneously upon the establishment of the independent multiracial nation.[15] "Deeply engrained in Cuban dominant ideology," based on Martí's signal phrase—"there is no racial hatred, because there are no races"—the silencing of race facilitated pervasive racism in the early Republic (Casal 1979c: 22; Martí 2002: 295; Arredondo Gutierrez 1939).[16] The insistence on a post-race *cubanía* resulted in the elision or destruction of cultural survivals, archives, and memory in the neocolonial and revolutionary governments, all of which has made it more difficult to redress discriminatory assumptions and actions (Ferrer 1998; Benson 2016).

Against Martí's incorrect notion that establishing a multiracial nation was all that was necessary to heal centuries of slavery and colonialism, Casal's writings in the 1970s indicate that the longed-for Cuban republic only barely masked profound anti-Black sentiments. The nation for which mostly Black Cubans fought and died ended up carrying out violent policies of whitening, as Casal (1979c: 13) notes:

> Deeply felt racism, even if it allowed for convenient reclassification of light mulattoes as whites, is behind the immigration policies followed by the Early Republic, and the massive attempts to import white workers from Spain. Even the relative facility of reclassification can be considered

as an assimilationist weapon which effectively functioned *against the development of race consciousness among Cuba's blacks.* (emphasis added)

Rather than inaugurating a period of racial harmony, much less equality, the republic that formed less than two decades after the official end of slavery in 1886 maintained an explicitly racist program of importing light-skinned immigrants, mainly from impoverished parts of Spain, as part of a policy of *blanqueamiento*, which promoted "reclassification" or the abandonment of Black identification in legal documents (Morrison 2015; De la Fuente 2001: 45). This long-standing procedure of claiming legitimacy and upward mobility through white identification or passing into whiteness had peculiarly problematic consequences for Black women.[17] Black congress members in Estrada Palma's republic received an invitation to a reception at the presidential palace that excluded their Black wives (Casal 1979c: 14). Parks, private schools, social clubs and beaches were segregated, before and after 1959 (Díaz [1987] 1997). Defying this de facto segregation had violent repercussions: Casal (1979c: 25–26) cites the anti-Black riot in which a mob assassinated Feliz Justo Proveyer, a Black journalist, in Parque Céspedes in Las Villas Province, Trinidad, in January 1934 for challenging the "customary division" of city parks according to skin color.[18] This violence extended inward to suppress memories and acknowledgment of this historical violence for generations.

A first-person account informs Casal's (1979c: 15) discussion of the "understudied" 1912 massacre of thousands of Black Cuban men, women, and children who died in what Casal forthrightly names "a nationwide extermination of blacks" (Schomburg 1912: 143; Valdés 2017: 75–78).[19] Defining a "heritage of oppression" dating back centuries and passed on by Cubans of all shades, Casal draws on the now classic Black lesbian and woman-of-color feminist rhetorical device of self-inscription of her body to reveal the effects of unspeakable history. She denounces the repression of an organized antiracist Black-led voting rights group (with white and Black members) that became the Partido Independiente de Color (PIC) before, during, and after the so-called Race War ("la Guerrita") of 1912. As in the narrative of her own radicalization after the death of Salvador Allende, she points out that the Martín Morua Delgado amendment that shut down space for the legal activities of the PIC left them little choice but to militantly protest the Gomez administration. Thus the highest-ranking Black congressmember, Morua Delgado, became responsible for the amendment that "legalized" this massacre. Prefaced with a reprinting of the United Nation's Declaration of Human Rights, Casal's essay claims that such acts of anti-Black violence—a fact looming large in any reader's mind in the wake of the assassinations and imprisonment of Black leaders Martin Luther King Jr., Malcolm X, Medgar Evers, Assata Shakur, and Angela Davis at the time of Casal's publication—should be tried as human rights violations.

The essay's visceral account of the suppression of race consciousness refers not just to a pre-revolutionary moment but also to hard-to-discuss forms of anti-Black discrimination encoded in the intimacy of the family (Casal 1979c: 22). Departing from social scientific academic conventions, Casal's essay stages a familial scene of retelling to make the present repercussions of the massacre palpable and undeniable:

> I still remember how I listened, wide-eyed and nauseated, to the stories—always whispered, always told as when one is revealing unspeakable secrets—about the horrors committed against my family and other blacks during the racial war of 1912. A grand-uncle of mine was assassinated, supposedly by orders of Monteagudo, the rural guard officer who terrorized blacks throughout the island. Chills went down my spine when I heard stories about blacks being hunted day and night; and black men being hung by their genitals from the lamp posts in the central plazas of small Cuban towns. (12)

Beginning with the fine grain of gruesome physical details, the phrase "I still remember" situates her in 1979 among the descendants of the victims, recalling an earlier scene alongside her grand-aunts and other survivors. The text registers the scene's ongoing effect on her body: chills, nausea, and the insistent request that her elders speak, to which they responded with whispers to teach the young listener to silence such "disagreeable" discussions, an admonishment she clearly ignored. Parallel to contemporary spectacles of U.S. lynching in the early twentieth century, this massacre desecrated Black lives. The massacre had the potential to catalyze a movement for Black lives like the widespread demonstrations that began in June 2020 after white police offer Derek Chauvin killed George Floyd, but the survivors in Cuba had to first overcome the tradition of silence and what Casal refers to as "the heritage of oppression."

This passage reads as if the repression's effects and resistance to them were happening in present time. With her body covered with goosebumps present on the page, the essay bridges continuities between the early republic and residual structures of anti-Black terror as a challenge to Fidelistas and to Latin Americanists. As Gwendolyn Midlo Hall (1995: 946) notes in her review of Aline Helg's (1995) study of the 1912 massacre, *Our Rightful Share*, Latin American historiography continued—up until the late twentieth century—to perpetuate myths of "mild slavery" or "racial equality" in Latin America. Observing the author reenact or relive the scene of attempting to remember, against the witnesses' reluctance to speak, the reader can no longer proceed as if "no hay problema, no ha pasado nada aquí" (there's no problem; nothing has happened here), which is the essay's paraphrase of a common reaction she encountered when probing her elders' memories (Casal 1979c: 12). This research forestalls a conclusion that racism no longer impinged on Cubans' psychic life, whether as victims or perpetrators.

Casal's tone becomes sarcastic with disgust as she revises the familiar and problematic historical terminology of *Race War*, or *La Guerrita del '12* (The Little War of '12), which suggests that a massacre of several thousand could be "dismissed or ignored" as "a quasi-farcical episode" and could therefore be reduced to a single line or a footnote in history books (12; Formoselle 1974). By contrast, Casal describes this massacre as "a nationwide extermination." Similarly, she asks how a massacre of that scale could figure as either Monteagudo's justifiable act of self-defense or a as "war" between two belligerent parties. Whether diminished as farce or mischaracterized as a war-like threat, this movement that began as a Black voting rights organization merited further study. How could historians remember this racialized violence with a cute diminutive, as a farce that merited no serious historical inquiry? Casal's (1979c) return to this history spotlights how invested white-dominant cultures—including that of Cuba—have been in suppressing memories of white racial terror.[20] As Jenna Leving Jacobsen (2018: 41) rightly notes, Casal brings to light "her homeland's misremembering."[21]

The effects of the terror and repression informed race relations in Cuba, but not merely as a result of the U.S. military occupations of the island in 1898–1902 and 1906–9. Casal (1979c: 18) emphatically diverges from the view that such racism should be attributed to the importation of U.S. race relations: "Homegrown racism, with the 'improvements' added by strong U.S. penetration during Republican times, was more virulent and insidious than most writers on the issue have been willing to admit." Casal refutes an argument that blamed the victims for their exclusion from power based on U.S. imperial-style racism or upon the victims' supposed lack of valor, educational preparation, or leadership skills. Against these efforts to elide Black resistance and the state's repression of it, Casal and others in Areíto sought to restore the memory of Black Cubans' struggle to end slavery and decolonize the island by naming a brigade of exiled Cuban youth after the Black military general, Antonio Maceo (Leving Jacobsen 2018; Latner 2017; Mirabal 2017; Hoffnung-Garskof 2019).

The essay alludes to a future present when describing the transgenerational effects of the massacre. With the phrase "never recovered," she indicates the persistent repercussions of the repression for future generations: "The black Cuban community never recovered from the heavy losses inflicted upon its most race-conscious male leadership. Since the Independientes were hunted down during the war and its aftermath, no other political organization of blacks emerged in the neo-colonial Republic" (Casal 1979c: 14). Here Casal reveals why she did not become a leader of a Black youth organization and instead became a youth leader in white-dominant women's sections of Acción Católica. The Cuban state terrorized and disarticulated Black political organizations that might have contributed to Cuban civil society, beginning with alternatives to the disarming or "pacification" mandated by William Howard Taft of the mostly Black Mambi army veterans and continuing into the twentieth century, as suggested by Helg (1995: 242). In an effort to end the political changes prompted by Black consciousness, the state drove the Afro-Cuban cabildos into hiding until incorporating them into government-run associations in the 1980s. Casal's leadership in (white-dominated) Catholic women's organizations bears the trace of the earlier eradication of (male-dominated) Black political organizations and asserts a role for women as leaders in race-conscious organizing and for Blacks in women's organizations. As an alternative to both roles, Casal intimates a "brave" woman-of-color position, which becomes available to Casal in the Afro-Cuban-American diaspora (López 2012; Bell-Scott, Smith, and Hull 1982; Lomas 2018). Thus, we can link anti-Black violence—including this massacre—to Casal's delayed identification as Black. Her Black consciousness became available—and perhaps unavoidable—after journeying to Africa and living in New York during the effervescence of Black power, feminist, and decolonial movements of the 1960s and 1970s.

According to Casal, in post-revolutionary Cuba, a "pervasive" "unwillingness to discuss racial issues" persists. As with the story about the suppression of memories, Casal (1979c: 13) notes that "this subtle racism affected even blacks which [sic] tended to deprecate black features as much as whites or even more." The breakdown of the meaning in this sentence, precisely at the site where the subject of the verb *tended to deprecate* goes missing, calls attention to the effect of racism's erasure, reclassification, and the long-standing suppression of Black protagonism.[22]

While it is true that Casal may have found it more possible to enunciate her position as Black and antiracist than as a lesbian, queer, or critical intellectual in circles that maintained a dialogue with the Cuban revolutionary government, and she does reproduce a male-dominated hagiography in her disidentifications, her research has an intersectional feminist and decolonial agenda. It would be a mistake to read her citation of Castro's March 1959 speech as a capitulation to government officialdom or, worse, an endorsement of or "selling out" to a white revolutionary elite, per Eldridge Cleaver's analysis.[23] Casal and her white Cuban collaborator Marifeli Pérez-Stable (1976) responded to Cleaver's insinuations of Castro's anti-Black elitism by suggesting that Cleaver had confused Castro with Monteagudo, the general in charge of the massacre in 1912. They argue that Cleaver makes a mistake in characterizing Cuba's leader as a "racista recalcitrante empeñado en exterminar a la población negra de Cuba" (recalcitrant racist obsessed with exterminating the Black Cuban population); they call instead for a critique of Cuban racism from a Cuban perspective (33). Casal's writings attribute such misreadings to a superficial knowledge of Black Cuban struggle.

Among Casal's last essays—"Revolution and Race" (1979d)—itself a transgressive alliteration and affirmation of the ongoing relevance of race in the context of revolution—demonstrates the contemporary legacies of denying the effects of white racist violence in the new republic and after. In her reading, the state's glaring omission of blacks as a protected category contradicts the official position that the deep wound of racism urgently needed to be addressed. Casal notes this omission candidly: "Blacks have been singled out for lack of special treatment. Programs addressed to the urban poor could have been instituted benefitting Blacks without fostering racial divisiveness" (7). This recommendation merits our attention. Acknowledging persistent microaggressions in 1970s Cuba, she observed—probably from her own experience—that "privately, many white Cubans, even solid revolutionaries, employ the old racist language" (1979c: 23). Casal prophetically calls for affirmative action programs to benefit Black Cubans who did not receive the compensatory programs the revolution offered to women and peasants: "It could be argued that unless some compensatory measures are taken, black Cuban children are going to find it very hard to compete given the heritage of oppression" (1979d: 23, 21). Interrogating the prohibition of "positive discrimination," Casal calls on the revolutionary government to "offset the residual differences in life chances, access to elite schools or top level appointments which are the legacy of hundreds of years of oppression and discrimination" (22). This argument deftly moves beyond the official position of color blindness to adopt a critical race theory and feminist method of "responding to the lessons of [the revolution's] own experience" (Casal 1976b: 24). Casal's critique of mainstream women-and-development disourse for its exclusion of socialist perspectives resonates with the demand here that the revolutionary government needed to acknowledge that the first two decades of revolutionary declarations and policy changes had not accomplished its goals.

Toward the goal of addressing ongoing racism by changing attitudes and behavior, Casal disidentifies with some of the most influential Cuban and Latin American thinkers and resignifies the Latin American master discourse of *mestizaje* away from criollo masculinity and whitening and toward cultural decolonization (I. López 2018: 80). Casal's disidentification adapts and reformats an enormously influential Cuban intellectual genealogy, from Martí to Roberto Fernández Retamar. Both have long enjoyed a monumental status as intellectual and political leaders who wielded extensive cultural power in the pre- and post-revolutionary periods. Casal's (1968; 1980a) writings about Martí and Fernández Retamar acknowledge their influence and share their investment in the Latin American essayistic tradition, especially insofar as it assumes the interrelation of aesthetics and politics. Whereas the *we* of Martí and Fernández Retamar refers almost exclusively to criollos or Cuban-born male leaders of white-passing or (predominantly) European heritage, Casal breaks open the borders of that "we" and replaces their embrace of the local and properly Cuban or Latin American territory with her own location in diaspora.

Fernández Retamar (1979) first publishes his "Calibán" in 1971, in the midst of the Heberto Padilla crisis, and through a critical inversion of Latin American *arielismo* articulated by the Uruguayan José Enrique Rodó. Rejecting Prospero's obedient servant Ariel as a symbol of Latin America's spiritual promise and dependence on imported European books (not including Karl Marx and Vladimir Lenin), Fernández Retamar claims Caliban as emblematic of Latin American anticolonial and nationalist militancy. If Rodó associated Caliban with the boorish, materialistic United States, Fernández Retamar draws on Martí and Che Guevara to limn a "New" or "Third" World Calibán, affiliated with a criollo masculinist revolutionary youth, and defined against the diasporic, the exilic, the lumpen, and the effeminate.

Casal's (1980a) "Re-lectura: Lo que dice Calibán (Re-reading: What Caliban Says)," which appeared in Areíto in 1980 after she had returned to Cuba for treatment of her advanced kidney disease, extends the redefinition of mestizaje to underscore and amplify rather than silence the fundamental role of non-European heritages in Latin American cultural expression. She concurs with Walterio Carbonell in defining Cuban culture, for example, as fundamentally Black and African, as she notes in "Race and Revolution":

> In spite of the efforts of the white dominant classes, in spite of their resistance, black cultural elements are integrated into Cuban music, Cuban popular lore, (including proverbs and sayings), Cuban plastic arts, poetry, etc., in such fashion that, without their component of black heritage, they would not be what they are; they would not be Cuban. And this must not be seen as the result of an assimilationist option, but rather at the consequence of a true mestizaje, of the complex interactions of two powerful cultural traditions. (Casal 1979d: 29)

Casal radically reformats and decolonizes the Latin American tradition of mestizaje, reorienting it against the logic of whitening, assimilation, and racial essence that undergirds it (Miller 2004). Diverging from Fernández Retamar's "culturalist" understanding of race, Casal foregrounds the class position and practices of diaspora that racialized working-class people were developing in urban metropolitan ghettoes. This acknowledgment of revolutionary creativity outside the nation challenges Fernández Retamar, Martí, and Castro to discern the limited ability of a white criollo elite in Havana to represent and define cubanía. Casal makes this critique through a "re-reading" of Fernández Retamar's influential essay, in which she assumes with pride the Calibanesque monstrosity that white male Cubans had long assigned to women like her.

In Conclusion: Casal as Calibán

> De lo que se trata es de asumir nuestra condición calibanesca, de blandir
> como arma, como penacho de orgullo lo que se nos imputó como insulto:
> nuestro carácter de pueblo mestizo, radicalmente *otros* con respecto a los
> europeos, aunque hayamos aprendido a hablar su lenguaje, que ahora nos
> sirve para maldecir.

> It is about assuming our Calibanic condition, to brandish it as a weapon,
> to wear as a plume of pride what they assigned to us as an insult: our char-
> acteristic mixture as a people, radically *other* with respect to the Europeans.
> Although we learned to speak their language, now it serves us to curse.
> —Lourdes Casal, "Lo que dice Calibán"

Not as the light-skinned daughter Miranda, not as Caliban's woman, nor as
Sycorax, but as a creative, outspoken, transgendered Caliban, does Casal
seize a place for herself in a mostly male tradition of Caribbean, Latin
American, and postcolonial writers who adapt the most memorable character of Shakespeare's *Tempest* (2004) to address questions of race and revolution.[24] Casal includes herself among Spanglish-cursing Calibans in the
empire's belly, assuming this condition with the third-person plural, as a
flamboyant plume or a weapon with which to fight back against insults and
exclusion. Whereas the dominant discourse of Latin American *mestizaje* is
defined by cultures of European origin displaced and inserted into New
World contexts, Casal's *mestizaje* is "radically *other* with respect to the Euro-
peans" in a way that foregrounds the African, Indigenous, and Asian creativity among working-class "colonized minorities."[25]

Appropriating this Calibanic condition away from the old guard of
Cuban institutions—whether in the United States or in Cuba, Casal privileges the critical angle of the diaspora at the height of the Mariel exodus in
1980, precisely when those who left the island figured in official and popular discourse as *gusanos* (worms), scum, traitors, effeminate queers, and
femmes. Casal's (1980a: 45) rereading decentralizes the focus from the
nation to the diaspora:

> Quizás sea precisamente en el interior de los EE.UU., al observar la evolu-
> ción y destino de los movimientos de las minorías colonizadas dentro de
> este país, que pueda verse con meridiana claridad la paradoja: la moviliza-
> ción de los grupos étnicos oprimidos sobre bases "culturales" entraña
> varias trampas. Por ejemplo, la idolización de "la raza," cuya genealogía

puede trazarse a Vasconcelos, desvirtúa la perspectiva clasista, debilita
(o imposibilita) la alianza con otros grupos oprimidos—aún hispanos—y
da pábula a una serie de mixtificaciones que dificultan la lucha contra las
clases dominantes.

It may be precisely in the interior of the United States, by observing the
evolution and destiny of movements of colonized minorities in this country, that it is possible to see with meridian clarity the paradox: the mobilization of oppressed ethnic groups on the basis of "culture" sets various
traps. For example, the idolization of "the race," whose genealogy
extends back to Vasconcelos, distorts a classist perspective, weakens (or
makes impossible) alliances with other oppressed groups—even
Hispanics—and feeds a series of "mix"-tifications that hobble the struggle against the dominant classes.

This critique of the category of race as elaborated by elites like José Vasconcelos (1920) anticipates a twenty-first-century assessment of the problems
of Eurocentric *mestizaje* when disassociated from material conditions and the
psychic trauma caused by racialized violence. By contrast, Casal's diasporic
"colonized minorities" were learning and bending the oppressor's language
to form a curse while dancing to salsa and listening to jazz in Washington
Heights, the East Village, and Newark. This Calibanesque condition, Casal
suggests in her critical race theory, pertains not to a racial, ethnic or national
essence (Fernández Retamar 1981) but to a relational perspective of the
racialized, of those considered "monstrous," on structures of power.

For Casal, a critique of anti-Black racism (and its related misogyny) is
not tantamount to co-opted dissident and pro-imperialist politics,
although this view has long circulated among revolutionaries and other
anti-colonial nationalists who have historically defined the antiracist, the
queer, the woman, and the translator as traitor.[26] Groundbreaking in
Cuban and Cuban exile culture in the late 1970s and still relevant today,
Casal's late writings on Cuban race relations offer a first-person, embodied
critique of attempts to eradicate or silence Black race consciousness, while
recognizing that racial identification can become a trap if not articulated
relationally and with attention to structural disenfranchisement. Casal's
disidentification and bridging extends to the Cuban revolution on her
return to Havana when she directs the attention of Cuba's leaders to the
disdained, dark-skinned, Spanglish-speaking, queer and working-class
diasporas, where she became a radically different Caliban, inventing the
tools we still need for dismantling racism.

Laura Lomas, a historian and cultural literary critic at Rutgers University-Newark, coedited the *Cambridge History of Latina/o American Literature* (2018) and authored *Translating Empire: Migrant Latino Subjects, José Martí, and American Modernities* (2009). Her current research is on the protagonism of New York Latinx writers in the emergence of the interdisciplines.

Notes

I wish to thank the Rutgers Research Council, the Institute for Latino Resesarch at the University of Texas at Austin, and the British Academy for supporting archival research toward the book-length project of which this essay is a small part. Special thanks to Enmanuel Martínez for encouraging me to pursue this connection between Casal and Fanon; to Ricardo Luis Hernández Otero for generously sharing his intimate knowledge of Casal's bibliography, and pointing me to the college yearbooks of La Villanueva at the Biblioteca Nacional de Cuba José Martí in Havana. I appreciate the anonymous reviewers at *Meridians* and Robyn Spencer, Yolanda Martínez San Miguel, and Kevin Meehan for indispensable feedback on earlier drafts of this essay. I also wish to thank Rubén Dávila, Marta Zabina Dávila-Lomas, and Amaru Dávila-Lomas for permitting me to engage in archival research away from home.

1   Cuba has faced setbacks and survived ongoing imperialist, white supremacist, and toxic masculinist aggressions from the United States, where I am complicit even as I am critical because I enjoy privileges as a white-passing, cisgendered, first-world documented citizen, and bilingual feminist of mixed ancestry working in Latinx and American studies. The remarkable phrasing here acknowledging a persistent colonial wound is Casal's (1979c: 19) transcription of Fidel Castro's March 25th televised speech, which she describes as a denunciation of racial discrimination "in the most sweeping terms ever heard in Cuba from a political leader holding political office." The speech impressed her because it thwarted what she calls the "traditional conspiracy of silence about racial matters so deeply ingrained in the Cuban dominant ideology" (19), an ideology that she speaks about in the present tense in the 1970s, and that the antiracist movement active in Cuba today has continued to denounce (Zurbano 2012).

2   Translations are my own unless I indicate otherwise. Happily, Zuleica Romay, the first director of the Programa de Estudios sobre Afro-America at Casa de las Américas in Havana, has expressed a desire to publish the first Spanish translation of Casal's essay, "Race Relations in Contemporary Cuba" in a projected anthology of African American thought (email correspondence with the author, February 1, 2018).

3   See Veltfort's *Adios mi Habana/Goodbye My Havana* (2017, 2019), which offers an insider's account of governmental persecution of two queer women walking together on the *malecón*, even though they were the victims (not the perpetrators) of violence. Casal (1973) describes her familiarity with the queer *ambiente*

in her fiction and evinces a non-heterosexual love object and queer persona in certain poems (1981), as Martínez San Miguel (2017) has demonstrated.

4   Higgenbotham to Barbara Gelpi (March 2, 1982), in *Signs* archives, Special Collections and University Archives, Alexander Library, Rutgers University, box 26, folder "Communities of Women." Juanita Ramos makes the point about how third world women needed to form alliances with non-feminist, non-lesbian men and women (Henry 1981: 3).

5   Sergio Chaple recounts Casal's meetings with members of anti-Castro exile groups in New Jersey during the same year as Eulalio Negrín's murder in Elizabeth. Interview on file with the author, April 2017.

6   There were one hundred bombings between 1973 and 1979 in Miami, but this did not deter Casal and her associates from their commitment to dialogue and to Cuba's right to exist and govern itself.

7   Michael Bustamante paraphrases how anti-Castro groups referred to victims like Carlos Muñiz Varela, but does not author these cariacatures.

8   Muñiz Varela was killed by gunshot on April 28, 1979, and a right-wing Cuban exile terrorist organization, Comando Cero in San Juan, claimed responsibility. Family members continue to call for justice. Muñiz Varela facilitated the visit of exiled Cubans to the island (cf. Ruiz 2019 and Arboleya Cervera, Álzaga Manresa, and Fraga Del Valle 2016). On Muñiz Varela and the homophobic tenor of the Cuban exile groups that "claimed" these assassinations, see Quiroga 2014. The right-wing Cuban exile group Omega 7 also claimed responsibility for the death of Negrín in Elizabeth, New Jersey, in 1979, and Casal notes in an interview with Lee (1984) that she received death threats indicating she was to be next.

9   Spanish chronicler Fernández de Oviedo refers to the term *"areíto"* as an Indigenous mode of telling history through singing and dancing that Cuba's original inhabitants practiced as a form of opposition to cultural colonization.

10 Miguel Barnet, unpublished interview by Iraida López, 2016. I appreciate Iraida López for sharing this interview and an editorial project of Casal's writings with me.

11 Born in New York, Miltona Mirkin Cade (aka Toni Cade Bambara) wrote, studied, and taught at Queens College and City College in New York, helping to develop City College's "Search for Education, Elevation, Knowledge" (SEEK) program. She taught English at the New Careers Program of Newark, in 1969, and at Rutgers's Livingston College between 1969 and 1974. Toni Cade Bambara traveled to Cuba to study women's political organizations in the mid-1970s, so it is possible that she and Casal crossed paths.

12 For more information on the LGBTQ and Chinese communities in Cuba, see Bejel 2001 and K. López 2013.

13 Jennine Capó Crucet (2015: 314) creates a light-skinned Cuban character whose father tells her that "Latino" refers to Mexicans and Central Americans and not to Cubans.

14 Nancy Morejón and Sara Gómez are two exceptions, both of whom knew Casal from having grown up with her in Centrohabana.

15 I intend this essay as an *autocrítica*, as I have published on Martí as antiracist
without fully engaging with the problematic effects of this antiracist doctrine
in the republican and revolutionary periods of Cuban history. The Cuban
government officially retracted this position and committed to grappling
with anti-Black racism in 2019. However, in November 2020, the San Isidro
movement staged a protest and many activists have faced or are enduring arrest,
surveillance, and house imprisonment, including Luis Manuel Otero Alcántara,
now recognized as a prisoner of conscience (Amnesty International 2020). Protests inspired by Afro-Cuban musicians Descemer Bueno, Gente de Zona, Yotuel
Romero in their song, "Patria y Vida," suggest a new dimension of tension
between Black Cuban social movements and the Cuban state.

16 Casal (1968) knew Martí's work well, claimed his influence in her interview
with Dorn and in a prologue to a Cuban edition of his prison writings, *El presidio
político en Cuba* (Dorn 1980).

17 This racist policy offered all-expenses-paid immigration to white Spaniards, an
extension of the *blanqueamiento* proposed by Francisco Arango y Pareña in the
early nineteenth century. A parallel policy existed in Brazil, thus the relevance of
publishing studies on Brazil and Cuba in the same volume, as Casal and Dzidzienyo do. As Cirilo Villaverde dramatizes in *Cecilia Valdés*, this policy demanded
Black women to become complicit vehicles of the politics of "whitening."

18 In this essay, Casal (1979c: 25n42) exclaims her "puzzlement" at how, on visiting
her family's hometown Alquízar, Artemisa, for *fiestas patronales*, her extended
family divided to participate in three *sociedades*, "according to skin color!"

19 Indeed, building upon Portuondo Linares (1950) and Rafael Fermoselle López's
(1974) *Política y color en Cuba*, Helg offers the first detailed history in English of
this massacre of between two and six thousand Cubans of African descent. She
uncovers an attempt to justify the massacre through dissemination of stereotypes and misinformation about Afro-Cubans' murdering white children
through "brujería" (witchcraft).

20 Alejandro de la Fuente (2001) cites Casal (1979c) to show how she gives the lie
to claims that Cuba was a racial paradise prior to the 1959 revolution, but he
does not discuss the essay's commentary on the afterlives of the massacre in
post-revolutionary Cuba.

21 Especially in Oriente, where the Partido Independiente de Color was born and
had its base of support, discussions of the massacre remain a taboo subject or a
source of shame for the victims rather than for the perpetrators. I draw this
conclusion based on informal interviews I conducted with people of different
skin colors in Santiago, Cuba, in 2016.

22 At this juncture, the reader mentally must replace *which* with *who*. This could be
a mistranslation of *que*, or a canny error that reproduces and thus makes visible
the reduction of persons to things as an effect of a racializing discourse.

23 In this view, Black Cubans working within the Cuban party structure headed by
the Castro family have sold out. Cleaver's (1976) *Time Magazine* column describes
Cuba's political elite as "more insidious and dangerous for black people than is
the white racist regime of South Africa."

24 In addition to Rodó and Fernández Retamar, see the work of Aimé Césaire (1992), Sylvia Wynter (1990), M. Nourbese Philip (2019), Suniti Namjoshi (2006), and Paget Henry (2000).

25 Hudes (2021) also emphasizes both the creativity of Spanglish-speaking urban barrios in her memoir and the psychic torment of a racializing discourse that attributes monstrosity to working-class Latinas.

26 Roberto Zurbano's *New York Times* editorial about racism in Cuba (2013), "For Blacks in Cuba, the Revolution Hasn't Begun," however distorted in translation, moved forward a public debate about racism in twenty-first century Cuba (Fogel 2020). Problematically, the public letter led to Zurbano's demotion from hard-earned decision-making positions in Cuba's most powerful cultural institutions, including Unión Nacional de Escritores y Artistas de Cuba's executive council and Casa de las Américas. See part 1, "El Caso Zurbano," *Afro-Hispanic Review* (Luis 2014).

Works Cited

Amnesty International. 2020. "Cuba: Harrassment of San Isidro Movement Exemplifies Ongoing Assault on Freedom of Expression." November 20, www.amnesty.org.

Anzaldúa, Gloria, and Cherríe Moraga. (1981) 1983. *This Bridge Called My Back: Writings by Radical Women of Color*. Rev. ed. New York: Kitchen Table Women of Color Press.

Arboleya Cervera, Jesus. 2013. *Cuba y los cubanoamericanos: El fenómeno migratorio cubano*. Havana: Casa de las Américas.

Arboleya Cervera, Jesus, Raúl Álzaga Manresa, and Ricardo Fraga Del Valle. 2016. *La contrarevolución Cubana en Puerto Rico y el caso de Carlos Muñiz Varela*. San Juan: Ediciones Callejón.

Arredondo Gutierrez, Alberto. 1939. *El Negro en Cuba*. Havana: El Alpha.

Behar, Ruth. 2018. "Introduction: Looking Back and Forward." *Cuban Studies*, no. 46: 3–9.

Bejel, Emilio. 2001. *Gay Cuban Nation*. Chicago: University of Chicago Press.

Bell-Scott, Patricia, Barbara Smith, and Gloria T. Hull. 1982. *All the Women Are White, All the Men Are Black, but Some of Us Are Brave: Black Women's Studies*. New York: Feminist Press.

Benson, Devyn Spence. 2016. *Antiracism in Cuba: The Unfinished Revolution*. Chapel Hill: University of North Carolina Press.

Bryce-Laporte, Roy S. 1981. "Obituary to a Female Immigrant and Scholar: Lourdes Casal (1938–1981)." In *Female Immigrants to the United States: Caribbean, Latin American, and African Experiences*, edited by Delores M. Mortimer and Roy S. Bryce-Laporte, 349–55. RIIES Occasional Papers No. 2. Washington, DC: Research Institute on Immigration and Ethnic Studies, Smithsonian Institution.

Bustamente, Michael. 2015. "Anti-communist Anti-imperialism? Agrupación Abdala and the Shifting Contours of Cuban Exile Politics, 1968–1986." *Journal of American Ethnic History* 35, no. 1: 71–99.

Cade, Toni, ed. 1970. *The Black Woman: An Anthology*. New York: New American Library.

Cannon, Terry, and Johnetta Cole. 1978. *Free and Equal: The End of Racial Discrimination in Cuba*. New York: Venceremos Brigade.

Capó Crucet, Jennine. 2015. *Make Your Home among Strangers*. New York: St. Martin's.

Carbonell, Walterio. 1961. *Crítica: Como surgió la cultura nacional*. Havana: Ediciones Yaka.

Casal, Lourdes. 1957a. "Calvinismo, caridad y segregación racial." *Quincena* 3, January 15, 1957: 2, 72.

Casal, Lourdes. 1957b. "Derechos civiles y discriminación racial en los Estados Unidos." *Quincena*, September 15, 12–13, 48–51.

Casal, Lourdes. 1962. "Africa ante el problema cubano." *Cuba nueva* 1: 11–17.

Casal, Lourdes. 1968. Prologue to *Presidio político en Cuba*, by José Martí, edited by Lourdes Casal, i–v. Havana: Ediciones Islas.

Casal, Lourdes, ed. 1971a. *El Caso Padilla: Literatura y revolución en Cuba: Documentos*. New York: Ediciones Universal.

Casal, Lourdes. (1971b) 1982. "Opinión." *Nueva generación*, nos. 22–23 (June–September); reprinted 1982. In *Itinerario ideológico: Antología de Lourdes Casal*, edited by María Cristina Herrera and Leonel Antonio de la Cuesta, 65–67. Miami, FL: Instituto de Estudios Cubanos.

Casal, Lourdes. 1973. *Los fundadores: Alfonso y otros cuentos*. Miami: Ediciones Universales.

Casal, Lourdes. 1974. "Dos semanas en Cuba." *Areíto* 1, no. 1: 20–28.

Casal, Lourdes. 1975. "Descarga no. 2." *Areíto* 2, nos. 2–3: 20–22.

Casal, Lourdes. 1976a. "Los revolucionarios 'ausentistas': Respuesta." Ms in María Cristina Herrera and Instituto de Estudios Cubanos archive, Cuban Heritage Collection, University of Miami.

Casal, Lourdes. 1976b. "Cuban Communist Party: The Best among the Good." *Cuba Review* 6, no. 3: 23–30.

Casal, Lourdes. 1976c. *Images of Cuban Society among Pre- and Post-revolutionary Novelists*. PhD diss., New School for Social Research.

Casal, Lourdes. 1977. "Reflections on the Conference on Women and Development: II." *Signs* 3, no. 1: 317–19.

Casal, Lourdes. 1978. "Memories of a Black Cuban Childhood." *Nuestro*, April: 61–62.

Casal, Lourdes. 1979b. "Cubans in the United States: Their Impact on US-Cuba Relations." In *Revolutionary Cuba in the World Arena*, edited by Martin Weinstein, 109–36. Philadelphia, PA: Institute for the Study of Human Issues.

Casal, Lourdes. 1979c. "Race Relations in Contemporary Cuba." In *The Position of Blacks in Brazilian and Cuban Society*, edited by Lourdes Casal and Anani Dzidzienyo, 11–27. London: Minority Rights Group.

Casal, Lourdes. 1979d. "Revolution and Race: Blacks in Contemporary Cuba." Working Papers, Woodrow Wilson International Center for Scholars, 39. Washington, DC: Woodrow Wilson Center, Latin American Program.

Casal, Lourdes. 1980a. "Lo que dice Calibán." *Areíto* 6, no. 24: 44–46; repr. abridged *Areíto* 9, no. 36 (1981): 115–16.

Casal, Lourdes. 1980b. "Revolution and *conciencia*: Women in Cuba." In *Women, War, and Revolution*, edited by Carol R. Berkin and Clara M. Lovett, 183–206. New York: Holmes and Meier.

Casal, Lourdes. 1981. *Palabras juntan revolución*. Havana: Casa de las Américas.

Casal, Lourdes. 1987. "Images of Women in Pre- and Post-revolutionary Novels," edited by Virginia R. Domínguez. *Cuban Studies* 17: 25–50.

Casal, Lourdes. 2011. "For Anna Veltfort," translated by David Frye. In *The Norton Anthology of Latino Literature*, edited by Ilan Stavans, 1189–90. New York: W. W. Norton.

Casal, Lourdes, and Marifeli Pérez-Stable. 1976. "Sobre Angola y los negros de Cuba." *Areíto* 3, no. 1: 32–33.

Casal, Lourdes, and Rafael J. Prohías. 1980. *The Cuban Minority in the US: Preliminary Report on Need Identification and Program Evaluation*. Boca Raton: Florida Atlantic University.

Césaire, Aimé. 1992. *A Tempest: Based on Shakespeare's The Tempest, Adaptation for a Black Theater*. Translated by Richard Miller. New York: Ubu Repertory Theatre Publications.

Cleaver, Eldridge. 1976. "My Turn: Fidel Castro's African Gambit." *Time*, May 3, 13.

Coogan-Gehr, Kelly. 2011. "The Politics of Race in U.S. Feminist Scholarship: An Archaeology." *Signs* 37, no. 1: 83–107.

Crenshaw, Kimberle, Neil Gotanda, Gary Peller, and Kendall Thomas, eds. 1995. *Critical Race Theory: The Key Writings that Formed the Movement*. New York: The New Press.

DeCosta-Willis, Miriam. 2003. *Daughters of Diaspora: Afra-Hispanic Writers*. Kingston, Jamaica: Ian Randle.

De la Campa, Román. 2006. "Revista *Areíto*: Herejía de una nación improbable." *Encuentro de la cultura cubana* 40: 137–41.

De la Fuente, Alejandro. 2001. *A Nation for All: Race, Inequality, and Politics in Twentieth-Century Cuba*. Chapel Hill: University of North Carolina Press.

Delgado, Richard, ed. 1995. *Critical Race Theory: The Cutting Edge*. Philadelphia: Temple University Press.

Díaz, Jesús. (1987) 1997. *Las iniciales de la tierra*. Barcelona: Editorial Anagrama.

Domínguez, Jorge I. (1977) 1981. "Letter to Abe Lowenthal." November 14, 1977. In *Areíto* 7, no. 26: 18.

Domínguez, Jorge I. 1995. "Twenty-Five Years of Cuban Studies." *Cuban Studies* 25: 3–26.

Dorn, Georgette. 1980. "Lourdes Casal Reads from Her Poetry." Washington, DC: Library of Congress, Hispanic Division. Audio recording made on August 28, 1979.

Fanon, Frantz. (1952) 2008. *Black Skin White Masks*, translated by Richard Philcox. New York: Grove.

Fermoselle López, Rafael. 1974. *Política y color en Cuba: La guerrita de 1912*. Montevideo: Ediciones Gemenís.

Fernández Retamar, Roberto. 1979. *Calibán y otros ensayos: Nuestra América y el mundo*. Havana: Editorial Arte y Literatura.

Fernández Retamar, Roberto. 1981. "Palabras de Roberto Fernández Retamar el entierro de la compañera Lourdes Casal, el 3 de febrero de 1981." *Areíto* 26: 4–5.

Fernández Retamar, Roberto. 1989. "Caliban: Notes toward a Discussion of Culture in Our America." In *Caliban and Other Essays*, translated by Edward Baker, 3–45. Minneapolis: University of Minnesota Press.

Ferrer, Ada. 1998. "The Silence of Patriots: Race and Patriotism in Martí's Cuba." In *José Martí's "Our America": From National to Hemispheric Cultural Studies*, edited by Jeffrey Belnap and Raúl Fernández, 228–49. Durham, NC: Duke University Press.

Fogel, Jean François. 2020. "Ending Systemic Racism Is the Revolution Cuba Needs." *New York Times*, January 25.

González Echevarría, Roberto. 2010. *Cuban Fiestas*. New Haven, CT: Yale University Press.

Grupo Areíto. 1978. *Contra viento y marea: Grupo Areíto*. Havana: Casa de las Américas.

Guerra, Lillian. 2014. *Visions of Power in Cuba: Revolution, Redemption, and Resistance, 1959–1971*. Chapel Hill: University of North Carolina Press.

Haggins, Bambi. 2007. *Laughing Mad: The Black Comic Persona in Post-soul America*. New Brunswick, NJ: Rutgers University Press.

Hall, Gwendolyn Midlo. 1996. "Review of Aline Helg, *Our Rightful Share: The Afro-Cuban Struggle for Equality, 1868–1912*." *American Historical Review* 101, no. 3: 945–47.

Helg, Aline. 1995. *Our Rightful Share: The Afro-Cuban Struggle for Equality, 1868–1912*. Chapel Hill: University of North Carolina Press.

Henry, Alice. 1981. "Isolation of Third World Women in Mostly White Feminist Organizations." *Off Our Backs* 11, no. 11: 3.

Henry, Paget. 2000. *Caliban's Reason: Introducing Afro-Caribbean Philosophy*. New York: Routledge.

Herrera, Maria Cristina. 2005. "Lourdes Casal." In *The Oxford Encyclopedia of Latinos and Latinas in the United States*, edited by Suzanne Oboler and Deena J. González, 274–75. New York: Oxford University Press.

Higgenbotham, Elizabeth, 1982. "Elizabeth Higgenbotham to Barbara Gelpi, typed letter dated March 2, 1982." *Signs* archives. Special Collections and University Archives. Alexander Library. Rutgers University, box 26, folder "Communities of Women."

Hoffnung-Garskof, Jesse. 2019. *Racial Migrations: New York City and the Revolutionary Politics of the Spanish Caribbean*. Princeton, NJ: Princeton University Press.

Hudes, Quiara Alegría. 2021. *My Broken Language: A Memoir*. New York: One World.

Jacobsen, Jenna Leving. 2018. "Race and Reconciliation in the Work of Lourdes Casal." *Cuban Studies* 46: 39–50.

Jiménez Román, Miriam, and Juan Flores, eds. 2010. *Afro-Latin@ Reader: History and Culture in the United States*. Durham, NC: Duke University Press.

Johnson, E. Patrick, and Ramón H. Rivera-Servera, eds. 2016. *Blacktino Queer Performance*. Durham, NC: Duke University Press.

Latner, Teishan A. 2017. *Cuban Revolution in America: Havana and the Making of a United States Left, 1968–1992*. Chapel Hill: North Carolina University Press.

Lee, Susana. 1984. "Entrevista con Lourdes Casal, de 23 de julio de 1980." *Areíto*, no. 36: 124–27.

Lomas, Laura. 2018. "On the 'Shock' of Diaspora: Lourdes Casal's Critical Interdisciplinarity and Intersectional Feminism." *Cuban Studies* 46: 10–38.

Lomas, Laura. 2020. "Lourdes Casal's Interdisciplinary Writing." In *The Oxford Encyclopedia of Latina and Latino Literature*, edited by Louis G. Mendoza, 934–50. Oxford: Oxford University Press. https://doi.org/10.1093/acrefore/9780190201098.013.406.

López, Antonio. 2012. *Unbecoming Blackness: The Diaspora Cultures of Afro-Cuban-America*. New York: New York University Press.

López, Iraida H. 2018. "Entre el ideal de la nación mestiza y la discordia racial: 'Memories of a Black Cuban Childhood' y otros textos de Lourdes Casal." *Cuban Studies* 46: 63–84.

López, Kathleen M. 2013. *Chinese Cubans: A Transnational History*. Chapel Hill: University of North Carolina Press.

Lorde, Audre. 1984. *Sister Outsider: Essays and Speeches*. Trumansburg, NY: Crossing Press.

Luis, William. 1997. *Dance between Two Cultures: Latino Caribbean Literature Written in the United States*. Nashville, TN: Vanderbilt University Press.

Luis, William, ed. 2014. *Afro-Hispanic Review* 33, no. 1.

Luis, William. 2018. "Cuban American Counterpoint: The Heterogeneity of Cuban American Literature, Culture, and Politics." In *Cambridge History of Latina/o American Literature*, edited by John Moran González and Laura Lomas, 435–51. Cambridge: Cambridge University Press.

Martí, José. 2002. *Selected Writings*, edited and translated by Esther Allen. New York: Penguin.

Martínez San Miguel, Yolanda. 2015. "Releyendo a Lourdes Casal desde su escritura en queer." *80 Grados*, October 16. www.80grados.net/releyendo-a-lourdes-casal -desde-su-escritura-en-queer/.

Martínez San Miguel, Yolanda. 2017. "Fantasy as Identity: Beyond Foundational Narratives in Lourdes Casal." *Cuban Studies* 45: 91–114.

Martínez San Miguel, Yolanda, and Frances Negron Muntaner. 2007. "In Search of Lourdes Casal's Anna Veldford." *Social Text* 25, no. 3: 57–84.

Meehan, Kevin. 2009. *People Get Ready: African American and Caribbean Cultural Exchange*. Jackson: University Press of Mississippi.

Miller, Marilyn G. 2004. *The Rise and Fall of the Cosmic Race*. Austin: University of Texas Press.

Mirabal, Nancy Raquel. 2017. *Suspect Freedoms: The Racial and Sexual Politics of Cubanidad in New York, 1823–1957*. New York: New York University Press.

Moore, Carlos. 1988. *Castro, the Blacks, and Africa*. Los Angeles: Center for Afro-American Studies, University of California.

Morrison, Karen Y. 2015. *Cuba's Race Crucible: The Sexual Economy of Social Identities, 1750–2000*. Bloomington: Indiana University Press.

Muñoz, José Esteban. 1999. *Disidentifications: Queers of Color and the Performance of Politics*. Minneapolis: University of Minnesota Press.

Namjoshi, Suniti. 2006. *Sycorax: New Fables and Poems*. New Delhi: Penguin Books.

Pérez Firmat, Gustavo. 1995. *Next Year in Cuba: A Cubano's Coming-of-Age in America*. Houston, TX: Arte Público.

Philip, M. NourbeSe and Scott Jordan. 2019. "'Sycorax, Spirit and 'Zong!' An Interview with M. NourbeSe Philip." *Jacket2.org*. https://jacket2.org/interviews/sycorax -spirit-and-zong.

Portes, Alejandro. 1969. "Dilemmas of a Golden Exile: Integration of Cuban Refugee Families in Milwaukee." *American Sociological Review* 34 (August): 505–18.

Portuondo Linares, Serafin. 1950. *Los Independientes de color. Historia del Partido Independiente de Color*. 2nd Edición. La Habana: Liberia Selecta.

Prida, Dolores. 1991. *Beautiful Señoritas and Other Plays*, edited by Judith Weiss. Houston, TX: Arte Publico.

Prieto, Yolanda. 2018. "Lourdes Casal and Black Cubans in the United States: The 1970s and Beyond." *Cuban Studies* 46: 51–62.

Quintanales, Mirtha N. 1987. "The Political Radicalization of Cuban Youth in Exile: A Study of Identity Change in Bicultural Context." PhD diss., The Ohio State University.

Quiroga, José. 2014. "The Cuban Exile Wars: 1976–1981." *American Quarterly* 66, no. 3: 819–33.

Ramos, Juanita. 1987. *Compañeras: Latina Lesbians—An Anthology*. New York: Latina Lesbian History Project.

Reddy, Chandan. 2011. *Freedom with Violence: Race, Sexuality, and the U.S. State*. Durham, NC: Duke University Press.

Ruiz, Albor. 2019. "El asesinato de Carlos Muñiz Varela: 40 años de impunidad." *Aldíanews*, May 1. https://aldianews.com/es/thought-leaders/lideres-de-opinion/40-anos-de-impunidad.

Schomburg, Arturo. 1912. "General Evaristo E. Estenoz." *Crisis: A Record of the Darker Races* 4, no. 3: 143–44.

Shakespeare, William. 2004. *The Tempest: An Authoritative Text, Sources and Contexts, Criticism, Rewritings and Appropriations*, edited by Peter Hulme and William H. Sherman. New York: W.W. Norton.

Sharpe, Christina. 2016. *In the Wake: On Blackness and Being*. Durham, NC: Duke University Press.

Sutherland, Elizabeth. 1969. *The Youngest Revolution: A Personal Report on Cuba*. New York: Dial.

Tinsley, Omis'eke Natasha. 2010. *Thiefing Sugar: Eroticism between Women in Caribbean Literature*. Durham, NC: Duke University Press.

Valdés, Vanessa K. 2017. *Diasporic Blackness: The Life and Times of Arturo Alfonso Schomburg*. Albany: State University of New York Press.

Vasconcelos, José. 1920. *La raza cósmica: Misión de la raza iberoamericana, notas de viajes a la américa del sur*. Paris: Agencia Mundial de Librería.

Veltfort, Anna. 2017. *Adiós mi Habana: Las memorias de una gringa y su tiempo en los años revolucionarios de la década de los 60*. Madrid: Editorial Verbum.

Veltfort, Anna. 2019. *Goodbye My Havana: The Life and Times of a Gringa in Revolutionary Cuba*. Stanford, CA: Stanford University Press.

Villaverde, Cirilo. 2005. *Cecilia Valdés, or El Angel Hill*, translated by Helen Lane, edited by Sibylle Fischer. New York: Oxford University Press.

Wynter, Sylvia. 1990. "Beyond Miranda's Meanings: Unsilencing the 'Demonic Ground' of Caliban's 'Woman.'" In *Out of the Kumbla: Caribbean Women and Literature*, edited by Carole Boyce Davies and Elaine Savory Fido, 355–70. Trenton, NJ: Africa World Press.

Zimra, Clarisse. 1984. "Négritude in the Feminine Mode: The Case of Martinique and Guadeloupe." *Journal of Ethnic Studies* 12, no. 1: 53–78.

Zurbano, Roberto. 2012. "Cuba: Doce dificultades para enfrentar al (neo)racismo o doce razones para abrir el (otro) debate." *Universidad de la Habana* 273: 266–77.

Zurbano, Roberto. 2013. "For Blacks in Cuba, the Revolution Hasn't Begun," translated by Kristina Cordero. *New York Times*, March 23.

Elizabeth Pérez

Remittances

Santiago de Cuba, 1996

Nephew my grandfather loved
(tanned man at my sunburned elbow):
you introduced me as myself to your wife,
circular visage burning
with the urgency of a silver bowl
tarnishing on your table.

Forty-some years ago
your father's blonde father (my great-grand),
distantly Italian,
forbid his son's marriage to a *Negra* in writing
that few in town could read.
Your parents eloped, snapping
sugarcane shafts underfoot,
the final crush
after snubbing a compulsory harvest.
As soon as your mother bore her sole child,
wriggling in the heat of a legendary fall,
my great-uncle
(your father)
leapt at a flight

MERIDIANS · feminism, race, transnationalism   21:1 April 2022
DOI: 10.1215/15366936-9554112 © 2022 Smith College

to the United States
with a bottle-redhead twelve years his senior.

His brother embarked on regular visits,
bearing wheeled toys and custard apple candy
from the capital.
Turning to purpose what he learned
from brotherless sisters
on the plantations of the interior,
he never stooped at your mother's door
(whistling apart his obsidian mustache)
without apologizing.
You called him *Papá*
even after he also went,
bequeathing the contents of his cabinets
and dribbling steady money via telegram until his death.

When you and I finally meet
we spend the short time budgeted for this
debating the relevance of revenants
in mannered Spanish,
sipping *café con leche*
out of my grandfather's indestructible Soviet glasses,
I not fond of you in the least
and neither of us named after him.

· ·

Elizabeth Pérez is associate professor of religious studies at the University of California, Santa Barbara. Her first book, *Religion in the Kitchen: Cooking, Talking, and the Making of Black Atlantic Traditions* (NYU Press, 2016) was awarded the 2017 Clifford Geertz
Prize in the Anthropology of Religion, and received honorable mention for the 2019
Barbara T. Christian Literary Award. Her poetry has appeared in several journals and
two edited volumes.

The title of this poem, "Remittances," refers to money transferred from a person in
one country to family members and friends in another. These payments are transnational gestures of care and sacrifice, tying immigrants to the lands of their birth, to
"faceless" flows of capital, and to relatives with whom they share intimate racialized

and gendered histories. "Remittances" begins by tracing back a legacy of misogynoir, as the term was coined and conceptualized by queer Black feminist scholar Moya Bailey. It then contemplates the intergenerational expressions of love available to cisgender men in post-revolutionary Cuba. It is the latest in a series of poems about Santiago, starting with "Six Eulogies for a Cuban Exile," published in the *Bilingual Review/ La revista bilingüe* in 1996.

Rachel Afi Quinn

....

La Reina de la Fusión
Xiomara Fortuna Coming of Age in the Dominican Republic

Abstract: Afro-Dominican singer-songwriter Xiomara Fortuna has enjoyed a career that spanned more than four decades and shaped the work of a new generation of Dominican musicians. In March 2017 she was bestowed a presidential award of honor and she accepted it barefoot, making a clear statement about her values and where she sees herself fitting in Dominican society. Drawn from three separate interviews conducted with Fortuna in Santo Domingo in July 2016, augmented by her extensive internet archive, this article frames a transcribed and translated testimonio that captures some of Fortuna's experiences while coming of age in the Dominican Republic in the late twentieth century. While much of Dominican society's African cultural history has been actively obscured by the ruling class, Fortuna has long celebrated Afro-Dominican culture through her life's work and her identity has shaped how she has navigated a neoliberal society as a black artist. Her insights provide an essential piece of Dominican historiography that includes Dominican youth organizing on the Left in the 1980s and 1990s, feminist activism, and cultural production.

....

I am Xiomara Fortuna. I was born in Monte Cristi at the border with Haiti—the Dominican Republic and Haiti—where I lived my early years. I lived my first 19 years there in Monte Cristi. I never left the community until age 19, when I came to the city of Santo Domingo, after traveling at that time to Cuba and Jamaica. This visit to Cuba had a great impact on my life. This was 1978.
— Xiomara Fortuna
....

MERIDIANS · feminism, race, transnationalism   21:1 April 2022
DOI: 10.1215/15366936-9554123 © 2022 Smith College

The Queen of Fusion

On International Women's Day in 2017, musician Xiomara Fortuna received a medal of honor from the Dominican president, Danilo Medina, in recognition of her lifetime of activism in women's rights, anti-racism, and environmentalism (see fig. 2). The award stirred controversy in the local media because Fortuna accepted it at the national palace *descalzada* (barefoot). While her rejection of upper-class Dominican rules of propriety scandalized some, the act was truly a testament to Fortuna's life-long political values and the place that she has made for herself as an artist in the Dominican Republic (DR). Known as La Reina de la Fusión (the queen of fusion), sixty-two-year-old Fortuna is a prolific cultural producer who began playing and writing music at an early age. She is recognized as a pioneer of *música raíz* in the Dominican Republic, a music that blends Afro-Dominican rhythms and sounds of *carabiné, la mangulina, la salve, la bambula, el merengue típico, congo, gagá,* and *palos* with hip hop, reggae, rock, jazz, and pop music (Guerrero 2011).[1] Her career has emerged in different waves over the last four decades. Although she found recognition for her music in Europe early in her career—when she says her music went from being referred to as "world music" to "Dominican fusion"—she was deliberate about returning to her homeland. Singing with the late Tony Vicioso in the band Kaliumbe greatly informed her sound and connected her to broader Dominican audiences. Yet her talent and abilities as a songwriter were being overlooked or ignored by many Dominicans for some time because of her gender and her blackness (see Austerlitz 1998; Davis 2012; Quinn 2015).[2] Her music has gained greater prominence in the last decade, however, and she has paved the way for a next generation of Dominican musicians known as "generación fusión." Numerous collaborations with younger musicians and recordings with queer artists like Rita Indiana and the group Mula (known for their futuristic sound and aesthetic) have helped her work reach "alternative" listeners.[3] Among Dominican musicians in their twenties and thirties, Fortuna is respected for her artistry and work ethic, while her signature sound inevitably elevates and inspires their own.

Today, Fortuna's music and her cultural aesthetic circulate via social media through sophisticated videos by Dominican media makers, and her new releases debut on YouTube and Spotify. It is possible to trace her musical contributions through the recent scholarship of Dominican ethnomusicologist Rossy Díaz and others, alongside a newly expansive internet archive (Díaz 2018; Sánchez 2016–17; Vargas 2014). Preceding the global pandemic, Fortuna performed regularly on the island, with concerts for audiences throughout the DR and Haiti. In 2019 she won a Soberano, the famed Dominican cultural award, for Best Alternative Music, and in August of that year, she held a forty-year retrospective concert at the National Theater (*Listín Diario* 2019).[4] She then won a Soberano again in 2021 in the same category.[5]

However, I did not seek an interview with Fortuna to learn more about her musical career. I wanted to learn about who she is, and how she has navigated a transnational life as an Afro-Dominican artist and activist; I hoped to learn about the ideologies she embraced along the way and how her thinking might be reflective of a generation of black feminist activists of the Spanish-speaking Caribbean (Laó-Montes 2016: 1–3). Her stories of coming of age in the northern region of the Dominican Republic during the second half of the twentieth century reveal much about who she is today; they illustrate her becoming. Her life story exposes the cultural and political context of the Dominican Republic in the decades following the dictatorship of Rafael Trujillo (1930–61), and later, Joaquín Balaguer, who continued Trujillo's legacy (Liberato 2013: 58–59). Throughout that period, a vibrant student movement at the Universidad Autónoma de Santo Domingo, where Fortuna studied, fostered a revolutionary legacy that continues to this day. She reveals how growing up in the 1960s and 1970s Caribbean meant that a leftist movement in the region informed her politics and her creative work. She provides insights into aspects of Dominican society that are often invisibilized by historians of the white Dominican elite.[6]

Fortuna's identification with blackness has always informed her career; it is reflected in the expansive archive of music she has produced over the last four decades, and it has significantly influenced how (and when) the Dominican music industry and its audiences have received her. Much cultural history tying the Dominican Republic to Africa has gone unrecorded or was erased, as the African heritage of Dominicans has been contested for centuries by a social elite of European descent who are invested in a national identity that is decidedly not black (see García-Peña 2016; Quinn 2015). It is this cultural dissonance that has motivated some scholars and visitors to the DR to proclaim that Dominicans do not know they are black, yet U.S. black identity and Dominican blackness are constructed through different histories and cultures. Moreover, as Brendan J. Thornton and Diego I. Ubiera (2019: 417) state, "Within the Dominican Republic, scholarly attempts to recover the African heritage of Dominican culture are not scarce but have tended to consign black traditions to the domain of folk-lore; that is, conspicuous cultural forms regarded as relics to be celebrated at specific times and in specific places." Fortuna's artistry is likewise interpreted in limited ways by a culture in which, as Thornton and Ubiera understand,

> black or "Afro-Dominican" culture can be found in magical religious beliefs (e.g., Dominican vodú), in carnival and festival traditions (e.g., el gagá), or in folktales, dance, and traditional music (e.g., palo) (see Andú-jar 1997; Tejeda Ortiz 1998; Aracena 1999), but not usually in everyday social and cultural life, conceding, however erroneously, that ordinary Dominican culture is inherently nonblack since black culture, to be pres-ent and operative, must be distinct or distinguishable from it. (417)

Although Thornton and Ubiera parenthetically suggest that "hyphenates like Afro-Dominican imply that Dominicanness on its own is absent of black cultural attributes and therefore requires a modifier," Afro-identified Dominicans, including many I have interviewed, would likely argue other-wise. Rather, today their claims on Afro-Dominicanness or blackness for many articulate lived experiences of being othered or of anti-blackness.

Until quite recently, Fortuna's work had been overshadowed because she is outspoken about anti-blackness in the Dominican Republic, and her blackness is undeniable; she celebrates *afrodominicanidad* through her sound and her aesthetic, inspiring other artists to do the same. It appears that increased claims to blackness among Dominican youth in the last decade—based on a new cultural currency placed on African heritage among transnational artists and cultural producers—may have countered some of Fortuna's earlier marginalization. New desires to either celebrate or merely consume Afro-Dominican culture provoke an increased interest in her oeuvre. Her music and its visual translations celebrate the diversity of Dominican life, particularly that of black and working-class Domini-cans, which for many seems to push the limits of respectability and chal-lenges how Dominicans of the dominant culture have long imagined themselves.

In the 2013 music video for Fortuna's classic rallying cry, "¡La calle será la calle!," her signature barefoot concert performance is interwoven with the story of a woman (played by comedian Lumy Lizardo) walking the streets at night in full drag (thick layer of makeup, fake lashes, short skirt, and high heels) looking for sex work; a rainbow-striped tie dangles around

her neck. Fortuna's 2021 music video *Afro E* with Dominican rapper
AcentOh further exemplifies her celebration of Afro-Dominican culture in
lyrics and rhythms but is also queered through the humor that it incorporates as well. A short clip at the end of the video that rolls after the credits
portrays a working-class Dominican woman (seemingly another performance of drag) sitting with a neighbor, her living room essentially set up on
the street. Wearing a house dress and skirt (over what appears to be a T-
shirt and shorts), house slippers, and the quintessential hair in curlers, she
places Fortuna's record on a record player beside her and then giddily
enjoys the African rhythms of the music that emerges.

A Different Story

This essay was initially to serve as a *testimonio*, an oral history of sorts, to
provide readers with Fortuna's voice at length, from her stories of street
theater and public education campaigns to a generation of lesbian feminists organizing, the impact of a proliferation of nongovernmental organizations (NGOs) on Dominican society, and the ways that her music
energized activist youth. Ultimately, the narrative she shares pays great
attention to the ways that the opportunities she had growing up, the
obstacles she overcame, the family of which she was a part, her personality,
and her desire to pursue the life of an artist have all uniquely shaped her
trajectory. Emerging from the details of Fortuna's life is her long-held
feminist politic, which she has used to empower other Dominican women.
I see her story as politically significant, with a keen sense that the insights I
am able to gather through ethnography can produce new theories about the
world as experienced by black people (Caldwell 2007: 178). Moreover, as
anthropologist Kia Lilly Caldwell affirms, "Scholarly production is insepa-
rable from researchers' personal identities, interests and politics" (xxi).
Fortuna's story not only teaches us about race in the Dominican Republic
but it also points to the influences of the Left in the Caribbean region in the
1960s and the Dominican feminist movements of the seventies and eighties that utilized the arts to disseminate feminist ideology.

   In July of 2016, I conducted a series of interviews with Fortuna in Santo
Domingo to piece together some aspects of the early part of her life that
shaped her unique outlook on Dominicanness.[7] I did not sit down with her
for an interview as a stranger but as someone who had met her before and
who held a deep respect for her knowledge of the world and her work in it.
As another black woman in diaspora, a U.S. scholar, I serve not only as an

interlocutor but as an erstwhile intermediary in my effort to convey biographic details about Fortuna's life to academic audiences. I lived for over a year in Santo Domingo and had met Fortuna in 2010. As an ethnographer, I have developed an understanding of Dominican life and culture over more than a decade thanks to the support of people like Fortuna who are willing to share their stories. I have actually had the opportunity to get to know Fortuna better in the years since I left the island, through WhatsApp messages, my return visits, our collaboration on the documentary film project *Cimarrón Spirit* (Durán et al. 2015), and through her online performances. I have witnessed her many new album debuts and other media events such as internet radio broadcasts, TEDX talks, and Instagram Live performances as well. I have sought to offer her words here at length, to make space for her storytelling and for her to speak for herself as she does with her music. Captured in this essay may be a different story than the one Fortuna might decide to tell today; most know her to be guarded about her personal life, or perhaps judicious about who she lets into it.[8]

Family Life in Color

Matter-of-factly describing her upbringing and family legacy as a source of pride, Fortuna tells me, "We always lived in the center of the city, my family, Las Taveras, in the community of Monte Cristi—my maternal family. It is a humble family, but very respected, since in small towns honesty is very important. And the people are educated, well-studied, with ideas ready to discuss them. This is important in a small town. My family is also a very honorable family." She explains how she was able to become an artist—and come into herself—in the world in which she grew up. Her experiences from a very young age would make her aware of the many injustices in the world:

> I first came in contact with art when I was twelve years old, since before that I remember I was in fifth grade and my teachers already recognized that I could sing and recite, even though I was very shy—well not shy enough to keep me from performing and reading whatever they gave me and such. So, in school I first learned to sing all of the hymns. The national hymn, the hymn of the mothers, the hymn of the trees, the hymn of the heroes, the hymn of the revolution. I learned all of these hymns at home with my mom and we sang them almost every day. We did it like a study session after dinner. We ate together and then stayed there with my mother, who wanted us to teach her to sing the hymns,

since she also liked them. We learned them bit by bit every day until we had learned them completely, everyone in the house learned them. There were eight of us. Three boys and five girls, so there was that dynamic. My mother drew us a lot of *historietas* [comics/illustrated stories]. I mention this because it shaped somewhat my interest in literature and the arts, since we always had stories, we sang, we told stories and we enjoyed the outdoors, the moon and the stars and the trees and the animals. My mother liked a natural environment, and we always talked about the planets and such and this shaped my thinking and perception of the world. Also, I was the oldest.

I am the only daughter of my mother's first marriage. My mother married a "foreigner," which is to say a man who wasn't from our city [Monte Cristi] but rather from the capital, from Santo Domingo, and, unfortunately, they divorced when I was born. Because of this, I never knew my father. My mother thought that he would come and get to know me, but we waited for many years and he never came. So, I was the oldest. Later, my mother married her first boyfriend who was from there, from our town, and had all the kids with him, the other seven children. I grew up in a family in which I was different, since I had a different father. I was also at the same time the daughter of a *black* father, and my siblings were the children of a man who was of German heritage, of German roots, and with a white mother and their white father. Well, with a little mix but . . . around here you call this "white"—a person with light skin, light eyes, fair hair. And my siblings came out a bit fairer and this brought about all the issues of racism (see fig. 1).

In this same house, my mother didn't want to dress me in bright colors, rather she didn't want me to wear red, and I loved red; she said that this wasn't a color for black people, so in this way she came to single me out as different because I had dark skin. I never realized it until my mother began to say this to me and my siblings. When we talked about it, we would fight. There was always this allusion to my blackness, which surprised me: "*Negra, negra, negra,*" "*negra del diablo,*" were some of the words they used most at home . . . "*negra de olla,*" like a cooking pot that is black on the bottom, that's an insult I heard at home, directed at me. My mother always said it wasn't important, that I was equal with my siblings, but this was very difficult. It was especially difficult for a child like me: very thoughtful since childhood, thinking about a lot. I learned very early that I was different and that this difference was often negative.

Figure 1. Photograph of Xiomara and her mother and sisters. Courtesy of Xiomara Fortuna.

A researcher of Dominican culture in her own right, Fortuna shared with me various stories of the racial discrimination and colorism she experienced, in part because these were questions that I asked about her life experience, but also because it was these experiences and not others that were the most profound examples of what had shaped her perspective in life. A hierarchy of color and class, and segregation in terms of race and gender, was produced and reinforced within the Dominican system of education. With a great deal of animation, Fortuna describes the details of how it played out in school for her:

At school I also began to feel this discrimination, this difference. Because at the school I always applied myself and wanted to sit in the front of the class to hear better and I always liked to study. But even if I arrived first and sat up front, the teacher moved me to a desk at the back, since the seats at the front of the class were for the whitest students and those with more money, who were usually the whitest. All of the blacks, always the poorest, we were seated in the back. The lightest, with good hair, were all seated in the front, well-dressed, wearing expensive shoes and all, and then us. They used to put me in the ninth row or beyond. There were something like sixteen rows for the whole school and the closest I got [to the front of the class] was seat number 7, when I was in primary school. Later, when I was in high school, I fought to be in front. So when I got there early I sat in front and everyone came with their chairs trying to pull them up in front of mine, then I pulled mine in front of theirs, until we were all the way at the wall, fighting. It didn't have to do with who was poor so much as we wanted to see who was studying more, who knew more, who was more intelligent. This was the competition between the youth and adolescents. So every day we did this until the teacher arrived and sent us back.

Fortuna said she eventually realized that the teacher was paying attention to how the students behaved and would allow well-behaved students to leave their desks up at the front of the class. It became a position that she would fight for throughout high school. She noted, "It was always a fight to be up front." As a child she received many messages about her position in society:

> This school was in the community, where the same things happened to me at school that happened at home. In this community in Monte Cristi, the people are a reflection of what's in the home. It's the same. The same thinking and the same "you must put your hair in curlers, you must dress in light colors." The same rules. The home is a reflection of the city and adopts the same codes that the city has, that the people have. If they don't adopt these things, they are out of order, out of context, and the people don't like it. It appears that the whole world thinks the same, the Dominican people don't like difference.

Furthermore, as Fortuna tells us, one learns early on that being different is not a good thing, particularly in a society in which there is constant pressure to conform. Yet, being unable to conform to the expectations of those around her in terms of race and gender is precisely what gave Fortuna insights about how the world works, or as Audre Lorde (1996: 112) identified: "those of us who stand outside the circle of this society's definition of acceptable women; those of us who have been forged in the crucibles of difference." Fortuna's way of navigating the world as a youth was founded in not only a feeling of difference but also *being* different from her own family. As such, her worldview was a theoretical framework through which she was able to make sense of her experiences of racism from an early age. Her stories of colorism and systemic racism were familiar to me and similar to those of other "visibly black" Dominican women I interviewed in Santo Domingo from 2006 to 2016.[9]

The Cost of Resistance

Fortuna explained her own coming into consciousness about gender inequity first in her childhood home, where she realized that inequitable labor divisions based on gender were something that her mother maintained:

> I always wanted to be close to my mother, so I wanted to learn to cook. I like to cook. Because I was the oldest, my mother sent me to clean up the bedrooms. Yes, and I rebelled. I first rebelled at age twelve when my mom wanted me to every day go out and pick up the boys' rooms. The girls picked up their clothes and brought them to wash and the boys did not. We lived in a house with three floors, so I had to go up to the second floor to pick up the boys' bedrooms, and I was the oldest and saw how they sent me basically to pick up the socks, pants, and shoes and such. I rebelled at twelve years old and at that moment gave a feminist speech to my mother. I told her that no, I would not pick up my brother's things that I had to pick up when I was their age. So, this was also important to my mother. She always noticed it, but I always, always, always brought it up.
>
> She would say to me, "You aren't going to do such and such a thing," and I would always say, "Yes, I am." She never gave me a reason why not. I asked her "Why not?" She would say, "Because I said so." Even though she said this, I would not abide. I would continue saying, "Yes, I will. Yes, I will. Yes, I will."
>
> "No, because you can't. Because you are skinny. You can't because you are this, you can't because you are that. You don't have a father. I don't want the responsibility, I . . . " You know? So I was always very "Yes, I will." "Yes, I will." I hardly spoke but was very contemplative about what I wanted. Always intent, very precise about what I wanted, and I defended my decisions when questioned.

Fortuna was very much the "willful girl" that Sara Ahmed defines for us in *Living a Feminist Life*, who refuses to submit to the will of her parents or others with power around her. As Ahmed (2017: 71) recognizes, it is no surprise that "this figure of the willful girl, the one who is becoming feminist, who speaks the langue of injustice to mask her own desire or will for power, creates such a strong impression." Moreover, the point Ahmed is making, which Fortuna relays in her telling of her childhood, is the reality that "to become a feminist is to be assigned as being willful: you are not willing to recede" (75). Notably, these moments of "willfulness" emerge out of a recognition that one is being treated differently because of one's gender and because of one's race, as Ahmed highlights. However, according to Fortuna, it is her personality, forged in response to the day-to-day discrimination that she faced, that determined her life course. As she understands it, such a willful orientation to the world always has a cost. While Fortuna does not necessarily want to share with me in her interview what it has cost her, examples she describes in our conversation provide enough of an explanation of how doing this work of remembering is very much about "putting a body into words," and, as Ahmed so aptly describes it, the injury is cumulative, like "gathering things in a bag, but the bag is your body, so that you feel like you are carrying more and more weight. The past becomes heavy. We all have different biographies of violence, entangled as they are with so many aspects of ourselves: things that happen because of how we are seen; and how we are not seen" (23). The experience is no different for Fortuna, who theorizes it thus:

> I was always different. I never liked to be like others. And I paid for this. I paid because the people on the island don't want to talk with you. They bully you. They say, "What are they thinking?" "What is this?" "They think they are some big deal." You know? People don't understand that you have the right to be however you want to be. And to go out however. People won't accept this; they still work to be the same. My family was like this. They didn't wear red lipstick because it seemed too *black*. They conformed to the same social codes. I think this came to a head and became the rule under Trujillo, but it is from much further back, emerging from colonization, from what was brought from Africa to America. And so, what came with the Spanish as they worked to make one race superior to another. Yes, this is the project of colonization, I believe. And Trujillo, what he did, was to make these beliefs into laws, to institutionalize this.
>
> As a society, colorism is really terrible. My mother had to go to school with me many times to say to them, "Look, she has a mother and I am her mother, even though she is black." My mother said, "She is *india* [in color], she has a mother who is *india*." She would go and defend me there. "She is black but she has a mother who is not black," my mother would tell them. Of course, she is *mestiza* and she always had to go and show her face. Because she always told us that fighting was bad, and if people mess with you, you don't have to fight them. And I never fought. They bullied me, and my mom would go to school and come up with

ways to punish the people who bullied me without me having to fight. . . . If I'm in line and someone shoves me aside, well the next day they'd want to fight because I pushed them. There was a lot of violence. I grew up in this environment, but thankfully my mother understood that violence is not the right way to defend oneself. Rather, one has to talk.

Through Fortuna's willfulness, or resistance to being marginalized in the classroom, in the home, and beyond, she became acquainted with the workings of power in her world. She learned early in life that she would not be conceded any power, and her choice was to fight or not to fight in the hardscrabble world of her youth. Rather than retreat, Fortuna joined in where she was able, and with talent and determination she became a leader among her peers: "I participated in all of the cultural movements in the town with the youth, in theater, in chorus, sports, all throughout my adolescence I participated. In Monte Cristi, I started a theater group and we did plays with social content. We denounced poverty. We did a piece where we spoke out against the rape of a woman by a man. We came to work on the issue of imperialism, too. . . . Various themes like that, with social content."

Fortuna's political engagement started locally, but eventually her world expanded. As a black girl from a town in northern Dominican Republic, growing up not far from the site of the massacre of tens of thousands of Haitians and Dominicans of Haitian descent at the border town of Dajabon, she made a profound journey into consciousness about the workings of the world. In telling her life story, she returns to the spaces in which she was able to engage with art: "I was also in a poetry group—a group that recited poetry. So I learned a lot of poems by great poets like Pablo Neruda, everything Latino. We learned them in order to recite them. And it also brought me into social consciousness, which would appear in my work much later."

Leaving Home

As a teenager, Fortuna started to separate from her family, leave her hometown, and take some distance from her relationship with her mother: "I went to Cuba after many problems with my mother, who didn't want me to go." Fortuna's motivation to forge her own path led her on a life-changing adventure that she repeatedly points back to when she tells her story today:

I didn't have much opportunity to leave my town, my mom couldn't afford to pay for university and I could not afford life in the capital. Because of this, when I graduated from high school, I spent a couple more years in my community. I was teacher in the private school, where I saved up money to come to the university. I worked two years. Then my mother said no, that she would not send me to the university. That happened. I never thought that I would travel but I always wanted to travel. I am a lover of cultures. And in my little head I wanted to know them, the other countries and the culture of our country. I wanted to do what I wanted to do. And I got the opportunity when there was a very important festival in Cuba, organized by students. It met in Cuba with students from all over Latin America. So for those of us from the provinces, they saw it as an opportunity for a young person, just one person, from all of Santiago and below. So we were well-organized, the youth, at that time. We were organizing the towns and their organizations—every neighborhood had a group. We built a trust for the election of groups of youth, at the national level. So, at my level, the confederation to the north elected only one person to go to Cuba. The youth understood that the best person to go and represent them was me. I could sing. I was the best actor. No other youth knew how to do much. So there was voting, and then there was voting, and then there was voting, and I won my town. First, I won my town and after winning my town, I won.

So I had the opportunity to travel to Cuba and also spend some time in Jamaica. That's because I had the luck of coming all the way from Monte Cristi, and when I arrived at the office of those organizing the youth that would go to Cuba, they told me that on that day there was no delegation going and that it would be two more weeks to go to Cuba. So they said, "There's a group going tomorrow to Jamaica, you want to go?" And I spent twelve hours in the office and they organized everything and the next day I went to Jamaica. I spent about ten days there and then I went to Cuba. This was a trip for me that, as my mother said, was *antes y después* [before and after]. I had not even been on a donkey. Not a car, not anything. And in this trip, I rode in everything that there was to ride in: ship, train, plane, *guagua*, car, even an elevator. Everything, everything, everything. For me it was a trip of discovering the world. And so I sang in Cuba with artists that I heard on the radio. Very famous artists that were like idols, and some of them were my idols too. I sang with them there in Cuba, and I was the youngest and I was very successful. Dani Rivera,

Lucecita Benitez from Puerto Rico; from here Sonia Silvestre, and Luis Días, who already lived in the capital and had made a name for himself, and me, living in the countryside, *el pueblo*. Well, I was totally unknown. No one knew me. But I showed up with my guitar, and I had quickly memorized all the poems by Don Pedro Mir, our national poet, and that's what I sang at the concert there in Cuba.

I lost my clothes and luggage on that trip. I went the whole month without clothes, without anything, without a brush, without clothes, without a toothbrush or toothpaste, without anything. Nothing more than what I had on. What happened was that my hair grew out, and I discovered my hair because my mother had always straightened it. But I was there, and I didn't have a thing, and my hair began to grow, and grow, and grow. It got big, and I liked it. I left my hair natural. I didn't see other women like this. Dreadlocks in Jamaica, but not on women. I think I was— yes, I was the first woman here, I think. I was the first woman here that went natural. I can say that because it was terrible. I had to be very strong. They threw stones at me, they threw combs. They said all kinds of things. They shouted at me in the street and wouldn't allow me to get into the public cars. If I got in, people would pull my hair. I had to sit in back because if I sat in front they pulled my hair and shouted *loca* [crazy]. They shouted many things at me. The first time I went on television with my hair natural and big like this, they threw things at me while I sang. Yes, yes, yes.

Hair is a critical marker for black women worldwide in terms self-expression, performance of gender, and self-actualization, no matter the era. In 1978 it was equally important for Fortuna. She explains:

I'm telling you about this hair, and when I decided to be a singer, because it is a decision. In my house my father didn't want me to—my stepfather—he didn't want me to pursue art. At that time, still to be an artist was something bad. For women it was like prostitution. It was as if, it was seen as something negative—for a woman, for a decent young lady—they prostitute themselves. So I always said that I am going to show them that one can be an artist and not prostitute oneself. I have endeavored to be an artist that does what she wants to do. I didn't do it for anyone else. If I didn't do what I needed to do, what I had to do, I wouldn't have done anything I didn't want to do. Nothing. No, no, not anything, not a career. I was feisty, with a lot of strength and strong beliefs. I had a lot of faith in what I wanted, and I defended my beliefs above all else, before money, fame, wellness, and whatever else. I didn't care. I said I was going to be a different kind of artist, I was going to do what I wanted to do, and I didn't care if I starved in the streets. I decided this very young, because my father always said I was going to be a prostitute, that it was prostitution. He even came to take me out of the cultural movement of the theater troupes and all that. He took my guitar. He didn't want me learning guitar, and when he took it and took me out of the group, I held a hunger strike at home. I sat in the living room and would not speak, would not eat, nothing. And all the neighbors came by to say to my mom, "Let her be, let her be, let her go. Let the child be. This girl that has so much talent, this girl is an artist. Let her go to her group. Don't take her out. This girl is so sad." And there I was, mute, striking for almost fifteen days. Until it made my mother so sad and she said, "No! Get out of here! No man is going to tell me what I need to do with my daughters." She said it like that, "No man is going to tell me what I need to do with my daughters. Get out of here!" This was when I was fourteen or fifteen, that age, when I lived the whole day with my guitar, and at my house more than forty youth would come by daily, to be with me. I was a leader without realizing it. Yes, my house was *como un dulce* [like a sweet], everyone was drawn to it.

Forty youth came by my house every day. And the neighbors said that—after I went to Cuba—the neighbors said I had gone to Cuba for weapons training and that I was teaching communism to the youth. When I arrived back from Cuba, then, the police were waiting for me, to take all of the things I brought from Cuba, and I brought many things. I brought many books, I brought a lot of propaganda on T-shirts, on brochures that they make, the hat, I brought posters too, of Che, of Fidel, of anything at all Cuban. I brought a lot of posters and such. I brought the poster of the symbol of liberty, and I covered the town with the poster—yeah, we did it bam-bam-bam and took all the posters that I brought and put them up in town. So what happened then was the police came after me. But my mom had an idea. She told me that I needed to hide all the things I had brought. And you know how my house is? A big house with three floors? We had something like a water tank on the second floor, in between the floor and ceiling. It was impossible for someone who wasn't from the household to know where it was. So that's where we hid all of the things that I brought from Cuba. And it's there that I also hid when they came to look for me. I hid inside the water tank. Eighteen or nineteen years old . . . yeah. I was thus, well politicized.

Self-Making and Political Education

Fortuna's experience in youth organizing would help her find others with shared values around issues of social justice. Her interest in cultural exchanges and her desire to learn about the world beyond her small town would lead her to significant transformation during her adolescence. More than once in our interview, she recalls this moment of politicization and of becoming, as marked by a before and after moment.

> Cuba was an opportunity to make connections with others. The political part was voluntary, say, to inaugurate something and there would be speech, or two, or three, political speeches, but it was an event with a lot of music, and a lot of exchange. We spent two hours daily at talks, but this was voluntary, you didn't necessarily have to go. The lectures were about the rights of the people and liberty, la lucha [the struggle], you know? I already had this in me. I arrived there with a desire for this, that's why I went. There I was left with nothing, and I discovered how to be a warrior. I became much stronger on this trip. It made me. . . . I went as a girl whose hair my mother combed, as my mom said, that would do anything for her mother. . . . But there, surviving a month on my own, I discovered my strengths, and so I began to present myself in a different way. For example, I was no longer a mama's girl. I came into myself. That's why she always said there was "before Cuba and after Cuba." Because I didn't ask her to do my hair anymore. She could no longer tell me how to do my hair, how to dress, what colors I should wear, nothing. That was it. Not where I could go, or where I was going, or with whom I could or could not go. I already learned how to grow up the hard way, on this trip. For me, it was definitive because it framed my life, significantly. I was able to come to the university and I came prepared. Because I had to confront all the professional artists when I arrived with my guitar, and I already had status, like a confidence to say, "This is who I am," not, "This is what I want to do." Yes, that happened in for me in Cuba: "This is who I am."

Women's Movement

Fortuna sought out and was sought out by other Dominican feminists who wanted to create a community with aligning values. Through music, she was able to build community and help mobilize an activist movement among youth. However, only a small fraction of their efforts have been documented. She laughed as she described to me their attempt to do it all themselves as feminist activists:

When I came here to Santo Domingo in the eighties, there were already feminist events, they had started feminist movement and women's movements. So since I sang, I found myself with a group of women that played women's music, and they sought me out so I would sing with them. They were women who played guitar, percussion, bass, violin, so I was the singer. It was an idea of a group that never was, but we got together, talked, selected short feminist songs to put together, and then I discovered the world of women and of feminism—through this idea that never was. But without a doubt much later, two years after, we created a feminist theater troupe. We called it *Las Marchantas*.

There was already a strong women's movement behind the NGOs. All of the NGOs now had offices that worked on the theme of women, the problems of women, so we created the plays, writing the *libretos collectivos*. We did the lighting, we did it all. We didn't want men to put a finger on anything! We all did the work. We had a little truck that we drove. We would go to the countryside bringing the stage. For three years. There were five of us. Five actresses. At that time, I didn't know if I would dedicate my life to theater or to song. It was Arlette Oleka Fernández, Josefina Stubbs—who is now the second rank at Banco Mundial—it was Rita Mella, who is the first Latina judge. It was Ginny Taulé, who is also a big deal, working at Brahma, the beer company, and there was me. It was us five. All of them have become tremendous women and have worked outside of the country and made many decisions together. Oleka married and had children. The others didn't have children because the work was hard, and sometimes you can't have children and then be able to do other things. And sure, out of all of us the other four were lesbians, but we were not lesbians *para siempre* [forever], but on the road it happens. So many ideas, so many ideas and so much thought in search of something better, that's all. *Nada*, everyone was pursuing her work. I do my work as an artist, the other her work as a judge, the other as an actress. We didn't work on the theme of lesbianism, the theme of pure feminism. At that time, no one spoke of a lesbian feminism, of a black feminism, of a white feminism, nor rich, or poor, they didn't talk about it. Only "feminism."

I don't think feminism of the U.S. arrived here. The movement, I think, evolved into another thing and other forms because the NGOs covered everything. . . . The people, if they didn't have any money, they didn't do anything, but if *we* didn't have any money we [still] handled everything. Because when there's money, those that have the money decide what the issues get addressed. Therefore, with the NGOs' involvement, things became more individualized: a lot of everyone doing whatever they could from wherever they were.

Fortuna's memory work recalls an early period of neoliberal influence through the NGO-ification of the DR in the 1980s, when she made her way to Santo Domingo. Dominican feminists were well aware of the damaging effects of neoliberalism's commitment to individualism, and as Ochy Curiel (2016: 46) and others would argue, the ways that a neoliberal politic "makes collective action more difficult."

At University

The activism Fortuna recalls at the University Autónoma de Santo Domingo (UASD), the public university in the capital, captures a moment of feminist activism and revolutionary influences from other parts of Latin America and the Caribbean.

> So I arrived at la UASD, and at la UASD I had to study and I looked for a major that would allow me to continue to explore art. I declared a major that at that time they called advertising arts, but it gave you exposure, it offered two semesters of all the majors that had to do with art: architecture, design, advertising, sculpture, history of art, psychology of art, and such. I studied all of these fields, these theoretical subjects, about all of the theory of art, psychology of art, which I loved, because I already came from that and I didn't have books to study. I did my studies without books. My mom could not buy books, so I studied with the *Larousse* dictionary. Like, for example, the question, "What were the planets?" I looked up in my dictionary, "What were the planets? The planets were—" I studied everything in the dictionary, because the dictionary had a section that had to do with art. All of the definitions of the artistic movements— the Renaissance, impressionism, all of this, I studied this. I had studied this in my town. I could look at the little pictures. Mine was a big one, a larger *Larousse*. I studied everything with the *Larousse* and the Bible.
>
> When I arrived at la UASD, I became famous in the socialist movement. I sang every day at the university. Songs with social content. The professors were with me because I was filling their classrooms. I did not have a notebook, I did not have a book, I went as a listener. I knew that I wasn't going to graduate. I would go to learn whatever interested me; I listened. This I was always clear about. And so learned as I went, and I came to understand the university and beyond. After this I came to the feminist movement, where I was always singing as well.

As Fortuna described it, when she got to la UASD in the 1980s she discovered that the students were so politicized and each political party had students within the university that represented it. The parties on the Left wanted her to join them because of the content of her songs: "So now I was able to do this work and was useful to the parties of the Left."

Well, reluctantly I did more with the militants of the PCD [Dominican Communist Party] and all of the big leaders that were now involved in that movement. All of them are now representatives. I don't know all of those people that were part of this movement. I also got close to the PLD [Dominican Liberation Party] that was in power. We had concerts every Friday on the patio of the party headquarters. We also sang children's songs. And from these two platforms we built a lot of solidarity with the people, which was important. We built a lot of solidarity with Cuba; we built solidarity with Nicaragua, with the Sandinista movement. We built solidarity with Haiti, and with El Salvador. From this platform, then, I went two times to Cuba, to youth festivals. Nicaragua, a couple times too, facilitated by the same president, Daniel Ortega [Saavedra]. I went to sing in El Salvador, and I went around as an activist revolutionary.

○ ○ ○

Never did they pay me. Never did they value my work in other ways more than someone who could represent their interests. So in this way I was welcomed, and the two parties that chose me at that time were the PCD and the PLD. It isn't so much that I was resentful; it was good for the artists who at the time were very important in this genre of protest music, of protest songs. But I didn't have support. I was not well received. In fact, it was the opposite—from the beginning, I experienced discrimination for being young, for having a good reputation, you know. I was someone very compromised by my career choice. I didn't go with any movement at the time that used drugs, you know, there's always peer pressure. And if you don't participate it's a little like, "Ah, don't invite her to this, there's the other thing." A little "no, no, no, not for this." I wasn't cool, in a way. I had to win my space as a singer and composer, I had to insert myself in a way, but I was fortunate that the parties saw something in this handsome-feminine that I was, that could in that moment represent their interests in the fight for a chance, once again, through song.

This was the environment in which I developed at the university, and from there, little by little, I was soaring to new heights. This included my screenings, television, and such, but always with a protest song. And from there, of the other groups that were movements, like the women's movement, the feminist movement, the worker's movement, the peasant's movement, all of these movements began to see in me the possibility that my songs could reach across class to the people, and so they began to see me as someone essential to the cause because there were almost no women, maybe two, maybe three, but not very active in the movement nor with the clarity of calling that I wanted to transmit—thinking about struggle, about change, for equality, these types of symbols. So, I was very clear about this and because of this: "Ay, here she comes, she's coming." And they opened up the space to me. In this space, I spent all of the eighties singing. I don't remember how I survived because I was never paid a cent. I really don't know how I did it. But I did it. And I lived by myself, I had an apartment, nicely set up, and I lived for my work and I had a job in the morning.

I worked in a popular barrio named Guachupita. I worked in a medical center, a health center. My work was to offer education about prevention of illness through theater. So I created a puppet theater, with women and the people of the community, the doctors at the center, and I did short plays. Every day I would go into the community and bring a message of illness prevention. And this helped me pay for my studies, pay for my house and everything. I worked there for three years; it was very important for me because I could interact with the people most in need. My first contact with poor people, really. People really, really, really, precarious, living precarious lives. That was where I had my first contact with this reality. At the time, it was something in my head: the poverty, the inequality, the food and the hunger, these concepts that appear in the literature of the greatest poets, and philosophies that up until that moment I had only read about. There I had direct contact, and this was a good compliment to my ideas, to reaffirm my ideas, my desire to fight, my interest in equality for all. All of this was reaffirmed in my work.

Like many graduates of la UASD whom I encountered in my ethnographic research in Santo Domingo, Fortuna took advantage of the opportunity to wander through her studies. All aspects of her education would inform her music:

I studied the arts. I took other classes they gave. They offered anthropology, and I could say I have done anthropological work because I have been in contact with and draw my music from my research when I was investigating Afro-Dominican roots. Also, I know a very important Haitian singer, named Toto Bissainthe. I also knew an American anthropologist that lived here and developed the anthropology department at la UASD.

She refers to anthropologist June Rosenberg, who spent three decades as a professor la UASD, researching Dominican cultural traditions that tie the Dominican people to many African traditions. Rosenberg (1979) worked alongside a whole generation of Dominican scholars—Dagoberto Tejeda Ortiz, Frank Moya Pons, Carlos Esteban Deive, and others—who were equally committed to defining Dominican culture beyond the official line of the state and the Dominican elite about the roots of Dominican culture. In interviews Fortuna often credits Rosenberg with this education that changed her. Spending time doing anthropological research in rural Dominican communities and a training in the methods of ethnography altered her outlook and understanding of not only the society in which she lived but also how she saw herself.

With June Rosenberg, the American anthropologist, and Toto Bissainthe, who were great friends, I began to visit the ceremonial centers of what we call Dominican *vudú*. With her and with Doña Rosenberg, I would go and study. I would sit beside them, I would sit beside Haitian singers as well, and we would, as June said, dig into those realities, of Afro-Dominican religion, and all that it brought. Because it brought with it dance, and it brought a worldview, and it brought music, rhythm, the drums, the melodies. All of this for me was a discovery that I enjoyed. Until that moment, I had not had contact with any folklore. Nothing. I arrived at college at twenty-two years old without having exposure. Only what we sang at church, the hymns, and those sorts of things. And I liked to listen to songs of different genres. Otherwise, I had to hear this music during my Cuban hours. I had to listen to it at dawn, since after 2 a.m. I could get radio signals from Cuba, two stations. One was called *Radio rebelde*. So there I was hoping they would play the songs of Sergio Rodriguez, of Pablo Milanés, and everybody, impassion and all that. Mercedes Sosa. This represented the genre of *música de trova*, protest music, freedom songs. I would do it, so that I listened and learned these songs. I remember one time spending a whole month trying to be able to write out an entire song that they put on at night—so that I could write all the words out. I did my best because I could not write as quickly as the ideas came. But I would record and write songs and afterward look for the music, sound it out on the guitar to teach myself the songs so that I could sing them. This helped me a lot too, it helped me become who I am now with all the interest that I have in social justice, in these types of ideas.

So with this work in Guachupita, this poor community and with June Rosenberg and Toto Bissainthe, on the other hand, investigating folkloric Dominican music, basically religion—*el gagá*, the drums. Well, I was discovering in myself an identity. Not something theoretical, but an identification that was very real. Then came the concept: I am black, I make music, all this pertains to me. And later, that I had to preserve this, that I also want to promote this, that I want it to reach more people, that it is my identity, and I want Dominicans to know that it is part of us, that we can encounter it in our cultural identity and in our African origins, and value this, and carry it with pride. This has been a very important objective of the work of *la lucha* [the fight].

With her music and in her political efforts Fortuna was part of a network of activists who make black identity central to their revolutionary feminist resistance. Her consciousness raising came about through an immersion in and discovery of Dominican blackness. Institutionalized narratives of Hispanicity and Indigeneity, as key components of Dominican identity, would have otherwise kept her from embracing blackness (Candelario 2007: 85; Ricourt 2016: 46). Though not all Dominicans who claim *afrodominicanidad* as an identity present phenotypically in ways that outsiders might perceive as "black," the term *Afro-Dominican* names both an inheritance and a bodily experience that Fortuna has described above. Her consistent and overt commentary on race and her claims on Africanness in her music resist the social norms under which she grew up (Whitten and Torres 1992).

As Fortuna shows us, her embrace of blackness has been a process: "I began to study this and I met a Dominican musician named Tony Vicioso. He was doing jazz, and they introduced us. He brought me into the jazz band that he had, and I began to sing his music. Then he began to write, and I started to make lyrics for his music; later we separated." But as is common in the small artist's community of Santo Domingo, presumably much smaller than today, Fortuna would circle back into this collaboration: "We made a band called Kaliumbé, where he made music and I made music and I sang. He had a little guitar and had the band. This was at the end of the eighties—eighty-five, eighty-six, eighty-seven. This all happened, and from this we made an album together." Fortuna's musical trajectory has taken many paths with numerous collaborations—arguably a feminist approach to cultural production—and perhaps this is why she has hardly been recognized as a composer in her own right. Since the 1980s, her artistic projects have been motivated by her politics, and her musical talents have served as an opportunity to respond to the society in which she lives:

> I did this work with the movement of women poets, the circle of Dominican women poets that was like eleven or twelve women that got together to study and share ideas and their poetry. They made me an honorary poet in this group . . . and we did an investigation of the writings of women in the countryside, about songs, because there was already a women's movement, and they were creating women's associations. The women, when they got together, sang songs with misogynist content that were playing on the radio. So they reproduced the values of songs written by men, with very violent content, that was extremely demeaning towards women. I remember that there was a song that said one should be careful of women today, that you needed to tie them up with a rope, and if they chewed through the rope, tie them up with a chain, and if they chewed through the chain, then let them go, they aren't worth it. Something like that. So the women sang this at their gatherings. We realized that they had to make lyrics that women could sing and with an NGO called MUDE (Mujeres en Desarollo Dominicana [Dominican Women in Development]) that we worked with, they had many connections at the national level that worked specifically with campesinas, supporting initiatives for them to have their own land, and an association that helped them to start small businesses in order to have some resources.
>
> So, then here comes me and the women poets. And we decided to offer a contest in which the women would write, and we had the campesinas submit their ideas. There were hundreds of poems written by these women and we chose ten. Then we made an album from them, which we called De la Loma al Llano, which was the first work I did. We recorded it between eighty-three and eighty-four. I think it was released in eighty-four or eighty-five. So we gave the women that tool, those songs with content of their own. When you see this record, you can have an overview of what the campesina women's movement was about then: what their concerns were, and

Figure 2. Fortuna was awarded a Medal of Excellence in the Arts from the President of the Dominican Republic and the *Ministerio de la Mujer.*

what their limitations were, and what their dreams were. You'll find it in that work. This is how I participated in the movement of women poets.

Fortuna proudly describes this moment in the 1980s of a feminist intervention that involved poetry writing with poor and rural women and publishing their work on albums. Her faith in the transformative nature of art and cultural production is as powerful as her personal narrative, through which she was changed by her experiences abroad, the music she could access on the radio, and opportunities she had to organize with others around art and performance that continue to this day.

Rather than a story of childhood trauma and marginalization because of her blackness, Fortuna provides us with a clear-eyed take on what it has meant for her to navigate Dominican society as a rebellious Afro-Dominican woman of her generation. Plans for a documentary film on Fortuna—aptly titled *Descalzada*—emphasize the significance of her life and legacy. She continues to be driven by her values and is a staunch environmentalist amidst a tourist economy in which the DR produces a literal sea of plastic bottles.[10] In 2001, Fortuna founded the ecotourism project Rancho Ecológico el Campeche, an organization and foundation that fosters environmental education, grassroots development, and sustainable tourism in the region. By hosting guests from across the island and abroad at her ranch just south of the capital, Fortuna seeks to promote "respect and love for nature" among those who visit. The space is also used for transnational black feminist retreats organized by the next generation of Dominican activists.

When she had the opportunity to tell her own story to an audience for TEDx in Santo Domingo in 2016, Fortuna signaled her arrival onstage with warm, deep vocals that invited response, and she told the audience that the reason she went without shoes to receive her award from President Medina was simply because as an artist she "didn't have the right shoes for the occasion" yet did not want to miss the opportunity. Of course, it is more than that, she explains; to arrive *descalzada*—to be barefoot on the stage as she has done on several other occasions—is an act of humility.

. . . .

Rachel Afi Quinn is an associate professor in the Department of Comparative Cultural Studies and the Women's, Gender and Sexuality Studies Program at the University of Houston. Her first book, *Being La Dominicana: Race and Identity in the Visual Culture of Santo Domingo* was published in 2021. She has published in *The Black Scholar*, *Small Axe*, and *Latin American & Latinx Visual Culture*.

Notes

1   Her albums, many of the last decade recorded with members of the Sinhora Band, include *De la Loma al Llano* (1985), *Balbuceos* (1996), *Pan Music and Música Raíces* (1997), "Baisabi" on *Putumayo Presents Latinas: Women of Latin America* (2000), *Kumbajei* (2001), *Ella ta'í* (2002), *Tonada Para un Querer* (2004), *La Calle Será la Calle* (2009), *Pa' Cantarte a Ti* (2010), *Son Verdad* (2017), *Rosa y Azul* (2018) with the Sinhora Band, *Canto de Abril* (2020), and *Viendoaver* (2021). Fortuna has produced some twenty albums with ILé Akwa Productions and collaborated with Dominican artists such as Vakeró, Rita Indiana, and AcentOh, to name a few.

2   While I recognize the reasons that publishers have moved to capitalize the word *Black*, I use the word in lowercase to talk about blackness in the Dominican Republic as a social construction that is different from African American claims on Black identity in the United States. I find that capitalizing the term to affirm it as a political identity obscures some of the nuances of the racial category across different contexts in Latin America and the Caribbean.

3   With a limited background in music, I find myself hesitant to write about Fortuna's particular sound; I encourage readers to explore the visual and audio archive of her work online.

4   Special guests included local favorites Raulín Rodríguez, Covi Quintana, Vakeró, La Marimba, El Prodigio, Techy Fatule, Janio Lora, Diomary La Mala, Roldán Mármol, Mula, and Cheddy García.

5   There is much more to be said here about how Fortuna's work has been categorized and assessed by the judges of this Dominican award and the fact that she

won only one previous award for her music before the category for Best Alternative Music was created. She had received a Casandra (what would become the Soberano) award for Best Female Solo Artist in 2002.

6 She is less forthcoming about lesbianism among feminists in the DR, and while she doesn't gloss over it entirely, I quickly understood that queerness would not be at the center of our interview.

7 My conversations with Fortuna took place in Spanish at the recording studio in her home in Santo Domingo; I recorded on my ipad, and for some of the interviews, Fortuna did her own recording on her phone. I transcribed and translated our three interviews and sorted the content in ways that highlight moments of her becoming. Scheduling these interviews required time and persistence, as ethnographic work so often does, and although I was often reminded that my priorities were not always hers, I felt an urgency to record her story.

8 My 2015 essay, "No tienes que entenderlo," conveys Fortuna's sentiments about what information should be available to whom. Our conversation continues, as I seek her permission to publish her thoughts and reflections in this format, and in English, a language that she does not read.

9 Fortuna's experiences of having her body "policed" are not unlike the stories of many Dominican women I interviewed o. er the years. It is something that I, too, experienced firsthand while visiting and living in the DR between 2006 and 2017.

10 More than once, I have seen Fortuna reject a single-use plastic bottle of water when handed to her.

Works Cited

Ahmed, Sara. 2017. *Living a Feminist Life*. Durham, NC: Duke University Press.

Austerlitz, Paul. 1998. "The Jazz Tinge in Dominican Music: A Black Atlantic Perspective." *Black Music Research Journal* 18, nos. 1–2: 1–19.

Caldwell, Kia Lilly. 2007. *Negras in Brazil: Ere-envisioning Black Women, Citizenship, and the Politics of Identity*. New Brunswick, NJ: Rutgers University Press.

Candelario, Ginetta E. B. 2007. *Black behind the Ears: Racial Identity from Museums to Beauty Shops*. Durham, NC: Duke University Press.

Curiel, Ochy. 2016. "Rethinking Radical Anti-racist Feminist Politics in a Global Neoliberal Context," translated by Manuela Borzone and Alexander Ponomareff. *Meridians* 14, no. 52: 46–55.

Davis, Martha Ellen. 2012. "Diasporal Dimensions of Dominican Folk Religion and Music." *Black Music Research Journal* 32, no. 1: 161–91.

Díaz, Rossy. 2018. *Diez años blogueando música*. Santo Domingo: Luna Insomne Editores.

Durán, Rubén, dir. 2015. *Cimarrón Spirit*. Santo Domingo and Houston: Cab 95 Films and Cosmic Light Productions.

Fortuna, Xiomara. 2016. "Haz lo que hable de tu identidad." TEDxSantoDomingo, November. TEDx video, 17:48. www.ted.com/talks/xiomara_fortuna_haz_lo_que_hable_de_tu_identidad.

García-Peña, Lorgia. 2016. *The Borders of Dominicanidad: Race, Nations, and Archives of Contradiction*. Durham, NC: Duke University Press.

Guerrero, Teresa. 2011. "Música raíz, tambores de resistencia: Impronta imperecedera de la identidad." *Acento*, October 10. https://acento.com.do/cultura/musica-raiz-tambores-de-resistencia-impronta-imperecedera-de-la-identidad-7880.html.

Laó-Montes, Agustín. 2016. "Afro-Latin American Feminists at the Cutting Edge of Emerging Political Epistemic Movements." Special issue, *Meridians* 14, no. 2: 1–24.

Liberato, Ana S. Q. 2013. *Joaquín Balaguer, Memory, and Diaspora: The Lasting Political Legacies of an American Protégé*. Plymouth, UK: Lexington Books.

Listín diario. 2019. "Xiomara Fortuna celebrará entre amigos y artistas." August 2. listindiario.com/entretenimiento/2019/08/02/576647/xiomara-fortuna-celebrara-entre-amigos-y-artistas.

Lorde, Audre. 1996. "The Master's Tools Will Never Dismantle the Master's House." In *Sister Outsider: Essay and Speeches by Audre Lorde*. Freedom, CA: Crossing.

Quinn, Rachel Afi. 2015. "'No tienes que entenderlo': Xiomara Fortuna, Racism, Feminism, and Other Forces in the Dominican Republic." *Black Scholar: Journal of Black Studies and Research* 45, no. 3: 54–66.

Ricourt, Milagros. 2016. *The Dominican Racial Imaginary: Surveying the Landscape of Race and Nation in Hispaniola*. New Brunswick, NJ: Rutgers University Press.

Rosenberg, June C. 1979. "El Gagá: Religión y sociedad de un culto dominicano—Un estudio comparativo." Santo Domingo: Universidad Autónoma de Santo Domingo.

Sánchez, Edis. 2016–17. "Xiomara Fortuna: La reina de la fusión." In *Una isla es un universo: Bianuario de la música alternativa dominicana*, compiled by Rossy Díaz and Cecilia Moltoni, 263–65. Santo Domingo: Fundación Retajila. retajila.com/descargas/UNA_ISLA_ES_UN_UNIVERSO_2016_2017.pdf.

Thornton, Brendan J., and Diego I. Ubiera. 2019. "Caribbean Exceptions: The Problem of Race and Nation in Dominican Studies." *Latin American Research Review* 54, no. 2: 413–28.

Vargas, Tahira. 2014. "Xiomara Fortuna, 'solo poemas,' propuesta educativa-cultural." *Hoy digital*, September 6. hoy.com.do/xiomara-fortuna-y-su-cd-solo-poemas-una-propuesta-educativa-e-identitaria/.

Whitten, Norman E. Jr., and Arlene Torres. 1992. "Blackness in the Americas." In *Report on the Americas* 25, no. 4: 16–46.

Constance Bailey

Signifying Sistas
Black Women's Humor and Intersectional Poetics

Abstract: This article explores the evolution of Black women's humor from its historic origins to its contemporary manifestations. The author argues that Black women humorists, including Zora Neale Hurston, the Queens of Comedy, and comediennes on A Black Lady Sketch Show, interrogate the daily and varied oppressions that Black women face. In doing so, they reveal not only the intersectional nature of Black female comedy but also the previously unexplored political aspects of Black women's humor.

With the notable exception of *Key & Peele*, when *Chappelle's Show* abruptly ended in 2006, there was a conspicuous absence of African American sketch comedy on television. Much like *Chappelle's Show*, *Key & Peele* amassed its own cult following while introducing viewers to the comic talents of Keegan Michael Key and Oscar winner Jordan Peele in the process. Almost five years after *Key & Peele* ended and more than a decade after *Chappelle's Show*'s untimely demise, HBO's *A Black Lady Sketch Show* arrived on the scene to fill a much-needed void. Not only does it build on the success of the handful of sketch comedy shows helmed by Black men that came before it, but it also centers the experiences of Black women in ways that no other sketch comedy series has done before. As such, *A Black Lady Sketch Show* articulates an intersectional feminist poetics that it may not even realize it possesses, but this humor does not exist in a vacuum.[1] Black women's humor has a long history that lays an important foundation for the success of the popular series and contemporary Black female comics. Part of this

MERIDIANS · feminism, race, transnationalism   21:1 April 2022
DOI: 10.1215/15366936-9554134 © 2022 Smith College

foundation includes Lucy Terry Prince, Sojourner Truth, Elizabeth Keckley, and Zora Neale Hurston, who would seem to have little in common with the self-proclaimed Queens of Comedy or the comics of *A Black Lady Sketch Show* save for the fact that they are all Black women. Yet these early women used wit to subtly differentiate their lived experiences from those of white women, a topic that has easily become part of the canon of Black women's humor. Unfortunately, because of this emphasis on Black women's daily lives, their wit has often been miscategorized as apolitical; however, as Melissa Harris-Perry (2011: 5) reminds us in *Sister Citizen: Shame, Stereotypes, and Black Women in America*, "the internal, psychological, emotional, and personal experiences of Black women are inherently political."

In her 2007 work *Mutha Is Half a Word: Intersections of Folklore, Vernacular, Myth, and Queerness in Black Female Culture*, L. H. Stallings observes that, "with the exception of Mel Watkins's *On the Real Side* and Elsie A. Williams's *Humor of Jackie Moms Mabley*, Black female comedic tradition continues to be undervalued, understudied, and misunderstood by mainstream critics and Black popular studies" (117). Over two decades later, this same observation holds true. Despite Stallings's assertion, in Watkin's comprehensive history of African American humor, women are almost nonexistent, and because Moms Mabley is the focus of Williams's (1995) volume, she does not engage in a thorough explanation of the contributions of other Black women comics. While Darryl Dance's *Honey Hush* (1998) does an excellent job of compiling examples of Black women's humor, there is very little analysis of this material. Bambi Haggins's *Laughing Mad: The Black Comic Persona in Post Soul America* (2007) and Glenda Carpio's *Laughing Fit to Kill: Black Humor in the Fictions of Slavery* (2008), are important contributions to the study of African American humor, but Black women are not the focal points of these studies. As a result, there is a dearth of scholarship about Black women's comedic tradition. The handful of articles or chapters in larger texts that do exist have not discussed the highly intertextual nature of Black women's humor in great depth, so while early Black women may have used humor to articulate their difference from white women, contemporary Black comediennes offer a vision of their lives distinct from that of Black men. As such, Black women's humor addresses the concerns of Black and intersectional feminism.

Black Women's Humor: A Historical Cross-Section

Any scholar of eighteenth- or nineteenth-century American literature will attest to the contributions of the lives and writings of Lucy Terry Prince,

Sojourner Truth, and Elizabeth Keckley, but most critical insight has focused on the content of the writings. Equally important is the manner in which these women conveyed their messages. By employing humor in various forms, Prince, Truth, and Keckley assumed familiarity with, and simultaneously distanced themselves from, their primary audience of middle- and upper-middle-class white women. Their facetious mocking of eighteenth- and nineteenth-century women's fashion expressed a latent hostility toward white women. Although these women almost certainly had grievances against Black men, when clothing or fashion is an element of their critique, it is specifically directed toward white women. For instance, Terry Prince denigrates white women's fashion taste when she uses signifying language in her poem "The Bars Fight." Similarly, in *Behind the Scenes*, Elizabeth Keckley cleverly uses double entendre and irony to condemn nineteenth-century women's fashion choices through her condemnation of Mary Todd Lincoln. Lastly, the historian Nell Painter (1996) portrays a Sojourner Truth who skillfully uses witticisms to mock her audience. When Truth attired herself as a docile former slave, her audience was often oblivious to the intensity of her critique of nineteen-century American society.

Of the aforementioned texts, this verbal play is most apparent in Terry Prince's "Bars Fight." In *Word from the Mother: Language and African Americans*, Geneva Smitherman (2006: 69) offers a concise definition of signifying when she states, "Signification/signifyin is a style of verbal play that focuses humorous statement of double meaning on an individual, an event, a situation, or even a government. Signifying can provide playful commentary or serious social critique couched in the form of verbal play." This definition of signifying informs the following interpretation of Terry Prince's poem and the subsequent texts that follow. The suggestion that "Bars Fight" was originally a ballad that was later transcribed supports this idea of Terry Prince signifying in her poem (Proper 1997: 17). An oral performance of the text would have included vocal nuances indicating that signifying is occurring in oral discourse. On one level, Terry Prince's poem appears to pay homage to the fallen citizens of Deerfield, Massachusetts, during the last Indian raid on the town. After all, Prince was an integral part of the community, and she was treated as if she were a member of the family, although she was technically a slave (though the preferred terminology in their community was *servant* [15]). If this was true, what, then, qualifies the poem as a signifying text?

Terry Prince's tone throughout "Bars Fight" suggests that the poem is more an ironic elegy than a deferential homage: "Given the play of doubles at work in the black appropriation of the English-language term that denotes relations of meaning, the Signifying Monkey and his language of Signifyin(g) are extraordinary conventions, with Signification standing as the term for black rhetoric, the obscuring of apparent meaning" (Gates 1989: 53). This reversal of meaning to which Henry Louis Gates Jr. refers is evident in several places in the poem. For instance, when she writes, "Samuel Allen like a hero foute / And though he was so brave and bold / His face no more shall we behold," the reader can almost hear Prince's sarcasm (qtd. in Proper 1997: 18). Terry Prince's lines might be best summarized in this way: although Samuel Allen fought bravely, he is still dead. Moreover, his strength pales in comparison to that of Indigenous peoples. Finally, the *we* in these lines is ironic. She asserts her membership in this community, although the very act of speaking about these events places her outside it. Ironically, her blackness and servant status cause her to be excluded from the excursion, and this is the reason she is not one of the "valiant dead."

The most interesting incident where apparent meaning is obscured in the poem involves clothing. Terry Prince writes, "Eunice Allen see the Indians comeing / And hoped to saved herself by running / And had not her petticoats stopt her / The awful creatures had not cotched her" (qtd. in Proper 19). Here, Terry Prince adopts a seemingly callous attitude toward her subject, while still managing to sound sorrowful. The suggestion that Eunice would not have been injured if she had not worn petticoats provides a subtle critique of eighteenth-century women's fashion. In *Pantaloons and Power*, critic Gayle Fischer (2001: 1) argues that fashion reformers "identi- fied fashion (and its attendant evils) as one of the ills facing nineteenth- century American society." Moreover, she contends, "clothing was (and is) a powerful cultural symbol that showed the constraints society applied to women" (4). Although Fischer is referencing fashion norms in the nine- teenth century, the norms she refers to were established during the eigh- teenth century, when Terry Prince is composing this piece. Like Fischer, Terry Prince suggests the impracticality of women's fashion by identifying Eunice's petticoats as the source of her destruction. Indeed, Eunice's pet- ticoats are merely a physical manifestation of the constraints placed on middle-class white women; however, this would not have been the case for Terry Prince. As a servant, she would have worn a more serviceable gown, which suggests that, even if she had been in that situation, her subjugated status would have proved to be her salvation. Once again, her blackness saves the day! Most importantly, the subtlety of this insult is a classic example of signifying.

The subtle use of signifying is also apparent in Painter's biography of Sojourner Truth and even in Keckley's *Behind the Scenes: Thirty Years a Slave and Four Years in the White House*. Painter's (1996: 128–29) biography offers profound insight into the paradox of Sojourner Truth:

> A reading of reports of Sojourner Truth's speeches, including the one at Akron in 1851, shows clearly that she was saying what needed to be said, sometimes indignantly. But her manner of speaking undercut the intensity of her language. To capture and hold her audience, she accompanied sharp comments with non-verbal messages: winks and messages provoking the "laughter" so often reported. . . . The humor was shrewd, for it allowed her to get away with sharp criticism, but it permitted some of her hearers to ignore her meaning. Even today, when Truth can symbolize the angry black woman for most in her audience, others can see her as a kind of pet.

This interpretation of Truth's identity suggests that she was adept at performing for the various audiences she spoke before. Unfortunately, this presentation of self that Painter refers to contributed to a prevailing misinterpretation of Truth as "simple," when nothing could be further from the truth. Joanne Braxton (1989: 45) similarly observes, "This studied deceit echoes the theme of disguise and concealment found in the narratives of Frederick Douglass, Harriet Jacobs, William & Ellen Craft, and Henry 'Box' Brown." Although Braxton excludes Elizabeth Keckley's autobiography *Behind the Scenes*, I would argue that an air of concealment and "double voice" pervades Keckley's narrative as well. Although she claims that she wants to clarify public opinion about Mrs. Lincoln, Keckley casts her confidant in an unflattering light by revealing her desperate financial state. When she reveals that the source of Mrs. Lincoln's debt is her wardrobe, Keckley effectively castigates other nineteenth-century women for creating a situation in which a woman—and not just any woman, but the wife of the president of the United States—cannot be accepted in society unless she is expensively attired. More importantly, Keckley subtly throws shade at Mrs. Lincoln by signifying about her financial state.

Probably the most well-known example of signifying language comes from Hurston, a woman whose writing is as well known for its humor as for its ability to convey southern African American folk idioms. Although Trudier Harris (1996) does not discuss Hurston's use of humor in *Their Eyes Were Watching God*, her observations about the performative aspects of

Hurston's identity as revealed through the process of collecting folklore for *Mules and Men*, might help us better understand Janie. Of Hurston, Harries writes, "She moves easily from being ingénue, to chef, to chauffeur, to collector, to singer, to desirable love, to cultural analyst, to anthropologist, to threatened heroine in a melodrama" (10). These same descriptors could easily be applied to Janie, especially when she transitions from desirable love to melodramatic heroine during her long marriage to Joe.

Readers see this melodrama and Janie/Hurston's trademark humor during the twilight of their relationship when Janie eviscerates Joe in a discursive practice that I refer to as ritualized rhetorical emasculation. While this may certainly involve the penis or a phallic equivalent, it is not a prerequisite. A ritualized rhetorical emasculation occurs when a man invites symbolic castration by deliberately and consistently provoking a woman using sexual innuendo or by questioning her womanhood, so it might also be understood as a very specific type of signifying that is a response to male provocation. The "ritual" is the continuous verbal assault, with no provocation, which suggests a subconscious masochistic desire for public humiliation. When Joe ridicules Janie for inaccurately cutting tobacco, saying "don't stand dere rollin' yo' pop eyes at me wid yo' rump hanging nearly to yo' knees" (Hurston 2009: 74), Janie's rebuttal provides the quintessential example of ritualized rhetorical emasculation. Her initial response was a mild rebuke, but as Joe continues to goad her, something breaks inside her at his continued public insult. When he points out that she's not a young woman anymore, she says, "Naw, Ah ain't no young gal no mo' but den Ah ain't no old woman either. Ah reckon Ah looks mah age too. But Ah'm uh woman every inch of me, and Ah know it . . . Humph Talkin' bout me lookin' old! When you pull down yo' britches, you look lak do change uh life" (75). Janie's verbal skewering of Joe speaks for itself.[2] He's so embarrassed at the insult to his masculinity that he resorts to physical violence because he knows there is no hope for verbal retribution.

Janie's verbal retaliation against Joe is only the first of many steps in her search for contentment, but it is an important one. Harris-Perry (2011: 6) argues that "Janie learns to express her own wit and intelligence, even if her ideas disappoint or scandalize others. In the end she learns that she must preserve herself even if doing so is painful. These lessons are as much about the collective struggles of Black women seeking their own freedom as they are about an individual Black woman's quest to find fulfillment." Whereas the Black women humorists who came before Hurston were trying to carve out their fulfillment in comparison to the white women who surrounded them, by the early twentieth century when Hurston is writing, Black women are struggling against the oppressive bonds of sexism and patriarchy, hence Janie's focus on the men in her life. Black women would continue to use humor to critique their secondary social status but also to try to articulate a burgeoning sense of self-identity.

Contemporary Comediennes: A Brief Analysis of Themes

Although numerous Black comediennes' oeuvres deserve critical scrutiny, I focus my analysis on the *Queens of Comedy* (Purcell 2001) and *A Black Lady Sketch Show* (2019) because, collectively, not only do these comics' works reflect their unique positionality as Black women, but their routines are often in direct conversation with those of Black men.[3] Released just a year after the Spike Lee-directed project *Kings of Comedy, Queens* focuses on the stand-up routines of Sommore, Adele Givens, and Mo'Nique. Hosted by Laura Hayes and featuring backstage footage between sets, the stand-up special was filmed at the Orpheum Theatre in Memphis, Tennessee, and originally aired on Showtime. *Queens* was then released in 2001 by Paramount Pictures, the same studio that released DVD footage of *Kings of Comedy* a year earlier. Over fifteen years later, *A Black Lady Sketch Show* sprang from the minds of Issa Rae and Robin Thede, one of the show's stars. Soon to have its own cult following due to the popularity and hilarity of many of its skits, *A Black Lady Sketch Show* featured the comic talents of Ashley Nicole Black, Quinta Brunson, and Gabrielle Denis (HBO n.d.). Though these comics broach numerous subjects, three of the most persistent are self-image/standards of beauty, male/female relationships, and parenting.

Self-Image/Standards of Beauty

Most comedy routines by women, especially women of color, will feature some type of rallying cry or call for unity, a female affirmation of sorts. *Queens of Comedy* is no exception, as it begins with a call for self-love among Black women. All three women express an admiration for Black women's expressive culture and Black women's bodies. Mo'Nique elaborates on how proud she is to be a Black woman, Sommore mentions the strength and resiliency of Black women, and Givens praises the "average" woman. Both Mo'Nique and Sommore create a culture of acceptance by addressing body type. In claiming that she wants a "big ass," one that is stereotypically associated with Black women, Sommore insists that she is less sexually desirable to Black men because she doesn't have one. This public praise of Black women's bodies is commendable, but claiming that she should change her appearance to become desirable to men undermines the very call for self-love that Queens is predicated on. If, however, we interpret Sommore's statement to mean that plus-size Black women are just as sexually desirable as smaller women, it seems much more progressive. After all, Lizzo, body-positivity movements, plus-size Sports Illustrated models, and Dove ads featuring "real women" were not a staple of mainstream media in 2001. Similarly, Mo'Nique argues for the beauty of large Black women. Her affirmation that "once you go fat, you never go back," "encourages women viewers to reject destructive objectifications in favor of a self-defined sexuality that is uncommon in mainstream American culture" (Fulton 2004: 83). Because body dysmorphia is increasingly common among young people—white, Black, male, and female—promotion of constructive images is crucial in reaffirming Black women's value despite what their bodies look like. Similarly, skits like "Invisible Spy" from A Black Lady Sketch Show imply that plus-size Black women are still rendered invisible in society. Trinity, a chubby Black woman who is the best CIA operative around, is juxtaposed with the svelte Kelly Rowland, whom everyone assumes is the spy but who actually "works in IT." The sketch also subverts the narrative that "overweight" people cannot participate in certain types of activities because they are unhealthy. In fact, it is her weight that allows Trinity to excel in espionage; because she is Black, a woman, and plus size, people are, ironically, unable or unwilling to "see her."

Givens extends Queens' (Purcell 2001) focus on self-affirmation by admonishing her audience to "know that you are beautiful." She further encourages Black women not to be fooled by unrealistic beauty standards displayed on television. Givens finishes this segment by emphasizing that these women are not "real" women because they suffer from ailments that the average woman does not, such as dehydration and exhaustion. She queries, "Now what bitch you know so tired she got to go to the hospital? I know some exhausted bitches. I know some women who got two jobs, six kids, no man. The bitch got things to do." The rhetorical question she poses followed by examples of the "typical" woman emphasize the chasm between the life of the upper-middle-class white woman and the working-class Black woman that she purports to represent. Indeed, "Givens undermines media representations of women with 'perfect' figures. She privileges the lives of working-class, 'ordinary' women—who survive alone in spite of enormous economic and familial pressures—as true reflections of beauty and human substance" (Fulton 2004: 85). At first glance, Givens seems to buy into the myth of the Black superwoman who stoically endures her struggles, but, in fact, Givens may be advocating for greater self-care among Black women.[4] Givens jokes that women who are exhausted should take a nap, encouraging Black women to seek economically viable ways to ameliorate the stress of their lives rather than drive themselves to the point of physical and mental exhaustion. The nap merely becomes one accessible, cost-effective method of attaining equilibrium.

A very different, but equally hilarious, take on the unrealistic standards of beauty appears in *A Black Lady Sketch Show's* "Bad Bitch Support Group" (HBO 2019a), which features guests Laverne Cox and Angela Bassett. The ladies in the support group play on familiar reality television stereotypes of Black womanhood—the proud Afro-Latina woman; the basketball wife who rarely, if ever, was married to a basketball player; and the groupie. Grievances in the support group range from having to "wake up one hour early to put on my Fenty highlighter before my man wakes up" to not ever being able to remove her makeup because the "athletes [she] dates wouldn't know what to do with a woman who takes her cheekbones off every night." When Maya, one of the young women in the group, expresses frustration about not being able to walk around with a flat face (a face without makeup), Bassett, the group facilitator who is also complicit in indoctrinating naive young women to buy into unrealistic beauty standards, asks her, "What's going on under that lace front?" Maya responds that sometimes she wishes that she was "not a bad bitch all the time; like sometimes I wish I was just an—okay bitch," to the horror of other group members. Even though an okay bitch should not be confused with a mediocre bitch, group members are still outraged, express concern for their personal safety, and object to her use of language such as "okay bitch" in what should be a safe space.

Maya further expresses her frustration because she says she saw a lady who seemed content not wearing false lashes. She says she would like to wear slippers without heels, walk around without fake lashes, and even sit down without wearing a waist trainer. The other women are appalled at her desire to take uninhibited breaths, proclaiming that breathing is overrated. They also reject her assumption that the woman she saw without lashes was an okay bitch. Cox's character asks, "How do you know she was an okay bitch? Maybe she was a bad bitch with alopecia." As the scene draws to a close, viewers see two women behind a glass, one who is a scientist and the other is an executive for a pharmaceutical company. The scientist exclaims that Maya appears to be building up an immunity to the "foxycodone," to which the executive replies, "Double her dosage. If women start rejecting impossible beauty standards, we'll go out of business." The scientist tries to object, saying that "it isn't safe; she's already at All Star Weekend level," but when the executive gets irate and bangs her hand on the table insisting that she increase the dose, the group thinks they hear something. Bassett then whispers "is everything okay" into her earpiece. She is assured that everything is fine, and that she should "keep going," implying that the idea of cultivating "bad bitches" is a social experiment.

Between popular culture references such as the affinity for middle-class Black women to purchase Black-owned brands, including Rihanna's Fenty cosmetic line, and the propensity for Black athletes and their fan base to be "extra" during All Star weekend, it is hard to know where earnest observation ends and social commentary begins.[5] Indeed, the two are blurred because the popularity and hypervisibility of "reality" television stars have made images of women like those in the support group a staple of cable television. The pervasiveness of such images through television and social media influencers seems to have moved these women much closer to the norm than they were twenty years ago, if anecdotal observation is any indicator. The sketch insinuates that "bad bitch" accoutrement includes flawless makeup, high heels, designer clothes, fake hair by way of a lace front if necessary, and a deep philosophical belief that women's sole purpose is for the pleasure of men. To be clear, there is nothing wrong with the tangible accessories, but because the bad bitches mention their appearance only in relation to "their men," it is clear that they are not meticulously coiffed or impeccably dressed because of personal preference. The hyperbole of "bad bitch" culture in the sketch clearly reveals its absurdity (i.e., breathing is overrated). Any and everything can be sacrificed in order for women—in this case Black women—to look good for their men. Although the episode critiques corporate interests through pharmaceutical companies who pawn off "foxycodone" on their hapless victims, Americans' inclination to become addicted to prescription medication comes under fire too. Most significantly, the scientist, the CEO, and Bassett reflect those powerful Black women whose machinations ultimately subvert the potential of other Black women. Although successful in their own right, these women are effectively the producers of this "bad bitch support group," such that the sketch provides a metacommentary of sorts. Their success is based on convincing other Black women that the social fiction of the "bad bitch" is a desirable reality. Most importantly, they economically exploit their sisters for financial gain.

In addition to the Bad Bitch Support Group's lampooning of unrealistic standards of beauty, through their embrace of the term *bitch*, the skit still advocates for Black women to self-define. Likewise, other Black women have alternatively embraced and critiqued the terms *bitch* and *ho*. These expressions dominate the work of Black female comics, and "although for many this word [*bitch*] is offensive and degrading, the flagrancy with which these comediennes toss the term about suggests an attempt to dispel the offensive connotations" (Fulton 2004: 86). A good example is when Mo'Nique embraces the term, claiming, "We give that word so much power and if it's used at the right time, at the proper time, oh, it's a wonderful word" (Purcell 2001). She uses the term both as one of familial affection and as an insult, indicating that the meaning is fluid and varies based on the context. Givens also attempts to subvert traditionally sexist language by using it frequently. Despite being criticized for the vulgarity of her speech, she asserts that her "Grandma told [her] that it's not what comes out of your mouth that makes it filthy, it's what you put in it" (Purcell 2001). Here she is advocating for adherence to her own moral compass rather than trying to exist within rigid social boundaries (Fulton 2004: 85). She continues, claiming her grandmother said to tell her critics that "you wash all the dicks you suck" (Purcell 2001), effectively distinguishing between sexuality and morality. Moreover, although discussing her granddaughter's sexuality, the grandmother ironically still fulfills the role of the elder who imparts wisdom via oral tradition (see Morrison 1984). The anecdote, likely fictional, still attests to the vitality of Black women's communal bonds, be they biological or constructed.[6]

Relationships

Not only do the routines of Black comediennes exemplify the love they have for other Black women, but they also reveal their appreciation for Black men. Relationship jokes often provide the funniest and most agonizing examples of Black women's humor because they reflect an ethos of "love and trouble" that displays Black women's ability to laugh to keep from crying.[7] In *Queens* (Purcell 2001), Sommore modifies her signature "ya'll don't know money like I know money" to "ya'll don't know dick like I know dick" to express her admiration for Black men, especially as it pertains to sex. Her subsequent description of her sexual prowess reflects her comfort with her sexuality. Though at times her discussion of sexuality can be explicit, this should not be conflated with pornography because, as Audre Lorde (2007: 54) reminds us, "the erotic offers a well of replenishing and provocative force to the woman who does not fear its revelation," emphasizing that, for women, tapping into the erotic, which may or may not include sexuality, is a source of power. Sommore's monologue functions in this spirit. Another great example of Black women's frank sexual discussions that reflect feminine power comes from Givens when she enacts the ritualized rhetorical emasculation previously referenced in the Hurston discussion.

In the midst of Givens's "Def Comedy Jam" set when she is sarcastically joking about how ladylike she is, a Black man in the audience mentions receiving oral sex because of the size of her lips. Rather than act as if she doesn't hear him, Givens encourages the exchange. After previously saying that "little dick men do stupid shit," she then casts him among this group when she correlates his small feet with his penis size. Givens says, "I couldn't give him no blow job. My big old lips, his little old dick, it wouldn't work. It'd be like trying to give a whale a tic tac. That shit wouldn't work. It wouldn't work." Aside from the laughs at his expense, there a couple things worth noting. Like Sommore, Givens openly embraces her sexuality: she is the first person to mention the size of her lips, and then she suggestively adds that they aren't the only lips that are big. Even when the audience member shouts out "blow job," she doesn't say she *wouldn't* give him a blow job. Rather, she says she *couldn't*—emphasizing that she is okay with oral sex, just not with him because he isn't sufficiently endowed, thereby using this opportunity to chastise him for his public disrespect of a Black woman. Because her critique specifically references his penis, she diminishes his sexuality while reaffirming hers. In this way, her symbolic castration is similar to Janie's public excoriation of Joe.

Mo'Nique also offers commentary on the Black man's penis in an attempt to pay homage to him, declaring that Black women would not dare cut off a Black man's penis because it is too valuable. She proudly boasts that she is the breadwinner while simultaneously acknowledging that she "submits" to her man, even going so far as to suggest that she would be willing to accept physical abuse from her partner. In some ways, Mo'Nique may be embracing the myth of the strong Black woman, which at times is an identity projected onto Black women, and at others, is a "self-construction" that idealizes "black women [as] motivated, hard-working breadwinners who suppress their emotional needs while anticipating those of others" (Harris-Perry 2011: 184). But Mo'Nique's claims also call to mind stereotypes of the hyper-sexed, violent Black man, though her reversal of stereotypical gender roles implies that Black men are both willing and comfortable accepting domestic responsibilities, potentially debunking the belief that toxic masculinity causes Black men to have fragile egos. To admonish Black women to treat Black men like kings no matter what is insulting to Black men and women because it implies that Black men don't have to make any meaningful contributions to a relationship—their mere presence, and their penis, should be enough to appease Black women.

Explicit references to male genitalia aside, Black female comics' admiration for Black men often expresses conflicting ideals as is the case with Mo'Nique's monologue. Their occasional defense of Black men despite injustices committed against Black women is troubling, but in some ways it speaks to the culture of silence that Black women activists and academics have been railing against for eons.[8] Collins (2009: 134) observes that "developing analyses of sexuality that implicate black men" is unacceptable to Black men because "it violates norms of racial solidarity that counsel Black women always to put our own needs second." Inasmuch as this is true, other Black women often intercede, encouraging their sisters to put themselves first, and they develop a sense of agency that is not dependent on a man. Such is the case with Patti LaBelle in the "On My Own" (HBO 2019c) sketch from *A Black Lady Sketch Show*.

Titled after Labelle's 1986 hit, the skit features LaBelle as a fairy Godmother-esque character who appears to a young woman named Denise every time a guy breaks up with her. Rather than accept the end of this relationship, Denise tries to reason with him, saying, "My parents have been married for forty years and they are not compatible." Yet when the ex says, "I just feel," she interrupts him with "Ew. I don't want to hear about your feelings. Gross." From this exchange we gather that Denise might be as much to blame for the failure of the relationship as he is, but she tries to reason with him to stay nonetheless. When he finally says it's over, Patti appears in a puff of smoke complete with microphone and backup singers who arrive shortly after, complimenting Denise on her new hairstyle. Rather than being awestruck like her ex, Denise is annoyed. While Denise is trying to express how frustrating it is that Patti keeps showing up at these inopportune times, her ex is taking selfies with the singer, waving a ciga-rette lighter around as if attending his own private concert, and telling Denise that she should be more grateful for Mrs. LaBelle's sacrifice. Patti does not show up simply because a relationship ends; she shows up when Denise has been dumped, the message being that even when men let you down, Black women have your back.

Meanwhile, Patti is ad-libbing while singing "On My Own" and saying that she "likes him [the ex] better than the last one" who was "too skinny; he looked like a black and mild." The ex tries to thank her, but she quickly interjects, "I said I like you better, but I don't like your ass," effectively put-ting him in his place. She then turns to Denise, saying, "Denise you need to find some real love sugar." Even though Denise tries to dismiss Patti, she ultimately concedes that Patti does have a great voice, but it is time for her to let the relationship go. When Denise finally breaks down and sings with the diva, Patti and her entourage disappear, but not before she tells Denise that she'll find true love and she'll see her soon, reassuring her that even if the next relationship does not work out, she, like the community of Black mothers and grandmothers she represents, will be there to support her. The star-struck ex says maybe they can work it out, but after Patti forces her to literally use her own voice, Denise can confidently say, "Didn't you hear me say I'm on my own. Get out my house!" Although the relationships that the Queens joked about primarily revolved around sex, they were illusory, much like what Denise tries to hold onto. While painful, such depictions are important to remind Black women that it is impossible to hold onto something that does not exist.

Parenting

Black parenting is probably the most common topic among Black comics, discussed by men and women alike. In fact, Black male comedians are just as likely to attribute their success to a strong mother or maternal figure as are their female counterparts, but when the specific household dynamics are mentioned, the discussion is quite different. Although Chris Rock jokes about Black parenting in most, if not all, of his stand-up specials, Black family dynamics are substantial in *Bigger and Blacker* (Truesdell 1999). He says, "If Johnny can't read that's momma's fault. If Johnny can't read cause the lights are out that's daddy's fault." He doubles down on the original statement that it is the mom's fault if a kid can't read or has to repeat the first grade because a mother of two should not be in the club on a weeknight when she has two kids at home. He later explains that if a child calls his grandmother mommy but "calls his mom Pam, he's going to jail." Although such statements reek of respectability politics, the bigger concern is that the jokes oversimplify Black households and make Black women culpable for the failures of Black children. Such jokes pathologize Black motherhood and Black households. This is not to say that Black women offer up idealized versions of Black parenthood—quite the contrary in some cases. However, visions of Black motherhood by Black women are necessary because "no matter how sincere, externally defined definitions of Black womanhood—even those offered by sympathetic African American men or well-meaning white Feminists—are bound to come with their own set of problems. In the case of Black motherhood, the problems have been a stifling of dialogue among African American women." (Collins 2009: 190).

An example from Givens's *Queens of Comedy* (Purcell 2001) routine addresses parenting and standards of beauty. When recounting the scenario of a white woman on a Jenny Craig commercial, she finds it strange that a mother would be compelled to lose weight because her child called her fat. Givens says she too would be forced to action if her child called her fat. Specifically, she claims that she would beat her child so thoroughly that she would lose fifteen pounds. For some, this anecdote reinforces images of the domineering Black matriarch, but the "beating" the child receives acts as a metaphor for the way that disrespectful behaviors (including ones that are interpreted as disrespectful when they may not be) are swiftly and sternly addressed in Black families. Even if she physically disciplines the child, we know that she cannot literally lose fifteen pounds in the process, and because hyperbole is frequently employed by comics, we should not assume that any of the story is literal. Rather, Givens's story exemplifies the difference between white and Black parents, namely, that Black parents have zero tolerance for disrespect. Givens also rejects prevailing beauty standards in this segment, proclaiming that a woman who needs to lose only fifteen pounds is not overweight at all, further admonishing Black women to love themselves.

A Black Lady Sketch Show's "Get the Belt" (HBO 2019b) skit also depicts Black households, but in this sketch, the mother/daughter power struggle in single-parent homes is facetiously mocked by casting it as a game show. In the opening description of the challengers, Tonisha's birthdate is given as born "at night, but not last night," and she has a 6–2 record. Kimber Zak, one of the hosts, notes that "she's been known to knock challengers into next week." Her oldest daughter Reniece sports a 4–0 record and is described as a "thirteen-year-old dynamo who's been really focusing on her obedience and this season she's undefeated." Winning is simply being able to make it inside her room without her mother saying, "get the belt," but to secure a win, Reniece has to resist the urge to be disrespectful despite her mother's provocations. According to Kimber, "many things can lead to a spank out including raising your voice, being disrespectful, or being told to 'fix your face.'" Tonisha first tries to provoke her daughter by asking her for the TV remote, which is clearly within her reach. After easily passing this first challenge, Reniece then has to find batteries for the remote, also known as the "dreaded if I have to get up and find it myself challenge," according to Carmen Sipp, the other host. The hosts point out that Tonisha has the home court advantage because Reniece hasn't paid "na'an one bill around here." After racing against time (there is literally a fifteen-second timer on the screen) and searching everywhere, including a blue cookie tin, Reniece passes this test as well. Because ManMan, Tonisha's son, "worked her last good nerve" earlier in the day, she starts to doze off, allowing Reniece a reprieve from the parental hazing she has endured. The cohosts ponder whether she will go to her room for the easy win or give into her childhood impulse to "watch something she has no business watching." Kimber recalls her own similar childhood dilemma, saying that she took the easy win because "she knew that if [she] didn't start none, there wouldn't be none."

When Reniece opts to sneak and watch TV, the hosts wonder whether her decision to adjust the volume reflects "an embarrassing lack of judgment" or if it is something that could "revolutionize the sport"; when she laughs out loud, Kimber exclaims, "Making noise while her mother is asleep. She's just showboating right now." Despite Reniece's progress, things go downhill when her little brother runs in the house and leaves the door open. Tonisha abruptly wakes, looks at Reniece, and asks, "You letting mama cold air out my house?" but when Reniece tries to explain that it wasn't her, Tonisha grabs the belt and ominously poses the rhetorical question, "And you talking back?" While the hosts are declaring Tonisha the winner, the game show theme music stops when Tonisha asks if someone has shoes on in her house. The camera cuts to the hosts standing in front of a green screen. We see Carmen's socked feet and she says, "No ma'am, I would never track outside on your floors." However, when Kimber realizes that she still has her sneakers on, she decides to break and run, announcing that on the next episode we'll find out if she is "too grown to get a whipping." The skit ends with Tonisha sprinting after Kimber while telling her that she'd better run faster because she "used to run track."

The very premise of "Get the Belt" satirizes Americans' tendency to make a "reality" television show about anything, including the most quotidian aspects of life. This might be the biggest joke of all; however, other commentary worth noting includes Tonisha's reference to her previous track days, which reflects the nostalgia for youth and the tendency to recount these stories that every parent is guilty of. There's also the playful use of popular clichés used by Black Americans, especially Black parents. Because of Black women's work both inside and outside the home, many examples of unique language in the sketch are specific to Black women. These would include those that convey concern about the cleanliness of the home (i.e., don't track dirt in the house/take your shoes off when you come inside), expressions that pertain to expenses (i.e., running up the electric bill by letting all the air/cold air out, you haven't paid any/nan/na'an bill), and those that reflect a bodily expression of emotion (i.e., fix your face). Other expressions showcasing African American verbal acuity and wit include "being born at night, but not last night" and "if you don't start none [nothing], there won't be none [nothing]." Another running joke in the sketch connected to some of these unique expressions is the exhaustive list of things that are taboo in a Black woman's home: tracking dirt in from outside, leaving doors open and letting out the cool air, talking, laughing, or making any kind of noise while she is sleep, the ever-ambiguous watching or doing something that he or she has no business watching or doing, and so forth. The skit also acknowledges Black women's ingenuity through examples such as the recycled blue cookie tin or light bulb box. Rather than being discarded, both items are repurposed for storage, a way for Black women to maximize a limited budget and create something useful from nothing.

Although lighthearted in many respects, "Get the Belt" alludes to some painful truisms about mother/daughter relationships in Black households. There is a palpable tension between Tonisha and Reniece that is not there between Tonisha and ManMan, although he is equally subject to her discipline. Tonisha certainly is stern, even instilling fear in grown women like Kimber, yet only Reniece seems to have a constant grimace on her face. Maybe because as eldest, she is held to a higher standard than her siblings, but this context is not in the skit. It is true that "U.S. black mothers are often described as strong disciplinarians and overly protective; yet these same women manage to raise daughters who are self-reliant and assertive" (Collins 2009: 200). However, "Get the Belt" implies that some of this self-reliance is born of defiance against the perceived authoritarian rule of Black mothers like Tonisha. For Reniece who derives pleasure in sneaking and watching TV, the issue may be that her mother is not a TV mom and can never be: "Black daughters raised by mothers grappling with hostile environments have to come to terms with their feelings about the difference between the idealized versions of maternal love extant in popular culture, whether the stay-at-home Mom of the traditional family ideals or the superstrong Black mother, and the often troubled mothers in their lives" (203). For her own part, Reniece appears to be trying to curb her willfulness and rein in some of her "black girl magic" while retaining her own identity, but striking a balance is difficult when she is held accountable for things that aren't her fault (i.e., ManMan leaving the door open). As is the case with real families, the Black families and Black motherhood in these monologues and sketches are imperfect, but, significantly, these representations are created by Black women and, I think, attempt to express the complexity of Black mothers' lives in a way that is not reductive.

Conclusion

In *Beyond Respectability*, Brittney C. Cooper (2017: 9) challenges us to see "Black female bodies as sites of theory production [which] allows us to move the work of Black women's intellectual history beyond triage," meaning that, once we have identified critical contributions of a Black woman, we should not just move on to the next. Essentially, we should tarry with these women and their ideas because the intellectual possibilities to be unearthed are limitless. Such is the case with Hurston and the other Black women considered in this piece. Mary Helen Washington's foreword to the 2009 HarperCollins edition of *Their Eyes Were Watching God* reminds readers that the most damning criticism of Hurston's novel came from Richard Wright, who famously "excoriated" the novel for "carry[ing] no theme, no message, no thought" (Hurston 2009: xxi). Wright (2011: xxi) further asserts that *Their Eyes* "exploited those 'quaint' aspects of Negro life that satisfied the tastes of a white audience."[9] In much the same way that Hurston was maligned for not offering an explicit indictment of white racism in her writings, the Black female comic gaze may seem myopic when compared with her male counterparts; yet this misunderstanding of what constitutes Black women's political engagement is not just relegated to comedy. Frequently preoccupied with addressing more "serious" issues such as the pernicious nature of racism through state-sanctioned violence against Black bodies, Black men often fail to consider the specific concerns of their sisters. Black women also address systemic racism, police brutality, and equally weighty subjects as Black men; however, they do not address them to the exclusion of their own specific bodily experience of racism. In response to their erasure, Black women have been writing, joking, and "me too"-ing themselves into existence. In this attempt to center their experiences, Black female comics occasionally paint unsettling pictures of Black life, but these images are necessary to complete an otherwise incomplete portrait. In this way, Black comediennes, and the humorists who came before them, are asserting the validity of their voices, and in the spirit of Anna Julia Cooper's 1892 declaration (1998), they are articulating "when and where they enter."

. . . .

Dr. Constance Bailey is assistant professor in the English Department at the University of Arkansas. She also teaches in the African and African American Studies Program. Dr. Bailey is currently working on her first manuscript, *The Predicament of Crossing: The Black Collegian in Popular Culture.*

Notes

1 Although I use the term *intersectional* to refer to Black women's engagement with multiple oppressions, Black feminism, womanism, or even Africana womanism are equally valid and at times I employ these. In doing so, I hope to avoid what Jennifer Nash (2019: 6) describes as "an impulse toward historicization [which] all too often becomes a battle over origin stories, a struggle to determine who 'made' intersectionality, and thus who deserves the 'credit' for coining the term, rather than a rich engagement with intersectionality's multiple genealogies in both black feminist and women of color feminist traditions." Moreover, I concur with Deborah King's observation that "'the necessity of addressing all oppressions is one of the hallmarks of black feminist thought' even as intersectional thinking has unfolded around different keywords, analytics, and theories" (6). These varied historical points of genesis of intersectional thought include Anna Julia Cooper, Kimberle Crenshaw, and the Combahee River Collective, among others.

2 Another popular expression that could be used to describe Janie's insult is "read to filth" or "read for filth," an expression that originates in the Black gay subculture. See E. Patrick Johnson's "Snap Culture!: A Different Kind of Reading" (1995) and the film *Paris Is Burning* (Livingston 1990) for more information

on "reading." Unlike ritualized rhetorical emasculation, which is directed from a woman to a man, reading can be done by men, women, or nonbinary individuals. Anyone can read anyone else.

3 Although the recent media saturation of Leslie Jones on television and Tiffany Haddish in film reflects increased exposure of Black women's humor to wider audiences, this is not an attempt to unearth the intellectual contributions of these women. Other than Moms Mabley and Whoopi Goldberg, only a handful of Black women comics have been given critical scholarly attention.

4 For an extensive discussion of the mythical superstrong Black woman/Black mother, see Patricia Hill Collins's (2009) "Black Women and Motherhood" in *Black Feminist Thought*.

5 "Extra" is to be excessive.

6 See Collins's (2009) "Black Women and Motherhood" in *Black Feminist Thought* for an extensive discussion on the concept of "othermothering."

7 Collins (2009: 165) cites writer Gayl Jones's use of the expression "love and trouble" to describe the blues relationships between Black men and women.

8 Notable examples include some Black women's vocal support of Clarence Thomas, or more recently Bill Cosby and R. Kelly, despite compelling and, in some cases, overwhelming evidence against them.

9 Wright's criticism of Hurston is somewhat ironic, given that Baldwin (1983) would level similar criticisms at Wright in "Everybody's Protest Novel" (1955). Though Bigger Thomas is far from Hurston's "quaint" characters, his brutality dehumanizes Blacks and panders to white audiences, according to Baldwin.

Works Cited

Baldwin, James. 1983. *Notes of a Native Son*. Boston: Beacon Press.

Braxton, JoAnn. 1989. *Black Women Writing Autobiography: A Tradition within a Tradition*. Philadelphia, PA: Temple University Press.

Carpio, Glenda. 2008. *Laughing Fit to Kill: Black Humor in the Fictions of Slavery*. Oxford: Oxford University Press.

Collins, Patricia Hill. 2009. *Black Feminist Thought: Knowledge, Consciousness, and the Politics of Empowerment*. New York: Routledge.

Cooper, Anna Julia. 1998. *A Voice from the South: The Schomburg Library of Nineteenth Century Black Women Writers*. New York: Oxford University Press. Ebook.

Cooper, Brittney C. 2017. *Beyond Respectability: The Intellectual Thought of Race Women*. Urbana: University of Illinois Press.

Dance, Daryl, ed. 1998. *Honey Hush: An Anthology of African American Women's Humor*. New York: W.W. Norton.

Fischer, Gayle. 2001. *Pantaloons and Power: A Nineteenth-Century Dress Reform in the United States*. Kent, OH: Kent State University Press.

Fulton, DoVeanna S. 2004. "Comic Views and Metaphysical Dilemmas: Shattering Cultural Images through Self-Definition and Representation by Black Comediennes." *Journal of American Folklore* 117, no. 463: 81–96.

Gates, Henry Louis Jr. 1989. *The Signifying Monkey: A Theory of African American Literary Criticism*. Oxford: Oxford University Press.

Givens, Adele. 2019. "I'm Such a Fucking Lady." *Def Comedy Jam*. Laugh Out Loud Network, uploaded August 23. YouTube video, 4:40. youtu.be/a6Kaoa_lkeI (accessed March 1, 2020).

Haggins, Bambi. 2007. *Laughing Mad: The Black Comic Persona in Post-soul America*. New Brunswick, NJ: Rutgers University Press.

Harris, Trudier. 1996. *The Power of the Porch: The Storyteller's Craft in Zora Neale Hurston, Gloria Naylor, and Randall Kenan*. Athens: University of Georgia Press.

Harris-Perry, Melissa. 2011. *Sister Citizen: Shame Stereotypes, and Black Women in America*. New Haven, CT: Yale University Press.

HBO (Home Box Office). N.d. "About A Black Lady Sketch Show." www.hbo.com/a-black-lady-sketch-show/about (accessed February 25, 2020).

HBO (Home Box Office). 2019a. "Bad Bitch Support Group." *A Black Lady Sketch Show*, uploaded August 3. YouTube video, 3:37. youtu.be/_7n65rVz95Y. (accessed February 13, 2020).

HBO. 2019b. "Get the Belt." *A Black Lady Sketch Show*, uploaded September 7. YouTube video, 5:46. youtu.be/Fnc5KHSASAE (accessed February 13, 2020).

HBO. 2019c. "On My Own." *A Black Lady Sketch Show*, uploaded August 24. YouTube video, 4:36. youtu.be/z1fNTu6gzg8 (accessed February 13, 2020).

Hurston, Zora Neale. 2009. *Their Eyes Were Watching God*. New York: HarperCollins.

Johnson, E. Patrick. 1995. "Snap! Culture: A Different Kind of Reading." *Text and Performance Quarterly* 15, no. 2: 122–42.

Livingston, Jennie, dir. 1990. *Paris Is Burning*. Lionsgate, 2012, DVD.

Lorde Audre. 2007. *Sister Outsider: Essays and Speeches by Audre Lorde*. Berkeley, CA: Crossing.

Morrison, Toni. 1984. "Rootedness: The Ancestor as Foundation." In *Black Women Writers (1950–1980): A Critical Evaluation*, edited by Mari Evans, 339–45. New York: Doubleday.

Nash, Jennifer. 2019. *Black Feminism Reimagined: After Intersectionality*. Durham, NC: Duke University Press.

Painter, Nell Irvin. 1996. *Sojourner Truth: A Life, A Symbol*. New York: W. W. Norton.

Proper, David R. 1997. *Lucy Terry Prince, Singer of History: A Brief Biography*. Deerfield, MA: Pocumtuck Valley Memorial Association.

Purcell, Steve, dir. *Queens of Comedy*. Paramount Pictures, 2001, DVD.

Smitherman, Geneva. 2006. *Word from the Mother: Language and African Americans*. New York: Routledge.

Stallings, L. H. 2007. *Mutha Is Half a Word: Intersections of Folklore, Vernacular, Myth, and Queerness in Black Female Culture*. Columbus: Ohio State University Press.

Truesdell, Keith, dir. 1999. *Bigger and Blacker*. HBO. HBO Studios, 2005, DVD.

Williams, Elsie. 1995. *The Humor of Jackie Moms Mabley: An African American Tradition*. New York: Garland.

Williams, Shirley Anne. 1994. "Some Implications of Womanist Theory." In *Within the Circle: An Anthology of African American Literary Criticism from the Harlem Renaissance to the Present*, edited by Angelyn Mitchell, 515–20. Durham, NC: Duke University Press.

S. Erin Batiste

Longer, Love

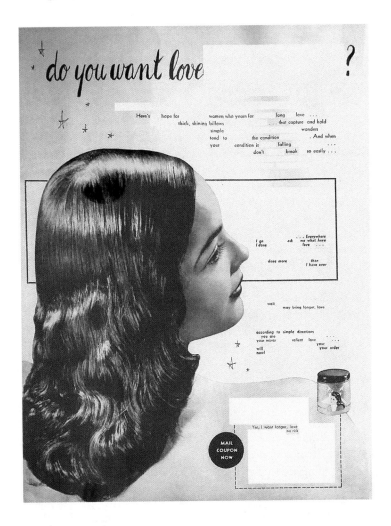

MERIDIANS · feminism, race, transnationalism   21:1 April 2022
DOI: 10.1215/15366936-9554145 © 2022 Smith College

Jennifer Williams

. . . .

Apologizing to Chavers
#Blackgirlmagic's Resilience Discourse and the Fear
of Melancholy Black Femme Digital Subjectivity

Abstract: On social media platforms such as Twitter and Instagram, Black
women create counternarratives to reclaim ownership of their representation from the anti-Black and misogynistic mainstream media. One example of their efforts is the proliferation of the hashtag #Blackgirlmagic,
which has become a device to herald Black women's unseen accomplishments. When Black femme social media users employ #Blackgirlmagic,
they feel a sense of control over their imagery, which contributes to the
hashtag's value as a political product. However, the technology underly-
ing #Blackgirlmagic is bound to corporate missions and deliberate algo-
rithmic limitations. This coupling of neoliberal capitalist interests and
Black femme liberatory politics causes the author to pause and interrogate the political and cultural efficacy of the hashtag. With an Afrofuturist
womanist framework, the author examines the vitriolic responses by
#Blackgirlmagic adherents to Linda Chavers's 2016 article, "Here's My
Problem with #Blackgirlmagic: Black Girls Aren't Magic. We're Human."
The author argues that these #Blackgirlmagic online adherents demonstrate the conflict between liberating Black femme imagery and the self-
commodification of Black womanhood via industrialized content creation. The marketability of the current iteration of #Blackgirlmagic diminishes the possibility of radical digital praxes such as protecting and holding virtual space for unpalatable and unprofitable Black femme affective
performances.

MERIDIANS · feminism, race, transnationalism   21:1 April 2022
DOI: 10.1215/15366936-9554156 © 2022 Smith College

Introduction

On January 13, 2016, *Elle* magazine posted an op-ed by Linda Chavers (2016b) on its social media, "Here's My Problem with #Blackgirlmagic: Black Girls Aren't Magic. We're Human." Her primary criticism of the hashtag is its similarity to the strong Black woman archetype, "the persistent image of a Black woman who perseveres, who survives, who continues on. In pain. In Suffering." She argues that being magical, similar to being strong, marks Black women as unneeding of care and consideration by people and institutions. Moreover, #Blackgirlmagic encourages Black women to see themselves as winners in a game of survival, overshadowing other responses Black women have to oppression. Chavers references the tragedies of Sandra Bland, Renisha McBride, and Miriam Carey—Black women who "failed" to survive oppressive institutions—to stress that the use of the hashtag creates a counterproductive standard by universalizing this magical quality as an attribute of Black womanhood. In such a construction, Black women who do not or cannot speak about their resilience receive few accolades of magic when compared to their counterparts who testify to surviving acts of anti-Black and misogynistic violence. Chavers refuses to identify herself with "magic" because she believes it calls back to the superhuman trope that sets unrealistic expectations for Black women's physical bodies to overcome obstacles easily. To emphasize her corporeality, she discloses how she copes with her chronic illness and pain with breathing exercises and other self-healing rituals and distances herself from others' optimism about her ability to heal. For her, truncating the possibilities of Black women's emotional response to their material reality continues mechanisms of othering, and she would prefer Black women to "be treated like human beings—who very much can feel pain, who very much can die" (Chavers 2016b).

Within a few hours of *Elle* posting the article, the online discourse about Chavers leaned toward the hostile. In 140 or fewer characters, social media users critiqued Chavers's argument, psyche, and politics. After reading the piece, Ashley Ford immediately contacted Chavers through Twitter's direct message program to ask Chavers why she was uninterested in the #Blackgirlmagic project. By the end of the day, Ford (2016b) had written and published a rebuttal, "There Is Nothing Wrong with Black Girl Magic," on *Elle*'s website where she argued that the strong Black woman archetype was put on Black women to mythologize them; however, #Blackgirlmagic was created by a Black woman—for Black women—to recognize their humanity, as they defy the expectations set by others. Ford explained that #Blackgirlmagic "has never been about being in possession of superhuman mental or emotional strength. . . . [It's] about knowing something that others don't know or refuse to see." Many social media users took Ford's approach of publicly defining the term and commenting on the inaccuracy of Chavers's comparison between #Blackgirlmagic and the strong Black woman archetype. One commenter (@Kaidavispoet) wrote, "#Blackgirlmagic celebrates our capacity to survive, to be vulnerable, to excel, to love. Not pretending we have superpowers," and another commentor (@ImVictoriaaRyan) responded, "Idk about her but me and the black women I know & love are all pretty damn magical. We are very different and will forever remain that way."[1] Some commenters accused Chavers of self-hate, and although she identified as a Black woman, they believed she did not support the uplift of other Black women. One commented, "Black writer at @Ellemagazine u insulted not only #Blackgirlmagic but THE iconic @essencemag & blackppl Ur Self hate is real #Elle #Essence."[2] Others included memes—images (often animated GIFs) derived from popular media that signify language—that insinuated they were dismissing Chavers's claim altogether. There were GIFs of Black women dropping something or walking away from a person—indicating the users' rejection of the article. Another directly replied to *Elle*'s tweet promoting the article: "the responses! We need someone to show Linda we're really magic. Someone throw me a disappearing spell."[3] Attached to the tweet was a GIF captured from the music video *No Problems* by Azalea Banks, in which the artist dismissively waves her fingers toward the camera with the lyrics displayed in white text, "poof, poof, be gone bitch." While many posters criticized Chavers, a few voiced their desire for Chavers to recognize that she can embody #Blackgirlmagic. They expressed pity at her choice to exclude herself from the #Blackgirlmagic love fest. Another user wrote, "Please tell Linda that she is Black Girl Magic fighting through and having a PhD."[4]

When I first read Chavers's article, I agreed with the commenters that her argument was outdated. It felt like a rehashing of Michele Wallace's (1999), "The Myth of the Superwoman," and Black women, including myself, were well aware of the effect of the trope on our psyches and fought for many years to heal from its destructive influence. I embraced the "girl, bye" attitude and decided that I did not need to give much mental space to Chavers's perspective. In retrospect, I feel shame in my choice to jump on the bandwagon of distancing myself from an alternative opinion toward

#Blackgirlmagic. When her article was first published, I was a PhD candidate who believed my future success was a measure of my resilience and evidence of my ability to survive despite the odds. I, too, had conformed to a singular practice of Black vocality that privileged a progressive narrative over a human one. Black femmes of 2016 intrinsically understood the need for a motto that embraced their beauty, contributions, and successes in the face of invisibility and erasure within and without Black communities. #Blackgirlmagic appeared as a form of public resistance in which Black women proclaimed the unique and amazing things about themselves and their sisters. Unfortunately, this self-congratulatory attitude among Black women has made it impossible to criticize the hashtag because it sanctions a vocal majority that uses social media to testify about their aspirations to overcome oppressive limitations or how they already have done so as the voice of the community. The vitriolic rejection of Chavers and her argument showed the allegiance of online #Blackgirlmagic adherents to a positivistic performance of Black femme identity. In silencing Chavers, #Blackgirlmagic adherents claimed standardization of "magic" over a diversity of Black femme affective labor.

I argue that social media users strongly associate #Blackgirlmagic with a Black femme performance of overcoming adversity. Black femmes participate in digital platforms to challenge who controls the consumption and interpretation of their embodiment; however, in their digital interventions, they produce counternarratives that unify the spectacle and marketization of identity with their version of the rhetoric and visual power of Black womanhood (Hobson 2016; Perry 2018). Although their personal meaning of #Blackgirlmagic may include a diversity of Black femme experiences, the culture of social media compels Black women who contribute to the hashtag to construct signifiers that conform to the structures of the platform. #Blackgirlmagic visualizes Black women's survival within the limiting and violent system as something aesthetically and affectively pleasing. Users like and follow the hashtag because the overcoming actions of the individuals they scroll through are legible and appealing, while the misdeeds of the state and society are a noninteractive subtext.

Black women's responses to the systemic damages they encounter, such as being silenced, sexually objectified, economically marginalized, and bullied, often reify scripts of an individualized or communal effort to overcome limitations (Whitefield-Madrono 2016). Resilience discourse has been used to explain the methods in which marginalized populations have physically and emotionally adapted to their historical and contemporary lack of protection from the state (Tierney 2015). #Blackgirlmagic rationalizes why Black femmes cling to inheritable magic to honor their adaptability to state- and society-sanctioned oppression, why their liberatory praxis works in conjunction with neoliberal capitalist exploitation, and why they react so viscerally to a Black woman who rejects a script of self-assurance and mires herself in her vulnerability. Chavers's criticism of #Blackgirlmagic is an example of Robin James's (2015) melancholic response. Melancholy does not reproduce identities or emotions that are (easily) consumable; it aligns with traits and ideas hostile to an optimistic-narrative marketplace. Chavers exhibits "a refusal to do the affective cultural labor white supremacist capitalist patriarchy requires of potentially resilient people" (141). She divests from the normative catharsis of "how we got over" and instead amplifies the substantiality of the acts of violence Black women endure.

I claim that the response to Chavers's article reflects a moment of intersectional failure within the Black community. Because she maligned a favored hashtag, the online adherents of #Blackgirlmagic dismissed and chastised a Black woman with a chronic illness who testified about her and other Black women's frailty. I examine this moment with an Afrofuturist feminist lens to illustrate how the adoption of technologies based in neoliberal ideologies diverts Black social media users' attention from practices that aim to free Black femme representation from palatable (i.e., emotionally "genteel") configurations that benefit systems of white supremacist capitalist patriarchy.

Background of the Hashtag

In 2011 *Psychology Today* published a blog post by Satoshi Kanazawa claiming that Black women were less attractive than women of other races. Kanazawa's unscientific study (which was eventually removed from the *Psychology Today* website), along with articles about Black women having an increased rate of sexually transmitted diseases and being the least likely to marry, were a part of a stockpile of internet paraphernalia that sustained the mythology that Black women had no value. CaShawn Thompson, a Black woman from the Washington, DC, area, held a different perception of Black women from what was being distributed online. When Thompson was a little girl, she recounts watching "the women in her family running businesses, raising families, making a way out of no way . . . it seemed like magic" (Ebony F 2017). Driven by her admiration of Black women, she felt compelled to produce a counternarrative to these denigrations of Black womanhood. In response, she began selling T-shirts with the phrase, "Black girls are magic."

To increase her sales, Thompson asked social media influencer Feminista Jones (Michelle Taylor) to promote the hashtag and the T-shirts. Feminista Jones bought a shirt and began posting images and links to articles of Black women's activities, categorizing them with #Blackgirlmagic. On March 2, 2014, when Lupita N'yongo won the Academy Award for best supporting actress for her role as Patsey in Steve McQueen's *Twelve Years a Slave*, Feminista Jones included the hashtag #Blackgirlsaremagic when she retweeted a photograph of N'yongo waving the golden statue over her head while wearing a bright blue dress and silver headband that contrasted against her dark skin and short curly hair. Hundreds of Black women social media users liked and retweeted the image to show their pride in this professional and cultural accomplishment. This social media discourse reclassified N'yongo's win as an exemplar of #Blackgirlmagic.

Feminista Jones regularly posted similar triumphs of representation between March and December 2014, highlighting celebrities such as Simone Biles, Mo'ne Davis, Alysia Montano, and Gabourey Sidibe. Her posts received hundreds of likes on average, a small percentage of her more than one hundred thousand followers at the time. Feminista Jones's campaign and Thompson's shirts gave #Blackgirlmagic the visual grammar that reified the term for wider cultural distribution.

Arguably, #Blackgirlmagic went viral in the following year because it emotionally resonated with hundreds of thousands of Black people. It became a shorthand to describe Black femmes' struggles and achievements, and their unique attitudes and behaviors. *Essence* contributor Bene Viera (2016) affirms, "[Black girl magic is] the sway in our hips, the way our melanin glows in the sun, how our coils grow upward, how we intuitively understand the difference between a 'girl' and a 'girrrrrrl' response, how we feel like a win for one is a win for all." #Blackgirlmagic grew from a T-shirt design to a cultural phenomenon that symbolized Black women's active resistance to the white supremacist capitalist patriarchy that invisiblizes, hypersexualizes, "mammifies,"[5] zombifies,[6] de-intellectualizes, and misrepresents Black women. The number of Black women posting words, images, memes, and links that show their accomplishments, beauty, and unique cultural experiences has influenced Black women's cultural identity and media representation in the early twenty-first century.

According to Thompson and Feminista Jones, #Blackgirlmagic

articulates the possibilities that Black women create despite the systemic inequalities they face. As the hashtag's political message was reified through social media practices such as reposts and likes, #Blackgirlmagic became visualized as neoliberal success. In her book, *Reclaiming Our Space*, Feminista Jones (2019: 93) writes,

> When some people would use [#Blackgirlmagic], it would be to celebrate accomplishments, right? It would be like a gold medal Olympian and some kind of thing like that, so they started feeling like maybe [#Blackgirlmagic] was only for celebrating those major accomplishments, but that's not what it was going for. . . . Black girls are magic is an action—it is an existence, it is a living thing. It is a moving thing which suggests perpetuity. . . . When talking about Black Girl Magic as a thing, as a noun, it almost becomes a commodity.

Feminsta Jones's comment identifies the complication with the marriage of antiracist and feminist intention with internet culture practices. Users, corporations, and social mores all contribute to transforming, and possibly incapacitating, tools used for critique and liberation. As #Blackgirlmagic proliferates to combat misrepresentation in digital environments and beyond, the capitalism, neoliberalism, and individualism that constitute that space can corrupt its utility.

Black Women's Digital Subjectivity

People living in the twenty-first century have grown dependent on digital environments for socialization, education, and interactions with the state and its benefactors. It is almost impossible to delete oneself from the ubiquitous practices of engaging in or spectating on digital discourse. As the division between the real and virtual worlds becomes less significant, social media becomes another location to interrogate how humanity defines itself. In addressing humanity's growing acceptance of becoming cyborgs—humans with digital identities—Imani Perry (2018: 130) notes, "Who we are—is cultivated and exists inside of digital platforms. The self emerges in the context of digital self-representation and communication, on phones, screens, and hard drives." In the lateral move from subjectivity to digital subjectivity, agency in the virtual environment almost necessitates expertise in the performance—or acting in character—of a digital self as well as how to perform one's own self virtually.

Feminist scholars have questioned the practices that signify a person as a digital subject or mark someone as an "inter-subjective" being because they were reared with both biological and digital impulses. In their infamous essay "A Cyborg Manifesto," Donna Haraway speaks to the idealistic complexity of the human/machine composite, and their optimism for a boundless subjectivity because a cyborg identity refuses divisions and cherishes the interplay between manufactured and socially constructed identities. Black studies and Black feminist/womanist scholars doubt the utopian ideal of the cyborg's manifesting amorphous beings and ideologies. When interrogating how virtuality impacts materiality, they recall the genealogy of racialization and heteronormativity and how Black gendered subjects have been misrepresented when they participate or attempt to construct themselves as technological subjects.

Amiri Baraka (1971: 157) warned that technologies—the techniques and mechanisms that extend the human ability to realize some specific purpose—reflect "the values, beliefs, and behaviors of their creators, and the cultures in which they are created, developed, and deployed," in other words, the modern Western technologies evolved from white cultural domination and anti-Black racism (Coleman 2009). He was concerned that Black people were ignoring their own creative impulses while blindly praising the Western innovations that generate their dehumanization. Safiya Umoja Noble (2016) follows Baraka's cynicism of Western technology, expressing that "digital technologies, social media, and computing systems, intersect with hegemonic and imperialist processes and structures that control the distribution and representation of material and ideological resources, many which are based in historical and contemporary patterns of oppression and privilege." Noble specifies that the internet has been marketed to marginalized communities as a space of liberatory expression, where the unheard can promote activism, counternarratives, and cultural practices. She urges for a critical engagement in the material conditions that maintain internet structures, particularly the mining of cobalt on the continent of Africa, as well as the labor of marginalized individuals who maintain user interest in the medium. Over the last decade, research on the online presence of race, gender, and class-based counternarratives endorses the idealistic view of a transformative internet.

Hashtags—words or phrases preceded by a # sign that categorize posts and indicate particular cultural and/or political meanings—have become devices used to network across geographic and digital spaces and coalesce people and ideologies into accessible and scrollable locales (Johnson 2019: 60). Researchers of marginalized communities' hashtagging practices laud social media for being an alternative source for distributing information to those who lack access to news outlets and other corporatized news media. They argue that hashtags allow people to "bypass the gatekeepers" and reach more individuals concerned with their cause or interest (Stache 2014). They claim that #sayhername, #oscarssowhite, #bringbackourgirls, #metoo, and other hashtags critical of in real life (IRL) injustices "do the labor of consciousness-raising" and create an archive for others to engage in political discourse. BlackTwitter—the assemblage of social media users and posts used to construct and convey Black identity, personally, thematically, and topically—circulates hashtags that demonstrate how Black people "subvert normative, linear, and objectivist ways of knowing" and produce nondominant epistemes (Clark 2015; Prasad 2016: 57). Andre Brock (2016: 6) claims that BlackTwitter hashtags, for example, #SolidarityIsForWhiteWomen, #PaulasBestDishes, #BlackSalonProblems, #AskRachel, #ThanksgivingWithBlackFamilies, and #StayMadAbby, are signifyin' devices that resist, disrupt, and play with mainstream conventions and norms from a Black cultural and historical perspective. They "link experiences of Blackness to one another," forming a curated image of Africana relational paths and recognition devices (Clark 2015).

In real life, government policies backed by media have exaggerated and demonized Black womanhood to devalue Black women and justify their exclusion and oppression (Noble 2016). As social media becomes an opportunistic landscape for all those who maintain or challenge the status quo, Black women participate in this grab for public attention to claim ownership over their narratives and images. They partake in visibility politics—the "political engagements with the meaning of Black femmes' raced and gendered embodiment which also intertwines with their access to media technologies and their acknowledgment of power dynamics that frame not only which bodies gain visibility but also who controls how that visibility is consumed and interpreted" (Hobson 2016). Hashtags have been indispensable in the struggle for visibility because they are part of the indexing that constitutes an ever-growing and ever-changing self-perpetuating archive that works to disempower stereotypes (e.g., the Jezebel, Mammy, and Sapphire) and other controlling images that "guide behaviors of and towards Africana women, and profoundly influence Black Women's self-perception"—repeated in the mainstream (Beauboeuf-Lafontant 2009: 22). Black women social media users found that by using relevant intersectional hashtags (e.g., #BringBackOurGirls,

#Sayhername, #BlkWomenSyllabus, #youoksis, #Blackwomendidthat, #Blackwomenatwork, #Whatadoctorlookslike), they could participate and witness how Black women reclaimed power over the public dissemination of their characteristics, imagery, and issues.

While Black women flood media with self-generated alternative performances of Black womanhood, their cyborg subjectivity may contribute to the neoliberal project embedded within social media platforms. Twitter, one of the largest social media platforms, is an application in which users write 280-character messages,[7] or tweets, which are aggregated into a feed—a continually updating list of user-generated content. Users interact with the posts presented on their feed by viewing the words and images and clicking on icons indicating that they like the tweet, they want to repost it or reply to it, or they want to forward the post to their followers. The simplicity of the interface, its user-relevant discourse, and the immediate feedback encourages users to habitually engage with Twitter, as well as other social media platforms.

Twitter's intention is to keep its advertiser clients satisfied. Its business model depends on its users' engaging with and returning to the platform, where they are exposed to advertisements. The company relies on its users to produce compelling content that brings their followers back. Most social media platforms mirror this practice, especially those like Instagram and TikTok that distribute primarily image and video content. Social media companies use algorithms to curate users' feeds so that messages that have many likes and/or are posted by influencers are seen as soon as a user opens the application. Users must scroll extensively to experience content that they find boring, provocative, or subversive, which would take away from the compulsive experience that social media relies on to be profitable. While curated feeds make for a stimulating individualized social media experience, they also falsify the idealistic heterogeneity of the internet. A user has access to a wide variety of content created by a wide variety of people; however, creators must still compete for their followers' time and likes to stay relevant to the algorithm and receive positive feedback. It becomes a cycle in which users copy the structure and style of posts that they like, which then others will like and then copy. The content that becomes widely circulated often is homogeneous because it is easy to replicate and interpret as likable.

Consumerism depends on capitalists' convincing consumers to buy into particular tropes, even using the language of the counterculture to do so. In the latter half of the twentieth century, many femmes bought products that would aid in their mimicking a norm of the slim-bodied, lighter-skinned, young-looking women promoted by fashion and beauty corporations. In the twenty-first century, social media and the heterogeneity of the internet space have altered how norms are promoted. Instead of a faceless corporate body dictating unrealistic ideals, individuals brand themselves for others to consume. Black women then, can and do become influencers who contribute to challenging negative imagery in media; however, their actions support social media companies' intention to make their platform indispensable with imagery and text that their users want to see more of.

Users creating ideal, authentic, and popular Black womanhoods may find themselves in conflict with Black feminist praxis. The strategy to delay or hinder the social and physical death hovering over Black people in a system founded on their negation by ideological warfare (as optimistically employed through visibility politics) is deployed through the marketing of Black womanhood and Black femme bodies combined with the immediate gratification of scrolling through and liking posts. When users engage in the transactional space of social media, they gain a feeling of satisfaction and accomplishment because they believe they are advocating for the Black feminist/womanist ideologies embedded in the posts they like, retweet, and comment on. When others use these posts as templates, they copy the style and structure to brand themselves as empowered digital agents. However, their actions are dictated, regulated, and endorsed by social media companies (Perry 2018). The consequence of this concoction of activities is a Black femme digital subjectivity that is "as marketable as possible" because it mirrors advertisement schemas of beauty and success that align with the neoliberal capitalist mission. Marginalized folks are enticed to participate in "bourgeois individualist cultural forms," such as commodifying their identity, to gain nominal inclusion into powerful, but oppressive, institutions.

Commodification and Resilience Discourse Online

Digital subjectivity may allow users to "rematerialize their bodies . . . and assert the fundamental value and particularity of their embodiment both on- and off-line"; however, users' hashtag protests have relied on mainstream sensibilities to set the standard for empathy and humanity (Bonilla and Rosa 2015: 9). An example of this practice is the unintentional neoliberal framework used in #iftheygunnedmedown posts. Pritha Prasad (2016:

Figure 1. #Iftheygunnedmedown tweet.

62) explains how "#Iftheygunnedmedown drew attention to the ways
media creates racial bias when reporting on the lives and deaths of Black
people and how these framings dehumanize Black bodies." Black social
media users created posts including the hashtag and attached two photographs of themselves. One image included items, clothing, or gestures that
news media would depict as deviant behaviors or impoverishment; the
other image included indicators of success, happiness, or social worth (fig.
1). Their desired pictures included graduation gowns, military uniforms,
business attire, and other symbols typically valued within the dominant
social and economic structures. The racially biased photographs showed
users raising their middle finger, wearing hoodies, smoking weed,
drinking alcohol, and brandishing guns. Despite their efforts to challenge
racism in media, Black social media users unintentionally agreed that
deviancy or unrespectability does not elicit sympathy on the stage of
public opinion. #IfTheyGunnedMeDown and similar digital protest performances reestablished "Black humanity and corporeality within liberal
humanist frameworks of subjectivity" (60).

Since #Blackgirlmagic went viral, individuals, cultural producers, and businesses have adopted the hashtag to proclaim their support of and relationship to Black femme visibility. *Ebony* and *Essence*, two of the leading lifestyle magazines for African Americans, have used "Black Girl Magic" in taglines and headlines to sell copies. In February 2016 "BlackGirlMagic: Class of 2016" headlined *Essence's* Black History Month issue, and the magazine published several covers featuring prominent Black women to celebrate "those shaping our future" (*Essence* 2016). The hashtag seems ubiquitous. Appearing in business missions, academic articles, television and movie scripts, and everyday speech, #Blackgirlmagic has become part of an arsenal that virtual and IRL Black femme empowerment advocates wield to destabilize stereotypes and marginalizations used to dehumanize Black femmes. The popularity of #Blackgirlmagic signifies Black women's recognition of their human complexity through visual and textual media. The use of the tag with selfies, blog posts, news media links, and other social media redirects the focus of Black women's identity construction from reacting to problematic representation to creating and disseminating authentic Black womanhoods. Nevertheless, when visibility is the primary choice for political action against historical and systemic erasure and misrepresentation, it can appear as though Black women are requesting validation from oppressive structures.

Janelle Hobson (2016) argues that Black women—influencers and followers alike—use social media to push Black aesthetics as a form of protest and "to reframe Black embodiment beyond commercialized spectacles." However, their action reflects their "investment in . . . the respectable body," a concept drawn from Evelyn Brooks Higginbotham's (1993) "politics of respectability" and Tanisha Ford's (2013) work on the history of clothing as political speech. As a strategy, the politics of respectability exhibits images of Black life that are perceived as positive and acceptable to counter the anti-Black racism propaganda that often exclusively shows grotesque or downtrodden exaggerations, generalizations, and outright lies about Black people. A consequence of this tactic is that Black people may internalize the validity of these ideas and images of Black inferiority and, consequently, police any identity performance that differed from the politicized "positive" Blackness. Ford's (2013) concept of the respectable body supplements the ideologies underpinning this contentious strategy. She posits that the body is a site of resistance and that Black people have used clothing, shoes, accessories, and nudity to react to systemic injustices. Focusing on civil rights and Black power movement activists, she explains how Black women hoped that, by wearing the costume of the middle class, they could "transgress the social hierarchy of the South that relied on dress as a marker of one's social status" and protect their bodies and image from defilement and exploitation (Ford 2013: 632).

Black women social media users exercise their digital subjectivity to extend how they use their bodies to subvert stereotypes and promote authenticity. Yet, in framing themselves as "respectable" digital subjects, white supremacist, capitalist, patriarchal aesthetic values overdetermine the value of their performances of digital Black womanhood. When *Vogue* featured Solange Knowles's wedding pictures on their physical magazine and website, social media users celebrated. The online picture gallery circulated widely, owing to Solange's inclusion of different bodies and styles of Black womanhood, and because Solange tends to be associated with the "woke" side of Black culture. Hobson (2016) remarks that, while Solange's wedding aesthetic attempted to decouple itself from colorism and texturism, it was still enveloped in the respectable markers of sophistication and heteronormativity. Social media corporations and users associate #Blackgirlmagic with sanctioned examples of Black femmes self-fashioning for public consumption, thus contributing to an unfamiliarity with and erasure of Black digital subjectivities that have not been embraced by the neoliberal marketplace.

Hunter Ashleigh Shackelford (2016) explains the violent reality of white supremacy when Black women maintain a bourgeois, middle-class Black femininity as the exemplar of visibility politics. They remarked that the most lauded examples of visibility tend to be people and events palatable to white audiences and Black grandmothers. The lighter-skin, looser-curl pattern, formally educated, well-spoken, smiling, and other visual and inherent qualities privileged in many #Blackgirlmagic posts and articles are praiseworthy. However, these traits take up a lot of virtual and mental space and affect how users make meaning of all Black femme digital performances. Shackelford writes, "Hood femmes, ratchets, thotties, poor folx, fat femmes, gender and sexuality queer folx, differently abled, and/or neuroatypical folx are denied the same platform or praise for representing or speaking on issues important to Black women." These genres of Black womanhood are often underrepresented in the most popular or liked #Blackgirlmagic paraphernalia, and therefore mainstream media overlooks their presence when attempting holistic portrayals of Black femme humanity.

Social media platforms' algorithms and users' attention spans shape the possibility of an atypical #Blackgirlmagic post appearing on one's feed. On average, Americans spend three to four hours a day on different applications (ranging from fifty-three minutes on Facebook to one minute daily on Twitter) (BroadbandSearch 2020). On their internet-connected devices, they scroll through hundreds if not thousands of user-generated posts and advertisements. Each post receives little attention and time. Posts with pictures, links, and/or relevant and engageable content tend to receive the most replies, retweets, or likes; due to increased user engagement, these posts become highly ranked by the platform's algorithm, which pushes the posts onto more feeds and makes them visible to millions of users. #Blackgirlmagic posts displaying people who exist at the margins of the margins are not as far-reaching in impressions (the number of times the content is delivered to a feed) and reach (the number of users scrolling the content). When these nonconforming Black womanhoods do appear in someone's view, they take more time to grasp because they clash with what people typically like or retweet as #Blackgirlmagic (and the act of scrolling itself distracts users from careful or deep reading). Both the structure of social media and people's online behaviors decrease the variety of Black womanhood stylings distributed online, rendering many nuanced and diminished Black femme experiences subservient to the dominant narratives of their peers who have the privilege to testify how they overcame race and gender oppression within the current system. When people use #Blackgirlmagic to act on their digital agency, they inadvertently participate in a "sisterhood and community that revolves around the creation and upkeep of a respectable, palatable [virtual] body" for status and profit (Ford 2013: 650).

Who/what is represented in #Blackgirlmagic deserves as much criticism and transformative action as who/what is represented when challenging visibility in mainstream society (Shackelford 2016). Black women's "magic" takes on new life in the neoliberal spaces of digital culture because it empowers voices who perform a resilience discourse. James (2015) defines resilience discourse as a type of speech that "normalizes the sexist, racist damage traditional white supremacist capitalist patriarchy inflicts on Black femmes as innocuous damage that they are individually responsible for overcoming. It transforms efforts to resist oppression into practices that reinforce and augment the status quo" (7). As they do with visibility politics, Black women recognize the systemic damage they encounter and tailor their responses to correspond with preexisting strategies, such as inclusion and diversity in media. Narratives that describe individual or communal efforts to overcome systemic limitations are lucrative. Black women who advertise their victories over hardships demonstrate that "with their strong, loud, resilient voices . . . they have the kind of agency demanded of all full participants in the state and market" (James 2017: 29). The popularity of resilience discourse in social media makes it appear as a proper response to white supremacist, capitalist patriarchy "because the individual's testimony of resilience boosts the perception that individuals should be adaptable to difficult socio-economic conditions, and that societal success, requires some damage" (James 2015: 6).

To refute Chavers's implication that #Blackgirlmagic is a reiteration of the strong Black woman archetype, Ashley Ford (2016b) explains, "Black girl magic moves way beyond the trope of impenetrable strength; [CaShawn Thompson] helped us name the unique experience of living in this world as Black women and finding a way to cross that line." Naming the process of surviving and thriving is a useful epistemological practice. The phrase reifies emotions and perspectives that often go unsaid and recovers cultural knowledges to intervene in dehumanization processes. The hashtag gave Ford, Thompson, and many others the language to describe the generations of Black femme ontological choices to reject assaults on their humanity. However, in the virtual environment, #Blackgirlmagic is entangled with the supply and demand of engaging online content. Having a social media presence and promoting one's digital identity is essential for twenty-first-century counternarrative distribution. As Perry (2018: 108) states, "Corporate and commercial digital platforms have become locations where attention and spectacle are mechanisms for participation. Self-marketing is de rigueur to get in the conversation." #Blackgirlmagic monopolizes the rhetoric of Black women overcoming sexism, racism, and other marginalizations (or at least finding personal and community reward) and transforms Black femme counternarratives into currency. Those with the most palatable narrative of pain and conquering barriers may benefit from more visibility through followers or widespread media distribution. Their digital identity performance "generates surplus value for hegemonic institutions," such as social media platforms, and affective value for others to feel catharsis when they consume Black women's achievements (James 2015: 7). #Blackgirlmagic becomes a repository where users voice their oppressive condition and develop the most marketable symbols of their virtual Black womanhood under a limiting framework of resilience (102). Black women social media users may find themselves alienating others who deviate from the norms of an ableist, misogynist, patriarchal, capitalist, white supremacist society because those others perform identities that are not quickly and easily commodifiable.

With her doctoral degree and chronic illness, Chavers could have been an exemplar of respectability and resilience; however, she objected to her identity's becoming a commodity that renders racial and gender discrimination as processes of the private realm and thus outside the authority of state regulation and society transformation (Higginbotham 1993: 203). Her #Blackgirlmagic commentary is unpalatable because she reclaims death, brokenness, and weakness as essential aspects of Black femme humanity and anti-Black and anti-misogyny resistance discourses; Chavers's ideas disrupted #Blackgirlmagic adherents' laudatory social media experience, and they reacted with discontent. With the tools provided by social media companies, #Blackgirlmagic and its adherents appeared successful in promoting resilient imagery as effective against misrepresentation. However, they also established an environment where it was almost impossible to disseminate criticism of such a celebration of conquering barriers because it incriminated them in blindly participating in the marketing of their identity for status. I posit that, albeit briefly, Chavers disrupted the unquestioned consumption of resilience as part of Black femme liberation and made a discursive space for melancholy engagements in Black femme digital subjectivity.

The Fear of a Melancholy Blackness

By the end of 2015, #Blackgirlmagic was praised as the best illustration of Black women's reclamation of their representation and declaration of support for Black women by Black women. When Chavers's article appeared the following year, social media users defended their version of #Blackgirlmagic. Commenting on the *Elle* tweet linked to the article, they posted their own definitions of #Blackgirlmagic and accused Chavers of being a "hater" trying to "denounce the movement" (Mayo-Lee 2016). Others just trolled Chavers with memes and jokes. In an era of #Blacklivesmatter, online #Blackgirlmagic adherents mocked a Black woman's expression of vulnerability because it pointed out the exclusionary nature of a construct. Instead of celebrating Chavers's Black woman voice being published in a magazine that historically idealized white womanhood, the online advocates for #Blackgirlmagic maligned Chavers for publishing what they felt was a divisive criticism in *Elle*. They policed her voicing her nonmagical, flesh-and-blood humanity because they believed it was an "unattractive" performance of digital Black subjectivity. Perry (2018: 133–34) acknowledges that such a reaction is a consequence of the marketplace of digital subjectivity. Sanctioned voices on social media that are manufactured by algorithms and digital culture have more privilege than others because they create wealth for the platform; smaller voices who have new or contrarian perspectives have to find space and purchase in the social media landscape. Sometimes they lose.

Neoliberal capitalism (with white supremacist patriarchy) assimilates marginalized communities' narratives as part of its marketing strategy; it turns around and indoctrinates them with the false hope that, by raising their voices, the oppressed will gain a seat at the table. Those who testify to their resilience are rewarded with social and/or financial wealth. The narratives of these exceptional community members are distributed widely as a model for how marginalized people can achieve inclusion in the current social structure. Stories about being damaged by anti-Black racism, sexism, homophobia, and so on, and personally overcoming these historical and systemic traumas become the idealist mythologies that all groups celebrate, sell, and repeat.

Melancholy is a challenge to these mediated and politicized mechanisms, which declare that marginalized people can thrive within oppressive structures if they perform a mass marketable subjectivity that enervates radical criticism. The marketplace of social media depends on affective labor that is easily and immediately satisfying, be it enjoyable, salacious, or somber. People who embrace melancholia fight against their emotional labor being of value to the current system; they embody and encourage affective discourses and practices that are unexpected, undesirable, or unmanageable to neoliberal capitalist norms of human valuation. They call for nuance and pause in the digital environment. They shame and incriminate institutions and individuals for past, present, and future damage and death and choose "[to fail at dying] in the right way, at the right time, or at the right pace" (James 2015: 20). In her article, Chavers (2016) highlighted how others used #Blackgirlmagic to aggrandize striving Black womanhood performance, which in turn, overshadows the affective responses of those who cannot overcome and die from oppression. She renounces mythologizing language about Black femme experiences and prefers to position Black femmes, women, and girls as just human. In stating that "Black girls and women are humans. That's all we are," Chavers declines to sugarcoat Black coping strategies and opts for candor.

James (2015) argues that melancholy is a queered resilience that produces narratives of damage that do not have enough optimism or that go in unexpected directions. It decouples itself from liberatory futurism and uplift; it redirects attention to presentism of one's material and social conditions. As resilience narratives draw attention to marginalized individuals' successful adaptation to state systems, melancholic responses get bogged down in the inability to adapt and the ceaseless struggle to sustain oneself within such systems. Melancholic behaviors invoke jarring, disquieting, haunting, and other unconventional emotional responses in audiences, who then "judge [them] to be insufficiently resilient" (20). Chavers's centering her narrative on the unique circumstances that impact how she navigates her humanity does not fit Black uplift rhetoric. When describing herself "as someone who has lived with the chronic, incurable illness MS for almost ten years," she recognizes that her condition impacts how she embraces optimistic outcomes. "I know that illness and disability can make the person who has it feel like a failure." She refuses hope in her own instance and denied others from using her narrative for Black uplift.

Her choice to act out of character from previous exemplars of digital Black womanhood leaves readers uneasy. They cannot perform the typical and easy social media interactions when faced with her text (or its marketing). In reaction, social media users took time to ridicule and refute Chavers's melancholic response to #Blackgirlmagic. Many posters' comments implied that Black women should embrace their magic because it is good for the individual and the group. Demetria Irwin (2016) typifies this perception when she writes, "BGM does not turn every Black woman into her own personal Jesus but rather a genuine cheerleader of her own awesomeness as well as that of her fellow sisters. Goodness knows Black women do not frequently get enthusiastic support (usually it's quite the opposite), so it makes sense for Black women to do for themselves." Some claimed that if Chavers had just internalized #Blackgirlmagic, it would help her as it helped them. One commenter (@i_am_eB) has experienced having cancer and takes ownership of #Blackgirlmagic: "As a Black woman that has beat cancer once, and continues to beat another, hell yes, I have #Blackgirlmagic."[8] Another expressed disappointment because they believe Chavers focuses on her illness too much: "If you allowed your magic to be dwarfed by an illness, not only is that sad, it is a marked indicator of WHY #Blackgirlmagic."[9] These posts attest to Feminista Jones's remark that #Blackgirlmagic has been co-opted by a segment of the Black digital public to establish an archetypical reaction to anti-Blackness and misogyny rather than describe a fluid expression of agency as the originator of the term and early adopters intended. Because users employ the hashtag to affirm the group and themselves, any challenge to its meaning is interpreted as a threat. James (2015: 143) reasons that they may "feel cheated out of the cultural work of defying stereotypes with the magic of performed pain visibility and packaging it for other Black women to consume." Ashley Ford's (2016a) tweet directed to Chavers reflects this effect: "People feel you attempted to take something from them without making a fair or strong argument. When you call something people find uplifting 'dangerous' and 'damaging,' it feels like taking." By publicly criticizing and rejecting an appreciated cultural article, Chavers appeared antagonistic to community harmony. To reinstate equilibrium in the Black community, #Blackgirlmagic users chose to bully Chavers into accepting #Blackgirlmagic as a better way of performing her digital Black femme subjectivity.

Chavers owns her corporeality and its fragility. She testifies that she is made of flesh and blood with "bad signaling," and multiple sclerosis affects how she embodies Black womanhood. When emotionally managing her chronic illness, Chavers chooses to cope. According to James (2015: 168), resilient women demonstrate their strength against patriarchy and sexism by claiming "self-love" and care for their bodies. They parade how they "transformed their damaged psyches and flawed bodies into normal bodies and healthy psyches. Body image narratives that rebel against this damage-transformation-spectacle logic, such as veiling/modesty or fat positivity, are seen as pathological, and their practitioners are unintelligible as (real) women." (168). To Chaver's critics, it appears as if she wants to remain damaged despite the availability of a healing tool and therefore is giving up and giving in to her situation. Resilience discourse adopters register her choice as unhealthy, toxic, and/or pathetic. To feign support for Chavers while dismissing the idea that #Blackgirlmagic is problematic, they attempt to intimidate her with their positivity and confidence because they believe healthy bodies and attitudes are necessary to fight anti-Blackness and misogyny. The ableism in the rhetoric of #Blackgirlmagic is the source of much of Chavers's concern with the hashtag, as well as how it repackages Black women's commitment to empowering respectable bodies (Hobson 2016). She provides her detractors a space to contemplate how frailty is possible as a location for resistance. Chavers flaunts her flawed body and its limitations as a fixed condition; it does not efficiently produce commodifiable affective labor under oppressive conditions and therefore is unproductive to the system that wants her to hide her damage and flaws. The exhibition of Black femmes' "getting over" due to their achievements and aesthetic practices coerces Black women to believe they are deficient because their bodies heal slowly or not at all, or they have defeatist and/or melancholic responses. Chavers (2016b) expresses apathy or annoyance toward others' insistence that she should hope for recovery or espouse a normative attitude about her own and other Black femmes' bodies: "No matter what doctors, friends, and family members say–no matter what the scientific establishment says, she can carry around a sense that she did something wrong. She might think that if she'd just done something different, something better, something magical, then maybe things would not be as they are."

Chavers acknowledges that she is not immune to #Blackgirlmagic's positive effect. She admits she enjoys "the sight of happy Black girls and women"; however, the good feeling is fleeting when Black women focus on "Black girl joy." The compendium of #Blackgirlmagic images generates an expectation (at least on social media) of a Black femme performance whereby their maligned social status has not kept them from finding spouses, rearing children, traveling around the world, and so forth. It is nice to look at their empowerment and live vicariously through them. Visibility politics, as currently practiced, depends on exceptional Blackness to open up access to neoliberal resources. But again, Chavers "bends this positive feedback loop into a vicious melancholy circuit" that her audience finds dissatisfying (James 2015: 159). Her arguments reveal that this survival by neoliberal productivity is a privilege: "Most [Black women] fail miserably, by the way; when one of us doesn't, we call them magical" (Chavers 2016b). Labeling what some Black femmes do as "magic" and then celebrating them for it constructs the belief that certain types of survival deserve amplification, since they generate more visibility and accolades that are quickly distributed through various platforms. The distribution of Black (femme) success should work to empower Black people; however, the medium of distribution warps how the information is engaged with and diverts some of the benefits from Black people to the platform and its advertisers.

Black women who succumb to damage or death or promote nonnormative success and aesthetics find themselves without an equivalent or consistent fanfare. In these cases, the visibility politics strategy is exclusionary to the wide range of outcomes to oppression. When white supremacist, capitalist, patriarchal institutions and people damage and murder Black women, many Black femmes take on strategies and tactics to avoid such harm, but falling into death and damage is a valid response that receives less public community support and is harder to perform in digital spaces.

At the end of her piece, Chavers (2016b) melancholically directs attention to Black women who were harmed or killed by state-sanctioned violence, highlighting those who "might think that if they'd just done something different, something better, something magical, then maybe things would not be as they are." She cites incidents of police violence against Black women and highlights the murders of Sandra Bland, Renisha McBride, and Miriam Carey. James (2015) notes that melancholy discourses often labor to resound death and amplify its dissonance. Here Chavers pushes her readers to occupy its discomfort and invest in its difficulty to reproduce labor. In the 2016 moment, #Blacklivesmatter and #Blackgirlmagic are contemporaries in the social media landscape, and yet they feel like disparate ideologies when analyzing the dehumanization of Black women by physical and emotional destruction. Chavers attempts to echo the absurdity that Black femme death is normalized while the best emotional response at the time was, "I'm here, I got over." The absence produced by overemphasizing inherent magic is recognition of not just the proximity of death but also of the ugly feelings that erupt: the morbid, the grotesque, the ugly. If exhibiting joy and gratitude is revolutionary for Black femme representation, then so is popularly exhibiting the affective responses to achievements and aesthetics of Black women who are closer to dying due to inequity, ignorance, and invisibility. To achieve catharsis from the effects of systemic oppressions, many Black women seek treatments such as #Blackgirlmagic. These salves are good and do alleviate external pressures; however, not everyone feels the sweet release. Those Black femmes who cannot be healed by #Blackgirlmagic and who fall into melancholia— they exist, and their discomfiting voices should be heard as loudly and clearly as the voices of those who espouse the "survival magic" rhetoric.

In an interview published a day after her *Elle* article, Chavers (2016a) states: "I will always talk about our bodies having violence enacted upon them, being raped, being maimed. I'm always going to talk about that because it keeps happening. I'm not going to say #BlackGirlMagic when this is going on." I suggest that her article (and the firestorm it generated) lays the foundation for a strike against Black femme visibility politics. If #Blackgirlmagic does not change the regularity of Black death and destruction, then Black femmes should consider non-participation as a tactic of visibility politics. If #Blackgirlmagic aids in maintaining oppressive structures and benefits the status and finances of a few people, mostly non-Black femmes, then Black femmes should funnel their resources toward strategies that invest in the death of anti-Black and misogynist institutions, and not a half-life of a group in which some can recoup their magic, and some cannot. They should "kill some of the joy that . . . contributes to the ongoing viability of white supremacist capitalist neoliberalism, and push their oppression into death" (James 2015: 164).

Chavers produces a counternarrative in which Black femme subjectivity, in digital spaces or elsewhere, includes Black women who are "unable to recover from damage" and fail to perform resiliency (James 2015: 163). She divests from narratives of untenable Black productivity and uplifts Black femme humanity that appears to be a drain on resources or is generally unproductive to neoliberal systems. She highlights the quieter voices of those Black women who may need lifelong health care, die of depression, or call for an end to capitalism and its subsidiaries. In writing "Here's My Problem with #Blackgirlmagic," Chavers embodied an irrational choice to produce uncommodifiable virtual Black femme subjectivity. Her testimony remains neither cathartic nor pretty.

Conclusion

In an interview, Thompson commented that "[#Blackgirlmagic] is for every Black woman—the ratchet girls, the hood girls, the trans girls, the differently abled girls. Black Girl Magic is for all of us" (Ebony F 2017). And yet, inclusive and multifaceted identity performances struggle for visibility when online strategies against misrepresentation develop within corporate-operated social media platforms. A post from July 2018 shows a Black little person posing in front of a cream-colored wall, wearing jean shorts and a yellow flower print shirt. She writes, "Look it's me. #Blackgirlmagic ???" (fig. 2). Many would (and did) respond with an emphatic affirmative, and her likes and reposts have increased since I took the screenshot. By exhibiting her post, I am not claiming that this Black woman presents a resilience or melancholic discourse that limited her

Figure 2. A social media user asking if she is #Blackgirlmagic.

reach and impressions or positioned her as inadvertently maintaining or destroying oppressive structures. Instead, I question why she used the hashtag as a query instead of a declaration of her affiliation with #Blackgirlmagic in the first place; it feels as if she worried the hashtag insinuated barriers to ownership—an aspect that confused Chavers (2016a) as to why she was punished for her definition of the hashtag if all Black femmes own its meaning. This person's question marks and the attack on Chavers are just a few moments that raise doubts about whether #Blackgirlmagic is effective in challenging misrepresentations of Black womanhood.

#Blackgirlmagic is just one possible marker of digital identity performance for Black femmes. However, in the battle for accurate and authentic representation, it is frequently used to combat invisibility in a white supremacist, patriarchal system. When Chavers said she had a problem with #Blackgirlmagic and compared it to the strong Black woman archetype, social media users reacted in a way that showed their preference for a strategy in which Black women resist oppression by parading their best and most beautiful for the mainstream to see. The hashtag echoes the "culture of dissemblance" in which the inner lives of Black women remain secret for the benefit of racial uplift, but the women appear poised and pretty for public consumption. When Chavers expressed her non-magical humanity and her belief that Black femmes may feel stressed trying to embody #Blackgirlmagicness, #Blackgirlmagic adherents responded with jokes and dismissal. Their censorship of Chavers's melancholia arises from a combination of the historical reactions to anti-Blackness and misogyny and the contemporary social media practices and algorithms. The consequence is a standardizing of the characteristics of the hashtag and, in some respects, the construction of a new archetype of an empowered resilient voice that oppressive systems often co-opt. In 2016 social media users took to Twitter and other platforms to popularize "correct" ways of experiencing #Blackgirlmagic, thereby confirming that unpalatable, unattractive, and weird testimonials are unacceptable for Black liberatory discourse.

Noble and Baraka suggest that Black people should interrogate the unintended consequences of adopting technologies created with the same moralities that oppress Black people. When social media users shunned Chavers, they proved their allegiance to a device over their mission to authentically represent Black femme humanity in media. The intermixing of their politics and cultural imperatives with corporate missions may appear beneficial to gain visibility, but visibility is only one aspect of revolution. Black people must envision other techniques and tools that protect multiple forms of affective Black femme performance in real and virtual spaces. The archive of #Blackgirlmagic can serve as a warning that, in the absence of criticism, radical concepts become conventional and Black people will police each other to conform to commodifiable subjects so that they gain access to mainstream discourses.

In conclusion, I appreciate the visibility of #Blackgirlmagic discourse. It has expanded the distribution of Black women's narratives and encouraged the practice of solidarity in social media and reality. However, I fear that digital subjectivities that express chronic pain, pessimism, depression, failure, and other affective states that social media or other institutions cannot capitalize on will find no place in Black liberation strategies. Black femme suffering will be visible only when it is trendy or valuable to supremacist, patriarchal capitalism or discussed as insufficient for progressive Black futures. I question if Black femmes, women, and girls can disentangle the neoliberal marketplace from their digital subjectivities without directing a critical eye toward the practices that keep them passively engaged in the medium. There might have to be a contingent of digital tricksters who interact "badly" with social media to maintain conflict and generate Black liberatory possibilities within the medium (Stallings 2007: 283). I stand with Chavers and contend that a focus on the "magic" of Black womanhood denies Black women the ability to express the complexity of their humanity. In the fight against marginalization and oppression, Black women must identify with the whole of their humanity and emotions—including the sacred, the profane, and the abject.

....

Jennifer Williams is assistant professor in the Department of African American Studies at Loyola Marymount University. Her research and teaching interests include African American women's history, Black queer studies, Africana nerd culture, and Afrofuturism. Her current research interrogates social media practices of Africana people.

Notes

1   @ImVictoriaaRyan, "Idk about her but me and the black women I know & love are all pretty damn magical. We are very different and will forever remain that way," Twitter, January 13, 2016; @Kaidavispoet, "#Blackgirlmagic celebrates our capacity to survive, to be vulnerable, to excel, to love. Not pretending we have superpowers," Twitter, January 14, 2016.

2   @Academicdiva, "Black writer at @ELLEmagazine u insulted not only #blackgirlmagic but THE iconic @essencemag & blackppl Ur Self hate is real #Elle #Essence," Twitter, January 13, 2016, 1:54 p.m.

3   @sendmemyangel, "the responses! We need someone to show Linda we're really magic. Someone throw me a disappearing spell," Twitter, January 13, 2016. 12:31 p.m.

4   @Coach_Thumper, "Please tell Linda that she is Black Girl Magic fighting through and having a PhD," Twitter, January 13, 2016. 12:15 p.m.

5   "Mammification" is the set of interactional and historical racial and gender dynamics that pressure Black women to assume status—reassuring deference to whites, particularly in workplaces. It is drawn from the historical characterization of Black women as innately more capable of caring for others, and the mythology that they enjoy doing this practice freely. Therefore, they are pushed to perform emotional labor in which they "represent, defend, counsel, and console their peers, superiors, and those who work under them, without any additional compensation, or acknowledgment of that labor" (Beauboeuf-Lafontant 2009: 29).

6   Since the 1960s, zombies have been associated with societal fears such as mortality or psychological dehumanization due to consumerism. For Africana people, the fear of zombification has its origins in slave owners' appropriation of Vodun religious beliefs and practices to assert control over the enslaved. Vodun priests knew of a powder that could immobilize a person and slow their heart

rate and breathing to the point that they appear dead. After the powder is metabolized, the "zombie" appears to come back to life. As the undead, they would be forced to work for those who zombified them. This process was a cautionary tale for Africana workers who feared that they would internalize their captors' beliefs that they were slaves—mindless, unfeeling laborers with no control over their actions. While the powder did claim a few victims, it was the consistent and degrading conditions of enslavement and post-enslavement marginalization (such as rape, terrorism, police brutality, hindering access to resources, and other dehumanizations) that created zombies who have lost the will to resist (Ginali 2014).

7   Twitter doubled the character limit for posts from 140 to 280 in November 2017.

8   @i_am_eB, "As a black woman that has beat cancer once, and continues to beat another, hell yes I have #BlackGirlMagic," Twitter, January 13, 2016.

9   Linda Chavers (@BtotheApp), "[Chavers Twitter handle], If you allowed your magic to be dwarfed by an illness, not only is that sad, it is a marked indicator of WHY #Blackgirlmagic," Twitter, January 13, 2016.

Works Cited

Baraka, Amiri Imamu. 1971. "Technology and Ethos: Vol. 2 Book of Life." In *Raise, Race, Rays, Raze: Essays since 1965*, 155–58. New York: Random House.

Beauboeuf-Lafontant, Tamara. 2009. *Behind the Mask of the Strong Black Woman: Voice and the Embodiment of a Costly Performance*. Philadelphia, PA: Temple University Press.

Bonilla, Yarimar, and Jonathan Rosa. 2015. "#Ferguson: Digital Protest, Hashtag Ethnography, and the Racial Politics of Social Media in the United States." *American Ethnologist* 42, no. 1: 4–17.

BroadbandSearch. 2020. "Average Time Spent Daily on Social Media (Latest 2020 Data)." BroadbandSearch.net. www.broadbandsearch.net/blog/average-daily-time-on-social-media (accessed June 3, 2020).

Brock, André. 2012. "From the Blackhand Side: Twitter as a Cultural Conversation." *Journal of Broadcasting & Electronic Media* 56, no. 4: 529–49.

Brock, André. 2016. "Critical Technocultural Discourse Analysis." *New Media & Society* 20, no. 3: 1–19.

Chavers, Linda. 2016a. "Dr. Linda Chavers on #BlackGirlMagic and the Article That Started a Firestorm." Interview. *For Harriet*, January 15. http://www.forharriet.com/2016/01/dr-linda-chavers-on-blackgirlmagic-and.html.

Chavers, Linda. 2016b. "Here's My Problem with #BlackGirlMagic: Black Girls Aren't Magic. We're Human." *Elle*, January 13. www.elle.com/life-love/a33180/why-i-dont-love-Blackgirlmagic/.

Clark, Meredith. 2015. "The Truth About Black Twitter." Interview. *The Atlantic*. April 10. www.theatlantic.com/technology/archive/2015/04/the-truth-about-black-twitter/390120/.

Coleman, Beth. 2009. "Race as Technology." *Camera Obscura: Feminism, Culture, and Media Studies* 24, no. 1: 177–207.

Ebony F. 2017. "As #BlackGirlMagic Turns Four Years Old, CaShawn Thompson Has a Fresh Word for All the Magical Black Girls." *Blavity*, August 29. blavity.com/as -blackgirlmagic-turns-four-years-old-cashawn-thompson-has-a-fresh-word-for -all-the-magical-black-girls.

Essence. 2016. "Essence Celebrates #BlackGirlMagic Class of 2016 on February Cover." *Essence*, January 6. Updated October 27, 2020. www.essence.com/celebrity /essence-celebrates-blackgirlmagic-class-2016-february-cover/.

Ford, Tanisha. 2013. "SNCC Women, Denim, and the Politics of Dress." *Journal of Southern History* 79, no. 3: 625–58.

Ford, Ashley (@ismashfizzle). 2016a. "People feel you attempted . . . " Twitter, January 14. twitter.com/iSmashFizzle/status/687670333592203265 (accessed May 3, 2018; removed by user July 2018).

Ford, Ashley. 2016b. "There Is Nothing Wrong with Black Girl Magic." *Elle*, January 14. www.elle.com/life-love/a33251/there-is-nothing-wrong-with-black-girl-magic/.

Ginali, Elizabeth. 2014. "Zombification Process." *Nathan S. Kline's Zombi in Haiti: Created by Bokor's Sorcery or Drugs?* (blog). sites.duke.edu/ginalisgh323/zombification -process/ (accessed May 3, 2018).

Haraway, Donna J. 1991. "A Cyborg Manifesto: Science, Technology, and Socialist-Feminism in the Late Twentieth Century." In *Simians, Cyborgs, and Women: The Reinvention of Nature*, 149–82. New York: Routledge.

Higginbotham, Elizabeth B. 1993. *Righteous Discontent: The Women's Movement in the Black Baptist Church, 1880–1920.* Cambridge, MA: Harvard University Press.

Hobson, Janell. 2016. "Black Beauty and Digital Spaces: The New Visibility Politics." *Ada: A Journal of Gender, New Media, and Technology*, no. 10. adanewmedia.org/2016 /10/issue10-hobson/.

Irwin, Demetria. 2016. "Let Me Explain #BlackGirlMagic to Elle.com." *Grio*, January 14. thegrio.com/2016/01/14/black-girl-magic-elle/.

James, Robin. 2015. *Resilience and Melancholy: Pop Music, Feminism, Neoliberalism.* Winchester, UK: Zero Books.

James, Robin. 2017. "Post-feminism's 'New Sexual Contract' and Electronic Dance Music's Queered Femme Voices." *Dancecult: Journal of Electronic Dance Music Culture* 9, no. 1: 28–49.

Johnson, Paige. 2019. " 'You Ok Sis?': Black Vernacular, Community Formation, and the Innate Tensions of the Hashtag." In *#Identity: Hashtagging Race, Gender, Sexuality, and Nation*, edited by Abigail De Kosnik and Keith P. Feldman, 57–67. Ann Arbor: University of Michigan Press.

Jones, Feminista. 2019. *Reclaiming Our Space: How Black Feminists Are Changing the World from the Tweets to the Streets.* Boston, MA: Beacon.

Mayo-Lee, Stephanie. 2016. "BlackGirlMagic, A Debate?" *Literary Lovin' Lady* (blog), January 14. literarylovinlady.wordpress.com/2016/01/14/Blackgirlmagic-a-debate/.

Noble, Safiya Umoja. 2016. "A Future for Intersectional Black Feminist Technology Studies." *Scholar & Feminist Online*, nos. 13.3–14.1. sfonline.barnard.edu/traversing -technologies/safiya-umoja-noble-a-future-for-intersectional-black-feminist -technology-studies/.

Perry, Imani. 2018. *Vexy Thing: On Gender and Liberation.* Durham, NC: Duke University Press.

Prasad, Pritha. 2016. "Beyond Rights as Recognition: Black Twitter and Posthuman Coalitional Possibilities." *Prose Studies* 38, no. 1: 50–73.

Ramsey, Donovan X. 2015. "The Truth about Black Twitter." *Atlantic,* April 10. www .theatlantic.com/technology/archive/2015/04/the-truth-about-black-twitter /390120/.

Shackelford, Hunter Ashleigh. 2016. "Hood Femmes and Ratchet Feminism: On Amandla Stenberg, Representation, and #BlackGirlMagic." *For Harriet,* January 28. www.forharriet.com/2016/01/hood-femmes-ratchet-feminism-on-amandla .html.

Stache, Lara C. 2014. "Advocacy and Political Potential at the Convergence of Hashtag Activism and Commerce." *Feminist Media Studies* 15, no. 1: 162–64.

Stallings, L. H. 2007. *Mutha' Is Half a Word: Intersections of Folklore, Vernacular, Myth, and Queerness in Black Female Culture.* Columbus: Ohio State University Press.

Tierney, Kathleen. 2015. "Resilience and the Neoliberal Project: Discourses, Critiques, Practices—and Katrina." *American Behavioral Scientist* 59, no. 10: 1327–42.

Viera, Bene. 2016. "#BlackGirlMagic: Why Black Women Have 'That Thing' and You Don't Have to Understand It." *Essence,* January 14. www.essence.com/2016/01/14 /black-girl-magic-bene-viera-february-cover-story.

Wallace, Michele. 1999. "The Myth of the Superwoman." *Black Macho and the Myth of the Superwoman,* 87–178. New York: Verso.

Whitefield-Madrano, Autumn. 2016. *Face Value.* New York: Simon & Schuster.

Malia Lee Womack

....

An Intersectional Approach to Interrogating Rights

How the United States Does Not Comply with the Racial
Equality Treaty

Abstract: The United States does not meet global human rights standards
regarding economic, social, and cultural rights. In 1994 the United States
ratified the United Nations core anti-racism treaty, the International Convention on the Elimination of All Forms of Racial Discrimination (ICERD).
However, the United States still does not fully comply with the multilateral
agreement. Malia Lee Womack explores the United States' poor compliance
with the treaty's protections concerning 1) Black women's economic, social,
and cultural rights (regarding housing, education, and health) and 2) concerning the U.S. prison industrial complex (its "school to prison pipeline,"
discriminatory sentencing practices, as well as police and prison workers'
violence against women). The author applies intersectional theory developed by Black feminists to UN Working Group reports, ICERD's shadow
reports, and ICERD's monitoring body's reports to reveal how Black women
experience racism differently than men and other racial groups. ICERD
implementation strategies must include Black women's intersectional
needs which are often marginalized in anti-racism strategies. This article
documents how Black women experience compounded and interrelated
forms of oppression due to their intersectional identities. Homogenizing
people of color cannot effectively address each group's specific needs concerning U.S. lack of compliance with ICERD (despite some similarities in
their experiences). Therefore, the author focuses on one collective identity
(Black women) yet also recognizes that other collective identities deserve
attention.

MERIDIANS · feminism, race, transnationalism   21:1 April 2022
DOI: 10.1215/15366936-9554167 © 2022 Smith College

The United States is a leading economy in the world yet does not meet global human rights standards regarding economic, social, and cultural rights. In 1969 the United Nations' (UN) core binding anti-racism treaty came into force and is referred to as the International Convention on the Elimination of All Forms of Racial Discrimination (ICERD). The multilateral agreement has 88 signatories and 182 state parties. In 1994 the United States ratified the treaty yet still does not fully comply with the statute. Scholarship that investigates this lack of compliance is commonly "gender neutral" and ignores women's specific needs. To address this gap in scholarship, I explore the United States' poor compliance with the treaty's protections concerning 1) Black women's economic, social, and cultural rights (regarding housing, education, and health) and 2) concerning the U.S. prison industrial complex (its "school to prison pipeline," discriminatory sentencing practices, as well as police and prison workers' violence against women).

Article 2 of ICERD insists that its member states must "in the social, economic, cultural and other fields, [take] special and concrete measures to ensure the adequate development and protection of certain racial groups or individuals belonging to them, for the purpose of guaranteeing them the full and equal enjoyment of human rights and fundamental freedoms." I apply intersectional theory developed by Black feminists to UN Working Group reports, ICERD's shadow reports,[1] and ICERD's monitoring body's reports published through 1995 to 2016 to provide insight about U.S. lack of compliance with ICERD. Discrimination is not a static issue, and forms of discrimination transform throughout each decade. This article engages with a spectrum of reports published between 1995 and 2016 to document how during these years Black women consistently experienced multiple forms of discrimination regarding the prison industrial complex and economic, social, and cultural rights. These reports, which were published throughout a twenty-one-year period, reveal how, despite the evolution over time of forms of discrimination Black women experience in the United States, there are primary issues that remain relevant as decades pass.

This research reveals how Black women experience racism differently than men and other racial groups and lobbies for ICERD implementation strategies that include Black women's intersectional needs, which are often marginalized in anti-racism strategies. Black women experience compounded and interrelated forms of oppression in relation to their intersectional identities. Homogenizing people of color cannot effectively address each group's specific needs concerning U.S. lack of compliance with ICERD (despite some similarities in their experiences). Therefore, I focus on one collective identity (Black women) yet also recognize that other collective identities deserve attention.

This publication is useful in a variety of other ways. For example, it 1) provides a multiple issue examination of the United States' poor compliance with ICERD's protections for Black women; 2) demonstrates that an intersectional analysis of U.S. noncompliance is crucial to fully acknowledge the potential of the treaty; 3) documents how intersectional foci in the human rights system are marginal but emerging; and 4) describes why human rights in general must be implemented using an intersectional methodology. I contribute to conversations among scholars including but not limited to Sylvanna Falcón, Kimberlé Crenshaw, and Stanlie James, who advocate for an intersectional approach to human rights. Collectively with such scholars, I aim to influence the human rights system to make intersectional methodology its central mode of operation. The pages below demonstrate that some content in UN Working Group reports, ICERD's shadow reports, and ICERD's monitoring body's reports address intersectionality; however, such attention to intersectionality is limited. I, therefore, also apply an intersectional feminist analysis to content in the reports as well as in ICERD that does not explicitly address intersectionality. While such content may not explicitly address intersectionality, the content applies to Black women's specific needs. Therefore, I argue for a more robust interpretation of human rights to account for intersectionality and to more fully meet ICERD's potential.

Intersectionality as Methodology

In the United States in the 1960s and 1970s, Black feminists collectively organized from the grassroots to highlight the compounded and interconnected discrimination they experience toward their race, gender, sexuality, and social class (Collins 2015). They constructed and dispersed poetry, publications, edited volumes, pamphlets, essays, and other creative works to draw attention to compounded discrimination they endured (Collins 2015). By 1977 the Combahee River Collective (a Black lesbian organization that arose from the movement) published the influential and extensively cited Combahee River Collective Statement. The statement insists that racism, classism, patriarchy, and homophobia must be addressed simultaneously because they are inextricably linked and that anti-racism or anti-sexism strategies that do not focus on these issues ineffectively address Black women's needs (Collins 2015). In 1991 African American law professor Kimberlé Crenshaw (1991) built on this movement and coined the term *intersectionality* to refer to intersecting forms of discrimination. Crenshaw acknowledges that she is not the founder of an intersectional analysis (despite often being accredited as such) and instead situates her work within the historical grassroots movement among Black feminists (Hong 2015; Collins 2015; Collins 2019). Crenshaw and the Combahee River Collective have prompted diverse academic disciplines to incorporate an intersectional methodological approach in their fields. Gender studies scholars, for example, commonly utilize an intersectional approach and in some cases expand their analysis beyond the intersections of race, gender, social class, and/or sexuality. Some gender studies scholars, for instance, include dis/abilities, age, sex, religion, skin color, ethnicity, geographical location, immigration status, country of origin, language(s), body type, family history, family design, experiences with gender-based violence, and/or other defining traits. In fact, in 2017 the National Women's Studies Association (NWSA) aimed to commemorate the Combahee River Collective Statement's influence and thus titled its annual conference "Forty Years after Combahee: Feminist Scholars and Activists Engage the Movement for Black Lives."

Intersectionality as methodology means that mono-categorical investigations into discrimination are not inclusive because discrimination is experienced by individuals in multiplicity. Identity traits are not unitary or mutually exclusive entities; rather, they interlock, and each human experiences their identity traits concurrently in systems of power. Depending on their intersectional identity, individuals experience multiple forms of oppression simultaneously, multiple forms of privilege simultaneously, or multiple forms of privilege and oppression simultaneously. All humans are intersectional beings. For example, Black lesbians experience compounded oppression regarding their race, sexuality, and gender; heterosexual Chicanas experience heterosexual privilege while simultaneously experiencing compounded ethnic and gender oppression; in comparison, white heterosexual males experience multiple forms of privilege concurrently because of their race, sexuality, and gender. Likewise, while there are profound trends in collective identities' experiences with discrimination and/or privilege, every human's experience is partially unique in relation to their unique individual lives. People's experiences in power hierarchies are also context specific. While they may normatively experience compounded forms of oppression or privilege, there are some contexts in which this experience is reduced and other contexts where the experience is magnified.

Identity traits are also fluid/not fixed because they are constantly reconstructed and reinterpreted because of historical, social, economic, political, legal, structural, institutional, and ideological transformations and influences. The transformations and influences impact how identity traits are experienced, perceived, and treated in identity-based power hierarchies. I utilize an intersectional methodology to argue that adverse interconnected legal, institutional, political, and ideological constructions of and treatment toward Black women must transform in the United States. ICERD can be a resource for this transformation.

Mainstreaming Intersectionality into Human Rights

International human rights treaties are not static. They are constantly reinterpreted and new understandings of human rights are constantly discovered. Stanlie James (2002), a Black feminisms scholar, describes how human rights are social constructions that manifest in various ways in relation to systems of power and temporal settings in which they exist. James notes that since human rights are always evolving, they can be used as tools to expose not yet recognized forms of domination and exploitation.

Kimberlé Crenshaw (1989) insists human rights violations are not mutually exclusive and are often experienced concurrently, and thus human rights institutions and instruments must adopt an intersectional approach. She argues that the human rights system does not comprehensively address racial discrimination or gender discrimination because it does not effectively acknowledge the interconnected nature of such discrimination. In agreement, a prominent Black feminist scholar Patricia Hill Collins (2015) criticizes that the founding 1948 Universal Declaration of Human Rights (UDHR) is not intersectional: the UDHR mandates that everyone must be equally protected by the document (regardless of their race, skin color, sex, language, religion, political affiliation, national origin, or other traits) yet does not examine these traits in relation to one another. Similarly, the United Nations' core racial equality treaty, ICERD, is underused to lobby for policy changes regarding Black women. The treaty's purpose is to protect against discrimination (anti-racism); thus the treaty must also not be a force for discrimination (sexism) by centering men's needs. To deepen its commitment to combat racial discrimination, ICERD must address how Black women's experiences with racism are gendered (Crenshaw 1989). Likewise, the United Nations' core gender equality treaty, the Convention on the Elimination of All Forms of Discrimination Against Women (CEDAW), must integrate an intersectional approach to address how women of diverse intersectional identities uniquely experience gender discrimination.

Transnational feminist efforts are beginning to draw attention to intersectionality in human rights discourse. For instance, Sylvanna Falcon (2016), a human rights scholar, describes how feminist activists of color from the late 1990s onward encouraged the United Nations to address how racism, sexism, classism, and geographical location are interconnected in systems of power. Crenshaw (2002) contributed to recognizing intersectionality in human rights in a UN background paper she wrote that examines the intersections of race, gender, and human rights. Conversations about intersectionality likewise emerged at the Beijing World Conference on Women, the Durban World Conference against Racism, in CEDAW's monitoring body reports, and in United Nations Development Fund for Women reports (McDougall 2002; Crenshaw 2002; Crooms 2003; Chow 2016).

ICERD's monitoring body also finds that racial inequality is in some cases gendered. For example, ICERD's committee published General Recommendation 25, which pinpoints circumstances in which women are uniquely impacted by racism in ways that intersect with sexism in the public and private spheres, physical and sexual violence, employment discrimination, and institutionalized power frameworks (CERD 2001). Monitoring bodies for individual treaties, including ICERD, publish general recommendations that advise UN member states about how the treaty in question should be interpreted. U.S. Constitutional amendments may be supplemental to or interwoven directly into the Constitution. In contrast, general recommendations exist as separate publications that each treaty's committee produces to provide insight about how the treaty should be interpreted. Articles in treaties are sometimes vague and/or broad; thus general recommendations more succinctly advise what the treaty's mandates require. ICERD, despite being the United Nations' core anti-racism treaty, does not explicitly address gender. Similarly, CEDAW, the United Nations' core gender equality treaty does not explicitly address race. However, since racial inequality is gendered, ICERD's committee's General Recommendation 25 advises that ICERD implementation strategies must be gender sensitive.

Despite the achievements noted above, human rights mechanisms are only slowly beginning to recognize intersectionality (de Beco 2020). Human rights continue to fail to adequality address intersectionality at length. Crenshaw (2002) as well as James (2002) agree that ICERD and CEDAW are not effectively addressed through an intersectional lens. Crenshaw (2002) insists that intersectional protocols designed to interpret the treaties must be developed that examine the intersections between racism and sexism to more adequality address Black women's intersectional needs. Likewise, James (2002) criticizes how human rights data has commonly been disaggregated by race and gender, yet this approach must be revised to more effectively collect nuanced data about Black women's experiences with human rights violations.

Loretta Ross (2017), a prominent African American activist, insists human rights are the end goal, yet intersectionality should be the process to reach this goal. She contends that human rights are universal and indivisible yet should be approached and interpreted through an intersectional lens to account for differences in human experiences. Intersectional theory should be put into practice in the operationalization/implementation of human rights to reconceptualize rights abuses in more inclusive manners (Bond, 2003; Wing 1997). Mainstreaming an intersectional approach in the human rights system will inspire new forms of identity politics, community organizing, information sharing, coalition building, allyship, and resource mobilization, all of which can combat interrelated systems of oppression and will enable human rights to become more inclusive, comprehensive, and robust.

Human Rights Contextualized

Nation-states have profound power over how human rights are operationalized into their national contexts. UN members co-construct human rights treaties, then individually decide 1) which treaties they will ratify, 2) how they will modify the treaties to suit their national preferences, and 3) how they will implement the multilateral agreements if at all. Therefore, ratification is predominantly a symbolic commitment without efficient global regulatory mechanisms to enforce the treaties and often with minimal intention by states to implement the multilateral agreements. Nation-states are also commonly the primary violator of their residents' human rights, despite being provided the responsibility to define and implement their human rights. Treaties' monitoring bodies' reports, nongovernmental organizations' shadow reports, scholarly works (such as this publication), and international pressure work to shame nation-states to comply with human rights treaties (Dietrich and Murdie 2017; Vadlamannati, Janz, and Berntsen 2018).

However, nation-states still resist treaties' mandates. The U.S. ratification of ICERD was primarily symbolic. The United States ratified ICERD with a series of Reservations, Understandings, and Declarations (RUDs) that conflict with some of the treaty's requirements. When a state submits a reservation to a treaty, it asserts that it is not accountable to the provision in question (Herndon 2013). States submit an understanding to describe (often inaccurately) a general international consensus on a particular provision's meaning (Herndon 2013). States submit declarations to describe how the state regards itself in relation to a provision (Herndon 2013). When the United States ratified ICERD, it submitted 3 reservations (about freedom of speech, private conduct, and resisting the International Court of Justice's power), one understanding (protecting states' power in federalism), and one declaration (that insists the treaty is not self-executing) (Herndon 2013). ICERD's monitoring body urges the United States to withdraw or narrow the scope of some of its RUDs such as those related to private conduct and freedom of speech (Herndon 2013).

The United States rarely ratifies human rights treaties, and when it does (as do some other nation-states), it declares that the treaties are not self-executing. Expectedly, the U.S. declared ICERD is not self-executing. In other words, this means the convention will not be directly applied in courts unless domestic legislation is first implemented related to the treaty. Moreover, when the United States ratifies multilateral human rights agreements, it modifies them with extensive RUDs. The Harvard law professor Jack Goldsmith (2005) contends that extensive U.S. RUDs are not out of the norm compared to other liberal democracies.

The United States insists to ICERD's monitoring body that its Constitution, Bill of Rights, and domestic laws sufficiently fulfill the statute's expectations (Harris 2008; Herndon 2013). Congress reported to ICERD's committee that "U.S. law is in conformity with the obligations assumed by the United States under the treaty" and that U.S. "policies and government institutions are fully consistent with the provisions of the Convention" (U.S. Department of State 2000: 4). The United States asserts that Congress has implemented anti-racism policies since 1863 (when slavery was abolished) and thus "the principle of non-discrimination is central to governmental policy throughout the country" (United States 2000: 4–7). While some of the United States' policies comply with the treaty, language noted above such as "U.S. law is in conformity" and U.S. "policies and government institutions are fully consistent" with ICERD is dubious. Such sweeping generalizations are fallible and do not account for specific areas in which the United States is not compliant with the treaty. The United States does not acknowledge, for example, that its institutions are systematically racist and instead blames individuals, select states' behaviors, and individual courts for perpetuating racism (United States 2000).

While the United States did not intend to extensively change its domestic policies when it ratified ICERD, it has repeatedly urged other governments to sanction the statute to remedy their racist practices (Herndon 2013). Goldsmith (2005) contends that the United States is an enthusiastic supporter of human rights. However, the United States' "support" for human rights is questionable because the support is generally unilateral. The United States rarely incorporates human rights treaties in its domestic operations, yet in some cases coerces particular states to comply with human rights mandates. For example, the United States may wield its influence over states' human rights practices by minimizing its economic exchanges related to aid, foreign investment, and trade with those states (Ignatieff 2005). The United States strives to coerce some states to comply with human rights statutes while not holding itself entirely accountable to those statutes. The U.S., for instance, participated in negotiations of the Rome Statute to establish the International Criminal Court in 1998; however, it is not a signatory to the multilateral agreement (Ignatieff 2005). Likewise, the United States participated in negotiating the Land Mines Treaty but "sought exemption for [U.S.] military production and deployment of land mines in the Korean Peninsula" (4). Therefore, the U.S. government views itself as exceptional to human rights law, misleads a global community about its human rights obligations, judges other countries for not respecting human rights norms despite not holding itself entirely accountable to them, and hinders the United States' international credibility regarding human rights (Mayer 1996).

Changes in U.S. administrations is another significant obstacle to implementing human rights treaties in the United States. Each administration's support and/or lack of support for human rights vary. Thus, it is difficult in the United States to follow through with substantial implementation of human rights. Some administrations extensively resist human rights while others have demonstrated support for some human rights initiatives. The Carter administration, for example, advocated for human rights domestically as well as internationally. Administrations that followed (such as the Reagan administration) were often not as supportive of human rights. In fact, some administrations advocated for human rights violations. For example, post 9/11 the Bush administration developed "anti-terrorism" policies that condoned and practiced torture and detention without judicial review (Soohoo and Stolz 2008). The Obama administration, in contrast, expressed its commitment to implement U.S. treaty obligations and also appointed a cabinet-level U.S. ambassador to the United Nations (Crooms 2010). The Trump administration, unfortunately, counteracted much of the Obama administration's progress, withdrew from the UN Human Rights Council, and aggressively distanced the United States from UN human rights institutions in general. Regardless which administration is in charge, for the United States to ratify a human rights treaty, two-thirds of the Senate must vote in favor of the multilateral agreement. This requirement commonly produces slow or no ratification of human rights statutes.

The United States' Stance on Economic, Social, and Cultural Rights

The United States is a leading economy in the world yet does not meet global human rights standards regarding economic, social, and cultural rights (United Nations Working Group 2015).[2] The United States is a signatory to the International Covenant on Economic, Social and Cultural Rights (ICESCR)[3] but has yet to ratify the treaty and thus globally declares that it is not accountable to these types of rights. The United States favors civil and political rights over economic, social, and cultural rights, especially taking into account that the latter set of rights require substantially more expansive government action and resources than the first set of rights. "The U.S. government attempts to discursively disassociate 'prohibit' from 'provide' by suggesting that legally prohibiting discrimination does not need to accompany concerted efforts to ensure the meaningful fulfillment of all incarnations of human rights" (Falcón 2011: 58). In fact, this approach is a fundamental principle in interpretations of the U.S. Constitution (Bandes 1990). A prominent Black feminist legal scholar, Patricia Williams (1991), argues that U.S. failure to recognize the right to, for example, shelter, health, and education (which disproportionately impacts women, children, and communities of color) is a failure to recognize the right to survive and instead assumes these are a matter of "choice." ICERD's monitoring body likewise criticizes how several states need to improve their affirmative action policies regarding education (CERD 2014).

The United States' approach to rights is highly selective and envisions "choice" and freedom as attainable through civil and political rights (Forsythe 2000). The United States frames itself "as representing equal freedom and opportunity for all" (19). This misconception stems from U.S.

ideologies asserting that if a person works hard enough they can advance their socioeconomic positioning and thus there is little need for social, cultural, and economic rights (Forsythe 2000). Such a narrow vision of freedom, rights, and "choice" ignores historically formed identity-based power hierarchies in which marginalized groups' agency is constrained and their oppressed positionalities are produced, concretized, and passed down through generations.

Zenzele Isoke (2016), a Black feminist theorist, pinpoints how in the United States racial groups are ongoingly marked, categorized, and differentiated through an uneven distribution of life chances. She contends that racial difference is constructed through social, economic, and political hierarchies based on skin color, phenotype, culture, and legal discrimination. The United States' legal and cultural history and contemporary state has in fact framed people who are Black as less than human (Giddings 1984). Discriminatory power hierarchies and legal systems define who is fully "human" and who is "subhuman" by extending greater rights to privileged human identities while excluding other groups from rights protections (Isoke 2016).

In recognition of this fact, ICERD and its monitoring body mandate governments to adopt economic, social, and cultural rights related to housing, education, and health while expressing particular concern for people of African descent (Article 2.2, Article 5.e, CERD 2010). Likewise, General Recommendation 25 requires that the United States evaluate and monitor Black women's hindered access to these rights (CERD 2000). If the United States complies with these obligations, the interrelated and intersecting systematic discrimination Black women experience will begin to be dismantled. It is improbable that the rights can be implemented as a short-term goal because of the profoundly racist/sexist design of U.S. legal and policy frameworks. Rather, implementation is more realistically a long-term goal that can be achieved through mass allyship that pressures legislatures to support the cause. Scholars, lawyers, politicians, activists, nongovernmental organizations, and individuals are collectively organizing in support of implementation of economic, social, and cultural rights in the United States. I participate in such allyship.

In the following subsections I examine three areas (housing, health, and education) in which the United States does not provide economic, social, and cultural rights to Black women. These issues are each complex topics and all interrelate to assure that women who are Black experience profound oppression. ICERD mandates rights in these areas, and if the United States fully implemented these rights, Black women's suffering would begin to reduce.

Housing

ICERD mandates "economic, social and cultural rights, in particular: [among other rights] the right to housing" (Article 5.e.iii). The treaty's members are also required to condemn racial segregation, discourage anything that strengthens it, and to "prevent, prohibit and eradicate" segregative practices (Article 2.1.e, Article 3). Wherever segregation exists (regardless of whether states intentionally design their policies to create racial division), states must institute desegregation initiatives (CERD 2010). Historically, the U.S. government promoted racial segregation to preserve and advance white patriarchal domination over resources. For instance, from 1938 through the 1950s the Federal Housing Administration (FHA) insured mortgages on approximately one-third of new housing (CERD Task Force et al. 2010). The FHA's manuals declared that African Americans were "adverse influences on property values and instructed personnel not to insure mortgages on homes unless they were in 'racially homogenous' white neighborhoods" (CERD Task Force et al. 2010: 10). U.S. policies intentionally fostered isolation of Black communities from white residents. Moreover, when Black residents moved into predominately white communities that contained extensive economic, social, and cultural resources, white flight occurred (and thus the flight of white-dominated resources) (Gotham 2000). White flight still occurs today. In other cases, contemporary gentrification of Black communities increases policing, heightens rent and the cost of living, and coerces impoverished Black tenants to move out of their communities to more affordable neighborhoods.

The United States does combat housing discrimination in some cases. The 1968 U.S. Fair Housing Act prohibits discrimination in the sale or renting of dwellings based on race, color, religion, sex or national origin (U.S. Department of Justice 1968). Despite this legislation, ICERD's monitoring body chastises the United States for practices that still do not meet global human rights standards in the following areas:

- Home foreclosures
- Mortgage lending, steering, and redlining
- Access to affordable and adequate housing
- Providing compensation for housing discrimination and holding perpetrators accountable for such discrimination

(CERD 2014)

Housing discrimination is interrelated to other forms of discrimination Black communities experience: high rates of poverty, crime, and lack of access to quality health care, employment, and education (CERD Task Force et al. 2010). Given the failure to remedy these inequalities, it is imperative to locate other resources to address them. Implementing ICERD policies that promote economic, social, and cultural rights can be part of the solution.

The 2013 Home Mortgage Disclosure Act data provides evidence that lending discrimination is an issue that must be addressed. The data indicates that Black borrowers' share of home-purchase loans was about 5 percent in 2013 (down from approximately 9 percent in 2006) compared to white borrowers' share, which was approximately 70 percent in 2013 (up from about 61 percent in 2006) (Bhutta and Ringo 2014). Twenty-nine percent of people who are Black were denied conventional home-purchase loans, compared to 11 percent for people who are white (Bhutta and Ringo 2014). Lenders also charged Black and Hispanic borrowers the most expensive rates (relative to loan amounts; Bhutta and Ringo 2014).

Black women experience housing discrimination differently than Black men in a variety of ways. In general, people who are Black access subprime mortgage loans at a rate five times greater than people who are white, and women experience a rate five times higher than men (CERD Task Force et al. 2010; United Nations Working Group 2015; Haughwout, Mayer, and Tracy 2009). Next, housing discrimination and employment discrimination interrelate to produce compounded hardships on Black women. People who are Black are paid less than people who are white, and women are paid less than men (Whittier 2009). In 2013, women who are Black made sixty-four cents to every dollar a white male earned (Russell, Sheltone, and Eaddy 2014). Black women endure pay gaps in relation to their gender and race, which limits their means to secure and sustain housing. Black women commonly endure discrimination and/or abuse in the workplace, are subject to long work hours with low pay, and commonly perform unsafe or dangerous work, all of which make their employment and thus their economic resources available to pay for housing precarious (CERD 2008). Therefore, ICERD's monitoring body expresses particular concern for employment inequalities (CERD 2001).

Similarly, Black women's experiences with compounded discrimination are intensified by familial hardships. Black women, especially single mothers, are disproportionately impacted by decreased expenditures for social protection programs, yet teen birth rates are highest among Black and Hispanic females (United Nations Working Group 2015; CDC 2021). Hardships that Black women experience due to diminishing social protection programs, high teen birth rates, and Black mothers' need to secure housing for themselves as well as their children are compounded by the fact that 48 percent of Black female–headed households live below the poverty line (United Nations Working Group 2016). Moreover, the United States is one of only two countries in the world without mandatory paid maternity leave and also does not meet global workplace standards for postnatal mothers, pregnant women, and women with family care needs (United Nations Working Group 2015). Furthermore, because of mass incarceration of Black men, Black women's responsibilities to economically provide for their families are heightened, including in relation to securing and sustaining housing. In fact, some Black women are unable to economically maintain housing and thus experience a cycle of housing evictions in which they and often their children live in a residence for a few months before being forced to move only to face another eviction (Duck 2015). Congress offers public housing programs; however, the government does not equip the programs with enough resources. This shortcoming results in long waiting lists to access such housing. Moreover, children of families living in public housing are moved to the top of the waiting list when they become eighteen years old which further hinders access to resources (Duck 2015). Similarly, private housing that is affordable and not rundown or a risk to residents' health and safety is extremely limited in predominantly Black neighborhoods. All of these factors contribute to the substantial and growing homeless population in predominantly Black neighborhoods.

It is vital to utilize an intersectional approach when addressing housing inequalities to avoid ineffectively designing housing empowerment initiatives. Strategies to alleviate prejudice (such as racism) must be intersectional in design so they are not exclusionary. ICERD implementation strategies regarding housing must address the complex nature of sexism and racism as interacting and dependent occurrences because Black women's intersectional identities make them vulnerable to interrelated forms of discrimination. Black women do not experience sexism or racism autonomously in housing; instead the collective identity experiences the prejudices simultaneously. This intersectional experience increases the adverse impacts of each form of prejudice. Thus, ICERD must be implemented with an intersectional approach.

Health

ICERD mandates the right to medical care and public health (Article 5.e.iv). In the United States, people who are Black are less likely to have health insurance than people who are white (McMorrow et al. 2015). In 2001 ICERD's monitoring body criticized the United States' inadequate provision of affordable and quality health care for racial minorities, then reinforced this criticism in 2014 (twenty years after U.S. ratification of the pact) (CERD 2001, 2014). The committee commended the 2010 Patient Protection and Affordable Care Act, otherwise known as Obamacare, yet disapproved of how many states with substantial racial minorities opted out of the Medicaid expansion program (CERD 2014). Racial minorities suffer due to inadequate health-care provisions; however, Black women endure added hardships because of sexism in the health-care system.

The United Nations Working Group (2015) insists that the U.S. must improve women's access to reproductive health care. Women's reproductive capacities are legislated by an overwhelmingly white male–dominated political system. Influential movements that resist reproductive rights also aggressively strive to minimize access to reproductive technology that enables women to control the number and spacing of their children. Impoverished women (which relative to population size are disproportionately Black) are most affected by expanding restrictive reproductive rights legislation, unnecessary medical procedures designed to prevent abortions, and the Hyde Amendment that outlaws public funding for abortions except in cases of incest or rape (United Nations Working Group 2015). Moreover, influential movements that resist reproductive rights strive to minimize women's access to free or low-cost birth control and to overturn the 1973 *Roe v. Wade* ruling that legalized abortion. Although abortion is legal, Black women often do not have the financial resources to access it (Smith 2005).

These realities correspond with how many institutions fail to provide objective science-based sex education and instead teach ineffective abstinence-only strategies (United Nations Working Group 2015). Inadequate sex education and fewer reproductive rights lead to high rates of unintended pregnancies and abortions in Black communities (CERD 2008). Systematic employment and housing discrimination discussed above contribute to Black women's inability to afford costs associated with abortions and/or unintended pregnancies. The hardships Black women endure are compounded by the interrelated nature of health-care, employment, and housing discrimination. The adverse effects of each form of discrimination on Black women are magnified by the other forms of discrimination.

Public programs for impoverished parents and children are also under constant attack. The term *welfare queen* is commonly used in the United States to falsely describe Black women as irresponsibly draining the U.S. welfare system, despite the fact that 1) low-income white parents numerically outnumber low-income Black parents and 2) the welfare system provides insufficient economic resources for impoverished parents. Race and law scholar Dorothy Roberts (2012) also describes how child protective workers subject Black women to heightened scrutiny and child removal in reaction to stereotypes that Black mothers are irresponsible, unreasonably hostile, mentally unfit, and/or drug addicts. In addition, intervention into Black mothers' homes occurs because of the state's approach to addressing poverty among children, which focuses on child removal from homes rather than providing impoverished families services and resources (Roberts 2012). Moreover, Black families' access to welfare services has declined since the 1970s; comparatively, the number of children in foster care has dramatically increased (Roberts 2012). In 2011, Black children comprised 15 percent of children in the United States but made up 30 percent of children in foster care (Roberts 2012).

Inadequate human rights for Black women is also a fatal matter. Compounded systematic and institutional discrimination hinders Black women's ability to control their pregnancies and lowers the chance of them and/or their children surviving childbirth (United Nations Working Group 2016). Black children are at high risk of infant mortality (CERD 2014). Likewise, from 1990 to 2013 maternal mortality rose by approximately 140 percent, and Black women are three to four times more likely than white women to die from pregnancy-related complications (United Nations Working Group 2015; United Nations Working Group 2016). Thus, compounded discrimination increases the numbers of deaths of Black mothers and Black children, which hinders their basic human right to life.

Motherhood is not the only threat to life Black women endure. Black women are at high risk of HIV/AIDS yet are subject to discrimination in health-care initiatives designed to prevent the disease (CERD 2008; CERD Task Force et al. 2010). The interconnectedness of classism, sexism, and racial discrimination, along with the stigma of HIV/AIDS and the United States' failure to provide economic, social, and cultural rights (including but not limited to health care, housing, and education) hinder Black women's agency to prevent and be treated for the disease. People who are Black are 12 percent of the U.S. population yet are 44 percent of people living with HIV/AIDS and are 42 percent of people newly diagnosed with the disease (Travaglini, Himelhoch, and Fang 2018; CDC n.d.). Sixty-two percent of women with HIV/AIDs are Black, and they are diagnosed with the disease fifteen times more often than white women (Travaglini, Himelhoch, and Fang 2018). Black women also have shorter survival rates than white women after they contract the disease (CERD Task Force et al. 2010; Daskal and Parker 2008). In fact, Black women account for 61 percent of HIV/AIDS deaths among women (Ojukwu 2019). One in five new HIV/AIDS cases are a result of drug injection, yet the U.S. government systematically prevents the use of federal funds for harm reduction strategies such as needle exchanges (Daskal and Parker 2008). The government's uncomprehensive and neglectful response to the epidemic undermines potential solutions to combat the disease (Daskal and Parker 2008). Government strategies for health care must instead take into account the intersectional and heightened needs of Black women to begin to remedy these discriminatory and dangerous policies.

Black women's lives are also at risk because of violence against women. While such violence is an epidemic among all racial groups, Black women experience it in unique manners. Predominantly Black communities are subject to classism, racism, and difficult living conditions, which are stressors that may contribute to gender-based violence. Black men may conduct gender-based violence to gain power in response to their male privilege being hindered by more powerful racial groups in a racist patriarchal system (Crenshaw 1991). Moreover, gender-based violence is caused by other interconnected systematic inequalities such as pay gaps, employment discrimination, media stereotypes, the naturalization of women as unpaid reproductive laborers, and legal solutions that prosecute a perpetrator after being convicted of the crimes rather than working to eradicate causes of violence against women. Black women are unlikely to report gender violence because of the following interrelated factors:

- Racism, classism, and sexism in policing and the criminal justice system
- The hesitancy to report one oppressor (Black males) to another (the police)
- The government's inadequate remedy for gender violence (conviction of a perpetrator), which marginally addresses survivors' trauma
- Limited if any benefits of reporting the crimes as well as low prosecution rates of perpetrators

- Fear of victim blaming or not being believed
- Threats of retaliation or social isolation from their families and/or community members
- Black women's concern that their mothering will be subject to surveillance and intervention after they report the crimes

Black women are also hesitant to seek assistance or refuge in domestic violence shelters because they fear child protective services' discriminatory surveillance of and intervention in their mothering (Gengler 2011). The interacting forms of oppression described in this paragraph and article in general assure that Black women are particularly vulnerable to gender-based violence and have only meager resources to address such violence. ICERD's monitoring body condemns the high rates of physical violence, sexual assault, and rape that Black women experience, in part because of insufficient and discriminatory prevention programs, service programs, counseling services, temporary shelters, early assistance centers, and federal and state action against such violence (CERD 2014, 2008). Moreover, the committee advises the United States to expand awareness-raising campaigns, improve prosecution rates for the crimes, improve procedures to address gender-based violence, and more promptly and thoroughly address the abuse (CERD 2014).

The spectrum of forms of discrimination described in this section (regarding reproductive health and effective sex education, public programs for impoverished parents and their children, the monitoring and surveillance of Black mothers, infant and maternal mortality among people who are Black, disparities in the prevention and treatment of HIV/AIDS, and policies and practices regarding violence against women) are compounded and interconnected in nature. Strategists can utilize ICERD to pinpoint how U.S. domestic behavior should change to simultaneously address these injustices. If interpreted through an intersectional lens, human rights can address compounded forms of inequality that Black women experience (Ross et al. 2017). An intersectional approach to human rights is revolutionary compared to commonplace arguments for simply including Black women in discriminatory mainstream rights frameworks that will inevitably still marginalize them (Ross et al. 2017). Black women and their allies can use the rights set forth in ICERD to inform the U.S. government about Black women's specific intersectional needs and to demand that intersectional solutions be operationalized.

Education

ICERD mandates the right to desegregated education and training (Article 5.e.v, Article 3). The 1954 Supreme Court *Brown v. Board of Education* ruling outlawed public school racial segregation, yet de facto[4] segregation and its effects continue to exist (Bell 1980). ICERD's (2014: 6) committee finds that Black students who attend racially diverse schools are "frequently assigned to 'single-race' classes [and are] denied equal access to advanced courses." Black students most frequently attend racially segregated schools with unequal facilities (CERD 2014). During the 2002–2003 school year, 71 percent of Black students, compared to 28 percent of white students, attended low-income public schools (CERD Task Force et al. 2010). U.S. practices discussed above regarding housing segregation are related to racial segregation in schools. The concentration of Black students in low-income neighborhoods adversely impacts the education they receive because local property "taxes typically make up a substantial portion of public school funding" (11). In areas that are impoverished, there is less funding obtained from local property taxes to assure quality education compared to areas that accrue greater monetary resources from taxes. Therefore, the committee advises the United States to improve the quality of education for Black students (CERD 2008). In addition, state parties must increase the rate of Black students' school enrollment and adopt immediate and effective measures to eliminate racial prejudices in education (Article 7; CERD 2014). ICERD mandates that state parties combat racially discriminatory approaches to education and instead educate about inclusivity and understanding of racially marginalized groups (Article 7). Zero-tolerance discipline policies and educators' prejudices have led to high rates of racist expulsion, suspension, and in-school arrests of Black children, as well as high rates of Black students dropping out of school (CERD 2008). Racist disciplining and criminalization of Black students also results in funneling them into the criminal justice system (referred to as the "school to prison pipeline") which produces high rates of incarceration among people who are Black (Crenshaw, Ocen, and Nanda 2015).

An intersectional analysis reveals that Black female students experience increased risks of unjust punishment because they are subject to compounded oppression. In the 2011–2012 school year, Black boys were three times more likely than white boys to be suspended, yet Black girls were six times more likely than white girls to be suspended (Crenshaw, Ocen, and Nanda 2015). The U.S. government boasts that zero-tolerance policies make schools safer; however, Black female students often disagree. They commonly envision that the policies and presence of security/law enforcement in their schools contributes to an environment that is chaotic, unsafe, not suitable for learning, and in which educational achievement is treated as less important than discipline (thus Black girls are discouraged from attending school) (Crenshaw, Ocen, and Nanda 2015). Black female students also experience high rates of interpersonal violence, yet school staff regularly do not intervene in cases of sexual harassment and gendered bullying, which contributes to unsafe and stressful learning environments for girls (Crenshaw, Ocen, and Nanda 2015). In fact, victims risk being penalized if they defend themselves against such behaviors or if they act out, while their counseling needs are disregarded or overlooked (Crenshaw, Ocen, and Nanda 2015).

As mentioned above, Black girls are also at high risk of teen pregnancy. Pregnant female students may become segregated from their peers and stigmatized in educational settings in ways that Black males do not experience (Crenshaw, Ocen, and Nanda 2015). Moreover, pregnant teens endure the physical and financial burden of pregnancy while a student. If they terminate a pregnancy, they must endure the economic, physical, and emotional impacts of the termination and may be stigmatized for their decision. If they birth and rear a child, they encounter economic stresses and barriers to find time for academic training because of social expectations for mothers to be children's dominant caregivers (Crenshaw, Ocen, and Nanda 2015). In some cases, teen mothers put their child up for adoption or permit their child to live in a different household, which can contribute to the teens' stress and ability to focus on their studies. Sexist and racist pay gaps, sexist and racist employment discrimination, workplace discrimination against pregnant teens and teen mothers, and the lack of financially adequate jobs for teens assures that in any of the cases above the teens will face economic hardships that will hinder their choice-making abilities and scholastic opportunities. Despite the educational disparities Black females endure, discourse about educational inequalities largely ignores their gendered needs (Crenshaw, Ocen, and Nanda 2015). ICERD strategies must prioritize the intersectional needs of Black female students so their needs are no longer marginalized.

The Prison Industrial Complex

U.S. failure to provide economic, social, and cultural rights overtly hinders Black communities' freedom. ICERD outlaws discrimination in criminal justice systems, and its committee chastises the racist prison industrial complex and economic, social, and cultural discrimination that makes Black communities susceptible to mass imprisonment (Article 5.a, Article 2.1.a; CERD 2001). ICERD's Article 5.a requires the "right to equal treatment before the tribunals and all other organs administering justice." Article 2.1.a insists that each member state "engage in no act or practice of racial discrimination against persons, groups of persons or institutions and to ensure that all public authorities and public institutions, national and local, shall act in conformity with this obligation." The United States imprisons the greatest number of people in the world (ICPR n.d.). The U.S. is only 5 percent of the world's population but imprisons 25 percent of prisoners in the world (NAACP 2021). People who are Black are approximately six times more likely to become incarcerated than people who are white (NAACP 2021). In 2001, one in six Black men were imprisoned at some point in their life (NAACP 2021).

Black women experience emotional, financial, and social stresses because of Black males' mass incarceration yet are also vulnerable to imprisonment. Black females are the fastest-growing population in the criminal justice system (Crenshaw, Ocen, and Nanda 2015). They are approximately six times more likely than white women to enter the criminal justice system and are eight times more likely than white women to receive jail sentences in court decisions; likewise, in most cases, they receive more severe sentences than white women (Crenshaw 2012; Russell, Sheltone, and Eaddy 2014; Steffensmeier and Demuth 2006). When sentenced as juveniles, they receive harsher sentences than females of other races (Crenshaw, Ocen, and Nanda 2015). The "war on drugs" that stigmatizes Black women as deviant drug users also increased mass imprisonment of Black women. Between 1986 and 1991, revisions in drug related sentences increased dramatically because of the "war on drugs," yet imprisonment of women of color for drug related offences grew by 800 percent, compared to 400 percent for white women (Crenshaw 2012). In addition to discriminatory sentencing practices, the United States does not meet global human rights standards for women in detention regarding solitary confinement, over-incarceration, health-care and reentry programs, free and high-quality legal counsel, shackling of pregnant women, and services for pregnant women and women with dependent children (United Nations Working Group 2015). Scholarship that advocates against the prison industrial complex, the "school to prison pipeline," and the "war on drugs" is most commonly from a patriarchal lens that marginalizes Black females' gendered needs. Therefore, while experiencing systematic discrimination in the prison industrial complex, Black women and girls also experience discrimination in advocacy against it.

Likewise, ICERD outlaws unjust violence by public authorities (Article 5. b). The treaty's monitoring body asserts that the United States must improve its training of correctional officers about violence against women (CERD 2014). Black female inmates are vulnerable to physical and sexual assault by prison workers. Inmates may fear reporting the crimes because in some cases the guards threaten violent retaliation against the accuser or threaten to revoke privileges such as their child and visitation rights (Russell, Sheltone, and Eaddy 2014). Female inmates also sometimes perform sexual acts for the workers to avoid punishment (Russell, Sheltone, and Eaddy 2014). If such crimes are reported and a prison worker is found guilty, the punishment is often merely to transfer the perpetrator to a different facility (Russell, Sheltone, and Eaddy 2014). Similarly, ICERD's committee contends that the United States must improve its training of police officers about violence against women (CERD 2014). Police officers are known to use excessive force against people who are Black (including women) without being properly disciplined for the excessive force (CERD 2001, 2008). Furthermore, Black women are vulnerable to sexual harassment, sexual assault, and rape by police officers. In 2010 sexual misbehavior was the second most commonly recorded police misconduct but was rarely adequately punished (Packman 2011). Police and prison guards are trained to assert their masculinity, repudiate femininity, and humiliate anyone who challenges their masculinity by defying their orders or by verbally shaming them (Cooper 2008). This volatile hyper-masculinized environment creates significant risk of sexual and/or physical assault against Black females.

Conclusion

Human rights practitioners must conduct their work with the awareness that collective identities are constantly reconstructed because of social, cultural, economic, institutional, and ideological transformations. Such practitioners must also conduct their work unrelentingly conscious that all people have intersectional identities (as all people possess compounded identity traits that are either privileged and/or discriminated against in systems of power). Identities themselves can be subversive (Butler 1990). There is revolutionary potential when an intersectional analysis is applied to human rights. To examine an international treaty with an intersectional analysis is to more fully understand and envision the potential of the multilateral agreement (Womack 2015, 2017).

This article draws from Black feminist intersectional approaches to examine U.S. noncompliance with the United Nations' core racial equality treaty, ICERD. Normative approaches to address racial equality are most commonly from a "gender neutral" perspective that prioritizes the needs of men of color. This article instead argues for an inclusive definition of racial equality. I use an intersectional analysis to reveal that systematic, structural, and institutional racism is gendered and that Black women experience compounded forms of discrimination. The pages above reveal that Black women experience disproportionate and compounded discrimination in economic, social, and cultural rights (regarding housing, education, and health) and in the U.S. prison industrial complex (its "school to prison pipeline," discriminatory sentencing practices, and police and prison workers' violence against women). The United States must abolish these behaviors to comply with the treaty. Moreover, the United States must acknowledge and address how diverse forms of discrimination related to education, health, income, housing, policing, and gender violence are inextricably linked. Consider that without quality education, economic advancement is unlikely. Without economic advancement, attaining adequate health care and housing is unlikely. Without adequate health care and housing, the government might revoke parenting rights. When parenting is policed, Black mothers may become imprisoned. If imprisoned, Black women may experience gendered violence. The list continues. Black women do not experience forms of discrimination autonomously; rather, they experience the forms simultaneously, which increases their adverse effects.

However, approaches to antidiscrimination legislation are most commonly not intersectional. Commonplace approaches generally focus on one issue and one identity trait at a time, yet this approach is not comprehensive and does not allow advocates to use the legislation to its fullest potential. Focusing on one identity trait at a time in antidiscrimination legislation tends to privilege the desires and needs of those most powerful in the group in question (for example in anti-sexism legislation white women or in anti-racism legislation Black men). Therefore, antidiscrimination legislation can in fact discriminate. Noting this reality, ICERD proponents should apply an intersectional approach to the treaty to avoid reproducing what they aim to diminish—identity-based power hierarchies.

Applying an intersectional analysis to ICERD holds the United States more accountable to the treaty, which can maximize its effects. Moreover, intersectional approaches to ICERD and other anti-discrimination legislation are useful for people other than Black women. Patricia Hill Collins (2004, 2015) contends that people who are not Black should consider in what ways an intersectional analysis is useful for their own social justice projects. Everyone has an intersectional identity, and people with any mixture of intersecting identity traits can use this theoretical approach to advocate for their rights. People of diverse intersectional identities can provide unique insight into power and oppression from their unique positionality. Intersectional analyses can operate in conjunction with one another, to inform one another, and to positively transform one another. Only then can a more comprehensive definition of rights become institutionalized.

· ·

Malia Lee Womack earned a bachelor of arts in Gender and Women's Studies with a minor in Global Poverty from the University of California, Berkeley, and a master of arts in Human Rights Studies with an emphasis in Women's, Gender, and Sexuality studies from Columbia University. She then concurrently earned a PhD in Women's, Gender, and Sexuality Studies and a master of arts in Latin American Studies from The Ohio State University, while finishing her PhD coursework without extended time. In 2001, Womack completed her dissertation "Puerto Rico in Crisis: Intersectionality, Activism, and Transforming Globalized Human Rights from the Grassroots." She is an intersectional transnational feminist scholar whose work focuses on advocating for intersectional approaches to human rights and activist movements in order to make their reach more inclusive and robust. Womack has served on the faculty at California State University, Sacramento; Saddleback College; Golden West College; College of Charleston; University of California, Riverside; and Purdue University. She has extensive participant experience in a wide spectrum of activist movements within the United States and abroad. For inquiries about Womack's publications and background, she can be reached at malia.lee. womack@gmail.com or found on academia.edu by the name Malia Lee Womack.

Notes

1   Nongovernmental organizations construct shadow reports to critique government reports summarizing their compliance with human rights treaties.
2   The phrase "economic, social, and cultural rights" describes a set of rights that are interdependent rather than being staunchly distinct from each other.
3   The ICESCR, the Universal Declaration of Human Rights, and the International Covenant on Civil and Political Rights (and its Optional Protocols) create the UN International Bill of Rights.
4   De facto refers to discrimination that is unintentional but still factual yet not officially recognized in law. De jure, comparably, refers to intentional discrimination that U.S. courts officially recognize in law.

Works Cited

Bandes, Susan. 1990. "The Negative Constitution: A Critique." *Michigan Law Review* 88, no. 8: 2271–347. papers.ssrn.com/sol3/papers.cfm?abstract_id=1242162.

Bell, Derrick. 1980. "*Brown v. Board of Education* and the Interest-Convergence Dilemma." *Harvard Law Review* 93, no. 3: 518–33. doi.org/10.2307/1340546.

Bhutta, Neil, and Daniel Ringo. 2014. "The 2013 Home Mortgage Disclosure Act Data." *Federal Reserve Bulletin* 100, no. 6: 1–37. papers.ssrn.com/sol3/papers.cfm?abstract_id=3280286.

Bond, Johanna. 2003. "International Intersectionality: A Theoretical and Pragmatic Exploration of Women's International Human Rights Violations." *Emory Law Journal* 52: 71–186. heinonline.org/HOL/LandingPage?handle=hein.journals/emlj52&div=10&id=&page=.

Butler, Judith. 1990. *Gender Trouble: Feminism and the Subversion of Identity.* New York: Routledge.

CDC (Centers for Disease Control and Prevention). 2021. "About Teen Pregnancy." https://www.cdc.gov/teenpregnancy/about/index.htm.

CDC (Centers for Disease Control and Prevention). n.d. "HIV and African American People." www.cdc.gov/hiv/group/racialethnic/africanamericans/index.html (accessed August 5, 2021).

CERD (Committee on the Elimination of Racial Discrimination). 2001. *Report of the Committee on the Elimination of Racial Discrimination (Fifty-Eighth Session and Fifty-Ninth Session).* UN General Assembly, Official Records, Suppl. 18. www.refworld.org/pdfid/3f52f3ad2.pdf.

CERD (Committee on the Elimination of Racial Discrimination). 2008. *Consideration of Reports Submitted by States Parties under Article 9 of the Convention: Concluding Observations of the Committee on the Elimination of Racial Discrimination: United States of America.* UN CERD, May 8. www.refworld.org/docid/4885cfa70.html.

CERD (Committee on the Elimination of Racial Discrimination). 2014. *Concluding Observations on the Combined Seventh to Ninth Periodic Reports of the United States of America.* UN CERD, August 29. https://docstore.ohchr.org/SelfServices/FilesHandler.ashx?enc=6QkG1d%2FPPRiCAqhKb7yhspzOl9YwTXeABruAM8pBAK1Q%2FDZ6XAqlyobgtsizwlHPkQhsSqMrVxuS6brQbHYpDYGXBUCX1bgRtTg3HaweAr5PBs9soaesD5KdByekI9OS.

CERD Task Force, Cidadao Global, Women's HIV Collaborative, Women of Color United, CADRE, Atlanta Public Sector Alliance, Thandabantu Iverson, and Malcolm X Grassroots. 2010. *From Civil Rights to Human Rights: Implementing US Obligations under the International Convention on the Elimination of All Forms of Racial Discrimination.* U.S. Human Rights Network. cwgl.rutgers.edu/docman/economic-and-social-rights/348-april-2010-cerd-report/file.

Chow, Pok Yin Stephenson. 2016. "Has Intersectionality Reached Its Limits? Intersectionality in the UN Human Rights Treaty Body Practice and the Issue of Ambivalence." *Human Rights Law Review* 16: 453–81. doi.org/10.2139/ssrn.2753549.

Collins, Patricia Hill. 2004. *Black Sexual Politics: African Americans, Gender, and the New Racism.* New York: Routledge.

Collins, Patricia Hill. 2015. "Intersectionality's Definitional Dilemmas." *Annual Review of Sociology* 41: 1–20. https://doi.org/10.1146/annurev-soc-073014-112142.

Collins, Patricia Hill. 2019. *Intersectionality as Critical Social Theory*. Durham, NC: Duke University Press.

Cooper, Frank Rudy. 2008. "'Who's the Man?': Masculinities Studies, *Terry* Stops, and Police Training." *Columbia Journal of Gender and Law* 18, no. 3: 671–742. scholars .law.unlv.edu/facpub/1122/.

Crenshaw, Kimberle. 1989. "Demarginalizing the Intersection of Race and Sex: A Black Feminist Critique of Antidiscrimination Doctrine, Feminist Theory, and Antiracist Politics." *University of Chicago Legal Forum* 139: 139–67. chicagounbound .uchicago.edu/cgi/viewcontent.cgi?article=1052&context=uclf.

Crenshaw, Kimberle. 1991. "Mapping the Margins: Intersectionality, Identity Politics, and Violence against Women of Color." *Stanford Law Review* 43, no. 6: 1241–99. https://doi.org/10.2307/1229039.

Crenshaw, Kimberlé. 2002. "Documento Para o Encontro de Especialistas Em Aspectos Da Discriminação Racial Relativos Ao Gênero" ("Document for the Meeting of Experts on Gender-Related Aspects of Racial Discrimination"). *Revista estudos feministas* 10, no. 1. https://doi.org/10.1590/S0104-026X2002000100011.

Crenshaw, Kimberlé. 2012. "From Private Violence to Mass Incarceration: Thinking Intersectionality about Women, Race, and Social Control." *UCLA Law Review* 1418: 1420–72. www.uclalawreview.org/pdf/59-6-1.pdf.

Crenshaw, Kimberlé, Priscilla Ocen, and Jyoti Nanda. 2015. *Black Girls Matter: Pushed Out, Overpoliced, and Underprotected*. Center for Intersectionality and Social Policy Studies and African American Policy Forum. https://www.law.columbia.edu /sites/default/files/2021-05/black_girls_matter_report_2.4.15.pdf.

Crooms, Lisa A. 2003. "'To Establish My Legitimate Name inside the Consciousness of Strangers': Critical Race Praxis, Progressive Women-of-Color Theorizing, and Human Rights." *Howard Law Journal* 46, no. 2: 229–68. heinonline.org/HOL /LandingPage?handle=hein.journals/howlj46&div=14&id=&page=.

Crooms, Lisa, and Dawinder S. Sindhu. 2010. "The Future of the United States Commission on Civil Rights." *University of Pennsylvania Law Review PENNumbra* 159: 127–54.

Daskal, Jen, and Alison Parker. 2008. *Submission to the Committee on the Elimination of Racial Discrimination*. Human Rights Watch, February 6. www.hrw.org/report/2008 /02/06/submission-committee-elimination-racial-discrimination/during-its -consideration.

de Beco, Gauthier. 2020. "Intersectionality and Disability in International Human Rights Law." *International Journal of Human Rights* 24, no. 5: 593–614. https://doi .org/10.1080/13642987.2019.1661241.

Dietrich, Simone, and Amanda Murdie. 2017. "Human Rights Shaming through INGOs and Foreign Aid Delivery." *Review of International Organizations* 12, no. 1: 95–120. https://doi.org/10.1007/s11558-015-92428.

Duck, Waverly. 2015. *No Way Out: Precarious Living in the Shadow of Poverty and Drug Dealing*. Chicago: University of Chicago Press.

Falcón, Sylvanna. 2011. "U.S. Treaty Obligations and the Politics of Racism and Anti-racism Discourse." In *Anti-racism and Multiculturalism: Studies in International Communication*, edited by Mark Alleyne, 55–72. New York: Routledge.

Falcón, Sylvanna. 2016. *Power Interrupted: Antiracist and Feminist Activism inside the United Nations*. Seattle: University of Washington Press.

Forsythe, David. 2000. *Human Rights and Comparative Foreign Policy*. Tokyo: United Nations University Press. www.corteidh.or.cr/tablas/27531.pdf.

Gengler, Amanda Marie. 2011. "Mothering under Others' Gaze: Policing Motherhood in a Battered Women's Shelter." *International Journal of Sociology of the Family* 37, no. 1: 131–52. www.jstor.org/stable/23029790.

Giddings, Paula. 1984. *When and Where I Enter: The Impact of Black Women on Race and Sex in America*. New York: HarperCollins.

Goldsmith, Jack. 2005. "The Unexceptional U.S. Human Rights RUDs." *University of St. Thomas Law Journal* 3, no. 2: 311–27. ir.stthomas.edu/cgi/viewcontent.cgi?referer=&httpsredir=1&article=1085&context=ustlj.

Gotham, Kevin Fox. 2000. "Racialization and the State: The Housing Act of 1934 and the Creation of the Federal Housing Administration." *Sociological Perspectives* 43, no. 2: 291–317. https://doi.org/10.2307/1389798.

Harris, Hadar. 2008. "Race across Borders: The U.S. and ICERD." *Harvard BlackLetter Law Journal* 24: 61–67. heinonline.org/HOL/LandingPage?handle=hein.journals/hblj24&div=5&id=&page=.

Haughwout, Andrew, Christopher Mayer, and Joseph Tracy. 2009. *Subprime Mortgage Pricing: The Impact of Race, Ethnicity, and Gender on the Cost of Borrowing*. Federal Reserve Bank of New York Staff Reports 368 (April). www.newyorkfed.org/medialibrary/media/research/staff_reports/sr368.pdf.

Herndon, Lisa. 2013. "Why Is Racial Injustice Still Permitted in the United States? An International Human Rights Perspective on the United States' Inadequate Compliance with the International Convention on the Elimination of all Forms of Racial Discrimination." *Wisconsin International Journal of Law* 31, no. 2: 323–51. heinonline.org/HOL/LandingPage?handle=hein.journals/wisint31&div=17&id=&page=.

Hong, Grace Kyungwon. 2015. *Death beyond Disavowal: The Impossible Politics of Difference*. Minneapolis: University of Minnesota Press.

ICPR (Institute for Crime and Justice Policy Research). N.d. "Highest to Lowest—Prison Population Rate." www.prisonstudies.org/highest-to-lowest/prison_population_rate?field_region_taxonomy_tid=All (accessed August 6, 2021).

Ignatieff, Michael. 2005. *American Exceptionalism and Human Rights*. Princeton, NJ: Princeton University Press.

Isoke, Zenzele. 2016. "Race and Racialization." In *The Oxford Handbook of Feminist Theory*, edited by Lisa Disch and Mary Hawkesworth, 741–60. New York: Oxford University Press.

James, Stanlie. 2002. "Racialized Gender/Gender Racism: Reflections on Black Feminist Human Rights Theorizing." In *Still Brave: The Evolution of Black Women's Studies*, edited by Frances Foster, Beverly Guy-Sheftall, and Stanlie James, 383–91. New York: Feminist Press.

Mayer, Ann Elizabeth. 1996. "Reflections on the Proposed United States Reservations to CEDAW: Should the Constitution Be an Obstacle to Human Rights." *Hastings Constitutional Law Quarterly* 23, no. 3: 727–823. repository.uchastings.edu/hastings_constitutional_law_quaterly/vol23/iss3/7/.

McDougall, Gay. 2002. "The World Conference against Racism: Through a Wider Lens." *Fletcher Forum of World Affairs* 26, no. 2: 135–51. www.staff.city.ac.uk/p.willetts/NGOS/WCAR/MCDOUGAL.PDF.

McMorrow, Stacey, Sharon Long, Genevieve Kenney, and Nathaniel Anderson. 2015. "Uninsurance Disparities Have Narrowed for Black and Hispanic Adults under the Affordable Care Act." *Health Affairs* 34, no. 10: 1774–78. https://doi.org/10.1377/hlthaff.2015.0757.

NAACP (National Association for the Advancement of Colored People). 2021. "Criminal Justice Fact Sheet." www.naacp.org/criminal-justice-fact-sheet/ (accessed November 16, 2016).

Ojukwu, Emmanuela. 2019. "Social Determinants of HIV Treatment Engagement among Postpartum Black Women Living with HIV (WLWH)." PhD diss., University of Miami. scholarship.miami.edu/esploro/outputs/doctoral/Social-Determinants-of-HIV-Treatment-Engagement-among-Postpartum-Black-Women-Living-with-HIV-WLWH/991031447530502976.

Packman, David. 2011. "2010 NPMSRP Police Misconduct Statistical Report—Draft." Marshall Literary Society, April 5. Posted May 19, 2017. taodannguyensuy.wordpress.com/2017/05/19/2010-npmsrp-police-misconduct-statistical-report-draft-by-author-david-packman-posted-on-april-5-2011/.

Roberts, Dorothy. 2012. "Prison, Foster Care, and the Systemic Punishment of Black Mothers." *UCLA Law Review* 59: 1474–500. www.uclalawreview.org/pdf/59-6-2.pdf.

Ross, Loretta. 2017. "Reproductive Justice as Intersectional Feminist Activism." *Souls* 19, no. 3: 286–314. https://doi.org/10.1080/10999949.2017.1389634.

Ross, Loretta, Lynn Roberts, Erika Derkas, Whitney Peoples, and Pamela Bridgewater. 2017. *Radical Reproductive Justice: Foundation, Theory, Practice, Critique.* New York: Feminist Press.

Russell, Leon, Hilary Sheltone, and Jotaka Eaddy. 2014. *Shadow Report of the National Association for the Advancement of Colored People.* Washington, DC: NAACP Washington Bureau.

Smith, Andrea. 2005. "Beyond Pro-choice versus Pro-life: Women of Color and Reproductive Justice." *NWSA Journal* 17, no. 1: 119–40. www.law.berkeley.edu/php-programs/centers/crrj/ashin/loadfile.php?entity_key=RD3G3J35.

Soohoo, Cynthia, and Soohoo Stolz. 2008. "Bringing Theories of Human Rights Change Home." *Fordham Law Review* 77, no. 2: 459–500. ir.lawnet.fordham.edu/cgi/viewcontent.cgi?article=4386&context=flr.

Steffensmeier, Darrell, and Stephen Demuth. 2006. "Does Gender Modify the Effects of Race–Ethnicity on Criminal Sanctioning? Sentences for Male and Female White, Black, and Hispanic Defendants." *Journal of Quantitative Criminology* 22, no. 3: 241–61. https://doi.org/10.1007/s10940-006-9010-2.

Travaglini, Letitia, Seth Himelhoch, and Li Juan Fang. 2018. "HIV Stigma and Its Relation to Mental, Physical, and Social Health among Black Women Living with HIV/AIDS." *AIDS and Behavior* 22, no. 1: 3783–94. depts.washington.edu /uwmedptn/wp-content/uploads/Feb-2019_HIV-Stigma-and-Its-Relation-to -Mental-Physical-and-Social-Health.pdf.

United Nations Working Group of Experts on People of African Descent. 2016. "Statement to the Media by the United Nations' Working Group of Experts on People of African Descent, on the Conclusion of Its Visit to U.S.A." January 29. Office of the High Commissioner on Human Rights. www.ohchr.org/EN /NewsEvents/Pages/DisplayNews.aspx?NewsID=17000&Lang ID=E.

United Nations Working Group on the Issue of Discrimination Against Women in Law. 2015. "United Nations Working Group on the Issue of Discrimination against Women in Law and in Practice Finalizes Country Mission to the United States." December 11. Office of the High Commissioner on Human Rights. www .ohchr.org/EN/NewsEvents/Pages/DisplayNews.aspx?NewsID=16872&Lang ID=E.

U.S. Department of Justice. 1968. "The Fair Housing Act." https://www.justice.gov /crt/fair-housing-act-2.

U.S. Department of State. 2000. "The Convention on the Elimination of All Forms of Racial Discrimination: Initial Report of the United States of America to the United Nations Committee on the Elimination of All Forms of Racial Discrimination, September 2000." https://1997-2001.state.gov/global/human_rights /cerd_report/cerd_intro.html.

Vadlamannati, Krishna, Nicole Janz, and Øyvind Berntsen. 2018. "Human Rights Shaming and FDI: Effects of the UN Human Rights Commission and Council." *World Development* 104: 222–37. https://doi.org/10.1016/j.worlddev.2017.11.014.

Whittier, Nancy. 2009. "Median Annual Earnings of Full-Time, Year-Round Workers by Education, Race, and Hispanic Origin." In *Feminist Frontiers*, 8th ed., edited by Verta Taylor, Nancy Whittier, and Leila Rupp, 206. New York: McGraw-Hill.

Williams, Patricia. 1991. *The Alchemy of Race and Rights: Diary of a Law Professor.* Cambridge, MA: Harvard University Press.

Wing, Katherine. 1997. "Critical Race Feminism and the International Human Rights of Women in Bosnia, Palestine, and South Africa: Issues for Latcrit Theory." *University of Miami Inter-American Law Review* 28, no. 2: 337–60. www.jstor .org/stable/40176422.

Womack, Malia Lee. 2015. "The Intricacies of Adopting International 'Norms' from the Bottom Up." *Wagadu* 13: 211–33. sites.cortland.edu/wagadu/wp-content /uploads/sites/3/2015/07/9-NINE-Womack.pdf.

Womack, Malia Lee. 2017. "Troubling Universalized Human Rights: The Complexities of Identity and Intersectionality." *Journal of Politics and Democratization* 1, no. 1: 56–61. jpd.gipa.ge/files/4%20-%20Womack(2)%202-1.pdf.

Raquel Wright-Mair and Milagros Castillo-Montoya

Sisterhood Birthed through Colonialism
Using Love Letters to Connect, Heal, and Transform

Abstract: It is already known that one of the ways in which colonialism operates and exerts harm is by dehumanizing Black, Indigenous, and other racially minoritized populations. Less attention has been paid, however, to the ways in which this dehumanization erodes relations among those colonized. Colonial logics designed to separate and alienate the colonized from each other have been internalized for centuries, preventing communities and individuals from recognizing how they connect. In this piece, the authors draw on their experiences as racially minoritized women in the U.S. academy to reflect on how this colonial legacy has shaped not only their identities but also their identifications—how and with whom they identify. The authors demonstrate what they refer to as a love letter approach that enables them to foster connection, healing, and transformation through dialogue. Most importantly, they highlight the radical potential of finding and articulating love for one another as a form of resisting the very colonial logics that would keep them apart. They conclude the piece with guidance on how to use this approach to connect individuals, communities, and organizations.

This piece began with a series of conversations about a trip we both took to the Netherlands to present our research on global racial equity in education. It was a trip mainly attended by scholars who, at the time, were in the United States and who are racially minoritized.[1] During this trip, we went on a Black heritage tour of the Netherlands that included a museum that was the former house of a key stakeholder in the slave trade. It included a powerful exhibit on Suriname, a former Dutch colony located off the coast of South America. The exhibit was located in the horse carriage area of the

MERIDIANS · feminism, race, transnationalism   21:1 April 2022
DOI: 10.1215/15366936-9554178   © 2022 Smith College

house—a location we instinctively felt was problematic and further dehumanizing of the people and history it was aiming to showcase. We each walked through the museum at our own pace with brief conversations here and there, but mostly independently processing the experience. It was painful for us in different ways to see the wealth made from trading and enslaving human bodies and reckoning with this being part of our personal history, whether we liked it or not. It was not until a few months after our trip that we had a conversation about this museum tour and realized that we both walked away feeling emotions that connected us more than separated us. This connection was the impetus for us to identify a way for us to connect, heal, and transform.

In what follows, we provide some context about who we are and why the colonial history we confronted in the museum binds us to one another. We then explain the approach we took to unpack this experience with each other in the form of love letters. We follow this introduction with the love letters themselves. After the love letters, we describe our understanding of how we are connected in a deeper way as a result of this process. We conclude by offering guidance to others who might be interested in engaging in connection, healing, and transformation through what we are referring to as the love letter approach.

Our Entering Points: Bounded by Colonialism

We both come from colonial contexts—Raquel from Jamaica, and Milagros from Puerto Rico. We moved to the mainland United States at different stages in our lives, but both have grappled with the impact of colonialism in various ways.

Raquel's Positionality Statement

I moved to the United States for college as an international student from Kingston, Jamaica. My identity as a first-generation, multiracial Jamaican woman would serve as an important foundation for my later career as a professor studying the experiences of racially minoritized populations in higher education. During my master's degree program, I was able to more pointedly explore the nuances of my racial heritage in a US context through various racial developmental theories. While I thought a lot about my racial and ethnic identities as a young child, I never had the language, tools, or space to make sense of my varying identities and contextualize their importance to me. I frequently wondered why my hair was a different texture from my mother's and why both sides of my family ranged in skin tones and racial composition. Navigating my identities in the context of being multiracial and an immigrant was a complex journey that included resistance and acceptance of a colonial past rooted in violence.

Milagros's Positionality Statement

I was born in Puerto Rico and as a young child moved with my family to the New York metropolitan area. I grew up in a low-income household and was the first one in my family to obtain a higher-education degree, making me a first-generation college graduate and now scholar. I am bilingual, with Spanish being my first language. I am multiracial with light-skin privilege. From a young age, I wondered why I was so light-skinned and had such straight and thin hair when others in my family had darker complexions. I learned about Puerto Rican history in college. Through my advisor and coursework, I learned how resilient and resistant Puerto Ricans have been against colonialism. I also became very clear about the pain, violence, and control the colonial state had and continues to employ over Puerto Rico and its people. I had a lot of questions about race and its meaning in a colonial context where almost everyone is racially mixed. I have mostly been trying to figure out these questions on my own, not knowing who to talk with about race in the Caribbean and who I am as a racialized being. I am still reconciling the meaning and impact of being a light-skinned Puerto Rican.

Our Differences and Commonalities

One of the first conversations we had as we wrote this piece was spent unpacking the complexity of being multiracial. Specifically, my (Raquel) racial heritage comprises Black, South Asian, and white ancestry, but I identify mostly with my Black and South Asian heritage, as these are my parents' salient identities. My white lineage is important to note as we nuance our complex racial identities as scholars who seek to dismantle systemic racism. It is not a lineage that I connect with, and, in fact, it is a lineage that would likely not acknowledge or accept me. But simply ignoring it erases the colonial reality that is part of my family stemming from white slave owners in Jamaica dating back to 1690, with the other part being poor South Asian immigrants to Jamaica. In essence, not acknowledging the complicated lineage erases the reality of colonialism that is part and parcel of those of us who identify as multiracial.

Additionally, phenotype plays a role in how we identify, and how we feel we *can* identify based on our society's fixation on boxes and categorization. We discussed navigating the fact that our phenotype does not reflect an accurate composition of our racially mixed identities, which contributes to our grappling with and questioning how and why we racially identify in the way we do. For example, who do we leave out when we choose one identity? Why does that matter? Does it matter? How do we reconcile these questions within ourselves when our racially mixed identities do not fit in a predetermined box?

In discussing my positionality with Raquel, I (Milagros) was struck by how similar our experiences were in having and living with racially mixed identities, but also the important differences between us, given the colonial history of our respective islands. I reflected on this experience with Raquel: "It became so evident that I was opening, revisiting, and exploring aspects of who I am and what contributes to my racial identity in ways I probably have not done with anyone else, ever. The more I poured out, the more my cup was filled."

We both agree that positionality statements are often fickle and lack the substance to do justice to one's own individual racial composition. In fact, we struggled about whether to include such statements here, for fear of producing an unfinished statement that barely scratches the surface of our unique and complex identities. But we decided to use the statements to describe how our unique identities shape our entry point to this work, even as we recognize the impossibility of capturing our identities and their influence on our work in a single paragraph. We hope this starting point highlights how we connect with, reconcile, and *continue* to grapple with the long-lasting effects of colonialism.

Why Did We Take a Love Letter Approach, and What Does It Mean?

Through a series of letters to each other, we experienced the process of witnessing ourselves in each other. By this, we mean putting our guards down and fully being open to and noticing each other's humanity. Through this process, we learned how sisterhood could be birthed through the collective naming, interrogation, and disruption of colonial logics. The letters took the form of a dialogue, moving back and forth as we shared our individual thoughts, processed each other's thoughts, and witnessed together the similarities and differences across our experiences. In this process, we advanced a reflexive praxis that, in many ways, mirrors what is often referred to as the LARA/I method of dialogue (listen, affirm, respond, and affirming/inquiry) used in intergroup dialogue—a pedagogy developed for dialogues across difference within the context of higher education (Program on Intergroup Relations 2014).

We recognize that dialogue is a valuable way of communicating and an approach that is part of our legacy. Black and Latina scholars have written about the powerful experience of creating spaces to dialogue, to be, with one another. bell hooks (2015: 42) writes of these spaces as a "homeplace," which she describes as "the one site where one could freely confront the issue of humanization, where one could resist." She further explains this homeplace construction as something Black women did so that Black people could "be affirmed in our minds and hearts . . . where we could restore to ourselves the dignity denied us on the outside in the public world" (42). In this homeplace, hooks notes, Black people could "heal many of the wounds inflicted by racist domination . . . and grow and develop, to nurture our spirits" (42).

Other scholars have written about sister circles among Black women that reflect the spirit of a homeplace (Davis 2019), and Latinas have written about creating spaces to learn, confront, heal, grow, and write together (Latina Feminist Group 2001). Some have used and written about *pláticas*—conversations and learnings about life as a way of sharing transgenerational knowledge, to disrupt academic spaces, and to resist dehumanization (e.g., Castillo-Montoya and Torrez-Guzmán 2012; Fierros and Delgado Bernal 2016). Given this legacy we have inherited from within and across racially minoritized communities, we understood that using dialogue to unpack our experiences and learn from one another was necessary to connect, heal, and transform our individual and collective perspectives. Dialoguing in person was not possible, however, given the reality that we were (and are still, at the time of this writing) living through the COVID-19 pandemic. Yet we knew that it was urgent and necessary work, given the persistence of racism. During the time that we worked on this piece, Breonna Taylor and George Floyd were both murdered at the hands of state-sanctioned police violence. Protests demanding racial justice unfolded throughout the world. Amid this pivotal moment, we committed to work toward racial justice by forming a stronger connection, engaging in healing, and striving for individual and collective transformation through dialogue that, at this time, took the form of letters.

What we did not know at the time we started was how well the format of a letter would fit our endeavor. Writing letters back and forth provided us with the space, time, and freedom to listen, process, and reflect on each other's words. What had begun as a necessary adaptation to the pandemic became the ideal medium for communication and connection between us as racially minoritized women. We each had space to be with the other person's words, to let them simmer within our own consciousness prior to responding or asking more questions. Letter writing gave us space to promote more reflexivity and, in so doing, deepened our self-awareness. It gave us space to ache on our own terms, to laugh and hold on to joy in the midst of disaster. It forced us to pause, to forestall the questions we might have immediately asked had we been in person, and to *really* listen instead. Our point here is not to devalue the insights that can be gained through in-person dialogue, which has its own benefits and challenges. Rather, we simply seek to share how much we cherished this opportunity—so rare within the academy—to embark on the healing process at a pace that recognizes the deep historical roots of harm. In this sense, our love letters became, themselves, another form of homeplace. Moreover, between us as a Jamaican woman and a Puerto Rican woman, it was a chance for some racial dialogues that we frankly have not always had with racially minoritized women, particularly those who are racially mixed. It was not the same homeplace created by sister circles of Black women connecting with Black women, nor was it fully a *plática*. It was a fusion, if you will, that created something altogether new.

Some of you may question the very idea and terminology of "love" letters, especially in our shared context as academics. But in developing these letters as a form of dialogue, we knew that love had to be at the core of what we aimed to do, because confronting and refusing colonialism requires its affective antithesis. As Paulo Freire ([1970] 1996: 70) so beautifully put it: "Dialogue cannot exist . . . in the absence of a profound love for the world and for people. . . . Love is at the same time the foundation of dialogue and dialogue itself. . . . Because love is an act of courage, not of fear, love is commitment to others. No matter where the oppressed are found, the act of love is commitment to their cause—the cause of liberation. And this commitment, because it is loving, is dialogical." Freire's powerful statement affirms that, to find liberation from oppression, we must anchor ourselves and our work in love. Aurora Chang (2018) similarly points out the importance of centering love when conducting research with vulnerable populations in an effort to open ourselves to the healing and transformative powers of love. In addition, we notice and value (and need) the love letters Black and other racially minoritized faculty have written to and for each other, as well as to and for students (e.g., Beatty et al. 2020; Calafell 2007; Kynard 2019; Paris 2014). The many love letters available online speak to the need for love to be poured into and within our communities. We also view these love letters as a tool for resistance, similar to the notes and messages written by and exchanged between enslaved people during the colonial era. Such messages served as a means of keeping hope alive, connecting to new friends, and affirming one's connection to the motherland. These notes between enslaved people also dispel false histories that Black people were not intelligent and could not read or write—or, for that matter, were not capable of as lofty and valued an emotion as love. With this history in mind, we were able to collectively commit to this dialogical process and to each other. We now share our letters with you.

Love Letters

July 10, 2020

Dear Raquel,

When we all met in the conference room in the Netherlands and introduced ourselves, I knew we were all connected because of our commitment to racial equity in education. As the days passed, I felt a sense of community building among all of us. The day we visited the museum, in the carriage house, I looked at a map of Suriname, the plantation divisions, and the picture with the big house on the plantation. And, something happened. I realized, more clearly than ever, that what bonded all of us on the trip was not only our scholarship and commitment to racial equity, but a family-hood birthed through the tragedy of colonialism. In other words, you and the other racially minoritized people on the trip are actually brothers and sisters. Not in a figurative way, but for real—the Atlantic slave trade birthed us a long time ago. Our ancestors are family. We are family. This feeling sank deep into my heart in that moment. My eyes welled up with the emotion of a sudden connection with a long-lost family member, but also looking around us and wondering why I didn't see this all along. Not just now, but always. I knew why in that moment: the colonial project split us up a long time ago, it split up our ancestors and does not want us to know or live like we are family.

I was born in Puerto Rico and grew up in the New York metropolitan area. My world growing up was mostly Black and Brown. We were the majority. I knew we were poor, and everyone else around me, for the most part, was poor too. In this sense, I felt . . . a solidarity across racial and ethnic communities, but family, for me, was more intimate. That shattered that day in the Netherlands looking at that map. We *are* family. My eyes welled up over the connection, but also of the pain and the loss; we don't live, act, work, or love like we, across racial and ethnic lines, are family. Or, maybe I should be saying I haven't lived, acted, worked, or loved like *we* are family. You might feel differently and I welcome hearing your thoughts on this. What would happen if we did? If I did? If we have a sisterhood birthed through colonialism, how does recognizing this explicitly and living it out change us? How would we see each other in each other? How does it change the way we, as a larger community, live, work, love with each other? How does it dismantle the power structure of colonialism? I'm even afraid to say this too loud. Will the colonial master hear me and start working to destroy the possibility of this family-hood?

I must give these very questions more thought. To borrow your words, I want to consider what it means to decolonize love—what it is, how it is offered, and to whom. Seeing love as including radical honesty (Williams 2016), showing up, giving space so wounds can heal, and planting new seeds that deepen and transform the connection between us. Love means your wounds are my wounds. Your hopes are my hopes. Your fears are my fears. Your joy is my joy. Your pain is my pain. It reminds me of the Mayan principle *In Lak'Ech*, meaning that you are my other me.

Love,
Milagros

o o o

July 12, 2020

Dear Milagros,

It is interesting that you mention our visit to the Museum Van Loon during our trip to the Netherlands, since I, too, had a profound moment during the tour. I was born and raised in Kingston, Jamaica, and grew up on an island that is predominantly Black. My immediate and extended family are multiracial (Black, South Asian, and white). I moved to the United States for college and graduate school, where I ended up making the United States my home (for now). I enjoyed every moment of my trip to the Netherlands and am still processing much of the self-reflection that took place and the moments of transformative learning that I totally did not expect!

For me, there were several visceral reactions taking place simultaneously during our museum visit. The irony of being in the "big house" and navigating its nooks and crannies made me nostalgic of the history I had learned growing up in Jamaica. In particular, the experience recalled the stories of wealthy merchants and directors of the slave trade who profited immensely from the bodies and souls of enslaved people. I remember thinking, as we stood in Van Loon's dining room, that he must be turning in his grave as I, a descendant of both enslaved people and colonizers, stood in the very location where plots of the slave trade ensued daily. I remember being disgusted by the very presence of the family crest that proudly boasted the heads of Black enslaved women and being angry at how colonizers took joy in the commodification of enslaved people. As I walked through the connecting garden into the carriage house, I was shaken by the powerful display of artifacts showcasing the cultural history of Suriname. Honestly, I teleported back to colonial Jamaica in that moment, as I observed pictures of landscapes and plantation houses similar to those in Jamaica.

For the rest of the tour, I reminisced about my childhood history classes in Jamaica, which taught brutal truths about the trials that enslaved people endured on Jamaican plantations. Many things struck me during this tour, but particularly the images that depicted enslaved people on plantations, looking "happy" or "indifferent." In many instances they seemed to be empty shells, just images without souls. Those pictures cut deep. I'm not sure why this moment impacted me so profoundly. Maybe sometimes it takes a physical separation from your comfort zone to really "feel" things and make sense of them. I also know in that moment I felt very alone, and while I know most of us on this trip came from racially and ethnically minoritized backgrounds, something about my own personal journey being raised in a former colony was immensely triggered.

Maybe it is the fact that, although I live in the colonizer's land, I have never truly felt like an American, because I have always been othered. Whether it is because of my accent, or immigration status, and most recently my naturalized status, I've always felt too Jamaican and not American enough. Perhaps the loneliness I felt on the tour stemmed from the realization that colonialism is global, far-reaching, and transcends language, culture, nationality but still upholds whiteness as absolute. The colonizers ravaged colonies, leaving little to no resources, and still, we continue to be sidelined and treated as second-class citizens always needing the help of "Massa." The cycle never seems to end. That day I heard the ancestral voices of enslaved people on Jamaican plantations loud and clear as I viewed pictures of Surinamese plantations.

We are indeed connected by a rich, painful colonial history that seeks to separate rather than unite us. Your question about what it would be like to see ourselves in each other is a great one, but in order to answer that I think we have to start from the beginning and understand how history has pitted us, and continues to pit us, against each other. We must reflect on how anti-Blackness, colorism, and access to privileges like "citizenship" creates an *us versus them* mentality. This mentality gives rise to feelings of resentment, fear, and marginalization in both our communities. I once read that the opposite of love is fear, not hate, and I believe that our inability to love is deeply rooted in our fear of each other, created mainly by our painful colonial histories.

Recognizing our past and examining how it has impacted us is the first step to embracing our sisterhood birthed through colonialism. It means understanding and contextualizing the privileges we do and do not hold as a result of those histories, unpacking how sisters could actually be family although they look and sound different. It means that our communities should live, work, and love each other for better or for worse. It means being willing to fight each other's fights for justice without playing "oppression Olympics." It means pledging to disrupt what we have learned from our own families about people from other racial, ethnic, and national backgrounds. It means holding ourselves and each other accountable and having honest, hard, transparent, and vulnerable conversations in which we push our boundaries and beliefs. It means understanding and being willing to forgive each other for our imperfections, while simultaneously allowing for growth and being unashamed to grow. Why is this so hard for us to do as human beings? Why do so many of us cower at the onset of feelings of shame?

But, alas Milagros, colonizers do not want us to be sisters, and do not want us to fight for each other. The system was intentionally created for us to live in silos and operate in isolation *against* rather than *alongside* each other. Think about how many times in our own families we have been conditioned to think of ourselves as better than others . . . how we have been pushed to only associate with people who can elevate us . . . or make us more like the colonizer. To facilitate "culture change" in both our communities, we must consciously engage in unlearning, relearning, and be willing to choose to partner with each other. As we both know, decolonization is a process, this is just the beginning! There is one picture that really left an imprint in my mind ever since our tour of the Surinamese exhibition in the Netherlands; do you remember the picture of the mannequin wearing the shirt, "Which Legacy Do You Choose?" It is a question I often reflect on and urge you to think about as well.

With Love,
Raquel

° ° °

July 15, 2020

Dear Raquel,

The picture you referenced brought up so many emotions. I remember seeing it, and it is a simple but such a powerful question for us to ask ourselves about the legacy we choose to honor. I find that I regularly choose the legacy of resistance. I think often and mostly as being from a people who have been and continue to be colonized, and yet we dance, we laugh, we dream, we hope, we love, we cry, we unite with nature, we go with an island vibe—not so stringent about life. I am in awe that we continue to find ways to reinvent and reimagine what is possible despite the suffering we have and continue to endure as a people and community. And this suffering, while broadly shared, is only deeper when it comes to Afro-Caribbean people.

Recently, I learned that Puerto Rico was one of the last islands to abolish slavery. While it was under Spain's control, Spain waited until 1873 to abolish slavery, but then still had enslaved people work for three more years before they could taste their freedom (Library of Congress 2011). And, you know who was compensated when all was said and done? The plantation owners! For their poor suffering of losing enslaved people, Spain "compensated" each owner "with 35 million pesetas per slave" (Library of Congress 2011). Ugh . . . the inhumanity. It's hard to stomach it. . . . In Puerto Rico, you can see the racial divide, especially since there are some towns (example: Loiza) that are majority Afro–Puerto Ricans. That is, Afro–Puerto Ricans are still mainly in towns where enslaved people were taken to and sold.

And, with all this history, in my experience within my own family we speak so little about race. . . . Everyone just says we are all Puerto Rican. I remember asking my dad when I was about ten years old why I was so light-skinned and he was so dark-skinned. He . . . said that underneath we were all the same.[2] So, I think that planted an early confusion about race: I could see it (not only in skin color, but also in [some of] our practices of spiritual healing, etc.), but no one else around me did. . . . Even our music, bomba, *plena*, salsa, all derive from West African roots.

A recent podcast from *Code Switch* (Florido 2020) helped me understand how we erase race (specifically Blackness) in Puerto Rico. It talked about how the census in Puerto Rico was revised a few decades ago to remove race questions because they were not relevant to us since we are all mixed (Spaniard, Taino Indian, and West African). I couldn't believe it! There it was—the colonial project well and alive, erasing race while leaving the consequences of racial suffering (particularly Black suffering) in place. This suffering and its erasure is something that came to mind a lot when we were taken on the Black heritage tour in the Netherlands and there was this portrait of a wealthy white lady with her servant boy (he was dressed up, but potentially her enslaved child worker). The tour guide said it was a common practice to have family portraits with servants because this was a symbol of wealth to have an enslaved house worker. And, then I saw this other picture later in the museum where in the sea of whiteness (in a ballroom) there was a Black servant in the back corner. He was there, but he almost blended with the wall. We could see him just enough, but not too much. He existed only enough to showcase him as property, to display white wealth through his dehumanization. So, about my legacy, I choose the legacy of resistance, a resistance against colonialism and the erasure of Blackness.

You asked great questions: why do we cower at the feelings of shame? Because shame is hard to not internalize and we must move the shame away from us as individuals and back on the system. Shame on colonization, not us. When I read this sentence you wrote, "But, alas Milagros, colonizers do not want us to be sisters, and do not want us to fight for each other," I felt sad. It is so true. The entire system not only does not want us to fight for each other, but intentionally wants us to fight each other. This happened with the way they pitted enslaved people in the house against enslaved people in the fields, and they pit us against each other now with more tools of oppression and domination. Anything so that we do not see each other in each other. I'm wondering of examples you have experienced where you have seen our communities not engage in the "*us versus them* mentality." Do you have any experiences that speak to that?

Love,
Milagros

o o o

July 22, 2020

Milagros,

Resistance is the word of the day for us both it seems; I too choose the legacy of resistance and have always chosen to resist even when there was no language to qualify what I was doing. As I have grown and developed into a scholar, I have realized that erasure is a direct and purposeful by-product of colonialism—an attempt to intentionally delete and wipe out the harm done to our communities for centuries. Colonizers have always been of the mindset that they can just wipe the slate clean, not realizing that trauma lives on and is passed on through generations, as our bodies, minds, and souls do not forget violence against us.

Many of my friends and family members also shy away from conversations of race. I push them and try to disrupt normative ways of thinking and try to educate them on how we come to know what we know. By default, knowledge, as we have learned it, is held as absolute. I am always intrigued by my fellow Jamaicans who discuss issues of "classism" without recognizing how much class is deeply rooted in racism. I, too, found a crutch in discussions of classism in my younger years because something about class felt easier to process than the messiness and deep digging associated with racism. Again, we try to avoid that which pains our conscious and unconscious mind. Being deeply immersed in racial equity work means always having to engage in hard conversations at work, school, or play—I find it never ends. I think it's the hardest part of my job as a professor who studies equity specific to racially minoritized populations, never being able to turn off my mind and always grappling with resistance in all its forms.

The picture you referenced in your letter also stirred many emotions for me—I remember it so clearly. I remember thinking he blended in so well with the curtains and canisters on the table but stood out just enough to prove the magnitude of wealth the slave owners had. How many examples of this dehumanization of Black people can we recall, and continue to see today? "White wealth," as you say, lives on in so many forms beyond just showcasing having financial capital. I think immediately about the academy: institutions of higher education proudly showcase "scholars of color" who do diversity work and are often the only ones in our departments. Yet our work is often devalued, not supported, misunderstood, and described as not objective or rigorous.

The white academy profits from our dehumanization (when our work is not valued and we are not tenured and promoted), yet it uses us to prove a point that institutions are honoring and supporting their "diversity and inclusion" commitments. How many years have Black women been talking about "white fragility" with little to no attention? Yet, when a white woman writes a book on the very topic, it is lauded in majority culture as the gospel, a number one best seller in teaching white people about themselves. That is not a personal attack on Dr. [Robin] DiAngelo, whose work is important, but rather on the system that elevates white voices and makes Black voices invisible. How many Black women authors can you name that spoke about the same thing over centuries? Or, the pride many non-Black people take in boasting about their Black/Jamaican/African/(insert other Black ethnicity here) friends, while still being reluctant to fight for equity, inclusion, and anti-Blackness. White wealth spans finances and also includes power that abuses and takes advantage of people and then profits from it.

I'm fascinated by the experience you shared of growing up and asking very pointed questions about race. I understand these experiences so well and have asked similar questions as well. Growing up in a multiracial family also yielded many of these emotions and questions for me. For me it was the obsession of having very different hair than my mother, and wondering why it was "too curly," "too thick," or "too unruly" . . . stereotypes that are often placed upon Black women's natural hair. Like you, many of my family and friends still gloss over race and focus more on national identity. Like Puerto Ricans, we *are* Jamaicans, but we are also Black, white, South Asian, and so much more, the latter of which we are often afraid to name. *Afro-Caribbean*, for example, is a term I only learned when I moved to the United States. How crazy is that? What I have learned in discussions with many of my Jamaican friends who also immigrated to the United States is that this is their experience as well. So, what does that tell us? Well, the colonizer lives on in our internalized oppression, and so does our fear to proudly embrace our deeply rich racial and ethnic histories. What I mean by this is when we fear discussing and embracing our varied racial identities we move away from what many of our ancestors fought for: the recognition, understanding, and acceptance of racially minoritized people as human beings who contribute richly to the world. I also want to acknowledge that within both our communities there are great inequities within racial groups. Colorism lives on, and just as enslaved people in the house were pitted against enslaved people in the fields, in many ways that continues today. People with darker complexions are often seen as "less than" their lighter-skinned counterparts, who are offered more opportunities and treated very differently. This is not unique to any one context: you have seen this in Puerto Rico, I have witnessed this in Jamaica, and we both experienced this in the United States as well. We must realize that these socially constructed categories serve to further divide, not unite us. We must actively work through them to disrupt our internalized oppression and the notion that white is right, or that proximity to whiteness is better. I see the work as always continuing, Milagros. We have spent centuries hating ourselves and our communities, so learning to love the very bodies we detest will take time, patience, and a willingness to unpack metanarratives and othering, taught to us by colonizers whose sole intentions were to divide and conquer.

The example that came to mind about our communities not engaging in *Us versus Them* Olympics is my friend Brenda. She identifies as Chicana and is the daughter of Mexican immigrants. She is also a professor in higher education. I noticed Brenda's activism very early after meeting her and remember being intrigued and truthfully somewhat shocked by her level of awareness, recognition, and support for Blackness in all its forms. She proudly supports and advocates for Black people and was always the first to speak up about anti-Blackness in Latino communities. Not only did I feel like Brenda *saw me* and others in my community, but she was willing to fight for equity in a way I never experienced, especially from someone who did not identify as Black or Afro-Latino. She understood the transnationalism of my struggle as a Jamaican immigrant navigating Blackness and multiraciality in a world that was unfamiliar and unwelcoming in so many ways. Activism runs deep in her bloodline, and it started at a young age through reinforced family values and television. She once told me that she found common ground with the struggles of Black people, as they reminded her of her own experience with racism, as a Mexican American growing up in a predominantly white farm town. She has no problem making people uncomfortable with her commitment to dismantling anti-Blackness, particularly in Latino communities.

Centering Black lives is instrumental to her existence; I have witnessed this firsthand over and over again: in her push back in our doctoral classes, professional conferences, and social settings (much to the dismay of others not ready or unwilling to *hear* her). As our friendship has grown over the years, I have come to understand that, for Brenda, centering Black lives is central to her existence and success, because she clearly understands that our battles are all connected and woven so intricately . . . so my fight is her fight and her fight is my fight. Part of the beauty of *our* sisterhood is that Brenda unapologetically pushes those in her community to see their own complicity in anti-Blackness. I have always felt a strong sense of security in our friendship. For this, and several other reasons, she is one of a few non-Black friends who I am confident would show up and wage it all for me.

For me and Brenda, we are sisters not just through the academy (though the academy brought us together) but we are connected by mestizo bloodlines, plantations, farms, sweat, slaughter, deep love, resilience, and so much more. How many people can say that about their friends, or communities?

Love,
Raquel

o o o

July 23, 2020

Dear Raquel,

I can see clearly from what you have written about why Brenda is your sister-friend. She stands up against anti-Blackness whether you are there or not and is unapologetic about why it matters. It sounds to me like someone you can fully trust and love because she is real—a real friend, a real co-conspirator in this struggle for Black liberation. That is beautiful. I think you are right that few people can say that about their friends or communities. I sat with that for a bit.

What can we do so that this is more the reality than not? How do we fight against how colonization has infiltrated our communities so that we are pitted against each other? It is not our fault because colonization is doing exactly what it is meant to be doing—breaking us down. But, how do we push against that and move toward love across our communities? So much of the conversations, scholarship, programming, is on this white-Black binary. We are working to dismantle whiteness, which we need to do. Yet, how much time and energy does that leave for us to not center whiteness, but to center our communities: to work on love within and across our communities? How do we shift some of the energy to seeing ourselves in each other?

Should fighting whiteness directly be primary in this struggle or should fighting whiteness indirectly through direct love-work in our communities be primary? Both are needed. No doubt. I'm wondering if our actions need to center Black, Indigenous, and racially minoritized people love way more than it currently does. What would that look like? What could result if this was the focus of our efforts? Much of the healing and reconciliation initiatives I've seen have focused on racially minoritized people healing and reconciling with whites. But, why? Why aren't we healing and reconciling with each other as a community? How did whiteness get centered? Do we even have a concept, theory, or community way of talking about, thinking about, engaging in, studying, community solidarity? There are such few examples that I can think of that focus on this type of solidarity within and across our communities. The thing that stands out to me, though, is that examples of this type of solidarity are not as pervasive as the focus on healing, calling in, calling out, dialoguing with, white people. What do you think of this?

Another thing that has been on my mind a lot lately is how, by using broad labels like diversity or People of Color, we get united, but we also get lumped together in a way that I'm not sure is fostering community. And, it erases distinctions that are important parts of the lived experiences and needs of each community. In particular, Blackness gets erased, and that only hurts all people of the African diaspora across the globe (Dache, Haywood, and Mislán 2019; Haywood 2017). There is this tension for me of wanting to connect us as a community because we are stronger together but also wanting there to be connection among us, even when we focus on the specific needs of each community.

I wonder if we, I, could benefit from a spiritual transformation. Could focusing on spiritual transformation support this work to heal and reconcile between communities? Could the poem "ritual . . . prayer . . . blessing . . . for transformation" (Anzaldúa 2002: 574–76) be helpful for guiding this spiritual transformation? In this poem, Anzaldúa calls on the spirits of nature and of our ancestors to help us "remember our interrelatedness" and the need for "transformation" so that we "create outrageously" and in the process "honor other people's feelings . . . as we do our own" as well as "heal the wounds of hate, ignorance, [and] indifference that break us apart" (574–75). It is such a powerful poem. And, of course, there is much more to it than I'm writing here. Could this be a call to action for us, for our communities, for healing, for coalition building?

With love,
Milagros

○ ○ ○

July 27, 2020

Dear Milagros,

I love that poem, as I do all of Anzaldúa's work! Thank you for including that; it undoubtedly captures many of the points you raise in your previous letter and provides an incredibly creative and powerful way to (re)imagine ourselves and each other. The inclusion of that poem grounds this dialogue and takes the discourse to an entirely new level. DEEP! It is absolutely a highly impactful piece that incorporates us seeing ourselves in each other and understanding what exactly it takes to do so. Seeing ourselves as intricately woven together throughout time, space, body, mind, and soul. Water for me, *agua* for you—it doesn't change what it is based on what it is called, or named. How can we connect and capture our experiences and lives across our collective and individual pain . . . *dolor* and healing . . . *curación?*

While reading Anzaldua's poem, the following really resonated with me as a strong call to action for what it takes to engage in community solidarity:

Agua, may we honor other people's feelings
respect their anger, sadness, grief, joy as we do our own.
Though we tremble before uncertain futures
may we meet illness, death and adversity with strength
may we dance in the face of our fears. (Anzaldúa 2002: 575)

This is how we move toward loving across communities! We honor and respect feelings and discomfort and recognize that it is through pain, grief, and adversity that we truly grow and develop while enacting meaningful change. This for many people is easier said than done—fear is paralyzing, and many do get caught up in the shame that ensues as a result of fear, and move away from the opportunity to learn, grow, and dare to be different. For many, it is easier to run, avoid, and hide, rather than embrace an opportunity to work toward doing the tough job of really, truly, and deeply illustrating and embodying loving actions. A call toward spiritual transformation as a collaborative vehicle fascinates me; it's not one I have given much thought to in regards to coalition building in our communities. However, in my own life, I ground myself and heal through connecting with spirit, so why should it be different in terms of coalition building? Spiritual transformation is certainly a starting place to deconstruct and reconstruct our own ideas and actions (or lack thereof).

You raise such great questions, and your question on why we consistently center whiteness is a great one. I think it depends on what the goal is within our communities and how we understand, recognize, and are willing to admit how much control whiteness has on us . . . we must examine that first in order to understand why we constantly center whiteness. Isn't this how whiteness works though? In order to focus on our own community wealth, resources, support, and love, this is crucial to name. Colonialism and racism have been internalized and centered by so many in and across our communities. Our task should be to (re)create our communities by naming how we embody these toxic traits, not be ashamed, and be willing and committed to work through it. We have to exhibit care and intentionality to ourselves while attempting to decenter whiteness; we work toward raising our voices, voices which have been so silenced and invalidated for SO long. It will be challenging, but it is possible. Active resistance requires deep digging and engaging in something larger than just ourselves. We must commit to discuss and understand how we perpetuate destructive rhetoric through our words, actions, and ideology, and mindfully disrupt these very oppressive systems that constrain us and indoctrinate our hegemonic notions of what is "real."

After George Floyd's murder, for example, I saw an article about many other racially minoritized groups that were "offended" that their lives didn't seemingly matter as much as Black lives. It pains me that other minoritized groups, especially, see this as a dismissal of their lives, when, as we clearly see, it is not. I have been really excited to see many of our colleagues in academe (both within education and outside of education) discuss these actions within their communities. They have made clear and constructive statements that in order to move toward equity for all, there has to be a centering of Blackness and a shift away from anti-Blackness. Again, there has to be a collective understanding among racially minoritized populations that we are stronger together, even while respecting and appreciating our individual differences.

You point out your struggle with the term *People of Color*. This is something I, too, grapple with, as it ignores racial hierarchy and we get lumped into one big category that almost never recognizes said hierarchy and the complicated histories that led us to this point. I actually also just detest the term, period! I make it a point to always say racially minoritized whether I am writing, teaching, or talking to family members, to ensure that I am making it clear that racially minoritized people were given minority status and deemed less-than in relation to white people and not by choice, or an accurate representation of the number of people in a group (Benitez 2010; Stewart 2013).

I am very reflective on your letter this week. I'm thinking about my own abilities to communicate to those who have caused me pain in and across minoritized communities in a way that seeks to educate rather than silence. I am particularly thinking about how in those moments, the rawness and bitter sting of pain paralyzes my own understanding and response to this very thing we are writing about.

Love,
Raquel

o o o

July 26, 2020

Dear Raquel,

I read your letter a few times. I relished listening and listening again to your thoughts as I read and re-read your letter. While the whole letter really captivated me, there are two points that made me pause, reflect, and imagine possibilities. The first is when you wrote, "However, in my own life, I ground myself and heal through connecting with spirit, so why should it be different in terms of coalition building? Spiritual transformation is certainly a starting place to deconstruct and reconstruct our own ideas and actions (or lack thereof)." It really made me pause to read this because this is also true for me. I pray daily. I read scripture daily. And, I do pray for God's words to guide my work, relationships, endeavors, but I do not think I pray explicitly for spiritual guidance, healing, and transformation in coalition building. Like you, I wonder why not, and call myself to make this a more active part of my spiritual work. What will be possible in coalition building if spiritual transformation guides the work?

Another part of your letter that I deeply reflected on is when you wrote, "I'm thinking about my own abilities to communicate to those who have caused me pain in and across minoritized communities in a way that seeks to educate rather than silence." I think this is something that is so hard to do in the moment of that raw striking pain that comes from those we most expect to be in solidarity with. I think when I am hurt by white people . . . while it still hurts it is a dull pain, one I anticipate before it even happens. When I am hurt by other racially minoritized people, the pain is deep, visceral, disturbing, and causes in me a brokenness that is hard to heal. Yet, in thinking about your words I reflected on family. The fact that family sometimes hurt us, but because they are family we find ways to forgive, to love, to heal, to connect. How might this be part of coalition building within and across our own communities? This thought is sitting in my heart, and I'm glad because I think it asks more of me individually and gives more to the collective.

Another thing I've been thinking about is how there is something beautiful and perhaps necessary in seeing each other in each other (tu eres mi otro yo). Yet, can we do this in a way that honors also how we are different in ways that matter to our lives and livelihood? For instance, I see much of me in you, but to see you I must see your experience as different too—as a racially mixed Black woman you confront, experience, and live realities that I will never live. I must see that to see you. And, there is so much even within that experience—pain, fear, but also hope and strength. There is so much to us all. What prism could help us see each other, *really* see each other and all the complexities that make us, us?

In thinking about what it will take to move toward more solidarity, I reflect on the transformation that seems to be happening right now in this moment in time around the world. There is something just striking about seeing a youth generation cross boundaries and stand together. Even in its imperfection, it calls for us to see that the next generation is moving us forward to something new, to something better. While our letters have been mostly focused on us, as two women, we are also two mothers and two educators—both roles that call us to shaping, informing, guiding, and supporting the next generation, while we also listen and learn from them. This is not to say it is only our role to do this, but I am embracing it as part of my role. This thought made me think of Sweet Honey in the Rock's (1988) song "Ella's Song: 'We Who Believe in Freedom Cannot Rest Until It Comes.'" The song highlights the pain of the past and the hope in the next generation. I wonder how our insights, writings, healing, loving, learning, sharing, reflecting, and growing will and can shape us as mothers and educators serving and working with the next generation—as "we who believe in freedom cannot rest until it comes."

Love, Milagros

∘ ∘ ∘

August, 8, 2020

Dear Milagros,

How relevant the song "We Who Believe in Freedom Cannot Rest Until It Comes" continues to be, and how sad that in 2020 we are still resonant with the lyrics and message captured. Everything Ella Baker fought for, still continues. I think including this song is relevant to our letters and also the conversations we have had in our collective fight for racial equity. I also strongly believe our reflections, like this song, and music, and stories have been for both our people, carry powerful messages and can be passed on through generations. Our responsibility will be to ensure these stories continue to be passed on through generations. We need to ask each generation to continue to complicate the work of those who have come before us. This includes equipping our children with knowledge that contextualizes their experiences, our experiences, and that of our ancestors. Only then can they fully understand the complexity of what it means to not rest until freedom comes. This is a shared responsibility that all members of our birth and chosen families should partake in. While we are mothers and educators, as you point out, it cannot be our sole responsibility to inform and guide the next generation. Collective transformation requires buy-in from all within our communities. The burden of informing, supporting, and guiding them should not necessarily be uniform. What I mean by this is our messaging should not only be academic, or gendered; rather, it should be a collection of knowledge. It is in doing so that our narratives are shared widely, broadly, deeply, and richly. This is how we cultivate in our children an appreciation and understanding for seeing ourselves in each other.

As I process our letters (which, by the way, I have enjoyed and looked forward to exchanging with you each week), I realize that engaging in the work of seeing ourselves in each other takes great vulnerability, reflection, reflexivity, patience, and understanding. However, if we are to enact meaningful change and create a culture of seeing ourselves in each other, it is absolutely necessary that we challenge ourselves AND each other to move past our hesitancy and unwillingness to engage in the hard work of disrupting what we have been socialized to think of as normal or right. Perhaps allowing ourselves to feel the emotions (positive or negative) that accompany our pain and committing to working through it—healing—could be a starting place. Sometimes I think our coping mechanism as humans is to deny or push aside our emotions and pretend we are ourselves.

Perhaps normalizing that we are not okay, or struggling, is a starting place for everything else I previously mentioned. In order to be vulnerable, reflective, reflexive, patient, and understanding we have to first understand what it is that causes us to think, feel, behave, or see things a certain way. These are not easy tasks, I realize, but as we make sense of our world today, the need to be all these things and more is so pertinent. Imagine being able for one moment to suspend our own judgments of each other and really focus on the root of our pain? I think we would realize we are more alike than different, and that through our differences we can learn so much about how and why we are who we are.

Communication is also key to seeing ourselves in each other. Talking about and being free to express ourselves without being judged as "too angry," "too sensitive," "too defensive," "too . . ." What would it mean to truly and honestly communicate with each other without worrying about backlash, judgment, punishment, and so forth? What if we actually communicated to listen, improve ourselves, and commit to coalition building, despite experiencing feelings of discomfort? Certainly I am not calling for a dismissal of discomfort but rather for an honoring of our discomfort and utilizing it productively. It truly takes a village to implement change in how we see ourselves and each other. It is my hope that we can unite within and across our communities to defy what the colonial project sought to do: divide and conquer. The work continues, and though our letter writing has come to an end, I look forward to seeing where this leads us both individually and collectively.

In solidarity (and always love),
Raquel

Healing and Transformation

Writing these love letters connected us, provided a space to process and heal, while helping us think about and engage in personal transformation and coalition building centered on love. Writing, reading, and reflecting on each other's letters provoked us to deepen our conversations about our positionalities, and in doing so we deepened our connection because we could more clearly see ourselves in each other, as well as honor our differences. We talked after writing these letters and not only shared what we gained from them but also reckoned with the work they left undone—because the work can never be done, but must be ongoing. Both of us found that there were deep personal aspects of our positionalities, the lived realities of which resisted capture through written discourse. For instance, Raquel's ancestors are connected by a web of racial hierarchy: enslaved Africans, poor South Asian indentured laborers, and wealthy white landowners all in her direct bloodline. Similarly, Milagros grapples with the African lineage that goes unspoken in her racially mixed Puerto Rican family. Sharing with one another our difficulties in conveying this complexity enabled a different form of connection that was not there or perhaps not even authentically possible before. Crucially, the temporality of letter writing provided the necessary space to build trust—a project that cannot, by definition, be rushed. Writing these love letters allowed us to arrive at a place where we could further interrogate what we know about ourselves and how it shapes us.

Growing in our capacity to witness ourselves in each other also offered us seeds of healing in the context of colonialism's past and present efforts to divide and conquer, a tactic that has been deployed in various ways against generation after generation. We are by-products of colonialism's hate. And we further entrench its legacy when we internalize that hate and leave its relations of alienation and antagonism intact. We must recognize and reject the hate we have been told (in ways both insidious and overt) to feel for each other, and reclaim our love for each other. Make no mistake: this healing will likely take generations, just as it took generations to instill. But we found this love letter process to be a great tool for facilitating the healing journey. The experience we had mirrored what other scholars have written about the healing spaces, the homeplaces, that Black and other racially minoritized women create and need (e.g., Davis 2019; hooks 2015; Latina Feminist Group 2001). What was unique in our experience is that, while we are both racially minoritized women, we experience this differently, given our own cultures and how society treats us because of the color of our skin. We had questions we never dared to ask others, we had answers we did not even know we had, and we shared tears and joy that we could only express in the process of building sisterhood together. It is a reckoning we think more of us Black, Indigenous, and other racially minoritized people could benefit from individually and collectively. We offer this love letter approach as another way to create homeplace across space and time.

Lastly, we want to note that we changed along the way and transformed individually and collectively. We clarified what is painful about our identities and the root of that pain. We also recognized that we can no longer proceed in our lives without this connection. We have a deepened commitment to coalition building across racial lines within racially minoritized communities. Our communities and our families deserve healing.

We did not center our experiences as women here, but we want to acknowledge that part of our connection did come through our specifically gendered experiences of being racially minoritized. We think this is powerful, given the legacy we inherit of women creating spaces for healing (hooks 2015). It is important to counter dehumanization by allowing ourselves to be fully human, in all its complexities. Given this insight, we share the following to guide others who might be interested in engaging in a similar process.

Engaging with the Love Letter Approach

We suggest that, prior to starting a love letter journey with someone else (or with a few people), each person engage in some personal reflection, addressing: Who do you need or want to have a dialogue with about race, and why? Are they interested in having this dialogue with you? Why do you need or want to have this dialogue? What do you hope to achieve through this love letter writing process? When will this process be possible and for how long? How will you engage in writing these letters (e.g., email, online platform, traditional mail)? We encourage an initial conversation addressing these important questions that center the *who, why, what, when,* and *how* of the process to ensure a shared perspective and commitment. This is something that we did prior to starting our letter writing, and it was beneficial to building a foundation for our process.

The love letter approach requires the following (we agreed on these prior to writing):

➤ **Legacy:** Understand that letter writing, creating homeplaces, dialoguing, and finding ways to foster healing are all acts of resistance that we, as racially minoritized people, inherit. It is a legacy with long colonial roots. As you engage in this approach, it is important to recognize this history. And, at the same time, it is also a great responsibility—creating another legacy for the generations to come.

➤ **Love:** Love for yourself and the other person. Even if love is an emotion that you might not feel yet, evoke love in the writing process. Do it for and out of love. Without love, this dialogue will reproduce a dehumanizing experience, however inadvertently. Love counters that possibility. It says and nourishes the sentiment: You are fully human. You matter. And I love you.

➤ **Bold courage:** To engage in this process, you must put fear down and pick up and embrace bold courage and vulnerability. By this we mean, say what you really need to say without fear that it will be used against you or that you will be wrong. Share what you are thinking and feeling with full and outrageous courage and a deep faith that, on the other side, there is someone waiting to receive your thoughts with love.

➤ **Respect:** You must be fully committed to respecting each other's journeys. No journey will be the same and no one has it right. There must be freedom from judgment, or the love letter writing approach can cause more pain than healing.

➤ **Confidentiality:** To be able to write with love, bold courage, and respect, there has to be a shared understanding of confidentiality. The content of the love letters belongs to the people involved, and nothing can or should be done with that content without agreement of the other people involved. It is their community property.

➤ **Center Race:** We have many aspects to our identities, and all of them shape who we are. We strongly encourage that these love letters centralize race. We believe that we must grapple with colonialism as a racial project in order to work toward liberation. We say this while also recognizing the ways in which we bonded over our womanhood—dialoguing about being mothers, partners, daughters, and more. This was another layer of connection and bonding. We also connected and bonded over our academic lives and discussed differences in our socioeconomic backgrounds. These all added to but did not distract us from our conversations on race. Instead, they added elements of identities that impact our lived experiences, but race remained in the forefront of our love letters.

➢ **Debrief:** The love letters can be a powerful tool for dialogue. Nonetheless, we also encourage live dialogue at some point, in which the people involved meet in person to discuss how the experience feels and why, what is surfacing, and where the dialogue needs to continue to go. Engaging in live dialogues periodically can support the love letter dialogue. We had an initial dialogue before we started letter writing, then we wrote these letters, and then we debriefed afterward, multiple times.

If you choose to engage in a love letter approach, we welcome you (with collective agreement to do so) to share these with us by emailing the corresponding author (contact information provided at the end of the piece). Our hope is to one day compile a collection of love letters that capture the essence and complexity of doing "race work." May the love letter writing begin!

With Love/Con Amor,
Raquel and Milagros

Dr. Raquel Wright-Mair is assistant professor of higher education in the Department of Educational Services and Leadership at Rowan University. Her research focuses on advancing social justice and equity and supporting the success of racially minoritized faculty members. Email: wrightmair@rowan.edu.

Dr. Castillo-Montoya is associate professor of higher education and student affairs in the Department of Educational Leadership at the University of Connecticut. Her research focuses on equity-based learning for Black and Latinx first-generation college students, equity-based teaching in higher education, and improving the experiences of racially minoritized faculty. Email: milagros.castillo-montoya@uconn.edu.

Notes

We want to take this opportunity to thank Dr. Frank Tuitt, Dr. Derrick Brooms, and Mikaela Levons for being a part of our love letter journey by providing their thoughtful feedback during our writing of this manuscript. We thank Dr. Tuitt for organizing, in collaboration with the Expertise Centre for Diversity Policy, the Racial Equity Summit in the Netherlands. It was an experience that continues to bear fruit.

1   We use the term *racially minoritized* to refer to people from diverse racial populations other than white people, who have little power in society based on a socially constructed status given to them by those in power (Benitez 2010; Stewart 2013).

2   I, Milagros, appreciate the way my dad grounded me in our common humanity when I was a little girl. I still had questions about race that I explored (and still am exploring) as I continue to grow. I am grateful too that as a result of this love letter experience with Raquel, I engaged in two meaningful conversations with my dad about his childhood, our family, his upbringing, and his thoughts on race. I now have much deeper understanding of his worldview and how it influences his thoughts on race. I, Raquel, similarly engaged my father in conversations about race and our family. I am grateful that through this process I was able to gather crucial historical documents dating back to the seventeenth century, as a result of my father's work on our family genealogy. During this time, my dad and I made several discoveries and processed everyone together.

Works Cited

Anzaldúa, Gloria E. 2002. "Ritual . . . Prayer . . . Blessing . . . for Transformation." In *This Bridge We Call Home: Radical Visions for Transformation*, edited by Gloria E. Anzaldúa and AnaLouise Keating, 574–76. New York: Routledge.

Beatty, Cameron C., Tenisha Tevis, Lorraine Acker, Reginald Blockett, and Eugene Parker. 2020. "Addressing Anti-Black Racism in Higher Education: Love Letters to Blackness and Recommendations to Those Who Say They Love Us." *Journal Committed to Social Change on Race and Ethnicity* 6, no. 1: 6–27.

Benitez, Michael Jr. 2010. Resituating Culture Centers within a Social Justice Framework: Is There Room for Examining Whiteness? In *Culture Centers in Higher Education: Perspectives on Identity, Theory, and Practice*, edited by L. D. Patton, 119–34. Sterling, VA: Stylus.

Calafell, Bernadette M. 2007. "Mentoring and Love: An Open Letter." *Cultural Studies↔Critical Methodologies* 7, no. 4: 425–41.

Castillo-Montoya, Milagros, and María Torres-Guzmán. 2012. "Thriving in Our Identity and in the Academy: Latina Epistemology as a Core Resource." *Harvard Educational Review* 82, no. 4: 540–58. doi.org/10.17763/haer.82.4.k483005176882in5.

Chang, Aurora. 2018. *The Struggles of Identity, Education, and Agency in the Lives of Undocumented Students*. Cham, Switzerland: Palgrave Macmillan.

Dache, Amalia, Jasmine M. Haywood, and Cristina Mislán. 2019. "A Badge of Honor Not Shame: An AfroLatina Theory of Black-imiento for US Higher Education Research." *Journal of Negro Education* 88, no. 2: 130–45. doi.org/10.7709/jnegroeducation.88.2.0130.

Davis, Shardé. 2019. "When Sistahs Support Sistahs: A Process of Supportive Communication about Racial Microaggressions among Black Women." *Communication Monographs* 86, no. 2: 133–57. doi.org/10.1080/03637751.2018.1548769.

Fierros, Cindy O., and Dolores Delgado Bernal. 2016. "Vamos a Platicar: The Contours of Pláticas as Chicana/Latina Feminist Methodology." *Chicana/Latina Studies* 15, no. 2: 98–121.

Florido, Adrian. 2020. "Puerto Rico, Island of Racial Harmony?" *Code Switch.* National Public Radio, April 24. www.npr.org/2020/04/23/842832544/puerto-rico-island-of-racial-harmony.

Freire, Paulo. (1970) 1996. *Pedagogy of the Oppressed,* translated by Myra Bergman Ramos. 20th anniv. ed. New York: Continuum.

Haywood, Jasmine M. 2017. "'Latino Spaces Have Always Been the Most Violent': Afro-Latino Collegians' Perceptions of Colorism and Latino Intragroup Marginalization." *International Journal of Qualitative Studies in Education* 30, no. 8: 759–82.

hooks, bell. 2015. *Yearning: Race, Gender, and Cultural Politics.* 2nd ed. New York: Routledge.

Kynard, Carmen. 2019. "On Graduate Admissions and Whiteness: A Love Letter to Black/Brown/Queer Graduate Students Out There Everywhere." Education, Liberation, and Black Radical Traditions for the Twenty-First Century: Carmen Kynard's Teaching and Research Site on Race, Writing, and the Classroom. January 24. carmenkynard.org/on-graduate-admissions-and-whiteness-a-love-letter-to-black-brown-queer-doctoral-students-out-there-everywhere/.

The Latina Feminist Group. 2001. *Telling to Live: Latina Feminist Testimonios.* Durham, NC: Duke University Press.

Library of Congress. 2011. "Abolition of Slavery in Puerto Rico." Hispanic Division, Library of Congress. www.loc.gov/rr/hispanic/1898/slaves.html.

Paris, Rae. 2014. "An Open Letter of Love to Black Students." December 8. *Diverse: Issues in Higher Education,* December 8. diverseeducation.com/article/68308/.

The Program on Intergroup Relations. 2014. *LARA/LARI and Empathy.* Association of American Colleges and Universities. www.aacu.org/sites/default/files/files/AM17/Difficult%20Dialogue%20Handout%201.pdf.

Stewart, Dafina Lazarus. 2013. "Racially Minoritized Students at U.S. Four-Year Institutions." *Journal of Negro Education* 82, no. 2: 184–97. doi.org/10.7709/jnegroeducation.82.2.0184.

Sweet Honey in the Rock. 1988. "Ella's Song: 'We Who Believe in Freedom Cannot Rest Until It Comes.'" Track 2 on Sweet Honey in the Rock, *Breaths.* Flying Fish Records.

Williams, Bianca C. 2016. "Radical Honesty: Truth-Telling as Pedagogy for Working through Shame in Academic Spaces." *Race, Equity, and the Learning Environment: The Global Relevance of Critical and Inclusive Pedagogies in Higher Education,* edited by Frank Tuitt, Chayla Haynes, and Saran Stewart, 71–82. Sterling, VA: Stylus.

2022 Paula J. Giddings Best Article Award

Winner

Rumya S. Putcha for her article "The Mythical Courtesan: Womanhood and Dance in Transnational India," *Meridians* 20:1

Bio: Rumya S. Putcha is assistant professor in the Institute for Women's Studies and the Hugh Hodgson School of Music at the University of Georgia.

Abstract: This article interrogates how and why courtesan identities are simultaneously embraced and disavowed by Brahmin dancers. Using a combination of ethnographic and critical feminist methods, which allow the author to toggle between the past and the present, between India and the United States, and between film analysis and the dance studio, the author examines the cultural politics of the romanticized and historical Indian dancer—the mythical courtesan. The author argues that the mythical courtesan was called into existence through film cultures in the early twentieth century to provide a counterpoint against which a modern and national Brahmanical womanhood could be articulated. The author brings together a constellation of events that participated in the construction of Indian womanhood, especially the rise of sound film against the backdrop of growing anticolonial and nationalist sentiments in early twentieth-century South India. The author focuses on films that featured an early twentieth century dancer-singer-actress, Sundaramma. In following her career through Telugu film and connecting it to broader conversations about Indian womanhood in the 1930s and 1940s, the author traces the contours of an affective triangle between three mutually constituting emotional points: pleasure, shame, and disgust.

Read the article: doi.org/10.1215/15366936-9554200

2022 Paula J. Giddings Best Article Award

Honorable Mention

Evelyn Asultany for her article "How Hate Crime Laws Perpetuate Anti-Muslim Racism," *Meridians* 20:2

Bio: Evelyn Alsultany is associate professor of American studies and ethnicity at the University of Southern California. She is the author of Arabs and Muslims in the Media: Race and Representation after 9/11 (2012) and coeditor of *Arab and Arab American Feminisms* (2011) and *Between the Middle East and the Americas* (2013).

Abstract: This essay focuses on two cases in which Muslim youth were murdered yet law enforcement refused to classify the murders as hate crimes. It examines the 2015 murders of Deah Barakat, Yusor Abu-Salha, and Razan Abu-Salha in Chapel Hill, North Carolina and the 2017 murder of Nabra Hassanen in Reston, Virginia. This author argues that the denial of these cases as hate crimes contributes to the diminishment of anti-Muslim racism and should be understood as a form of racial gaslighting—a systematic denial of the persistence and severity of racism. In conversation with those advocating for rethinking the criminal justice system through prison abolition and restorative justice, it posits that seeking state recognition for hate crimes cannot provide justice given that the state is responsible for constructing Muslims as a national security threat. It explores how anti-Muslim racism is upheld through extremely narrow and problematic definitions of racism and hate crimes, through an approach to hate crimes that prioritizes punishment over civil rights, and through creating a dilemma for Muslim communities who must seek recognition of anti-Muslim racism from the same state that enacts surveillance and violence on them.

Read the article: doi.org/10.1215/15366936-10059079

Teri Ellen Cross Davis

Black Berries

Abstract: Often the narrative on dark skin in America has been dominated by Eurocentric standards of beauty. White supremacy dictated dark skin to be unattractive and lesser than light skin. This poem explores the rich beauty of darkness in the natural world, from fruit in America to fruit in Ireland, unpacking and giving new energy to the old phrase "the blacker the berry, the sweeter the juice." By exploring the journey from wonderment to acceptance to love, the work is a refutation of lighter skin being the only pathway to beauty, not just in America, but globally.

I. Whidbey Island, Washington

Leave it to the seventy-year-old
Black woman, her honey skin
glowing, to tell me where
the best blackberries grow
on this island in the Puget Sound.

Reaching into the circular bushes
cautious of the cane's red thorns,
I hunt for the blackest berry.
A ripeness betrayed by fattened
drupelets, skin near bursting,
purple streaking my fingers
up to the elbows. Nature shows
her work, clusters on biennial vines.

MERIDIANS · feminism, race, transnationalism   21:1 April 2022
DOI: 10.1215/15366936-9554189 © 2022 Smith College

Know the tender ones won't satisfy,
persist, let your fingertips stroke
the yielding weight of sweetness
a near hidden whisper of a kiss,
blood berries, joyful and round
dappled in luster of late afternoon sun.

II. Limerick, Ireland

The blacker the berry
the sweeter the juice,
I told my Irish friend
his speckled hand reaching
deeper into a homegrown
bush of currants—searching
for the ripest for his Black
American guest. The young ones
a blushed violet, bled streaks
on his cream fingers but he kept
pushing, past crimson, dark garnet,
until sweet midnight unveiled itself.

The intermittent sun shed ribbons
of yellow light over the River Shannon,
the swimming swans' tragedy
a sole surviving gosling
—all eclipsed by the black currant
its tender rupture
on the hilt of my tongue.

III. Mombasa, Kenya

With long braids and dark skin
few knew I wasn't Kenyan.
Here, melanin was a blessing.
The batik bikini, baby oil,
equatorial sun—how Black
could I get? I never burned,

only burnished, strains of buttermilk
blocking anything deeper. I could not
have done this in the States. I would never
call it "tanning" having never been tan.
But in Mombasa, drunk on a camel
crossing the spilling evening sand,
ocean surf, my cover band
I chased my color, taunted it
to come out and play.

Teri Ellen Cross Davis is the author of *a more perfect Union*, the 2019 *Journal*/Charles B. Wheeler Poetry Prize winner and *Haint*, awarded the 2017 Ohioana Book Award for Poetry. A Cave Canem Fellow and member of the Black Ladies Brunch Collective, she's the Folger Shakespeare Library's poetry coordinator.

Mafalda Nicolas Mondestin

Ann fè on ti pale (The Meeting), 2016

Nicolas Mondestin's most recent body of work starts as an exploration of the relationship that exists between female bodies and the spaces they evolve in—in this case, nature. Bare female bodies are seen holding court evolving in a safe space, untouched by man-made constructions and constraints. The work questions not only the reciprocal influence between female bodies and nature, but also between the female body and society. It examines how bodies are shaped by societal views and how we transform them in return.

Mafalda Nicolas Mondestin is a Haitian visual artist born and raised in the United States, Haiti, and Canada. She studied graphic design at Valencia Community College in Florida. In 2012, Nicolas Mondestin moved to Haiti where she shifted her focus to the fine arts and pursued her practice full time, all the while working with nonprofit organizations such as Le Centre d'Art. Nicolas Mondestin exhibits in Haiti, the United States, and France, and has completed art residencies at the Cité International des Arts de Paris in France, and at the Taller Experimental Gráfica de la Habana in Cuba. Her practice encompasses multiple mediums such as painting, drawing, printmaking, and collage. She lives and works in Haiti.

MERIDIANS · feminism, race, transnationalism   21:1 April 2022
DOI: 10.1215/15366936-10059112 © 2022 Smith College